WARSHIPS
OF THE WORLD

TITLE PAGE
A 8th century BC Greek vase of the geometric type depicting a warship with the oarsmen on three levels. The bow, on the left, carries a ram, which was the preferred weapon for holing the hull on an enemy ship, which would then sink.

RIGHT
Defence of the Havana Promontory *by Rafael Monleon y Torres (1847–1900.) The complexity of the sailing rig, comprising the masts with their standing rigging and the sails with their yards and running rigging, was a huge target above the hull, and many ships such as this first-rate line-of-battle ship, were rendered impotent by the destruction of their ability to move.*

OPPOSITE
Engraved in the year following the event, this illustration of the attack on Cartagena by British forces under Admiral Lord Vernon in 1740 during the War of Jenkins' Ear (1739–43) wrongly claims that the British took the city. Note the several types of warship depicted in the harbour.

WARSHIPS
OF THE WORLD

CHRISTOPHER CHANT

LORENZ BOOKS

This edition published in 2011 by Lorenz Books,
an imprint of Anness Publishing Ltd, Hermes House,
88–89 Blackfriars Road, London SE1 8HA, UK;
tel. 020 7401 2077; fax 020 7633 9499

www.lorenzbooks.com; www.annesspublishing.com

UK distributor: Book Trade Services;
tel. 0116 2759086; fax 0116 2759090;
uksales@booktradeservices.com;
exportsales@booktradeservices.com
Australian distributor: Pan Macmillan Australia;
tel. 1300 135 113; fax 1300 135 103;
customer.service@macmillan.com.au
New Zealand distributor: David Bateman Ltd;
tel. (09) 415 7664; fax (09) 415 8892

ETHICAL TRADING POLICY
Because of Anness Publishing's ongoing ecological
investment programme, you, as our customer, can
have the pleasure and reassurance of knowing that
a tree is being cultivated on your behalf to naturally
replace the materials used to make the book you are
holding. For further information about this scheme,
go to www.annesspublishing.com/trees

PUBLISHER'S NOTE
Although the information in this book is believed
to be accurate and true at the time of going to press,
neither the authors nor the publisher can accept
any legal responsibility or liability for any errors
or omissions that may have been made.

The Battle of Trafalgar, *21 October 1805,*
by Thomas Whitcombe (1760–1824).

Contents

Chapter One
The Sailing Warship

Sailing ships are among the most graceful artefacts ever created by mankind. In the Western world today, the general perception of the sailing vessel is characterized by either the yacht at the smaller end of the size spectrum and, at the larger end, ships preserved as museums or sail training ships. This should not be allowed to obscure the fact, however, that in many other parts of the world the sailing vessel is still an everyday working mode of transport. In such ships men traverse lakes, rivers, the shallow waters of the coastal regions and, to a lesser extent, the deep waters of the oceans for a host of applications including trade, transport and fishing. In purely objective terms, it is arguable that the survival of many developing countries is largely dependent on the availability of sailing vessels, large and small, powered by the force of the wind that is free and in many parts of the world blows with great steadiness from different points of the compass at different times of the year. So while the world's more industrialized nations may no longer think it important to rely on the wind for the power to move ships, such wind power is to this day of crucial importance for less affluent and less industrialized countries that do not have either the financial resources or the technical skills to import or manufacture and then to operate the type of internal combustion

engine taken for granted in the West as the primary power source for ships.

Up to the first half of the 18th century, when the emergent age of steam began to make it feasible to introduce coal-fired steam engines that were practical for their task and also reliable, the wind was the only alternative to muscle power for the movement of large ships and small boats. It is also worth noting that even when the steam engine had entered the scene, it was a long time before sailing ships became obsolete for everything except pleasure. With a boiler fired by coal and later by oil, the steam engine had to prove itself first in terms of its reliability and then of its economy as a means of powering a system based initially on paddle wheels and then on propellers. Thus it was the beginning of

the 20th century before sail really gave way to steam.

For a period of perhaps 6,000 years before that, however, the sailing ship was among mankind's most important creations. It should not be imagined, however, that mankind 'invented' the concept of wind-powered movement along or across the waters of the world. From the earliest times the wind has propelled leaves across puddles, insects across ponds and branches down rivers. And it is believed that the wind, working with the waves and currents, was the motive power behind the migration of many plants, insects and even small animals from the adjacent mainland to several island groups. At some unknown time in this period, it is inevitable that a man saw that he could exploit the concept for his own benefit, first by riding a log down a river, then by using a pole or a paddle to control the motion of his load that was gradually developed into a hollowed-out canoe, and by rigging a primitive mast and sail (probably a pole and a fur) on a straight log to capture the wind's power and so speed his log, and steer his creation with his arms or a paddle. Such primitive sailing craft would have been able to cross wide rivers and perhaps even small lakes, but would have been unable to steer very far from the direction the wind was blowing.

Ever inventive, mankind was soon improving on this primitive system. It is thought that by 4000 BC the Chinese were using sail-driven rafts – a model of a sailing boat used on the Tigris and Euphrates rivers of what is now Iraq has been dated by archeologists to 3500 BC – and by 3400 BC the Egyptians were using sailing craft on the Nile river. From the use of sailing vessels on the comparatively placid and slow-moving waters of lakes and rivers, the next conceptual step was the use of sailing vessels on the sea, and before long the Egyptians had begun to trade along their coast and even across the Mediterranean Sea by sailing ship. It is likely that most river boats were made of reed bundles lashed together to make a hull with a wide and stable central section and a pointed bow and stern, which were lifted out of the water by the use of special lashings or by the use of a tensioned central rope connecting the bow and stern. Just forward of the central position, a short mast was placed (or stepped) with rope bracings (or stays) to the bow and stern and more bracings (or shrouds) to the sides of the hull formed by the reed bundles. These stays and shrouds held the mast upright in the fore-and-aft and lateral planes, and allowed it to carry a square sail hanging from a stout yard. The yard was controlled relative to the for-and-aft line of the vessel by rope braces running from the ends of the yard to the stern of the boat, and the bottom (foot) of the sail was controlled by other sets of lines (sheets). Steering was entrusted to a large paddle-bladed oar lashed to hang down into the water beside or behind the stern.

Sailing vessels intended for journeys more than a short distance from the coast were built to the same basic pattern but were larger and, when circumstances permitted, made of wood rather than reed.

The Egyptians lacked the type of tree that would provide long planks, so they made use of short planks (generally thick enough to be regarded as blocks) pinned together and made watertight by a wadding (or caulking) of papyrus reed hammered into the gaps and painted over with pitch or tree resin. In combination with the lack of any keel digging deep into the water to prevent lateral drift, the square sail (generally made of woven cloth or reed matting) was effective only for the purpose of making the vessel run directly before the wind or slightly away from this direction. As a result, vessels generally carried oars or larger sweeps as alternatives to sails when the wind failed or was blowing from the wrong direction. The oars were also important in manoeuvring the ship in harbours. These early sailing vessels were undoubtedly clumsy craft, but they did work and allowed countries such as Egypt to develop as important trading nations.

The sailing ship was also developed for fighting, and it is thought likely that this led to the development of the technique known as clewing. On the earliest ships the spar and sail were lowered to the deck by a rope halyard when not needed. For a trading ship this was fine, but the long yard and large sail would have been in the way of the soldiers who were embarked on warships as their 'weapons': the object of the ship's crew was to bring the vessel alongside the enemy, whereupon the soldiers boarded the enemy vessel and fought a pitched battle to

RIGHT
An Attic black-figure cup by Nikosthenes, depicting Greek warships with sails and rigging in evidence.

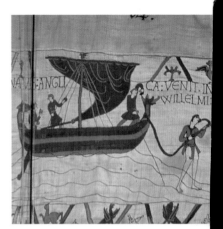

BELOW
Detail from the Bayeux Tapestry, showing Duke William of Normandy and his fleet crossing the English Channel to land at Pevensey, East Sussex.

LEFT
Duke William orders ships to be be built which the Normans drag down to the sea. (Detail from the Bayeux Tapestry which consists of wool embroidery on linen and was commissioned by the Bishops of Bayeux between AD 1066 and 1077.)

effect its capture. Such battles demanded that the deck be left as clear as possible for the movement of the soldiers, and for this reason, therefore, it was clearly a better arrangement in a warship to have the yard remain well clear of the deck toward the top of the mast with the foot of the sail lifted (or clewed) up against it, where it was firmly furled when not needed. It is believed that this development was first made on the northern shore of the Mediterranean, and is important as it left the deck uncluttered. It was then only a modest step from clewing to the development of reef points, which are transverse rows of short lines sewn into the sail so that they can be tied round the yard once the sail had been lifted slightly, and this provides a handy method of reducing the amount of sail offered to a rising wind. The use of several rows of reefing points allowed exactly the right area of sail to be furled as required.

Unlike the Egyptians, the Phoenicians of the Levant, or coast at the eastern end of the Mediterranean Sea (now Lebanon and Israel), had good supplies of timber suitable for shipbuilding purposes. Here the availability of Lebanese cedar, which can be sawn into long planks, allowed the creation of merchant ships that resembled Egyptian ships in shape but which as a result of the use of longer planks were stronger and could therefore sail farther from the coast, brave worse weather conditions and so undertake longer voyages. These included, it is possible, a three-year expedition right around Africa in the 7th century BC. The Phoenicians were also the first to develop a ship especially for war. This was a narrow type that could be sailed before any favourable wind for cruising but which was fitted with one, two or even three banks of oars for speed and manoeuvrability in naval battles. Despite these important developments, the Phoenicians lacked the engineering skill to make ships that were notably larger than those of the Egyptians.

It was the Greeks and to a larger extent the Romans who built the Western world's first large ships after developing the idea of a large and very strong frame on which was laid an arrangement of caulked planks to provide a watertight hull.

It was this type of ship that was used in one of the world's first decisive naval encounters, the Battle of Salamis, fought between the Greeks and the Persians in September 480 BC. This battle was part of the campaign launched by the Persian king Xerxes to bring the city states of Greece under Persian rule. The Persian forces had already revealed their maritime skills in the creation of two floating bridges across the Hellespont, where the waters flowing out of the Black Sea debouch into the Aegean Sea, to allow his army of some 200,000 men to march in parallel across the water gap separating Asia from Europe. That the Greeks were not devoid of martial skills was then revealed at the Battle of Thermopylae in August 480 BC, when a comparatively tiny force of Spartans under King Leonidas chose its ground carefully and delayed the far more numerous Persians from pressing their advance toward central and southern Greece, in the process buying time for the creation of a more effective Greek defence. Even so, after Thermopylae the Persians were able to resume their advance and capture Athens. The Persian army, which had suffered few casualties, had been augmented by contingents from Thebes and other northern Greek states. The Persian fleet probably totalled 700 or more fighting vessels, about double the number of Greek triremes. Themistocles, the Athenian leader, feared that the Persians would be able to secure a decisive victory if they played a waiting game and used their superior numbers to blockade the Greek fleet, lying in the waters just to the west of Piraeus, the

harbour of Athens, after ferrying most of the Athenian population to safety on the island of Salamis. This would allow a powerful element of the Persian army to be landed behind the defences of the isthmus of Corinth that connects the mainland of Greece with the Peloponnese and now the Greeks' main line of land defence. He therefore sent a secret message to Xerxes, saying that if the Persian fleet attacked, the Athenians would join the Persians and the rest of the fleet would flee. Xerxes felt that this was an opportunity too good to miss, and ordered the Persian fleet to move out that very night. While the Egyptian component of the Persian fleet blocked the western exit south of Salamis, the main fleet, at least 500 strong, formed in line of battle opposite the eastern entrance of the strait. Before dawn, a force of Persian infantry landed on the islet of Psyttaleia in the entrance to the channel between the mainland and the island of Salamis. On the mainland, overlooking the site of the forthcoming battle, Xerxes sat on his throne to witness the battle he thought would bring Greece into his empire.

Part of the Greek fleet was sent to hold the narrow western end of the strait, and the rest of the Greek triremes were drawn up in a line across the channel, behind a bend in the eastern strait, waiting for the main Persian fleet. A narrowing of the channel, where the Persians came around the bend after passing round Psyttaleia, now played into the hands of the Greeks as Themistocles had planned. The larger number of Persian warships found themselves in constricted waters and inevitably the gaps between the ships decreased, leading to an increasing level of confusion as the Persian ships were crowded together. This was the moment for which the Greeks had been waiting, and now they

fell on the Persians. With manoeuvre impossible and larger numbers a hindrance, the advantage was with the Greek ships, which were individually larger, heavier and more sturdily built than their opponents of the Persian fleet. The Greek triremes, with the Athenians on the left, allies in the centre, and Spartans on the right, were carrying the entire Athenian army of at least 6,000 men. Hundreds of what were in effect small land battles erupted on the decks of the jammed vessels. On a man-for-man basis, the Greek hoplite (heavily armed citizen soldier) was far superior to his Persian adversary, and although the battle lasted for at least seven hours the Greeks were in the ascendant throughout. The Persians lost half of their fleet sunk or captured, while the Greeks lost a mere 40 ships. The surviving Persians broke off the battle and pulled back, and a force of Greek troops, most of them Athenians, landed on Psyttaleia and destroyed the Persian force that had been abandoned on the island.

It was a decisive defeat in itself, and also gave the Greeks the overall naval advantage. This decided the outcome of the whole campaign, for Xerxes appreciated that his efforts in Greece were almost entirely dependent on supplies delivered by sea, and therefore decided to pull back.

Although navies generally decreased in size during the 4th century BC, they increased greatly in the following century. During the 1st and 2nd Punic Wars (264–241 BC and 218–201 BC respectively), the Romans and Carthaginians each frequently had at sea up to 500 warships, manned by as many as 150,000 seamen and marines, and individual fleets totalled as many as 350 ships. To control these vast maritime forces, Rome and Carthage each created an administrative organization comparable to a modern admiralty or navy department.

During this period, the trireme was generally displaced by larger warships, the first person to build such types being Dionysius the ruler of Syracuse in Sicily between 405 and 367 BC. By the time of the Punic Wars, the quinquireme had become the standard warship. The complement of these decked galleys consisted of up to 300 rowers and seamen, plus as many as 100 seagoing soldiers. Naval tactics remained essentially unchanged until the middle of the 3rd century BC, when the Romans, after appreciating the inferiority of their relatively slower and clumsier ships in the face of superior Carthaginian seamanship, introduced a new concept. This *corvus* (crow) was a combined grappling device and boarding bridge. In order to come close enough to ram or to break the oars of the clumsier Roman warships, the Carthaginians had to risk being caught by the *corvus*, which was followed by an irresistible charge of Roman soldiers.

There was little change in the concept and practice of naval warfare between this time and the end of the first millennium BC. The trireme and quinquireme remained the major types of warship, although the Romans were far-sighted enough to see the need for the special-purpose warships that would facilitate their creation and consolidation of a major empire. Such special-purpose warships included the *ponto*, which was derived from a type of river lighter which the Romans encountered in their conquest of Gaul. This flat-bottomed *ponto* was ideally suited to riverine operations, and became the core of the flotillas that the Romans created for operations on rivers such as the Rhône and the Rhine.

The standard battle tactics were still conditioned by the lack of any effective

projectile weapon, which dictated close-quarter combat. The main tactics for naval battles were ramming of the enemy's ships, or breaking their banks of oars, or setting them on fire, on boarding and capturing them. Given their high length/beam ratio, low internal volume and lack of good sailing and navigation skills, most navies preferred to operate close to the coast, which allowed the ships to be run ashore or anchored in shallow water so that the crew could camp on land during the night.

The one major change of the periods was the *harpax* or *harpago*, pioneered by Agrippa, the admiral whose support helped secure the position of Octavianus as Augustus, the first Roman emperor (27 BC–14 AD). This was in effect a catapult-launched harpoon with a substantial rope

attached to its rear: once the *harpax* had been fired into the side of an enemy warship, the crew could haul their own vessel close alongside to ease the task of boarding.

The *harpax* was important in the Battle of Actium (2 September 31 BC), the naval engagement off the western coast of Greece that ended the ambitions of Marcus Antonius to lead Rome. Each of the two fleets had about 400 ships available to it. Agrippa's fleet was deployed in a north-south formation of three squadrons each possessing about 130 ships, while Marcus Antonius deployed in the same basic fashion but with only about 340 of his available ships, the other 60 being held back in reserve under the control of the Egyptian queen, Cleopatra. Each commander tried to

A Polynesian war canoe. Although the Polynesians made some truly extraordinary ocean passages in large outrigger-stabilized canoes with sails, their warfare was restricted to island groups, and here speed and the carriage of large numbers of men were the vital requirements. War canoes therefore had a much finer hull and featured provision for as many men as possible to paddle them.

tacking. In their longships these adventurous people traded through the rivers of eastern Europe to reach the Black Sea, sailed round the coasts of western Europe to enter the Mediterranean through the Strait of Gibraltar, and most impressively of all sailed west into the Atlantic to discover and settle Iceland, Greenland and even North America before AD 1000.

These Viking ships were initially less than 100ft (30.5m) in length, and had provision for between 10 a·· 16 oars per side as well as the mast ····· ···· sail. These early Vik·· ··· ··· 60 t· 10·

envelop the other's northern wing, and at first it seemed that the squadron under the personal command of Marcus Antonius would prevail. Then the two other squadrons decided that discretion was the better part of valour and either surrendered or fell back into the bay of Actium and the protection of Marcus Antonius' land army camped there. Marcus Antonius realized that the battle was lost, signalled Cleopatra to save herself, and tried to fight his way out of the enveloping forces of Agrippa, one of whose squadrons was commanded by Octavianus. After a desperate fight, in which his ship was grappled by a *harpax*, forcing his to switch to another ship, Marcus Antonius managed to break free with just a few ships and escape to Egypt, also the destination of Cleopatra.

On land, Marcus Antonius' army was ordered to break out past the army of Octavianus, but generally mutinied against its officers and surrendered. It was now only a matter of time before this Roman civil war ended in total victory for Octavianus.

It was the Romans who were responsible for the creation of what can be called the modern sailing vessel. The Roman type of structure was based on a strong keel running from bow to stern, where uprights called the stem and sternpost rose to give the ship strength against the buffeting of the waves. The shape of the hull was created by large frames rising from the keel and held in place by the stringers that ran in wide curves from the stem to the sternpost. Over this frame was laid the planking of the hull and the deck sections to create a large, hollow interior. The system allowed the building of larger as well as more seaworthy ships, and this in turn opened the way for merchant ships that were short and wide, and also for warships that were long and narrow. The one- or two-masted merchant

LEFT
A galley on her oars. From La Pluche's Le Spectacle de la Nature, *Paris, 1735. By the 18th century, galleys were scarcely ever seen outside the Mediterranean, and they were generally powered by convict labour.*

OPPOSITE
Though this aquatint was made in the 19th century, it reveals the fact that the ships of the Normans were derived in concept from the longships of the Vikings, from whom the Normans were descended, with a larger hull for the carriage of a greater burden.

vessels were slow and decidedly unhandy, but were also well suited to the task of carrying the bulk of Rome's relatively enormous volume of trade including staples such as grain from the 'breadbasket' areas of Sicily, North Africa and Egypt. The warships were fast and manoeuvrable, on the other hand, the use of clewed sails allowing the crews to sail their vessels rapidly into battle and then get the sails out of the way so that the banks of oarsmen could get to work. Enemy ships were either rammed with the warship's long reinforced bow and left to sink, in the fashion also used by the Greeks, or boarded and captured by the soldiers carried for the task.

There were no other significant changes in the nature and practice of naval warfare in the period of the Roman empire under

imperial rule, when Rome faced no naval challenge. In addition to their flotillas of *pontones* for river patrol, the Romans maintained standing fleets in the Adriatic and Tyrrhenian seas as well as on the northern and western coasts of Gaul; but the task of these fleets was the checking of piracy rather than fighting for command of the sea with a foreign power.

The Roman type of building used planks laid side by side (carvel construction) to produce a smooth exterior finish next to the water, and this combination of framed internal structure with carvel planking was standard right across Europe up to the decline of the Roman empire in the 5th century AD. Thereafter it remained the norm for shipbuilding in the Mediterranean but, as Roman influence in northern

Europe grew less, the Roman techniques were largely lost.

There were no important improvements in naval warfare, such as there still was, in the period between the fall of Rome (and the western part of the Roman empire) in AD 476 and the end of the first millennium only genuinely effective navy was as the pan empire

envelop the other's northern wing, and at first it seemed that the squadron under the personal command of Marcus Antonius would prevail. Then the two other squadrons decided that discretion was the better part of valour and either surrendered or fell back into the bay of Actium and the protection of Marcus Antonius' land army camped there. Marcus Antonius realized that the battle was lost, signalled Cleopatra to save herself, and tried to fight his way out of the enveloping forces of Agrippa, one of whose squadrons was commanded by Octavianus. After a desperate fight, in which his ship was grappled by a *harpax*, forcing his to switch to another ship, Marcus Antonius managed to break free with just a few ships and escape to Egypt, also the destination of Cleopatra.

On land, Marcus Antonius' army was ordered to break out past the army of Octavianus, but generally mutinied against its officers and surrendered. It was now only a matter of time before this Roman civil war ended in total victory for Octavianus.

It was the Romans who were responsible for the creation of what can be called the modern sailing vessel. The Roman type of structure was based on a strong keel running from bow to stern, where uprights called the stem and sternpost rose to give the ship strength against the buffeting of the waves. The shape of the hull was created by large frames rising from the keel and held in place by the stringers that ran in wide curves from the stem to the sternpost. Over this frame was laid the planking of the hull and the deck sections to create a large, hollow interior. The system allowed the building of larger as well as more seaworthy ships, and this in turn opened the way for merchant ships that were short and wide, and also for warships that were long and narrow. The one- or two-masted merchant

LEFT
A galley on her oars. From La Pluche's Le Spectacle de la Nature, *Paris, 1735. By the 18th century, galleys were scarcely ever seen outside the Mediterranean, and they were generally powered by convict labour.*

OPPOSITE
Though this aquatint was made in the 19th century, it reveals the fact that the ships of the Normans were derived in concept from the longships of the Vikings, from whom the Normans were descended, with a larger hull for the carriage of a greater burden.

vessels were slow and decidedly unhandy, but were also well suited to the task of carrying the bulk of Rome's relatively enormous volume of trade including staples such as grain from the 'breadbasket' areas of Sicily, North Africa and Egypt. The warships were fast and manoeuvrable, on the other hand, the use of clewed sails allowing the crews to sail their vessels rapidly into battle and then get the sails out of the way so that the banks of oarsmen could get to work. Enemy ships were either rammed with the warship's long reinforced bow and left to sink, in the fashion also used by the Greeks, or boarded and captured by the soldiers carried for the task.

There were no other significant changes in the nature and practice of naval warfare in the period of the Roman empire under imperial rule, when Rome faced no naval challenge. In addition to their flotillas of *pontones* for river patrol, the Romans maintained standing fleets in the Adriatic and Tyrrhenian seas as well as on the northern and western coasts of Gaul; but the task of these fleets was the checking of piracy rather than fighting for command of the sea with a foreign power.

The Roman type of building used planks laid side by side (carvel construction) to produce a smooth exterior finish next to the water, and this combination of framed internal structure with carvel planking was standard right across Europe up to the decline of the Roman empire in the 5th century AD. Thereafter it remained the norm for shipbuilding in the Mediterranean but, as Roman influence in northern

Europe grew less, the Roman techniques were largely lost.

There were no important improvements in naval warfare, such as there still was, in the period between the fall of Rome (and the western part of the Roman empire) in AD 476 and the end of the first millennium AD. The only genuinely effective navy was that of the Byzantine empire, as the surviving eastern half of the Roman empire came to be called. Although its fleets generally declined during the early part of this period, allowing many of the peoples moving into the Mediterranean region, for settlement as well as for raiding, to make occasional use of ships, these fleets were brought up to a higher level of efficiency in the last 200 years before the end of the first millennium. Naval battles were in fact rare, since a fight at sea was the last thing a raider wanted. In the 10th century AD, however, the Byzantine navy became more capable in the face of increasing threats from raiders of several types, and was used in a systematic programme to hunt down and destroy the Moslem corsair and pirate fleets operating in the eastern Mediterranean from bases in the Levant and North Africa, resulting in several major sea battles, and also the Varangian (Scandinavian Russian) raiders operating in the Black Sea.

In the combined naval and land operations of Nicephoros Phocas against Crete in AD 960–961, the Byzantines demonstrated great skill and creativity in the novel art of amphibious warfare. Phocas' transport ships were equipped with ramps that could be lowered as soon as the ships came to rest on the beach, allowing cavalry to charge ashore directly onto the beach in the event of an opposed landing.

The new seafaring power that emerged in the northern part of Europe was that of the Viking people from Scandinavia. The

Vikings introduced a new type of sailing vessel, generally known as the longship for its considerable length/beam ratio. This was used for coastal and ocean voyages under sail or oar power, and was specifically created so that it could be beached as well as brought alongside a jetty. Large internal volume was required for the men and equipment carried on shorter raiding voyages, or for supplies and cargo carried on longer trading voyages, so the type of ship created by the Vikings had a high bow and stern for good sea-going qualities, and a capacious hull with a flat bottom that did not penetrate far into the water. This shallow-draught hull was well suited to conditions in northern Europe: the Vikings could beach their ships for safety in the winter, and in the summer use them to push deep into fjords and rivers on their raiding

and trading voyages. On the one hand, the Viking ships resembled those of the Phoenicians in being long and narrow, but on the other hand were akin to those of the Romans in being built up on a frame. Northern Europe had lost the technique of carvel planking, and the longships were clinker-built: in this type of planking, the lower edge of each plank overlaps the upper edge of the plank below it.

Driven before the wind by a single square sail or otherwise moved by its oars, the longship was ideally suited to the Vikings' way of life. It is believed that it was the Vikings who discovered that the yard could be braced far round so that the sail was angled more to the hull than running across it: this permitted the longship to sail crabwise into the general direction of the wind in a zigzag manoeuvre known as

tacking. In their longships these adventurous people traded through the rivers of eastern Europe to reach the Black Sea, sailed round the coasts of western Europe to enter the Mediterranean through the Strait of Gibraltar, and most impressively of all sailed west into the Atlantic to discover and settle Iceland, Greenland and even North America before AD 1000.

These Viking ships were initially less than 100ft (30.5m) in length, and had provision for between 10 and 16 oars per side as well as the mast carrying a square sail. These early Viking ships carried perhaps 60 to 90 men, but during the second half of the 9th century, the size of the 'typical' Viking ship became larger, and it is recorded that some of them carried as many as 200 men. Just as important as the general success of the Viking ship as an ocean-going, as well as coastal and riverine vessels, was the fact that Viking seamanship was of a notably high standard.

As the northern Europeans began to emerge from the so-called 'Dark Ages' that extended over much of western Europe in the aftermath of the fall of Rome, its seafaring peoples began to build up an important trade network using a type of small but notably stout ship that combined the layout of the Mediterranean ship (a hull of low length/beam ratio and carrying two or sometimes three masts) with the Viking type of clinker construction. The trade network grew rapidly up to about AD 1000, and during this period oared propulsion generally disappeared from northern European ships intended for seagoing service. The reasons for this were twofold: firstly, the merchants who were the force behind the revival of seagoing trade sought to economize on their manning costs by reducing the size of crews, among whom the oarsmen were the most expendable, and secondly the availability of an improved layout and greater seafaring skills opened the way for mariners to exploit the Vikings' discovery that ships could sail into the general direction of the wind by bracing the yards round. Such ships, with a small crew and a rig that may be regarded as practicable rather than generally efficient, were of necessity slow, but outright speed was relatively unimportant to traders, whose ships therefore had a low length/beam ratio to maximize their cargo-carrying capacity and make them simple to sail with small crews.

In naval terms, the most important development of the 200 years that followed the end of the first millennium AD was the significant rise of maritime states in Italy, and in particular Venice on the eastern side of the peninsula and both Pisa, and Genoa on its western side. The Norman kingdom of Sicily also developed a substantial naval capability. By the close of the 12th century, the navies of these four states dominated most of the Mediterranean. Over the same period the capability of the Byzantine navy went into a major decline, largely as a result of the devastation of the maritime areas of Anatolia after the Battle of Manzikert (AD 1071), in which the Turks under Alp Arslan decisively defeated the Byzantine forces

commanded by the Emperor Romanus
Diogenes as a result of treason in the
Byzantine camp. Most of Anatolia fell to the
Turks, and there followed a disastrous civil
war in the Byzantine empire.

Sea power was a decisive element in the
period of the Crusades as European armies
sought to wrest the Holy Land from
Moslem control and then keep it. During
the 12th century the states of Italy and
Sicily with any seagoing capability were able
to secure major payments as they
transported Crusader armies to the Holy
Land and then kept them supplied with
reinforcements, equipment and food.

The main type of warship in the period
between AD1000 and 1200 was essentially
similar to that which had been standard in
the Mediterranean for centuries, namely the
oared galley. This was long and lay low in
the water, and its oarsmen were generally
slaves. Given that the nature of the
'standard' warship had not changed, it is
hardly surprising that the tactics of naval
warfare also remained essentially unaltered:
the primary objective of any warship was to
ram the enemy and sink it, or to come
alongside it after shattering the oars on
either side, and then board and capture it.

At much the same time, larger carvel-
built merchant ships began to appear with
two or three masts. These each carried a
single square sail on each of the masts, but
as ships increased in size the masts were
lengthened by adding one or two more
sections above the main mast, each section
supported by its own standing rigging and
carrying its own sail in an arrangement that
allowed the spreading of exactly the right
quantity and arrangement of canvas for all
weathers and conditions. Ships were
becoming more manoeuvrable, and in the
12th century the sharply sloped stern began
to disappear in favour of a more upright

LEFT
*A drawing of a medieval
galley warship, a pen and
ink illustration from* De re
militari, *1460, by Roberto
Valturio (1405–75)*

OPPOSITE LEFT
*The first invasion of
Ireland, 1169: soldiers in a
boat approaching the Irish
coast. (English text with
Flemish illumination taken
from the St. Alban's
Chronical, late 15th
century.)*

OPPOSITE RIGHT
*Richard II's campaign in
Ireland in 1399. The ships
are bringing provisions to
the English troops.*

into the beginning of the 18th century.

The two primary types of trading ship found in the Mediterranean during the period from the 14th to the 17th centuries were the caravel and the carrack. Both of these had considerable freeboard (hull height above the waterline). The caravel was the smaller of the two types, and was a boat-built type in which the forward-curving beakhead and the after castle of the north European ships was replaced by a curved stem and a flat transom more suitable to the smaller seas of the Mediterranean. These vessels were generally two-masted, with a single lateen (triangular fore-and-aft) sail on each mast, and were able to sail closer to the wind than the square-rigged north European vessels. Both the Spanish and Portuguese began to use the caravel in the 16th century, and soon discovered that the lateen rig was not suitable for long sea-going voyages. These two great exploring nations therefore developed the caravel into a three-masted type with square sails on the two forward masts and a lateen-rigged mizzen mast. The three ships involved in Christopher Columbus' voyage across the Atlantic in 1492 were caravels, the *Santa Maria* being a 95-ft (28.95-m) vessel typical of larger caravels, and the *Pinta* and *Nina* 58- and 56-ft (17.7- and 17.1-m) vessels typical of smaller caravels: the *Nina* started the voyage as a *caravela latina* of the Mediterranean pattern, but this rig was found so difficult to control in the Atlantic that she was converted to the three-masted *caravela rotunda* rig in the Canary Islands.

The carrack was the larger trading ship used in the Mediterranean and also in northern Europe between the 14th and 17th centuries, and was in effect a cross between the lateen-rigged Mediterranean

LEFT
An Isnik dish from the second half of the 16th century painted with a ship and glazed in red, blue and green.

OPPOSITE
An engraving from the 16th century Italian School, depicting the Battle of Zarchio in 1499.

type that could take a hinged rudder. The introduction of the centreline rudder was followed quite swiftly by the disappearance of the side-hinged steering oar, and ships became not only easier but also more precise to handle. Working together, the true rudder and square sails that could be braced far round towards the side of the

ship provided the ability to sail in every direction except directly into or close to the wind, and progress in these directions was possible with the aid of tacking. This marked the end of oared ships in northern Europe, where still weather is very uncommon, but in the Mediterranean oared warships remained in service right

ship and the square-rigged north European ship. It was thus similar to the fully developed caravel with three masts, but was larger and broader in the beam up to a displacement of about 1,200 tons. The carrack was generally of sturdy construction, and carried both fore and after castles. The carrack was the first example what may be termed the 'typical' trading ship type that lasted until the arrival of steam, with square-rigged fore and main masts, and a lateen-rigged mizzen mast. The carrack's only real development was the galleon, which did away with the high fore castle to remove its tendency to blow the bow downwind, and the result was a ship able to sail closer to the wind.

The 15th century saw a complete revolution in naval warfare: the period of slightly more than 2,000 years in which the oared warship or galley had reigned supreme finally ended after reaching an apogee under Khair ed-Din, Andrea Doria and Don Juan of Austria, who were arguably three of the greatest naval commanders of the oared warship period. The end of the era of the galley did not mean, of course, that oared warships disappeared overnight, or the equivalent in historical terms, for they continued to operate in the Mediterranean with some success for more than another 100 years, but rather that they became of lesser importance than the new type of sailing warship based on the use of cannon, the weapon that had begun to make its appearance in land warfare in the middle of the 14th century and was becoming increasingly important in naval affairs in the first half of the 15th century. The introduction of the cannon as the primary armament of the warship for the first time made it possible for warships to stand off from each other and still fight with

projectile weapons capable of inflicting decisive damage, especially after the introduction of the broadside concept with one or more ranks of similar cannon disposed on each side of the deck to fire a simultaneous or rippled salvo at the enemy ship's hull, masts, rigging and sails.

The first naval leader to exploit the capabilities of the new type of warship was a Spaniard, the Marquis de Santa Cruz, but the first man to see the full extent of the revolution in naval affairs was an Englishman, Sir Francis Drake, and a number of his contemporaries.

In overall terms, naval tactics had changed little between the Battles of Salamis and Lepanto, the latter fought in AD 1571. The objective of each captain involved in the battle was to ram or board an enemy ship. With the exception of its larger masts and sails, the latter generally of the lateen type, the galley was a fragile warship that differed in no significant respect from the ships used by the Romans in their wars with Carthage. The galley had a high length/beam ratio, and in general was a low, single-decked ship some 150ft (45.7m) in length and 20ft (6.1m) in beam. In action the ship was propelled by some 54 oars, 27 on each beam, and for cruising there were two or sometimes three lateen-rigged masts, which were useful to rest the oarsmen and provided greater speed when the wind was favourable. Each oar was operated by between four and six men, usually slaves, and these men were protected from lateral fire by mantlets over the oar ports in ships of Christian navies. Including its sailors as well as the embarked party of soldiers, each galley therefore had a complement of about 400 men. The change in naval thinking was reflected in the fact that at the Battle of Lepanto, each galley of the Christian fleet generally carried five

LEFT
The caravel Santa Maria, *one of the boats used by Columbus in 1492. (From an engraving published in Paris in 1892.)*

OPPOSITE
The Harry Grâce-à-Dieu, *built for Henry VIII of England in 1512, from a drawing by Hans Holbein.*

Two examples of Tudor warships. Top: The Great Harry. *Below: The* Harry Grâce-à-Dieu. *(Engraving after a drawing in the Pepys Collection.)*

cannon in the bow to fire straight ahead or fire on each beam (broadside fire would have been dangerous with so low a freeboard and so high a length/beam ratio), but the Turkish galleys were generally smaller and mounted only three cannon. Just above the waterline, and extending straight forward from the bow, was a metal or metal-sheathed wooden ram some 10 to 20ft (3.05 to 6.1m) long with which they sought to strike the side of an enemy ship and pierce a large hole on the waterline.

Also involved at the Battle of Lepanto were two variants on the galley theme. One of these was the Turkish galliot, derived from Byzantine naval thinking: this was a smaller and faster type with a crew of about 100 and between 18 and 24 oars. The other was the galliass developed by the Venetians: this was the naval giant of its time, about twice the size of the typical galley, and was somewhat slower but considerably stronger than the galley with greater seaworthiness and also provision for the carriage of a larger number of soldiers. In overall terms the galliass should be regarded as an only partially successful attempt to combine the best features of the Mediterranean type of galley with the advantages of the new type of northern European warship characterized by greater seaworthiness and far greater firepower: in this latter respect the galliass had a gun armament of between 50 and 70 cannon, although the majority of these were of the falcon or smaller type optimized for the killing and maiming of men rather than the destruction or crippling of ships.

The Battle of Lepanto of 1571 was not only a milestone in naval history, but also marked the defeat of one of the final efforts by the Turks to extend their power into central Europe. The battle resulted from the launch by the Sultan Selim II in January 1570 of a war against Venice with the initial

campaign of seizing Cyprus, one of
Venice's prize possessions in the eastern
Mediterranean. Pope Pius V established a
Christian League to counter the Turkish
effort, but the concentration of an allied
force was slow, and in the meantime the
Turks took Nicosia and Famagusta,
Venice's two main fortress cities on Cyprus,
and Ali Monizindade Pasha's fleet attacked
Venetian possessions in the Aegean and
Ionian Seas before rounding the southern
tips of the Peloponnese before cruising into
the Adriatic Sea to a point within sight of
Venice. However, learning of the allied
concentration at Messina, Ali departed for
the Ionian Sea. The Christian fleet
gathering at Messina eventually totalled
some 300 ships under the command of
Don Juan of Austria, and this fleet sailed
on 23 September to bring the Turkish fleet
to battle.

When his fleet found the Turkish fleet at
Lepanto, Don Juan had under his command
108 Venetian galleys, 81 Spanish galleys and
32 other galleys provided by the pope and
other small states, as well as six Venetian
galliasses. The Turkish fleet sortied from
Lepanto with a strength of 270 galleys. The
fleets deployed in the battle formation that
had been standard since the Battle of
Actium: each fleet was in a long line divided
into three divisions (squadrons) with a
reserve to the rear. Under the command of
Ulugh Ali, the Turks' left wing was larger
than its right wing, suggesting that Ali's
overall plan was to envelop Don Juan's right
wing, under the command of Andrea Doria,
but in other respects neither side had a
cohesive battle plan other than a melee in
which success would fall to the fleet that
rammed or captured more of the enemy's
ships that it itself lost. The importance of
the boarding role is indicated by the fact
that of the 84,000 men manning the ships

*A model of a Portuguese
caravel. Note that the vessel
has four masts, square-
rigged on the foremast and
lateen-rigged on the other
three masts.*

25

The Battle of Lepanto in October 1571. Under the command of Don Juan of Austria, the fleets of Spain, Venice and the Pope defeated the Turks in the last great sea battle involving galleys.

of the Christian fleet no fewer than 20,000 were soldiers, while the equivalent figures for the Turkish fleet were 88,000 and 16,000. (Total strength of 84,000 on board the Christian fleet, and about 16,000 Turkish soldiers of a total of 88,000.)

At this point it is worth noting that the only genuinely significant difference between the fleets at Lepanto and those of some two millennia earlier was the existence of a few small cannon in the bows of the galleys and in the broadsides of the galliasses.

Each stretched out over a 5-mile (8-km) front, the two fleets meeting in a series of great engagements from about 10.30 a.m. By 12.00 a.m. the three main divisions of each side were completely engaged, and although the galliasses broke the Turkish line this was not crucial to the unfolding of events. The fighting was very confused and lasted for about three hours, the greater proficiency of the Christian sailors and the heavier armament and armour of the Christian soldiers gradually swinging the balance of the battle in the favour of Don Juan's fleet.

Under Scirocco, the Turkish right flank had not been able to move far off Cape Schropha, and was pushed back into shoal water by Barbario's squadron before being almost wholly destroyed. In the centre of the two battle lines the fighting was more protracted before Don Juan's squadron overwhelmed that of Ali. The fight between the Turkish left-wing squadron under Ulugh Ali, the Dey of Algiers, and the Christian right-hand squadron under Andrea Doria was more finely balanced until it became clear what was happening to the rest of the Turkish fleet. Ulugh Ali then broke off and managed to escape the scene of battle with 47 of his 95 ships, together with one captured Venetian galley. These were the only Turkish survivors of the

battle: 60 ships had gone aground, 53 had been sunk, and 117 had been captured, resulting in the release of 15,000 Christian galley slaves, although it is estimated that another 10,000 or more drowned as they went down with their ships. The Turkish losses were in the order of 15,000 to 20,000 men, and only 300 became prisoners. The Christian fleet's losses included 13 galleys, 7,566 men dead, and nearly 8,000 men wounded.

Because it was late in the season considered suitable for galley operations, the Christian fleet returned to Italy to await the return of good weather during the spring of the following year when it would try to exploit its crushing victory, which was not realized because of allied indecision before Venice decided to make peace with Turkey in March 1573 and forego its claim to Cyprus. Even so, Lepanto was one of the world's decisive battles, a victory that for a time united Christendom and terminated the threat of continued Turkish expansion engendered by its domination of the central and western Mediterranean.

In terms of the development of the warship, the Battle of Lepanto was something of a non-event, for by this time the future course of warship development had been decided in northern Europe. Before the start of the 16th century, the northern European warship had been seen, like its Mediterranean counterpart, primarily as a floating castle for soldiers who were to engage the soldiers carried by the enemy's floating castles: the floating platform on which the castle was based differed very significantly between the northern European and Mediterranean schools of thought, but in tactical terms there was little difference between the concepts. To this extent, therefore, the naval battle was little more than the land battle fought at

LEFT and OPPOSITE
*Two images of the famous
naval Battle of Lepanto.
The painting on the left is by
Antonio de Brugada
(d.1863), while the one
opposite is by Juan Luna y
Novicio (1857–1900).*

sea, the opening phase of the battle
beginning as soon as the enemy was within
bow or light cannon range and being seen
as a preliminary to the main task of closing
with the enemy with the object of boarding
and capturing his ship.

The warships of this period were little
more than adapted merchant 'round'
ships, whose lengths were only slightly
more than twice their beams. The initial
effect of the introduction of gunpowder
weapons was limited to a modest increase
in the range at which the fighting started,
for the light cannon of the time had little
real destructive power and were sited on
the fore and after castles, as well as along
the sides of the deck between these castles,
to supplement the efforts of the archers.
There were heavier cannon available, but
it was impossible to install these on the
castles or on the upper deck lest the added

The flagship of Henry VIII of England, the Mary Rose *was a great ship of some 600 tons with a crew of about 400 men and armament comprising 20 heavy guns and 60 light guns. The ship was a good sailer and a capable warship, but capsized and sank in July 1545 after being rebuilt to a standard that included a lower gun deck. The wreck was discovered in the Solent in 1968, and raised in 1982 before restoration as a museum exhibit.*

The flagship of Henry VIII of England, the Mary Rose *was a great ship of some 600 tons with a crew of about 400 men and armament comprising 20 heavy guns and 60 light guns. The ship was a good sailer and a capable warship, but capsized and sank in July 1545 after being rebuilt to a standard that included a lower gun deck. The wreck was discovered in the Solent in 1968, and raised in 1982 before restoration as a museum exhibit.*

top weight cause the ship to capsize.

At the start of the 16th century, a decisive moment arrived with the invention of the port, which was an opening in the ship's side, under a hinged cover, to allow the loading and unloading of cargo without it having to be hoisted over the side of the deck and down through a hatch. It is thought that the basic port was invented in France, but it was in England that the concept was adapted during the reign of King Henry VIII (1509–1547) to allow the installation of large and therefore heavy, but also longer-ranged and more devastating, cannon on a lower deck to fire through a port that was otherwise tightly closed to prevent the ship from flooding as it rolled in any sort of sea. This concept was the origin of the heavy cannon broadside, and after its introduction in England was soon copied in Spain to create the galleon. This type of warship was initially only 100ft (30.5m) long with a beam of 30ft (9.15m). With three square-rigged masts, the galleon in its initial form still had a small ram and tall fore and after castles that provisioned the area for the installation of a comparatively large number of small cannon.

The galleon was very far from perfect, however, for it was at best an indifferent sailer and, unlike the galley, decisively short of manoeuvrability and completely at the mercy of the wind. Improvements followed as the overall size and the length/beam ratio of the galleon both increased, and general improvement of the rig and sails allowed the galleon to sail closer to the wind. Other than its broadside armament, the feature that made the galleon decisively superior to the galley was its much superior seaworthiness, which made long ocean-going voyages perfectly practical.

It was the broadside that made the new type of warship, however, for the broadside finally removed the need to close and board an enemy ship: for the first time, naval warfare could be fought by ships that did not come into physical contact with each other. This was not completely appreciated at first, for the broadside was initially seen as a way of facilitating the approach to the enemy ship that was to be boarded, but during the reign of Henry VIII and his two successors, most especially that of his daughter Queen Elizabeth I (1558–1603), it was the English who first began to grasp the fundamental nature of the changes that were intrinsic in the broadside concept. This fact was reflected in the comparatively rapid fashion in which the English abandoned the ram, increased the ratio of large to small cannon, and lowered the height of the fore and after castles, which no longer needed to carry large numbers of archers for whom height above the water was vital for additional range.

The Spanish did not altogether agree with the English, and therefore retained the ram, kept greater parity between smaller man-killing cannon and larger ship-destroying cannon, and lowered the fore castle while keeping the large after castle as the site of a large battery of small cannon. What is evident from this is that the Spanish still retained an element of the 'floating castle' thinking in their naval

philosophy, which continued to emphasize the carriage of soldiers. Spain's large galleons were therefore something of a hybrid type reflecting old and new thinking, while the English moved swiftly to the new thinking that emphasized longer-range gunnery in ships that were generally smaller but always more handy than their Spanish counterparts. This latter reflected growing English expertise in ship-handling and in the creation of seaworthy ships, and also allowed the use of hull volume not for the accommodation of soldiers but for ammunition and powder as well as the additional stores that permitted longer voyages.

It was this more far-sighted approach to tactical and technical thinking that allowed the English to inflict a strategically decisive

defeat on the Spanish Armada in 1588 as the British ships used their greater manoeuvrability and seaworthiness to launch attacks on detached ships, and also used the longer range of their cannon fire to harass Spanish vessels that could not reply effectively. In the process, the English ships laid the foundations of a naval and directly related mercantile supremacy that was to last, with breaks, until well into the 20th century.

Before the start of the 16th century, naval strategy had been seen largely as a support to land strategy, for it was in land campaigns that the issue was decided. However, in the course of the 16th century, the development of merchant ships and warships with a genuine ocean-crossing capability changed this perception of naval warfare, which now started to become as important as land warfare in the furtherance of national interests at the political and economic levels. This was clearly reflected in the creation, by Alfonso de Albuquerque and Francisco de Almeida, of a number of carefully sited Portuguese bases around the Indian Ocean, resulting in the establishment of a virtually total Portuguese control of the coasts and sea routes of the Indian Ocean throughout most of the century.

While they may not have seen the implications of a carefully considered and implemented naval strategy as clearly as the Portuguese, the Spanish nonetheless made effective use of the more limited concept that they did possess. This was largely responsible for the overall Spanish superiority in the western hemisphere, and for the extension of this power to the sea routes of the Atlantic Ocean and the eastern part of the Pacific Ocean.

The implication of the Spanish domination of the Americas, based on carefully sited primary bases and control of

Henry VIII, after a painting by Holbein at Hampton Court.

Departure from Lisbon for Brazil, the East Indies and America, an engraving from American Tertia Pars, *1562.*

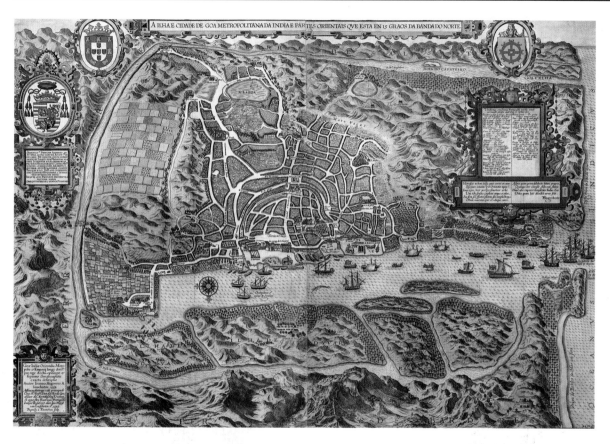

Map of the city and Portuguese port of Goa, India, an engraving of 1595 by Johannes Baptista van Doetechum the Younger (c.1560–1630). The voyages of the Portuguese and Spanish explorers from the later part of the 15th century, and their establishment of these countries' imperial and trading empires in the East and in the Americas, were instrumental in the development within Europe of the navigational skills and ships needed for long ocean voyages.

the sea lanes, was increasingly obvious to England's increasingly capable and ambitious maritime thinkers such as Drake, and these men were as much doers as thinkers. It was the confidence engendered in these men by their success against the

Armada using the latest broadside tactics, that paved the way for the emergence of the English and later British domination of the seas.

Turning back to the ships of the period once more, it is important to note that

apart from the lateen on the mizzen mast, ships were rigged with square sails until the middle of the 17th century. By this time the lateen had begun to give way to the more manageable spritsail rigged completely aft of the mast with a diagonal spar running from

A ship in full sail en route to Portugal. Although almost childishly simplified, and suffering from highly distorted proportions, this German illustration does serve to highlight the basic layout of a Portuguese caravel, which was square-rigged on its fore mast and main mast, but lateen-rigged on its mizzen mast.

low on the mast to the rear upper corner of the spritsail, and this process was completed when the spritsail was replaced by the four-sided spanker or driver with a boom at its foot and a gaff at its head. The driver was initially thought a fair-weather sail, but the ease with which it could be tacked meant that it finally replaced the mizzen course (the lowest square sail on the mizzen mast) from the middle of the 18th century.

Square-rigged ships are most effective when running before the wind, whereas ships with fore-and-aft rigs can sail closer to the wind. By the middle of the 17th century serious efforts were being made to combine the two types of rig to produce a sailing ship able to run before or tack into the wind with equal ease. The mizzen spritsail was a move in the right direction, but greater capability came from the adoption of staysails and jibs. Staysails are triangular sails set on the stays that brace the masts against fore-and-aft movement, while jibs are again triangular sails set on the stays bracing the foremast to the bowsprit running forward from the bow and previously carrying a spritsail and a small square sail below and above it respectively.

As trade increased in volume and importance during the 19th century, an increasing level of emphasis was placed on increasing profitability in merchant ships and overall efficiency in warships by an enhancement of speed and also by a reduction in crew numbers, although this latter was of more interest to the owners of merchant ships than to the operators of warships, which needed large numbers of men to sail the ship and man the guns in battle. The handling of fore-and-aft rigs requires fewer men than square rigs, and ship designers combined the two basic

types of rig into the ships of the period. The larger ships were the barque and barquentine. The barque displaced up to 5,500 tons and had between three and five masts, of which the forward two were always square-rigged. The barquentine had three masts and was square-rigged on only the foremast. The smaller ships were the brig and brigantine. The brig is a two-masted ship, square-rigged on both masts, while the brigantine is again two-masted but square-rigged on only the foremast. The ultimate in sailing vessels with high windward performance is the schooner, which began to appear at the beginning of the 18th century in Massachusetts as a comparatively small two- or three-masted vessel fore-and-aft rigged on all these masts. Schooners were fast and extremely weatherly vessels, at first carrying four-sided mainsails; but from the middle of the 18th century they were increasingly seen with the Bermudan rig: this replaces four-sided sails with triangular sails that have their heads at the top of the masts and so do away with the gaff and all its rigging.

To recapitulate: during the early part of the medieval period, comparatively little use was made of naval warfare, and when warships were needed merchant ships were used. The ships were loaded with men rather than cargo, and naval battles consisted of closing with the enemy so that the soldiers could board and capture the enemy ships – in short a land battle transferred onto the sea. But change became inevitable after the introduction of gunpowder weapons in the middle of the 14th century. At first, the warship was a comparatively simple development of the merchant ship with the fore and after castles revised for carriage of the light cannon that were typical of the period. As cannon became both more common and

LEFT
Sir Francis Drake (1545–96), English navigator and privateer.

LEFT
One of a set of contemporary playing-cards produced to celebrate the defeat of the Spanish Armada in 1588.

larger in size, however, this resulted in an increasing element of top-heaviness on the warships of the later part of the century. Inevitably, therefore, warships became longer and lower, with the cannon arranged in broadside rows along the length of the upper deck. At the same time the fore and after castles were made taller so that light weapons could be mounted in and on them to attack the enemy ship's crew and, in the event that the ship was boarded, to shoot down into the enemy fighting in the waist of the ship between the fore and after castles. The scheme worked well when the ships were in combat, but it also made the ships considerably more difficult to sail, the large area of the fore and after castles making it easier for the wind to push the ship sideways so that it slipped away downwind and therefore tended to lose the

weather gauge that was recognized as the single most important advantage that any warship could have in action.

These early warships were of about 500 tons, though some English warships were as large as 1,000 tons. Late in the 16th century English shipbuilders began to develop warships with lower castles, especially at the bow, and the ships of this revised pattern soon revealed that they sailed far more satisfactorily. Larger numbers of guns were installed by increasing the height of the hull above the water and by arranging the guns on separate decks, with the largest-calibre and therefore heaviest weapons on the lowest deck and the smaller and lighter guns on the higher decks. This English development was soon copied by other European navies to produce hard-hitting ships that could also sail well. This

An engraving of the final battle off Gravelines, France, during the engagement of the English and Spanish Fleets in July 1588.

established the pattern of warships until well into the 19th century. Refinements were made, but the basic pattern remained unaltered despite a growth in size to about 3,000 tons and 130 guns by the middle of the 19th century. The emphasis in warship design was given to speed and agility, which called for a long and comparatively narrow hull, and this also improved the warship's ability to carry the long rows of guns needed to fire effective broadside salvoes. By the middle of the 18th century, the

increasingly formal nature of naval warfare had led most navies to introduce special designations for their warships, and from this time onward warships were generally designated into six 'rates' on the basis of the number of broadside guns they carried: the first three rates and sometimes the fourth rate were 'line-of-battle ships', which meant that they were deemed sufficiently powerful to operate successfully within the line of battle that was the core deployment of all navies for fleet actions. The fifth and sixth

rates were frigates designed to scout for the heavier vessels. The exact number of guns that decided the rate varied slightly with date, but at the time of the Battle of Trafalgar in 1805 a first-rate warship had more than 100 guns on three decks, a second-rate ship between 100 and 84 guns on three decks, a third-rate ship between 84 and 70 guns on two decks, a fourth-rate ship between 70 and 50 guns on two decks, a fifth-rate ship between 40 and 32 guns on one deck, and a sixth-rate ship between 32 and 24 guns on one deck. Below this were sloops of war with between 24 and 16 guns, and these were two-masted vessels square-rigged on both in the case of brigs and square-rigged on only one (normally the fore mast) in the case of brigantines. Anything smaller than a sloop of war was generally designated as a cutter, and used for tasks such as delivery of dispatches and orders.

As noted above, the need of the larger ships to accommodate their guns on up to three decks led to the development of warships that were comparatively tall above the water, and to reduce the stability problems that might otherwise have affected the ships, their hulls were given great 'tumblehome', the attractive inward curve of the hull above the point of greatest beam. The heaviest guns were placed as low as possible to reduce stability problems still further, and the guns fired through ports in the hull that were covered by heavy port lids when the guns were not being used. The guns had long barrels and were extremely heavy, recoiling far inboard when fired and requiring heavy tackles to arrest them. The recoil brought the muzzle inboard of the port, which allowed these muzzle-loading weapons to be reloaded without undue difficulty before being run out again to their firing positions. The effective range of naval cannon was only about 100 yards, so naval battles were generally side-by-side slugging matches in which weight of fire (the weight of the ball fired and the number of rounds fired) in general counted more than pinpoint accuracy. The largest cannon carried by first-rate ships fired a 42-lb (19.05-kg) solid ball, and the lightest standard gun of frigates fired a 16-lb (7.25-kg) ball; smaller vessels were armed with guns firing 9-, 6- and 4-lb (4.1-, 2.7- and 1.8-kg) balls. The tendency toward weight of fire reached its height in the

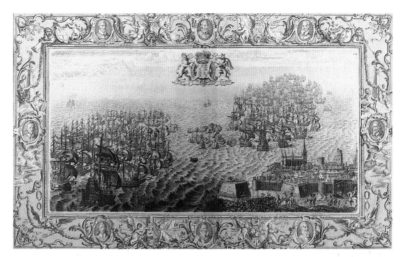

Another engraving of the Anglo-Spanish War of 1588.

Napoleonic wars, when the British introduced the carronade as a short-range 'smasher' weapon with a short barrel. To reduce its recoil this weapon was mounted on a slide rather than on a wheeled truck, and was a weapon of notable inaccuracy designed to fire a large ball over short range. Solid shot, designed to penetrate thick hull planking, was the norm, but there were available other types of projectile such as bar, chain and grape, that were designed to knock down masts, rigging and men.

The only two technical innovations in the first half of the 18th century were the replacement of the tiller by a wheel operating the rudder by means of ropes, and the adoption of copper sheathing to protect the parts of the hull below the waterline against attack by the teredo or shipworm.

The warships led the way in the development of sailing techniques during the 15th, 16th and 17th centuries. Where the low-cost movement of bulk cargoes was concerned, the owners of merchant ships still preferred large hulls moved by two square sails on each of three masts, and this is typical of the 250-ton caravel that was the most important trading ship up to the end of the 14th century and could be operated by a relatively small and therefore inexpensive crew. The opening of new trade routes across the world's oceans to the east and west of Europe, resulting from the expansion of the 'age of discovery', then demanded larger and more weatherly ships such as the Spanish high-forecastle carracks and succeeding low-fore-castle galleons of up to 1,600 tons, and the East Indiamen of the merchant companies formed by most northern European countries for the trade to India and the Far East. The development of this luxury trade began to place increasing emphasis on fast delivery, and these ships became larger than warships, with a basically

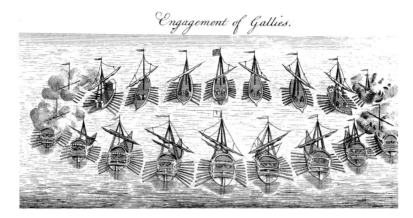

Engagement of Gallies.

slender hull for high speed combined with large carrying capacity. Tall masts with huge clouds of sail became common, and larger crews allowed these superb sailing vessels to be pushed to their limits over massive distances. The wool trade with Australia and the tea trade with China were dominated by the great clipper ships until the opening of the Suez Canal in 1869, when the steam ship began to rival the clipper on long routes to the eastern hemisphere. The last area where the great sailing ships still held an edge was South America, where European and American trade needed to round Cape Horn. This trade was better served by sailing ships than the steam ships of the period, and large four-masted barques and five-masted schooners were the best ships on this route until 1914. In that year the Panama Canal was opened, and this passage between the Caribbean and the Pacific Ocean removed most of the need for ships to round Cape Horn. World War I ended the day of the sailing ship as the chief trading type of the advanced countries:

German submarine and surface raiders sank many sailing ships that lacked the speed to escape, and the Allies concentrated their shipbuilding on the steam-driven ships that were already in a dominant position.

This simple overview of the development of the sailing ship in general jumps ahead of the story of the warship and naval warfare proper. By the start of the 17th century, and refined in the successes against Spain in the second half of the previous century, English naval thinking was decided superior to that of any rival power. This is decidedly odd as the secret of the English success was the broadside, which was not something that could be successfully concealed, but for reasons that have never been explained neither the Spanish nor the Dutch, the latter emerging as aggressive and far-sighted rivals to the English in terms of the use of sea power for mercantile purposes supported by naval power, appreciated this fact. The combination of European circumstance and an admitted English naval superiority meant

that there were no naval wars in the first half of the 17th century, and therefore no way for the British to test their newest ships and thinking in combat and thus gain the operational experience requirement for further improvement.

The only major development of the early part of the 17th century, apparently by the English, was the control of a gun's recoil with rope tackles in a manner that combined the least stress on the ship's structure and the tactical advantage of halting the gun far enough inboard from the port to make reloading simple and therefore quick. Before this invention, it had been the standard practice to lash the gun as hard as possible to the ship's timbers to prevent recoil: this required very strong (and therefore heavy) timbers, and made it very difficult for the gun's crew to reload its weapon. It was this fact that had led to the English tactic, which became very evident in the running battles against the Spanish Armada, of groups of about five ships attacking any one Spanish ship: each English ship attacked in turn, the time taken by the succeeding four ships providing the period required by the first to reload its broadside weapons and continue the cannonade.

The system of controlling and indeed exploiting the recoil of the cannon allowed the use of slightly less massive (and therefore lighter and cheaper) timbers and at the same time effectively increased the rate of fire of each ship by a factor of about five.

Using this development in combination with experience gained in the 1st Anglo-Dutch War (1652–1654), Admiral Robert Blake, the greatest English naval leader of the period, was able to formalize the 'line of battle' formation as the norm: the fleet's ships were deployed in single column, at regular intervals, to provide maximum broadside fire and also maximum control by the admiral. So far as the latter was concerned there were great difficulties, especially when the fleet was large or when visibility was reduced by natural (fog, mist, flying spray, rain etc.) and man-made (gun smoke) factors. These factors also combined with the size of the naval 'battlefield', which might stretch for several miles, to produce major problems in tactics and control. The concept of basic flag signals had already been devised, but even after it had been steadily refined in the period up to the end of the Napoleonic Wars in 1815, this system of signal communication was wholly inadequate to convey anything but general instructions.

It was this fact that induced the English navy to create a set of 'Fighting Instructions' that, it was hoped, would overcome or at least alleviate the problems associated with inadequate signalling by the establishment of a set of standard formations and tactics understood by all officers as relevant to the full gamut of naval situations likely to arise. The Fighting Instructions were amplified by detailed instructions issued by the admiral before his fleet put out to sea or at a meeting held in the flagship before the opposing fleets met.

The theory inevitably fell far short of the fact, for it was impossible to create a set of Fighting Instructions adequate to deal with everything that might happen under the spur of weather conditions, the actions of the enemy commander and other circumstances. As a result there emerged in England during the period between the 1st and 2nd Anglo-Dutch Wars, the latter taking place in the period 1665–1667, two schools of tactical thought. Each of these agreed that the approach to battle should be in line-ahead formation and preferably to windward of the enemy so that the English could dictate the time at which the battle began, but differed on the course that ought to be adopted after the battle had started. The adherents of what may be termed the 'formal' school of tactical thought held that the line-ahead formation should be maintained, no matter what happened, until victory had been secured: each ship would engage the enemy vessel

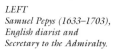

*Lord Horatio Nelson
(1758–1805) by Sir William
Beachy (1753–1839).*

closest to it, but would at the same time follow the course of the preceding vessel, and this would provide the admiral with the assurance that he knew the relative location of each of his ships, in action against the enemy ship opposite it, and could order the entire fleet to break off if necessary. On the other hand, the adherents of the 'melee' school thought that provision should be made for the admiral to free squadron and ship commanders to leave the line of battle to make a massed attack against portions of the enemy's fleet.

Both schools of thought had been tried by the end of the 17th century, and each were found to have advantages as well as disadvantages. In general, however, it was the adherents of the formal school who prevailed at the end of the century, and this established the pattern of naval tactics for the next 100 years as signalled by the 1691 enshrinement of the Fighting Instructions into law.

During the 2nd Anglo-Dutch War and then in the 3rd Anglo-Dutch War (1672–1674) the Dutch adopted the line-ahead formation pioneered by the English and also improved the efficiency of their ships' broadside force. Even so, the Dutch still believed in the primacy of boarding and capturing an enemy ship in hand-to-hand combat rather than destroying it with stand-off fire. This meant that even though the Dutch admirals were the equal of and in some cases superior to their English opponents, the Dutch challenge to English naval superiority achieved several successes but ultimately sailed in the face of the determination of the English and the superiority of their gunnery.

By the end of the Anglo-Dutch wars, a new naval rival to the English was emerging in the form of the French under the leadership of King Louis XIV (1643–1715) with the highly efficient Jean Colbert as the minister responsible for the navy in a fashion analogous to the position of Samuel Pepys under King James II (1685–1688), who as the younger brother of King Charles II (1660–1680) had been instrumental in creating the administrative framework under which the British navy flourished. Colbert saw that in the shorter term the way to rival

*A painting of the 1805
Battle of Trafalgar by
William Clarkson Stanfield
(1793–c. 1867).*

English naval power was the exploitation of science and technology to produce ships that were qualitatively superior to those of the English, and the French therefore adopted English concepts and improved them, with the result that French ships were generally faster and more seaworthy than their English counterparts. Quantity was then added to quality, and by the time of the War of the Grand Alliance (1688–1697) the French navy was arguably the finest in the world with a strength equal to those of the English and Dutch combined. The French failure to best the English in the naval aspect of this war thus reflected the essentially non-naval thinking of Louis XIV, who denied his finest admirals, Anne Hilarion de Tourville and Jean Bart, the right to fight the war as they thought fit. As a result, all France's naval efforts of the previous half century were wasted, and by the end of the war France had been reduced to commerce raiding.

British naval superiority remained supreme during the 18th century, although from the middle of the period there was clear evidence of a certain ossification of naval thinking, leading to slavish adherence to the Fighting Instructions rather than the development of new tactical thinking: this was perhaps inevitable after the Fighting Instructions had passed into law, and was characterized by the failure of Admiral Sir John Byng in the Battle of Minorca (1756), in which he refused to depart from the tactics laid down in the Fighting Instructions, an 'offence' for which he was court-martialled and executed by firing squad. Even so, the British continued to dominate the oceans of the world, and the implications of the Battle of Minorca finally persuaded farther-thinking admirals that the time was now more than ripe for the abandonment of the 'formal' interpretation of the Fighting Instructions in favour of the melee interpretation.

The tactical advantage offered by the adherents of the melee school, which included a large number of the younger captains of the Royal Navy, was that ships could turn out of the line toward the enemy's line and, after surviving the broadside raking fire that would be concentrated on the bows of the leading ship by several of the enemy's ships, break through the enemy's line, dividing it into a number of poorly coordinated elements that could be attacked and destroyed in detail by exploiting the superior seamanship and fighting powers (including rapid broadsides) of the British ships. This tactic was pioneered in action by admirals Sir John Jervis, Sir George Rodney and Lord Howe. The last of these used the concept to devastating effect during the classic tactical victory that the British scored in the four-day Battle of the Glorious 1st of June (1794), which ended when Howe committed his forces to attacks on the French centre: the French lost seven of their 26 line-of-battle ships in the form of six captured and one sunk, while the British lost none of their own 26 line-of-battle ships. The tactic began to reach its definitive form in the Battle of Cape St. Vincent (1797), when a British fleet of 15 line-of-battle ships under Jervis met a Spanish fleet of 27 line-of-battle ships under Admiral José de Cordova. Jervis sailed his fleet in line-ahead into the gap between the Spanish divisions of nine and 18 ships, and then turned on the latter, which might have escaped had not Captain Horatio Nelson, commanding HMS *Captain*, acted without orders and broke away from the British fleet in a wide-sweeping track that put him ahead of the larger group of Spanish ships. Nelson tackled the leading seven Spanish ships and

The Battle of Trafalgar, *by*
John Christian Scherty
(1778–1874).

Commencement of the
Battle of Trafalgar, 21
October 1805, *an
engraving by Thomas
Sutherland for J. Jenkins'*
Naval Achievements, *1817,
of a painting by Thomas
Whitcombe (1760–1824).*

so delayed them that Jervis had time to come up, and in the ensuing melee the British captured four Spanish ships.

This was the first example of the 'Nelson touch', and set the pattern for the naval warfare that took place in the Napoleonic Wars.

Gunnery was also divided into two schools during this period. One school, typified by the British practice, believed that as rapid a rate of short-range fire as possible should be directed at the hulls of the enemy's ships to pierce their sides and thus disable or sink them. The other school, typified by the French, adhered to the concept of longer-ranged and more carefully aimed fire directly at the masts, rigging and sails of the enemy's ships, which would thus be disabled for subsequent capture and, if possible, repair and addition to the French fleet. So strong was the belief of the British in the overall superiority of short-range 'smashing' fire that they introduced the carronade, which was a short-barrel weapon firing a 32-lb (14.5-kg) or heavier ball that at short range had far superior penetrating power than the longer guns that had been standard up to this time. Perhaps just as importantly, the carronade was also cheaper to manufacture than the long gun and was also easier to handle as it was lighter.

The carronade worked well against the French, but came to be seen as a limited weapon against the Americans in the War of 1812. Against the French, the British were able to exploit the better training and greater experience of their ships' crews to manoeuvre safely into the range at which the carronade was effective. Against the Americans, however, this was impossible, for the frigates that were the workhorses of the American effort in this war were large, fast, handy and manned by high-quality crews: they were therefore able to maintain

their distance and use their long guns to pound the opposing British frigates into submission.

Developments in technology allowed the British to pioneer several improvements in gunnery during this period, and in the process to assure their ships of superior fire power. These improvements included a more reliable firing system in which the original loose powder priming, fired by a linstock, was replaced by a flintlock device that flashed a spark into the touch hole; better bags in which the gunpowder was moved to the gun; the wetting of the wads inserted between the powder and the ball to prevent premature firings; addition of metal springs to the rope breechings used to check the gun's recoil; inclined wooden runways under the carriage wheels for a further easing of the gun's recoil; and, perhaps most importantly of all, tackles attached to the rear of the gun carriage to allow the traverse of individual guns to the right or left, which removed or at least reduced the gun's aim from the right angle to the ship's course that had hitherto been the norm.

Just as significantly for tactical success in naval warfare was a radical improvement in the signalling arrangements for ships at sea: the introduction of an improved and more versatile code of flag signals made it considerably easier for a commander to inform ships' captains of his intentions before battle was joined, and also to keep control of events after the fighting had started. The new system was introduced in 1800, and was the work of Admiral Sir Home Popham.

It was the combination of British determination and experience at sea, Popham's signalling and Nelson's operational genius that brought the fighting of the sailing ship era to its peak,

culminating in the Battle of Trafalgar on 21 October 1805. In April of the same year, Admiral Pierre Villeneuve had evaded the British fleet blockading Toulon, the main French naval base in the Mediterranean, and sailed into the Atlantic, where he joined forces with a Spanish fleet and sailed across the Atlantic Ocean to the West Indies. The 20 ships of the allied force were pursued by the ten under Nelson's command, and then returned to European waters where, after an action with a British force under Admiral Sir Robert Calder off Finisterre, resulting in the loss of two Spanish ships, they reached Cadiz and were reinforced.

Threatened by Napoleon Buonaparte with removal for cowardice, Villeneuve then sailed for the Mediterranean under orders to join forces with another French force from Cartagena and then support French land operations in southern Italy. Nelson was waiting for such a move with a fleet now numbering 29 line-of-battle ships, although on the eve of the battle only 27 of these were available to him, and intercepted the 33 French and Spanish line-of-battle ships. The allied fleet tried to return to Cadiz, but

so delayed them that Jervis had time to come up, and in the ensuing melee the British captured four Spanish ships.

This was the first example of the 'Nelson touch', and set the pattern for the naval warfare that took place in the Napoleonic Wars.

Gunnery was also divided into two schools during this period. One school, typified by the British practice, believed that as rapid a rate of short-range fire as possible should be directed at the hulls of the enemy's ships to pierce their sides and thus disable or sink them. The other school, typified by the French, adhered to the concept of longer-ranged and more carefully aimed fire directly at the masts, rigging and sails of the enemy's ships, which would thus be disabled for subsequent capture and, if possible, repair and addition to the French fleet. So strong was the belief of the British in the overall superiority of short-range 'smashing' fire that they introduced the carronade, which was a short-barrel weapon firing a 32-lb (14.5-kg) or heavier ball that at short range had far superior penetrating power than the longer guns that had been standard up to this time. Perhaps just as importantly, the carronade was also cheaper to manufacture than the long gun and was also easier to handle as it was lighter.

The carronade worked well against the French, but came to be seen as a limited weapon against the Americans in the War of 1812. Against the French, the British were able to exploit the better training and greater experience of their ships' crews to manoeuvre safely into the range at which the carronade was effective. Against the Americans, however, this was impossible, for the frigates that were the workhorses of the American effort in this war were large, fast, handy and manned by high-quality crews: they were therefore able to maintain

their distance and use their long guns to pound the opposing British frigates into submission.

Developments in technology allowed the British to pioneer several improvements in gunnery during this period, and in the process to assure their ships of superior fire power. These improvements included a more reliable firing system in which the original loose powder priming, fired by a linstock, was replaced by a flintlock device that flashed a spark into the touch hole; better bags in which the gunpowder was moved to the gun; the wetting of the wads inserted between the powder and the ball to prevent premature firings; addition of metal springs to the rope breechings used to check the gun's recoil; inclined wooden runways under the carriage wheels for a further easing of the gun's recoil; and, perhaps most importantly of all, tackles attached to the rear of the gun carriage to allow the traverse of individual guns to the right or left, which removed or at least reduced the gun's aim from the right angle to the ship's course that had hitherto been the norm.

Just as significantly for tactical success in naval warfare was a radical improvement in the signalling arrangements for ships at sea: the introduction of an improved and more versatile code of flag signals made it considerably easier for a commander to inform ships' captains of his intentions before battle was joined, and also to keep control of events after the fighting had started. The new system was introduced in 1800, and was the work of Admiral Sir Home Popham.

It was the combination of British determination and experience at sea, Popham's signalling and Nelson's operational genius that brought the fighting of the sailing ship era to its peak,

culminating in the Battle of Trafalgar on 21 October 1805. In April of the same year, Admiral Pierre Villeneuve had evaded the British fleet blockading Toulon, the main French naval base in the Mediterranean, and sailed into the Atlantic, where he joined forces with a Spanish fleet and sailed across the Atlantic Ocean to the West Indies. The 20 ships of the allied force were pursued by the ten under Nelson's command, and then returned to European waters where, after an action with a British force under Admiral Sir Robert Calder off Finisterre, resulting in the loss of two Spanish ships, they reached Cadiz and were reinforced.

Threatened by Napoleon Buonaparte with removal for cowardice, Villeneuve then sailed for the Mediterranean under orders to join forces with another French force from Cartagena and then support French land operations in southern Italy. Nelson was waiting for such a move with a fleet now numbering 29 line-of-battle ships, although on the eve of the battle only 27 of these were available to him, and intercepted the 33 French and Spanish line-of-battle ships. The allied fleet tried to return to Cadiz, but

Nelson had divided his force into two divisions abreast of each other and each deployed in a single line. These two lines struck at the centre of the allied fleet's disorganized deployment, cutting it into two parts. The resulting battle lasted for five hours in which British experience and gunnery prevailed: the allied fleet lost 18 ships captured and another four sunk as the other 18 broke off and tried to regain Cadiz: the British lost no ships, but Nelson was mortally wounded.

The combination of British seafaring capability, Popham's signalling system and the fusion of the formal and melee types of fighting as perfected by Nelson brought the naval warfare of the era of the sailing ship to a peak of perfection. Further development of naval warfare was now dependent on the emergence of new technologies, which were in fact already beginning to appear: it was in 1803, two years before the Battle of Trafalgar, that the first steamship was launched on the River Seine in France, and it was this novel type of propulsion that was to characterize the next step in the evolution of the warship.

Up to the middle of the 18th century there was no possible alternative to oars or sails as the motive power for ships of either the mercantile or naval type. The sailing ships of the time did possess the great advantage of using a source of power that is entirely free, namely the wind. This meant that primary motion was cheap because the sailing ship's equipment to exploit this free power, namely the masts, spars, sails and associated rigging, were fairly long-lasting. Only a small amount of the hull's volume was required for accommodation of spare sails and spars, and this left most of the hull free for the carriage of cargo in merchant ships or of men and armament in warships. However, it had been keenly appreciated

from the start of the sailing era that sail-propelled ships are limited by the prevailing weather conditions and cannot sail directly into the wind. The first of these limitations meant slow sailing speed in light winds or stormy weather, and the second required the ship either to tack upwind or to sail off course in the search of favourable winds: in both cases the result is a voyage lasting much longer than planned. This sometimes meant that the crew's food and water began to run short, a fact that was of only modest significance when the ship involved was a merchant vessel generally carrying a non-perishable bulk cargo such as timber or grain. For warships, the peculiar disadvantages of wind power often meant the difference between success and failure.

Mechanical propulsion obviously offered a way out of this problem, but was not available until the second half of the 18th century and the development of the first steam engines. The first practical steam engine was patented by a Briton, James Watt, in 1769; but the introduction of an entirely new concept of power was held back by a number of mechanical and design factors, and in the case of ships by the strongly conservative attitude of independently-minded sailors. The first recorded use of a steam engine in a waterborne vessel occurred in 1783 when a French nobleman, the Marquis Jouffroy d'Abbans, managed a trip up part of the River Saône in the paddle-wheel steamer *Pyroscaphe*. More important by far, though, was the development of the first successful steam-driven commercial vessel, the paddle-wheel tug *Charlotte Dundas*. She was a small wooden vessel with a steam engine designed by William Symington, and was built on the River Clyde in Scotland to the order of Lord Dundas, governor of the Forth and Clyde Canal. The vessel had a

single paddle wheel at the stern, and from 1802 proved her worth by towing two laden lighters 20 miles (32km) along the canal. The *Charlotte Dundas* was still largely an experimental design, and the honour of being the world's first steam vessel to maintain a regular schedule falls to the American *Clermont* designed by Robert Fulton and built on New York's East River. From 17 August 1807 the *Clermont* maintained a regular service along the River Hudson between New York and Albany. Displacing 100 tons and measuring 133ft (40.5m) in length, the *Clermont* had a British-built Boulton and Watt single-cylinder engine driving two 15-ft (4.57-m) diameter paddle wheels.

The single most notable feature of these early steam vessels is their use of one or two paddle wheels to transmit the power of the engine to the water and so propel the vessel. The use of paddle wheels was not in itself a complete innovation, as the Westerners of the time believed, for the use of wheels fitted with paddles or blades had been known to the Chinese and Egyptians several thousand years earlier, though of course with man or animal power. The first steam vessels readopted the concept, at first with a single wheel mounted between two hulls or within the stern (as in the *Charlotte Dundas*), but it soon became apparent that the use of two paddles, one on each side, offered a better way to use the modest power of the steam engines of the period. The paddles were mounted on a common shaft driven by the midships-mounted engine, and generally had six or more blades. The early steam engines were not very efficient, and their fuel consumption was high. This was not a particular problem for vessels that did not venture far from a coaling station, and most of the early steam vessels were therefore harbour and river

OPPOSITE
The Suez Canal was a classic example of the progress made in technological developments during the second quarter of the 19th century. The availability of the Suez Canal in itself drastically shortened the route from Europe to the East, removing the need for ships to round Cape Horn at the southern tip of Africa, and was geared to the transit of steam ships rather than sailing vessels, which were by this time becoming less important in terms of carrying high-value and time-sensitive cargoes.

HMS Glasgow, *a steam-and-sail wooden frigate, the last of its type and superseded by iron-clad corvettes and cruisers. 1861.*

tugs, gradually extending to coasting vessels that could come into harbour if coal stocks were low. But gradually, the advantages of steam for deep-ocean vessels became clearer, even though common sense dictated that a steam engine should be used to supplement rather than replace sails: should the wind be in the right quarter and of adequate strength the sails were used, but should the wind be wrong in strength or direction the steam engine could be used to maintain progress along the desired course. The tendency was not to use the engine unless absolutely necessary: the captains of merchant ships were under orders not to use expensive coal unless it was unavoidable, and the captains of warships disliked the damage and unsightliness inflicted on their sails and decks by the engine's smuts and smoke, and also had a concern that a devotion to the steam engine would reduce the emphasis placed on basic seamanship.

Given the emphasis still placed on sail, it was sensible to make the paddle wheels as units that could be dismantled and stowed on deck when not in use. The first ship to make a crossing of the North Atlantic entirely on steam power was the *Sirius*, a 700-ton British ship designed for ferry operations across the English Channel and powered by a 320-hp (238.5-kW) steam engine: the ship was chartered by the British and American Steam Navigation Company, which had pinned great commercial hopes on achieving the first steam-powered Atlantic crossing in a ship built especially for the task. But with its

LEFT
Brunel's Great Britain *leaving Liverpool.*

BELOW and BELOW LEFT
Great Britain *aground in Dundrum Bay. Twenty boxes of 30 tons of sand were used as leverage to raise the ship. Below left: Cutting a trench from the stern to seaward in attempts to refloat her in July 1847.*

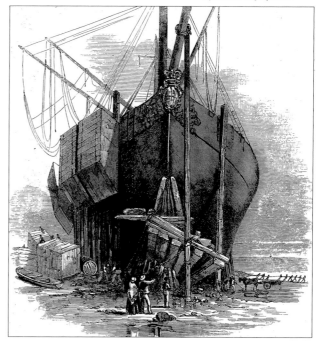

British *Queen* late in completion and
Isambard Kingdom Brunel's *Great Western*
nearly ready for a rival company, the
company chartered the *Sirius* in 1838 and
despatched her from Cork in Ireland on 4
April 1838 with 40 passengers: she arrived
in New York 18 days later after crossing at
an average of 6.7kt, beating the *Great
Western* by just a few hours despite the fact
that Brunel's ship had left Bristol four days
after the departure of the *Sirius* from Cork.

After using all her coal, the *Sirius* had been
forced to burn all the cabin furniture, the
spare spars and even one mast.

Typical of the early type of hybrid
warship was the British frigate HMS
Galatea of 1829.

By about 1840 it was common for the
blades of the paddle wheels to be fitted
with a feathering device (radial rods
operated by an eccentric wheel) to keep the
blades as nearly vertical as possible as they

entered, moved through and finally lifted
out of the water: this increased the
efficiency of the blades, and also reduced
wash with consequent improvements in
speed and fuel economy.

A major turning point in the
development of steam ships was the
construction of the first such ship designed
for the Atlantic run. This was the *Great
Western* designed by Brunel and built of
wood. She was 236ft (71.9m) long and of

Warships at anchor at the mouth of the Thames awaiting the tide. The one on the right is a sailing vessel while the ship next to her is transitional, possessing steam and sail. On the left are convict hulks used as prison accommodation. (Engraving by Arthur Willmore, 1814–1888).

HMS Invincible *(left) and HMS* Temeraire *(foreground) with HMS* Monarch *(behind).*

1,321-ton burthen, and just half of her hull volume was occupied by coal, four boilers and the two-cylinder Maudslay engine powering two paddle wheels. On her maiden voyage from Bristol to New York in April and May 1838, the ship averaged 8kt and achieved the crossing in 15 days. Carrying 24 passengers, the ship arrived in New York with 200 tons of coal remaining.

The success of the *Great Western* confirmed that purpose-designed steam ships were more economical than converted sailing ships or purpose-built hybrid types, and also proved that it was safe to operate long oceanic routes with ships powered entirely by steam. The result was considerable growth in the number and importance of paddle-wheel steam ships. Great Britain was by far the most important maritime power of the time, and the routes from British ports that saw the greatest growth in steam ship traffic were those across the Atlantic, to the Iberian peninsula (northern Spain, Lisbon and Gibraltar) and into the Mediterranean, and later in the century through the Suez Canal towards India and the Far East. Coaling stations were developed in strategically placed ports and islands, allowing the steady development of steam-powered trade routes to South America, South Africa and Australasia.

Even by this time, though, the paddle wheel was already entering its last phase as the means of transmitting the steam engine's power to the water. Merchant seamen had been aware all along that the ship's roll placed great strain on the drive shaft when one wheel was deep in the water and the other perhaps completely out of the water, a situation reversed as the ship rolled back in the other direction. Moreover, the fact that a lightly laden vessel had only part of its wheels submerged while a deeply

The Warrior, *the first iron warship, commissioned by the British government in 1859 and at sea by 1861. (A pencil drawing with white paint by William McConnell, fl. 1850–90.)*

laden ship had most of its wheels buried in the water made it difficult to plan the carriage of an economical load of coal. Naval officers were aware of the paddle wheel's limitations for another reason: even when protected by large paddle boxes, the wheels were highly vulnerable to the broadside typical of naval combat in

this period. Emphasis therefore turned slowly but inexorably to the propeller, which remains safely submerged in all but the most extreme circumstances, for ocean-going ships even though the paddle wheel remained standard for lake and riverine vessels.

The propeller was developed for ship

propulsion almost simultaneously by four men in the period between 1833 and 1838. These designers were the Englishmen Francis Pettit Smith and Robert Watson, the Frenchman Frederick Sauvage and the Swede Johannes (or John) Ericsson. Their designs were roughly similar, but that of Smith won a competition sponsored by the

Isambard Kingdom Brunel's steam ship Great Eastern *on the stocks at John Russell's Millwall shipyard on the Thames.*

British Admiralty and thus proved the basis for later developments. Smith's patent was granted in May 1836, just six weeks before that granted to Ericsson, and was initially proved on a 10-ton vessel as a two-blade unit driven by a 6-hp (4.5-kW) steam engine. This achieved fair success even in choppy water, and was followed by the 237-ton *Archimedes*, an appropriately named vessel that was used in 1839 for a number of official trials. The vessel achieved the speed of 10kt and made a voyage round much of the British coast as well as to Amsterdam in the Netherlands and Oporto in Portugal. The Royal Navy ordered its first propeller-driven ship in 1841 as HMS *Rattler*, which in 1845 was used for a decisive trial between propeller and paddle-wheel propulsion: in this trial the *Rattler*, an 880-ton frigate fitted with a 220-hp (164-kW) engine driving a two-blade propeller, was matched against HMS *Alecto*, an all but identical 800-ton frigate carrying a 220-hp (164-kW) steam engine powering two side paddle wheels. In a 100-mile (160-km) race the *Rattler* won comfortably by several miles and, when tethered by their sterns with engines going full ahead, the *Rattler* towed the *Alecto* stern first at 2.7kt. This proved that the propeller drove the ship faster through the water than paddle wheels on the same horsepower, and also exerted more power in the water. Fairly rapid development followed this trial, the two-blade propeller with long narrow blades being overtaken by three- and four-blade propellers with shorter and wider blades. The original arrangement of the propeller was as a single unit on the centreline of the hull, but to absorb the increased power of later engines this was steadily modified to two propellers installed as one on each quarter, three propellers as one centreline and two quarter

Isambard Kingdom Brunel's steam ship Great Eastern. (*From the* Illustrated London News, *1859.*)

units, and finally four propellers as two on each quarter.

Although initially sponsored by the Royal Navy, the propeller found its first real acceptance in merchant shipping. Brunel designed the 3,270-ton *Great Britain* as a side-wheeler, but then modified the design for propeller propulsion. In other respects, too, the *Great Britain* marked a new beginning in ship design. Laid down in 1839, launched in 1843 and commissioned in 1845, the ship was 322ft (98.1m) long, was the first transatlantic liner built of iron rather than wood, and for safety was divided into six watertight compartments separated by special bulkheads. The ship had six masts, but was designed principally for steam, her engines delivering 1,500hp (1118kW) to the propeller by an innovatory chain drive. On her maiden voyage to New

York the ship carried 60 first-class passengers, a considerably larger number of steerage-class passengers and 600 tons of cargo. Brunel build on all his experience in the construction of his third great steam ship, the classic *Great Eastern*. At a time when no other ship in the world displaced more than 5,000 tons, the *Great Eastern* was designed for 18,914 tons as the means of carrying 4,000 passengers (or as a troopship 10,000 soldiers) as well as 6,000 tons of cargo. As suggested by her name, the ship was schemed for service on the route linking Great Britain with India and Australia without the need to recoal, and 11,000hp (8202kW) was delivered by the separate engines installed for the two side paddles and one four-blade propeller of 24-ft (7.3-m) diameter. The ship was 692ft (210.9m) long and 82ft (25m) in beam,

and could achieve 15kt. Brunel introduced a power-operated rudder mechanism, and incorporated still more safety features, most notably a cellular double bottom to minimize the damage and the resultant flooding should the ship run aground. Laid down in 1854 and launched in 1858, the *Great Eastern* was too far ahead of her time, bankrupted her builder and broke Brunel's health, and was then wrongly used for the transatlantic rather than the antipodean run. As a result she was a commercial failure, but then achieved greater success as a telegraph cable-layer, placing four transatlantic cables as well as

another between Aden and Bombay. She was beached and broken up in 1888.

The adoption of iron rather than wood as the main structural material for hulls completely altered the nature of ships using both steam and sail propulsion. The first steam ship of iron construction was the *Aaron Manby*, which had a Bell engine and side paddles. She made her first voyage in 1820, carrying passengers from London round the coast of Kent, across the English Channel and up the River Seine to Paris at an average of between 8 and 9kt. The ship made this run several times and was then bought by a Parisian group for excursions

RIGHT
The Great Eastern *leaving Sheerness, Kent, with the French Atlantic telegraph cable. (From the* Illustrated London News, *June 1869.)*

OPPOSITE
The Great Eastern *being welcomed into New York for the first time in 1860.*

up and down the Seine from Paris. The ship was extremely important in the science of shipbuilding, and her novel construction rapidly became the norm for merchant ships in the 1830s and 1840s. Naval construction lagged, with even steam vessels built largely of wood, but commercial interests were quick to appreciate the advantages of the reliability and low maintenance costs offered by the combination of steam propulsion and an iron hull. As noted above, Brunel pushed forward the concept of iron construction with enormous far-sightedness, and by the 1870s and 1880s 20,000-ton passenger liners were relatively common as world trade and migration expanded. Iron was slowly overtaken as the main structural medium by steel, allowing the development of larger and stronger hulls, and this development in size was matched by improved engines so that performance did not suffer.

All these early steam engines were of the reciprocating type, in which one or more cylinders each contain a piston driven by steam for an up-and-down motion translated into the circular motion of the paddle(s) or propeller(s) by the throw of a crankshaft linked to the piston by a connecting shaft. In the early engines the steam was supplied from the boiler at low pressure, and after powering the piston was exhausted from the cylinder into a condenser that turned it back into water which was returned to the boiler for reuse. During 1854 John Elder introduced the compound engine, which had been patented as early as 1781 by Jonathan Hornblower but then had to wait three-quarters of a century before becoming practical after the development of boilers able to generate a sufficient pressure of steam, generally about 40lb/sq in (2.81kg/cm²). In the compound engine the steam exhausting from the main cylinder is passed through a

second, low-pressure cylinder before passing to the condenser: the compound engine's secondary use of the steam adds to the thrust generated on the crankshaft, thereby increasing the efficiency of the engine for a given quantity of steam.

Further development of boilers by the adoption of forced-draught measures allowed an increase in pressure to about 125lb/sq in (8.79 kg/cm²), making

possible the triple-expansion engine as first installed in the steamer *Propontis* during 1874. This was a logical development of the compound engine with high-, intermediate- and low-pressure cylinders to wring maximum effort out of the steam before it reached the condenser and became water once more. Limited use was also made of a quadruple-expansion engine.

Chapter Two
The Battleship &
Battleship Cruiser

As indicated by its name, the battleship was developed as the successor to the type of capital ship known in the navies of the sailing era as the line-of-battle ship which, with its armament of 60 or more guns on two or more decks, was regarded universally as the cornerstone of naval warfare in the period when the decisive maritime battles were fought by two fleets of ships sailing in lines of battle as ordained by the British Fighting Instructions and their equivalents in the other navies of the day. As the wind was replaced by steam as the primary motive power, and as wood was replaced by iron (itself soon replaced by steel) as the primary structural medium during the second and third quarters of the 19th century, the term battleship came into use to reflect the new type of modern warship. The creation of this new type was also facilitated, or arguably made inevitable, during the 1840s and 1850s by the development of the rifled gun initially to supplement and then to replace the shorter-ranged and less accurate smooth-bore gun, and of the explosive shell to supplant the considerably less damaging solid shot. In overall terms, therefore, a period of little more than 25 years saw the introduction of iron (and then steel), first for the improvement of protection and then as the basic structural medium; steam to create a propulsion arrangement that was independent of the wind

and therefore allowed, somewhat belatedly, the creation of tactics that were not derived ultimately from the need to gain and keep the weather gauge; the rifled gun to allow longer-range and more accurate engagement of the enemy; and the explosive shell to provide a far more effective scale of destruction on the sides of the enemy ship. These four factors combined in a period of between 25 and 50 years to render obsolete the line-of-battle ship that had reigned supreme on the world's seas for more than three centuries.

Arguably the first such ship of this type was the French *Gloire*, which was launched in 1859, but this was built primarily of wood with her sides provided with additional protection by a plating of iron. It is generally accepted, therefore, that the first true battleship was the British *Warrior*, which was launched in 1860 with a hull of iron construction. Both of these ships were officially rated as frigates and were completely ship-rigged, but this should not be allowed to disguise the fact that they were the harbingers of a new type of naval warfare, for with their auxiliary steam propulsion arrangements they could travel at 13kt, which made it possible for them to overhaul and outmanoeuvre, and so gain a decisive tactical advantage, over any line of battleship with its greater multitude of guns on several decks but wholly at the mercy of

LEFT
A chromolithograph published in 1864, entitled Wood and Iron. *It shows a traditional wooden warship on the left, beside HMS* Warrior, *the first iron-clad steam ship.*

OPPOSITE
HMS Caledonia *at general quarters. This is the second unit of the three-strong Prince Consort class that was conceived as a 91-gun second-rate ship type but then revised as a wooden broadside ironclad type. The Caledonia was laid down in 1860 and completed in 1865 as a square-rigged three-masted ship with a 1,000-hp (746-kW) single-shaft steam propulsion arrangement for a speed of almost 13kt. The armament was 10 7-in (178-mm) breech-loading rifled guns as well as eight 100-lb (45-kg) and 12 68-lb (31-kg) smooth-bore guns.*

the direction and strength of the wind.

This fact should not be read as suggesting that there was an immediate shift to the new concept of warship as a fully-fledged type, however, for in the absence of any major European war that might otherwise have provided both the stimulus and the operational validation of the concept, the process was gradual. The transition from ship of the line to battleship was therefore a process marked by two intermediate stages. In the first stage many line-of-battle ships were adapted toward the newer standard by the addition of a protective plating of iron sheets on the

outside of their hulls and the lengthening of their hulls to allow the addition of a primitive steam propulsion arrangement that supplemented but certainly did not replace their original complement of masts, yards, sails and all their associated spider's web of standing and running rigging. In the second stage, new iron-hulled and steam-powered battleships were built as such, but these nonetheless retained the sailing ship rig and massive gun batteries of

the earlier generations ships.

Thus it was only with the development of improved and considerably more reliable steam propulsion arrangements, offering an economically as well as tactically attractive combination of greater power and lower fuel consumption, that the battleship began to emerge in the third quarter of the 19th century as a type genuinely different, in concept as well as motive power and protection, from the line-of-battle ship.

The new breed of battleship was made possible not only by the latest steam propulsion arrangements but also by the adoption of more advanced guns with breech rather than muzzle loading, rifled rather than smooth-bore barrels and, late in the century, efficient smokeless nitro-cellulose propellant in place of the inefficient smoke-producing black powder; steady improvements in metallurgy allowing the construction of larger ships whose

armoured sides provided better protection against incoming fire; and the evolution of more advanced propulsion arrangements and hull designs for higher speeds. In this last respect, it is worth noting that although hull designs were generally improved in terms of a superior underwater line and a higher length/beam ratio, an anachronism that lasted until well into the 20th century, at least in vestigial form, was the ram bow: this had apparently proved itself by deliberate and successful use in the 2nd Battle of Lissa in July 1866, when the Austro-Hungarian flagship rammed and sank the Italian *Re d'Italia*, and by accidental but also successful use in 1893 when the *Victoria*, flagship of the Mediterranean Fleet, was rammed and sunk by another British battleship.

A circa 1890 chromolithograph of HMS Hero, a 2nd-class British battleship. It was an early form of monitor with light secondary armament and one very high-calibre twin-gun turret: it was principally used for bombarding shore installations.

The first battleships relying on steam rather than sail as their prime mover were generally known as mastless ships, and the first of these was the British *Devastation*. This ship was launched in 1869 as what was really a sea-going monitor as it was very low in the water and lacked any fore castle or poop. For some 20 years masted and mastless ships were produced in parallel, even though the masted ship was genuinely anachronistic, and it was nearly 1890 before the last masted iron battleships disappeared from the fleets of the major powers.

Such was the technical progress made in the period between 1870 and 1890 in the development of steam power, gun technology and armour protection, however, that these three factors ensured that the battleship did finally begin to emerge as a distinct type with the main guns mounted in trainable turrets. It was at this stage that the battleship began to emerge from experimental status, built in singleton units for the proving of particular ideas, to the level at which they could be produced by the world's leading maritime powers in classes of essentially identical ships: this greater facilitated production (and in the process lowered production and operating costs) and at the same time offered the invaluable tactical advantage of providing their operators with ships that could be grouped into class divisions and squadrons able to operate at a clearly established level of performance. Each generation of these classes introduced improvements in capability that were reflected in greater size and displacement, the latter increasing typically from the 9,200 tons of the *Warrior* to the 15,000 tons of the *Majestic*, a British battleship launched in 1895. Whereas the *Warrior* was a single-ship type 420ft (128m) long, fully ship rigged with an auxiliary steam powerplant delivering

5,267hp (3927kW) to one propeller for a speed of 14.1kt, protected by 4.5in (114mm) of iron over 18in (457mm) of wood, and armed with 10 110-lb (49.9-kg) and four 70-lb (31.75-kg) breech-loading guns as well as 28.68-lb (30.8-kg) muzzle-loading guns, the *Majestic* was the lead vessel of a 10-ship class to a standardized design that included a length of 421ft (128.3m), triple-expansion steam engines delivering 12,000hp (8947kW) to two propellers for a speed of 16.1kt, protection based on steel up to 14in (357mm) thick, and an armament of four 12-in (305-mm) breech-loading guns in two twin-gun centreline turrets supported by 12 6-in (152-mm) breech-loading rifled guns in

single casemated mountings, 16 12-pdr quick-firing guns and 12 3-pdr quick-firing guns.

The Majestic class was in effect the starting point for a series of a battleship type that became standard, with local changes, in most of the world's major navies and was built in large numbers in the period up to 1905 with changes limited in successive classes mainly to greater size and displacement to allow for the incorporation of thicker protection, a higher-rated propulsion arrangement for slightly greater speed, and an increase in the calibre of the secondary and tertiary gun batteries. This last is reflected in the evolution of the later British battleships of this type such as the

ABOVE
The Imperial Japanese Navy's battleship Hatsuse *shortly afer her launching onto the Tyne, 1899.*

RIGHT
HMS Albermarle *heads a line of battleships in 1903.*

OPPOSITE
HMS Goliath *was the third unit of the six-strong Canopus class of pre-Dreadnought battleships with a steam propulsion arrangement delivering 13,500hp (10065kW) to two shafts for a speed of 18kt, and was armed with four 12-in (305-mm) guns in two turrets, 12 6-in (152-mm) quick-firing guns in casemated mountings and numerous smaller guns.*

two Swiftsure class ships of 1904 with a secondary battery of 14 7.5-in (191-mm) guns, the eight King Edward class ships of 1905 with a secondary battery of four 9.2-in (234-mm) guns and 10 6-in (152-mm) guns, and the two ships of the Lord Nelson class of 1907 with a secondary battery of 10 9.2-in (234-mm) guns. The largest-calibre guns, normally mounted in pairs in two fore-and-aft centreline turrets, were seen as the primary armament for the engagement of opposing battleships, while the medium-calibre guns of the secondary battery, installed in casemated mountings on the ships sides, supplemented the main guns' efforts against an opposing capital ship while also providing a capability against secondary targets such as armoured cruisers, which could also be hit and moderately damaged (especially on their less well protected upper works) by the smaller-calibre guns of the tertiary battery that was provided mainly for the protection of the battleship against the attentions of the torpedo boat. First appearing in the 1890s

and then built in large numbers, the torpedo boat was generally regarded as a major threat to the battle fleet as it operated in flotillas designed to exploit their speed and manoeuvrability to get in close and decimate the battle fleet with waves of potent torpedoes, for which an exaggerated respect was held.

The performance of the guns arming the battleships of the period around the turn of the 19th century was considerable: the 12-in (305-mm) weapon, for example, could fire an 850-lb (386-kg) projectile out to a distance of more than 20,000yds (182.30m). Despite this fact, it was still standard at the beginning of the 20th century for the vast majority of naval officers to think of fleet engagements in

terms of a range of only a few thousand yards. This meant that range was relatively unimportant, and that virtually every gun of a battleships' primary, secondary and tertiary batteries would be able to strike the opposing ship. What was little appreciated at the time, largely as a result of a lack of practical experience resulting from the long period of maritime peace typical of the Victorian era, was that this fact raised enormous problems in spotting the fall of shot. With guns of three or more calibres hitting the target ship, it was of course crucially important to differentiate the explosions of the shells fired by the various guns: there was little point in an enemy capital ship being blanketed in the fire of the 6-in (152-mm) or smaller guns of the

HMS Hood *in 1904 trim. The* Hood, *completed in 1893, was the single ship of its class, and was completed with a steam propulsion arrangement delivering 11,000hp (8200kW) to two shafts for a speed of almost 17kt, and was armed with four 13.5-in (343-mm) guns in two twin turrets, 10 6-in (152-mm) quick-firing guns in casemated mountings, and numerous smaller guns.*

tertiary battery, which on their own could inflict only relatively little if any decisive damage, if this obscured the fact that the fire of the secondary and primary batteries was not hitting the target.

That this might well be the case was shown by Captain Percy Scott, a strong advocate of accurate gunnery at a time in which the Royal Navy, followed by most other navies, believed that protracted gunnery practice was expensive and unnecessary for the type of short-range engagements that were envisaged, in which the rate of fire and general accuracy would be of more importance than truly aimed

fire, and that gunnery practice also damaged the ships' paintwork and brightwork. Even so, it came as a shock in 1899 when Scott's ship, the cruiser *Scylla*, achieved an 80 per cent hit rate with its 4.7-in (120-mm) guns in the Mediterranean Fleet gunnery competition, easily winning over ships whose average score was a very indifferent 30 per cent.

Scott's technique was based on the use of a telescopic sight on each gun and the following of the target in elevation through his own ship's roll rather than firing only when the guns of his own ship were brought to bear by the ship's roll. Scott also

devised an effective training system for his gunners, who trained with the dotter, loader and deflection teacher aids for practice in roll, loading and allowance for the target ship's horizontal movement. Such was Scott's success that the long established resistance to any change in gunnery practice and training by the majority of British naval officers and the Admiralty was finally overcome, and by 1902 most British warships were using the same methods. Scott became Inspector of Target Practice in 1905, and in 1907 the average number of hits being secured by British ships had risen to 81 per cent. Scott returned to sea in 1908 as commander of a cruiser squadron in the Channel Fleet, but his involvement in the extraordinarily vitriolic quarrel between Admiral Sir Charles Beresford and Admiral Sir John Fisher, respectively the commander of the Channel Fleet and the First Sea Lord, ended his active career. Fisher was altogether too highly well aware of the importance of Scott's thinking to lose such a man, and Scott was encouraged to continue with his most important work. This was the creation of the director sight.

The director sight took overall control of each ship's complete gunnery package into a gunnery control position mounted in the battleship's foretop, now located at the junction of a sturdy tripod mast to ensure rigidity, from which a good view of the engagement could be obtained as it was generally above the haze of gun smoke that billowed round the ship as the guns were fired, and from which the laying and firing of all guns could be controlled. This system replaced the hitherto standard practice of individual aiming by turret or individual gun captains despite the fact that each such captain was located relatively low in the ship and could (or more generally would) have his sight of the target, especially as ranges

The Russian battleship
Tsarevitch *was Rear-
Admiral Vitgeft's flagship
in the Russian breakout
from Port Arthur to
Vladivostok during the
Russo-Japanese War. At
18.37 hours, Admiral Togo's
main battle squadron hit
Tsarevitch* with a salvo of
12-inch shells which wrecked
the bridge and conning-
tower, killing the Rear-
Admiral himself. The ship's
rudder was jammed to
starboard, causing the
warship to veer out of the
Russian battle line. She
managed to make one of the
neutral Chinese ports and
was interned. August 1904.

RIGHT
Another view of Tsarevitch *seen with damaged funnels at Port Arthur before the Battle of the Yalu.*

RIGHT
A contemporary chromolithograph depicting the death of Admiral Vitgeft.

OPPOSITE
The French battleship Jauriquiberry *proceeding at speed.*

met with considerable opposition from officers who claimed that reliance on a single director position and electrical controls opened the way to a disastrous failure as a result of a single shell hit, for reliance on this system would have ensured that little training was given to individual gunners. The matter was settled in 1912 by a trial between two battleships, one using the Scott system of director firing and the other relying on individual aiming: the director-equipped ship scored six times as many hits at a range of 9,000yds (8230m) as the ship using individual aiming, and as a result director firing was adopted by the British in 1913, only later being used by the Germans and Americans. It is worth noting that the accuracy of director firing was considerably enhanced from 1913 by the simultaneous adoption for the director position of the Captain Frederic Charles Dreyers fire-control table, which was in essence a mechanical computer for the

began to increase as a result of the Scott-inspired improvement of gunnery accuracy, obscured by spray, smoke, cordite haze, and mist or fog.

Director firing involved the use of a single telescopic sight in the director position. The target was held in this sight, located above most obstructions to its field of view, and the individual gunners had then merely to align their gun sights with a pointer controlled from the director position: once each gun sight had been aligned with the pointer it was accurately laid in azimuth and elevation, and then all the guns were fired electrically in unison from the director position, which ensured a higher level of accuracy and also simplified the spotting of the fall of shot and thus the generation of error corrections.

Scott perfected the system in 1910, but

solution of the fire-control problems on the
basis of data fed into the table for target
bearing, bearing rate change, range, range
rate change, and speed.

As this revolution in the nature and
practice of fire control was being planned

and proved, there took place the first major
battle or fleet engagement between the
naval forces of major powers for almost a
century. This took place toward the end of
the Russo-Japanese War (1904–05) after the
Russians, on the verge of losing their hold

on Manchuria and northern Korea after
losing their small naval forces early in the
war and then suffering a series of land
defeats, decided to reinforce the theatre
with ships of the Baltic Fleet.

Under the command of the wholly
indifferent Admiral Zinovy P.
Rozhdestvenskii, the Baltic Fleet left its
home ports of Revel and Libau (now known
as Tallinn and Liepaja) on the eastern side
of the Baltic Sea on 15 October 1904. The
fleet met its first mishap a few days later as it
was steaming across the North Sea: a false
alarm, indicating a surprise attack by
Japanese torpedo boats, resulted in the
Russian bombardment of a British fishing
fleet near the Dogger Bank. Several British
trawlers were damaged, and at least seven of
the men on them were killed. This incident
almost brought about a war between the
U.K. and Russia, and British cruisers
shadowed the Russian fleet until it had
passed the Bay of Biscay. Two battleships
and three cruisers were detached to pass
through the Suez Canal, while the main
body of the Baltic fleet took the long route
into the Indian Ocean round the Cape of
Good Hope. Problems of coaling and
repairs in neutral ports continually
hampered the seemingly interminable
advance of the Russian fleet. The two
elements of the Baltic Fleet joined forces
once more at Madagascar, and after a long
delay the fleet finally started across the
Indian Ocean on 16 March 1905.

One last stop was made at Van Fong
Bay in French Indo-China, where the
Russians prepared for battle as best they
could, even though their ships were in a
state of considerable disrepair after the long
voyage from the Baltic, and speed through
the water was further hampered by the
growths of barnacles and weed that had
attached themselves under the waterline in

the slow voyage through tropical waters. Accompanied by supply ships and colliers, the fleet steamed north toward Vladivostok, the main Russian naval base in the northern Pacific, on May 14. The Japanese had kept themselves fully informed of the progress of the Russian force.

As it approached the Strait of Tsushima between Japan and Korea, the Baltic Fleet comprised eight battleships, eight cruisers, nine destroyers and several smaller vessels. Although apparently potent, this force was in fact little more than a paper tiger based on obsolescent or obsolete ships, whose personnel was inferior in gunnery, discipline, and leadership to the Japanese fleet waiting under the command of Vice Admiral Heohachiro Togo. The Japanese strength was four battleships, eight cruisers, 21 destroyers, and 60 torpedo boats: though fewer in number of large warships, the Japanese force comprised more modern vessels that were well manned and well led.

On 27 May Rozhdestvenskii's fleet entered the Strait of Tsushima in line-ahead formation. To the north-west, Togo was steaming in a basically similar formation. Each admiral led the main body of his force, Rozhdestvenskii in the *Suvorov* and Togo in the *Mikasa*. The Japanese turned north-east, in the hope of using their greater speed to cross the Russian T and thus be able to concentrate the full firepower of their line on the leading ships of the Russian column. Rozhdestvenskii altered course to the north-east and then to east in an effort to evade this raking manoeuvre.

Fire was opened in early afternoon at a range of 6,400yds (5850m). The Japanese fleet, steaming at 15kt to the Russian ships 9kt, soon overhauled the ships of the Baltic Fleet and in less than two hours put two battleships and a cruiser out of action. The level of Russian losses then climbed as

The Japanese battleship Asahi *opens fire on the Russian Baltic Fleet during the Battle of Tsushima. From left to right are:* Asahi, Fuji, Shikishima *and* Mikasa. *27 May 1905.*

Togo, displaying a high degree of tactical skill, used the higher speed of his ships to manoeuvre his ships around the increasingly defenceless Russian vessels. By nightfall, Rozhdestvenskii had been wounded, three battleships (including his flagship) had been sunk, and the surviving Russian vessels, now under the command of Admiral Nebogatov, were in total confusion as they sought safety. Togo loosed the armoured cruiser force under the command of Admiral Kamimura, as well as his destroyers and torpedo boats, to maintain Japanese attacks on the Russians through the night. On the following day the Japanese completed the destruction of the Baltic Fleet. Only one cruiser and two destroyers escaped to Vladivostok, and three other destroyers got to Manila in the Philippines, where they were interned. The remainder of the Russian fleet was sunk or captured. The Japanese lost only three torpedo boats, and

while the Russian casualties reached some 10,000 men killed and wounded, the Japanese lost less than 1,000 men in all.

The Battle of Tsushima was the first genuinely decisive fleet engagement since the Battle of Trafalgar in 1805, and had very important lessons for all concerned, most notably in the importance of a wholly professional approach to seamanship and gunnery. Just as important, in terms of international politics, the battle was a clear indication that Japan must now be numbered among the great powers, the first time that this distinction had been paid to a non-European nation.

The Battle of Tsushima was fought without the gunnery advances that had resulted from Scott's thinking, and the director firing concept would have been useful for the type of battleship, described above with its three or even four calibres of guns, but in fact came into its own with a

RIGHT
*The Russo-Japanese War:
the Russian iron-clad*
Petropavlosk *sunk by
Japanese torpedo with a loss
of 600 lives, including that
of Admiral Makharoff. 13
April 1904.*

FAR RIGHT
HMS Dreadnought *at the
Spithead Review of 1886.*

OPPOSITE
*Japanese battleships at the
Battle of Tsushima, 27 May
1905.*

BELOW
A Ruggiero di Lauria*-class
battleship of the Royal
Italian Navy.*

new type of battleship that was conceptually simpler than those which preceded but offered a host of tactical advantages. Appearing in October 1906, this was the British battleship *Dreadnought*.

The spur to the creation of this new type and improved generation of battleships can be traced to 1896, when Germany passed the 1st Naval Law designed to pave the way for the creation of a German navy that would eventually rival the Royal Navy. This led to a numerical and strategic destabilization of the naval status quo throughout Europe at a time when the U.K. was already becoming concerned about the threat to its pre-eminent world position posed by Germany's growing industrial capability and ever-expanding mercantile navy, and coincided with the introduction, over a very short period of time, of several new technologies that were all to exert considerable influence on naval warfare. These technologies included the locomotive torpedo in a perfected form, the submarine, radio communication, the internal combustion engine including the very economical diesel engine, oil- rather than coal-fired boilers, steam turbines in place of triple-expansion engines for smoother running, as well as higher power in less volume, and the aeroplane.

These and other factors combined to make inevitable the introduction of what might sensibly be called the all big gun battleship. In this type of battleship, of which the *Dreadnought* was the first example, the armament arrangement of the typical pre-*Dreadnought* battleship, with its primary and secondary batteries of typically four 12-in (305-mm) primary guns in two centreline turrets fore and aft of the central superstructure and about 10 7.5-in (190-mm) secondary guns in casemated mountings round and below the

superstructure, was replaced by a larger number of turreted main guns. In the Dreadnought battleships, this battery of single-calibre main guns was installed in large turrets on or as close to the centreline as possible, and was complemented by large numbers of small guns located wherever possible: there were initially no secondary or tertiary batteries as such. The task of the main guns was to deal with major adversaries, and the function of the small guns was to provide protection against the attacks by torpedo boats, which were thought to offer a significant threat but which, to secure high speed, were also very lightly built and therefore seen as vulnerable to the fire of quick-firing weapons as light as 12-pdr guns.

A primary armament of single-calibre guns had been tested in the 1870s in a few British and Italian battleships, but the failure of these freakish vessels had led to the general retention of at least three main calibres for battleship armament. Then the Russo-Japanese War had revealed the limitations of such a mixed armament: the primary guns were used accurately at the unprecedented range of 20,000yds (18290m), and spotting of the fall of shot of the secondary and tertiary batteries proved almost impossible even at considerably shorter ranges.

The lesson was clear to all who considered the implications of the Japanese victory in the Russo-Japanese War: the day of the secondary and tertiary batteries as offensive weapons was over, and it was therefore sensible to concentrate all the offensive firepower in a larger number of main guns, which could concentrate an overwhelming weight of fire at very long range and sink or disable an enemy before it could close to a range at which its medium-calibre guns might become

effective. The Japanese were in the
position to reach this conclusion before
anyone else, and laid down the first all big
gun battleships as the *Aki* and *Satsuma*
with a planned armament of 12 12-in
(305-mm) guns in two centreline twin
turrets and, on each beam, one twin and
two single turrets. Completion of the ships
was delayed firstly by Japan's limited
industrial capacity, and secondly by the
realization that it was not cost-effective to

have two separate four-gun beam batteries
that would never be used simultaneously:
the decision was therefore taken to replace
the beam batteries of main-calibre guns by
beam batteries of intermediate-calibre
guns, these comprising 12 10-in (254-
mm) weapons in three twin turrets on
each beam.

Thus it was the British, now
thoroughly concerned about the pace and
extent of Germany's growing naval

strength and the combined naval and
mercantile ambitions that this strength
reflected, who produced the first all big
gun battleship as the *Dreadnought*, with
the Americans close behind them with the
South Carolina class and the Germans also
in the running with the Nassau class.

The *Dreadnought* of 1906 thus
pioneered a new type of warship and gave
her name to the new type of all big gun
battleship, and the ships of the previous

HMS Dreadnought. *A Dreadnought-class battleship of the Royal Navy shortly after completion. 1906.*

single exposed mountings.

The completion of the ship was a matter of enormous pride for the British people, but also a subject of much anxiety as the ship had, at a stroke, revolutionized naval warfare by making all pre-Dreadnought battleships obsolete. This meant that the Royal Navy currently enjoyed a numerical advantage of only one in terms of its best battleship strength, and naval superiority would therefore accrue to the country which could construct Dreadnought battleships more quickly in what came to be called the naval race.

The primary threat was Germany, but by striking first the U.K. had secured a significant advantage: at the time Germany had completed its first class of four Dreadnought battleships the U.K. had seven as well as three examples of the battle-cruiser, a still more revolutionary and controversial type of capital ship.

The origins of the battle-cruiser concept can be traced back to 1896 and the suggestion of Émile Bertin, the great French ship designer, for a large warship combining the speed and protection of the armoured cruiser with the main-calibre guns of the battleship to create a type notable for its great offensive power (speed and firepower) but only limited defensive capability: in short the Bertin type of warship would outpace any ship possessing the firepower to overwhelm its defensive strength, and outgun any ships possessing the speed to keep up with it. The concept appealed strongly to Fisher, who considered offensive capability to be all-important and saw in the concept a means of producing a cost-effective type that would be able to function in typical cruiser roles (scouting for the main fleet and protection of British maritime trade routes all over the world) but add to this the

capability for active participation in fleet engagements as a result of a main battery firing very large projectiles to great range.

The result was the battle-cruiser, of which the first three examples were laid down in 1906 as armoured cruisers. Completed at three-monthly intervals in 1908, the ships of the Invincible class were then revealed as vessels altogether different from anything that had gone before. Although their protection was along armoured cruiser lines, with a maximum thickness of only 7in (178mm), the main armament of these ships, each typified by a

full-load displacement of 19,940 tons, was eight 12-in (305-mm) guns in four twin turrets of which two were located on the centreline fore and aft of the superstructure and the other two in echeloned wing positions on each beam. A secondary armament more capable than that of the Dreadnought was installed, in the form of 16 4-in (102-mm) guns, and the other primary distinguishing features of these notably attractive ships was their fine lines on a length of 567ft (172.8m) and the high speed of 26.6kt provided by the delivery of 41,000hp (30570kW) to four shafts by four generation with mixed batteries were retrospectively designated as pre-Dreadnought battleships. The ship was laid down at Portsmouth Dockyard in October 1905 and launched in February 1906 for completion later in the year, and this was a truly remarkable construction effort made possible only by using matériel already ordered and built for other ships. The ship was described by Fisher, its conceptual father, as the hard-boiled egg – because she cannot be beat. The ship was the first capital ship in the world to be fitted with steam turbines as its primary propulsion

arrangement, in this instance four sets of turbines delivering 23,000hp (17150kW) to four shafts for a maximum speed of 22kt, which was considerably faster than any pre-Dreadnought battleship despite the ship's considerably greater length of 526ft (160.3m) and greater full-load displacement of 20,700 tons.

There is no doubt that Fisher had an overwhelming, indeed an almost mono-maniacal belief in the overall superiority of major warships that secured their tactical advantage through an offensive combination of firepower and speed rather than the

defensive strength of thick armour, and the Dreadnought was therefore only modestly well protected with a maximum thickness of 11in (279mm) on the waterline belt. It was in armament that the Dreadnought excelled, however, for the primary battery was 10 12-in (305-mm) guns installed in five twin turrets installed as one forward and two aft on the centreline, and the other two in wing positions abreast the superstructure for a broadside of eight 12-in (305-mm) guns. Intended only for the task of repelling torpedo boats, the secondary armament comprised 24 12-pdr guns in

The first Dreadnought built at the Elswick yard of Armstrong's, the Brazilian Minas Geraes, was the largest ship of her day. The Minas Geraes was the other unit of the two-strong São Paulo class of Dreadnought battleships, and was laid down in 1907. The ship displaced 19,280 tons on a length of 543ft (165.5m), and its triple-expansion steam-propulsion arrangement delivered 23,500hp (17520kW) to two shafts for a speed of 21kt. The armour ranged up to a maximum thickness of 9in (229mm), and the armament comprised 12 12-in (305-mm) guns in six twin turrets and 22 4.7-in (119-mm) quick-firing guns in casemated mountings.

The battleship USS Connecticut (BB-18) leads the American North Atlantic Fleet off the east coast of the U.S.A. 1909.

sets of steam turbines.

In overall terms, then, the battle-cruiser may be characterized as a development of the Dreadnought battleship with one fewer main turret, a protective scheme notable for the use of a considerably smaller area of thinner armour, and a combination of a longer and finer hull with a considerably more potent propulsion arrangement for significantly higher speed. The result was a highly impressive type of warship designed to outfight any ship it could not outrun, and outrun any ship it could not outfight.

As operations in World War I (1914–18) were to prove, however, the lack of effective protection was a fatal flaw in the concept of these fine ships.

The Dreadnought ships that followed in the period up to 1910 were the British Bellerophon class of three ships based on the Dreadnought but with two tripod rather than pole masts and a secondary armament

of 16 4-in (102-mm) guns, the generally similar St. Vincent class of three ships with slightly thinner bow and stern armour as well as 50- rather than 45-calibre main guns for higher muzzle velocity and therefore greater penetrative capability, the Japanese Satsuma interim type with its hybrid armament, and the German Nassau class of four ships with a main armament of 12 11-in (280-mm) guns in six twin turrets located as two centreline units fore and aft of the two superstructure blocks and four wing turrets, a secondary armament of 16 3.4-in (88-mm) guns, protection up to a maximum of 12in (305mm), and a propulsion arrangement based in triple-expansion reciprocating steam engines delivering 26,244hp (19568kW) to three shafts for a speed of 20kt.

It is interesting to note that after careful consideration the Germans had decided that the protection of the British ships was too

light, and therefore opted for the more capable defensive arrangement of larger areas of thicker armour. This would have resulted in heavier and therefore slower ships except that the Germans also believed that their guns were basically superior to British weapons and therefore opted for main guns that were slightly smaller in calibre and therefore lighter. The primary advantages of the Germans guns, other than the fact that they fired shells that experience was to prove superior to those of the British, were their high muzzle velocity (and thus good penetrative power) as well as a flatter trajectory that simplified the creation of a valid fire-control solution and also permitted the use of a lower and therefore lighter turret design.

As noted above, the completion of the Dreadnought gave the U.K. a considerable early lead in the naval race. From the end of the first decade of the 20th century, the pace of naval rearmament increased in direct

Blücher, *a Blücher-class battle-cruiser of the Imperial German Navy, 1910.*

British Bellerophon-*class battleships early in World War I.*

proportion to the worsening in international relations. The first evidence of this world-wide response to the British lead was the commissioning of the Nassau-class ships in 1909 and 1910, and then of the two American South Carolina-class battleships with a main armament of eight 12-in (305-mm) guns in four centreline turrets. Further Dreadnoughts were the two Minas Geraes-class ships built in the U.K. for Brazil, the two American Delaware-class ships with 10 12-in (305-mm) guns in five centreline turrets, the four ships of the German Helgoland class with 12 12-in (305-mm) main guns in six twin turrets disposed as in the Nassau class, the single British ship of the Neptune class with an armament of 10 12-in (305-mm) main guns in five two-gun turrets installed as three on the centreline (including a superfiring after pair) and echeloned wing turrets for the possibility of a 10-gun broadside, the two British Colossus-class ships similar to the Neptune class but with only one tripod mast, the two ships of the American Florida class as an improved version of the Delaware class with rearranged cage masts and turbine propulsion on four shafts rather than triple-expansion engines on three shafts, the two ships of the Japanese Kawachi class with an armament of 12 12-in (305-mm) main guns disposed as in the Helgoland class, the two ships of the American Wyoming class with a main armament of 12 12-in (305-mm) guns of a longer design in six twin-gun centreline turrets installed as a superfiring pair forward and two superfiring pairs aft, the four ships of the Austro-Hungarian Viribus Unitis class with an armament of 12 12-in (305-mm) main guns in four triple turrets located in fore and after superfiring pairs, the six ships of the German Kaiser class with an armament of 10 12-in (305-mm) guns in five twin turrets located as three on the

centreline (with the two after units in a superfiring arrangement) and two echeloned wing turrets, the single ship of the Italian Dante Alighieri class with an armament of 12 12-in (305-mm) main guns in four triple turrets on the centreline, the three smallest ever Dreadnoughts of the Spanish España class with an armament of eight 12-in (305-mm) main guns in four twin turrets located as two on the centreline and two in echeloned wing positions, the four ships of the French Courbet class with an armament of 12 12-in (305-mm) main guns in four triple turrets installed on the centreline in forward and aft superfiring pairs, the four ships of the German König class with an armament of 10 12-in (305-mm) main guns in five twin turrets located on the centreline, the single Rio de Janeiro class ship built for Argentina but taken over by the U.K. with an armament of no fewer than 14 12-in (305-mm) main guns in

ABOVE
A rudimentary flying platform on HMS Africa – built over the fore gun turret. A Short S27 was successfully flown from this construction on 4 July 1912.

ABOVE LEFT
The Regina Margherita, *a Regina Margherita-class battleship of the Royal Italian Navy.*

LEFT
The German battle-cruiser SMS Seydlitz of the first Scouting Group burning and sinking during the Battle of Jutland on 31 May 1916.

S. M. S. Deutschland

ABOVE
The battleship Deutschland
at sea during World War I.

ABOVE RIGHT
SMS Westfalen, *a*
Westfalen-class battleship of
the Imperial German Navy
during World War 1.

seven twin turrets located as five on the centreline (a superfiring pair forward and three aft including one superfiring pair) and two echeloned wing turrets, the two ships of the Rivadavia class for Argentina built in the U.S.A. with a main armament of 12 12-in (305-mm) main guns in six twin turrets located on the centreline and including superfiring forward and after pairs, the four ships of the Russian Gangut class with an armament of 12 12-in (305-mm) main guns in four triple turrets located on the centreline, the two ships of the Italian Caio Duilio class with a main armament of 13 12-in (305-mm) main guns in three triple and two twin turrets on the centreline with the twin turrets firing over the forward and after triple turrets, the two ships of the Italian Conte di Cavour class with basically the same armament as the Caio Duilio-class ships, and the three ships of the Russian Imperatritsa Maria class with a main

armament similar to that of the Gangut-class ships but in a revised layout, thicker protection, a heavier secondary armament of 18 5.1-in (130-mm) guns in place of 16 4.7-in (120-mm) guns, and reduced speed and range as the ships were designed for service exclusively within the confines of the Black Sea.

The same period saw the spread, although not to so large an extent, of the battle-cruiser concept. The three ships of the Invincible class found a German response in the single ship of the Von der Tann class with an armament of eight 11-in (280-mm) main guns in four twin turrets located as two on the centreline and the other two in echeloned wing positions. By comparison with the British battle-cruisers, the German ship had lower freeboard and superstructure in a combination that made it difficult to secure a good range figure, better armour protection and, for the first

time in a German ship, a propulsion arrangement based on two sets of steam turbines driving four shafts for high speed and great reliability. The British followed the Invincible class with the Indefatigable-class of three ships that differed from their predecessors mainly in the greater echeloning of their wing turrets, making possible an eight- rather than six-gun broadside. The Germans countered with the two ships of the Moltke class to an enlarged Von der Tann design with a fifth 11-in (280-mm) twin turret in a superfiring after position for a total of 10 such weapons. The single ship of the Seydlitz class that followed was basically an improved Moltke-class unit with the same armament on a longer and narrower hull for improved speed and better sea-keeping qualities. The final vessels of the pure Dreadnought type of battle-cruiser were the three ships of the Derfflinger class for

Germany, which differed quite significantly from the Moltke and Seydlitz-class ships in being flush-decked and in having their eight 12-in (305-mm) main guns in twin turrets located in superfiring pairs forward and aft of the superstructure, which contained the considerably enhanced secondary battery of 12 5.9-in (150-mm) guns.

In the last stages of the Dreadnought era's first stage, the building race between the U.K. and Germany was complemented by a technological race in which each side sought to create classes of capital ship in which each succeeding class offered advantages over its predecessor, and that of what had increasingly come to be seen as the enemy, in terms of firepower, protection and performance. Thus the Germans, who had initially been content to rival the British 12-in (305-mm) gun with their 11-in (280-mm) weapon firing a

lighter shell at a higher muzzle velocity for a flatter and therefore more aimable trajectory for roughly comparable armour-penetration capability, soon planned the switch to a 12-in (305-mm) weapon firing an 893-lb (405-kg) shell to a maximum range of some 21,000yds (19200m) for increased penetrative effect at longer range.

Anticipating this German switch, the British had already planned a development of the Dreadnought into the super-Dreadnought type of battleship with a primary armament of 13.5-in (343-mm) rather than 12-in (305-mm) guns. This larger-calibre weapon fired a heavier shell than the 12-in (305-mm) weapon at a lower muzzle velocity, resulting in more than adequate hitting power at long range in combination with greater accuracy and lower barrel erosion, the last providing a significant increase in barrel life. The first result of this process was the Orion class of

four ships, which introduced the new gun in five twin turrets located on the centreline (superfiring pairs of turrets fore and aft with a singleton turret amidships), and an increase in the height as well as the thickness of the armour belt: despite a significant increase in displacement, the Orion class was able to attain a higher speed than the Dreadnought as the result of its improved propulsion arrangement, in which four steam turbines delivered 27,000hp (20130kW) to four shafts for a speed of 21kt.

The British capitalized on the availability of the new 13.5-in (343-mm) gun by adopting it for a series of battleship and battle-cruiser classes. Among the battleships were the four ships of the King George V class with the same basic armament but an improved pattern of main gun, the four ships of the Iron Duke class with the same main armament as the King

ABOVE
HMS Bellerophon, a Bellerophon-class battleship of the Royal Navy during World War I.

ABOVE LEFT
The German Battle Fleet during firing practice in World War I.

ABOVE
The São Paulo, *a*
Dreadnought of the
Brazilian Navy at Rio de
Janeiro. 4 June 1918.

RIGHT
Surrender of the German
Fleet in 1918, with the
Queen Elizabeth *in the*
foreground.

George V class but the improved secondary armament of 12 6-in (152-mm) guns in place of 16 4-in (102-mm) guns supplemented, for the first time in a British battleship class, with anti-aircraft armament in the form of two 3-in (76-mm) high-angle guns, the single ship of the Reshadieh class built for Turkey but taken over by the U.K. as the Erin with the same basic armament as the Iron Duke class, and the single ship of the Admiral Latorre class built for Chile but taken over by the U.K. as the Canada with a primary armament of 10 14-in (356-mm) guns in the same dispositions as the British ships with 13.5-in (343-mm) weapons.

The first battle-cruisers with 13.5-in (343-mm) guns were the three ships of the Lion class, which were known as the splendid cats and were the largest warships yet planned when they were laid down in 1912 and 1913 with a full-load displacement of 29,680 tons and a length of 700ft (213.4m). The main armament was eight 13.5-in (343-mm) weapons in four centreline turrets, of which the forward two were installed as a superfiring pair, and this was complemented by a secondary

armament of 16 4-in (102-mm) guns. Protection was provided by armour up to 10in (254mm) thick, and the propulsion arrangement comprised four sets of steam turbines delivering 73,800hp (55025kW) to four shafts for a speed of 27kt. The *Tiger*, planned as the fourth unit of the class, was completed slightly later to a design that resulted from a measure of revision in light of British knowledge of the Japanese Kongo class, of which four were being built in the U.K. The *Tiger* therefore had the improved secondary armament of 12 6-in (152-mm) guns and slightly greater beam and displacement to allow an enlargement and reorganization of the machinery spaces to

allow the delivery of 108,000hp (80525kW) to four shafts for a speed of 30kt.

Detractors of the battle-cruisers protective arrangements felt that too much offensive power and performance had been built into the splendid cats, but it is worth emphasizing that at the Battle of Jutland in May 1916, the *Tiger* took hits from 21 (including 17 large-calibre) shells without suffering major damage, and was repaired in less than one month.

The major increase in operational capability represented by the Orion class, together with its battleship and battle-cruiser successors, meant that other navies could not ignore the super-Dreadnought

British warships at sea in the early stages of World War I.

Kongo-class battleship of the Imperial Japanese Navy in Sukumo Bay. 1913.

concept and had therefore to adopt larger-calibre main guns, improved defensive measures (secondary armament and armour) and, where they had not already done so, a centreline disposition for the main armament.

First off the mark was Japan with the four battle-cruisers of the Kongo class, of which the lead ship was built in the U.K. largely so that Japan could become accustomed to the latest design and construction techniques used by the British. The design was derived from that for the Turkish Reshadieh-class battleship and resulted in the most powerful battle-cruiser of its time, considerably improving on the standards set by the splendid cats in terms of protection (with a longer, deeper and thicker belt closed off at the ends by armour bulkheads as well as considerable internal compartmentalization) and gun

A British battle-cruiser squadron at sea in 1914.

ships were less well protected than these last American counterparts and carried their main gun in twin rather than triple turrets: this last factor meant that a main battery of 12 guns used six turrets rather than the American ships' four turrets, which required additional length. This meant a finer hull line, however, which translated into higher speed: 23kt was attained on the 40,000hp (29,825kW) delivered by the steam turbines to four shafts. The other details of the Fuso-class battleships included a main armament of 12 14-in (356-mm) guns in six turrets located on the centreline in superfiring forward and after pairs and two single turrets amidships, and a secondary armament of 16 6-in (152-mm) guns. The maximum armour thickness was 13.75in (349mm).

Although planned as standard Fuso-class ships, the last two units were completed to a

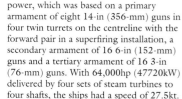

power, which was based on a primary armament of eight 14-in (356-mm) guns in four twin turrets on the centreline with the forward pair in a superfiring installation, a secondary armament of 16 6-in (152-mm) guns and a tertiary armament of 16 3-in (76-mm) guns. With 64,000hp (47720kW) delivered by four sets of steam turbines to four shafts, the ships had a speed of 27.5kt.

The battle-cruisers were matched by four battleships, namely the vessels of the two-ship Fuso and Ise classes that were originally to have been four units of the Fuso class. Entirely designed and built in Japan with Japanese weapons and equipment, the ships confirmed the full arrival of the Japanese navy to world-class status, for the Fuso-class battleships outgunned the contemporary Texas and Oklahoma-class battleships of the U.S. Navy and were basically equal to that navy's Pennsylvania-class battleships. The Japanese

LEFT
Rivadavia, a Dreadnought of the Argentine navy at Rio de Janeiro, 8 June 1918. The name ship of a two-strong Dreadnought battleship class, the Rivadavia was laid down in the U.S.A. during 1910 and completed in 1914. The ship displaced 28,000 tons, and its steam propulsion arrangement delivered 39,500hp (29450kW) to three shafts for a speed of 22.5kt.

BELOW LEFT
Äran, an Äran-class coastal defence battleship of the Royal Swedish Navy, in 1918. The name ship of a four-strong class of coast defence battleships, the frame was laid down in Sweden during 1899 and completed in 1902. The ship displaced 3,650 tons, and its steam-propulsion arrangement delivered 6,500hp (4845kW) to two shafts for a speed of slightly more than 17kt. The armour ranged up to a maximum thickness of 7.5in (190mm), and the armament comprised two 8.27-mm (210-mm) guns in two single turrets, six 6-in (152-mm) guns in single turrets, and several smaller guns. The ship was deleted only in 1947 and broken up in 1951.

HMS Indefatigable, *an Indefatigable-class battle-cruiser of the Royal Navy, 1912–1914.*

standard that was differed from that of the Fuso class sufficiently for them to be recategorized in their own Ise class. The main changes were the relocation of the two amidships twin-gun turrets as a superfiring pair, and the replacement of the 6-in (152-mm) guns of the secondary battery by more modern 5.5-in (140-mm) weapons.

The U.S.A. also opted for the 14-in (356-mm) main gun, but avoided the concept of the battle-cruiser. The Americans therefore opted for maximum firepower and maximum protection even if this meant a sacrifice in speed to typical battleship levels. The first of the U.S. Navy's ships to the super-Dreadnought standard were the two vessels of the Texas class to the typical U.S. flush-decked design derived from that of the beamy Wyoming class and originally designed for a primary armament of 15 12-in (305-mm) guns in five centreline triple turrets. Then the advent of the Orion class forced the U.S. Navy to rethink its concept and opt for a primary armament of 10 14-in (356-mm) guns in five centreline twin turrets (superfiring pairs forward and aft with a singleton unit amidships), a secondary armament of 21 5-in (127-mm) guns. Protection was provided by well arranged armour up to 14in (356mm) thick. A retrograde step, forced on the Americans by the inability of U.S. turbine manufacturers to meet the exacting official requirement, was the use of reciprocating machinery delivering 28,100hp (20950kW) to two shafts for a speed of 21kt.

Further development along the same

HMS Invincible, a *battle-cruiser of the Royal Navy during World War I.*

super-Dreadnought concept was to be found in the five ships of the two-ship Pennsylvania and three-ship New Mexico classes completed in the early part of World War I while the U.S.A. was still neutral. The Pennsylvania-class design was basically an improved version of the Nevada class with the earlier type's combination of two triple and two twin superfiring turrets replaced by four triple turrets in superfiring pairs. The same armament of 12 main-calibre guns was carried in the contemporary Fuso class for the Japanese navy, although in this instance the guns were carried in six twin turrets that demanded an additional 65ft (19.8m) of length and additional 15,000hp (11185kW) of power for a speed 2kt higher on the same displacement.

The New Mexico-class design was a much improved version of the Pennsylvania-class design with basically the same armament, although the main guns were mounted in separate sleeves to allow individual rather than collective elevation and the secondary guns were installed one deck higher. The main improvements in the class were a more refined hull, which introduced an elegant clipper bow and a bulbous forefoot, increased internal compartmentalization for greater survivability and, in the New Mexico, the first installation in a capital ship of a turbo-electric propulsion arrangement in which two steam turbines powered electrical generators supplying current to the four electric motors that delivered 27,500hp (20505kW) to four shafts for a speed of 21kt. Although bulky and heavy, the turbo-electric drive was highly economical and a decided asset to manoeuvrability.

The French had lagged somewhat behind in the Dreadnought race, and it was only in May 1912 that the first of three

basic lines resulted in the two ships of the Nevada class, which carried basically the same armament as the Texas-class ships but were considerably better protected. This latter resulted from firing trials against an old battleship, which revealed that light and medium armour were no protection against large-calibre shells. The Americans had therefore adopted the all or nothing principle for armour protection, demanding that all armour protecting the ships vital spaces and other essential areas should be proof against penetration by large-calibre shells fired at typical ranges, and that other

areas should receive no protection at all. The Americans now began to produce battleships with excellent firepower and protection although this inevitably meant a slight sacrifice in theoretical performance to typical battleship levels, and effectively ended any possibility of American battle-cruisers. The two ships of the Nevada class had armour up to 18in (457mm) thick. The propulsion arrangement was now based on steam turbines, in this instance delivering 26,500hp (19760kW) to two shafts for a speed of 20.5kt.

The final expression of the American

Rheinland, *a Nassau-class battleship of the Imperial German Navy.*

Provence-class super-Dreadnought-class battleships was laid down. This was based on the hull design of the Courbet-class Dreadnought battleship to save in design time, but marked a new departure for the French as it was armed with 10 13.4-in (340-mm) main guns in five centreline twin turrets (superfiring pairs forward and aft with a singleton unit amidships).

Meanwhile the British had been pushing ahead with their next development in response to the latest Germans ships.

These were now armed with 12-in (305-mm) main guns, which the British deemed to be comparable in operational terms to their 13.5-in (343-mm) weapons. The British response was the 15-in (381-mm) gun designed to provide a significant measure of advantage over the German 12-in (305-mm) gun and also the 14-in (356-mm) guns that was entering service with other navies. The 15-in (381-mm) gun proved itself an excellent weapon, with a 1,920-lb (871-kg) shell fired at a muzzle

velocity of 2,655ft (809m) per second to attain a range of 35,000yds (32005m); moreover, the gun soon revealed the additional advantage of suffering little barrel wear even in protracted firing, and this offered excellent economics. The additional weight of this larger gun, its mounting and the turret required to carry two such weapons, demanded a ship somewhat larger than had become the norm. The result was the Queen Elizabeth-class of five ships based on a hull design

The forward guns and bridge of HMS Queen Elizabeth, *a Queen Elizabeth-class battleship of the Royal Navy during World War I.*

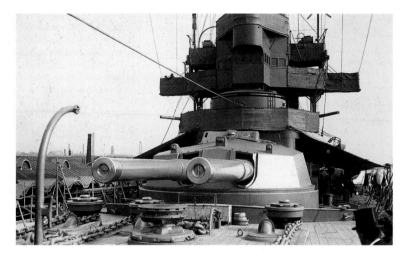

Guns aboard HMS New Zealand. The New Zealand was a ship of the Indefatigable class.

adapted from that of the Iron Duke class with an additional 2,500 tons of displacement provided by a lengthening of 20ft (6.1m) and a widening of 6in (0.15m). Another development was the introduction, for the first time anywhere in the world, of boilers that were fired exclusively by oil. The elimination of the bunkerage previously required for coal saved a considerable amount of weight, and this was used to improve the protection, which was based on a deeper belt up to 13in (330mm) thick, five armoured decks that yielded a greater overall thickness than the individually thicker decks of the Iron Duke-class ships, and two longitudinal bulkheads to provide improved underwater protection. On this massive hull, with a full-load displacement of 33,020 tons and capable of 23kt on the 75,000hp (55920kW) delivered to four

HMS Roberts, a Roberts-class monitor. Monitors were in essence floating gun platforms intended for shore bombardment purposes, and generally carried the primary armament of two battleship-calibre guns as well as smaller weapons for self defence.

shafts, the Queen Elizabeth-class battleships carried a main armament of eight 15-in (381-mm) main guns in four centreline turrets (superfiring pairs forward and aft) and a secondary armament of 16 6-in (152-mm) guns.

The Queen Elizabeth-class ships opened the definitive period in the development of the all big gun battleship, for further progress was now based not so much on any conceptual developments but rather on increased size for the greater power and thicker (as well as better disposed) armour that provided a higher speed and improved protection, in combination with a centreline main armament arrangement often involving larger-calibre guns, a better secondary

armament arrangement in which casemated single-purpose guns were generally replaced by turreted weapons that were often of the dual-purpose type, and a tertiary armament arrangement designed to supplement the secondary armament with a dedicated anti-aircraft fit to provide protection against the warplane that from the period after World War I became the primary threat to the capital ship.

This was still in the future, however, as countries started to respond to the British lead exemplified by the battleships of the Queen Elizabeth class and then exploited by the five ships of the Royal Sovereign class, which was a further development based on the hull design of the Iron Duke class with a primary armament of eight 15-in (381-

ABOVE
The after barbette aboard HMS Rodney. *Such was the weight of early breech-loading guns that they were carried, for topweight reasons, in open mountings at the top of a barbette. The* Rodney, *completed in 1888, was the first of the Admiral class with the primary armament of four 13.5-in (343-mm) guns.*

LEFT
Westfalen, *a Nassau-class battleship of the Kaiserliches Marine.*

99

SMS Friedrich der Grosse, *a Kaiser-class battleship at the surrender of the German Fleet in 1918.*

mm) guns in four twin superfiring turrets (forward and aft) and a secondary armament of 14 6-in (152-mm) guns. Revisions were incorporated to improve the design's steadiness, and to improve protection by an increase in the depth of the belt, the enhancement of the internal underwater protection and, in the last ship of the class, the introduction of the external bulges that became standard in the 1920s and 1930s. With a speed of 22kt on the 42,650hp (31800kW) delivered to four shafts, the Royal Sovereign-class battleships were for a time considered inferior to the Queen Elizabeth-class ships, but were in fact better ships as a result of their improved protection and better sited secondary armament.

The battleships armed with 15-in (381-mm) main guns were complemented by battle-cruiser equivalents, starting with the two ships of the Renown class with a main armament of six 15-in (381-mm) guns in three centreline twin turrets (a superfiring pair forward and a singleton unit aft), armour up to a maximum thickness of 11in (279mm) but only 6in (152mm) on the belt, and a speed of 32.7kt on the 126,300hp (94170kW) delivered to four shafts. The last three British battle-cruisers of World War I were distinctly odd ships reflecting Fisher's obsession with speed and firepower to the detriment of protection and, in this instance, his desire to undertake an amphibious landing, in collaboration with Russian forces, on the north German coast in the Baltic with the support of shallow-draught battle-cruisers. This resulted in the three ships of the Glorious class. The first two of these were completed with a main armament of four 15-in (381-mm) guns in two twin turrets and a secondary armament of 18 6-in (152-mm) guns in six triple turrets, an

A photograph of battle-cruisers HMS Inflexible *and* New Zealand, *taken from* HMS Indomitable *in 1918.*

armoured belt whose maximum thickness was only 3in (76mm), and a speed of 32kt on the 93,780hp (69920kW) delivered to four shafts. The result was a pair of magnificent but wholly impractical ships whose basic concept was taken to the limit, or indeed beyond it, by their half-sister *Furious* in which the main armament was two 18-in (457-mm) guns in single turrets and the secondary armament 11 5.5-in (140-mm) guns. Before completion the *Furious* was modified into a hybrid aircraft carrier with the forward main-gun turret replaced by a long flightdeck, and in 1918 the ship was revised as a true aircraft carrier, a standard to which the two half-sister ships were modified in the 1920s.

The German response to the British ships with 15-in (381-mm) guns was the Baden class projected at four units of which only two were completed. The design of this class reflected a change in German thinking from an original capital ship philosophy of gun-power inferiority but protective superiority vis-à-vis British ships,

to an equality of gun power and protection. This philosophy was posited on the new 15-in (381-mm) gun developed by Krupp, but this was in fact inferior to the British gun of the same calibre as it fired a lighter 1,653-lb (750-kg) shell at the lower muzzle velocity of 2,297ft (700m) per second to the shorter range of 22,200yds (20300m) at an elevation of 16°. Eight of these guns were located in four centreline twin turrets installed as superfiring pairs, and the secondary armament was 16 5.9-in (150-mm) guns in casemated mountings. The hull was basically an improved version of that developed for the König class but with greater length and beam for a larger displacement and room for a more powerful propulsion arrangement with three sets of steam turbines delivering 52,000shp (38770kW) to three shafts for a speed of 22.25kt.

German plans for the completion of the other two ships of the class, and also for the construction of other ships with 15-in (381-mm) guns, were overtaken by the end of the war, but British assessment of these and other German ships after the war revealed that the German ships were basically inferior to their British counterparts in structural integrity as well as a number of operational features.

At the beginning of World War I in August 1914, the British disposed of 20 Dreadnought battleships, eight battle-cruisers, 40 pre-Dreadnought battleships, 102 cruisers, 301 destroyers and 78 submarines. The equivalent figures for Germany were 13 Dreadnought battleships, five battle-cruisers, 22 pre-Dreadnought battleships, 41 cruisers, 144 destroyers and 30 submarines.

The first naval battles of World War I took place on the western and eastern sides of the South American continent as the German navy's Far East Squadron (two armoured and three light cruisers under the command of Admiral Maximilian von Spee) attempted to return home to Germany from China. In the Battle of Coronel on 1 November 1914, von Spee's forces overwhelmed Vice Admiral Sir Christopher Cradock's force of two armoured cruisers, one light cruiser and one armed merchant cruiser, sinking the two completely obsolete armoured cruisers. The situation was reversed in the Battle of the Falkland Islands on 8 December of the same year, when von Spee's force was surprised and comprehensively defeated by two Dreadnought battle-cruisers under the command of Vice Admiral Sir Doveton Sturdee.

The next significant confrontation between the British and German navies came on 24 January 1915 in the Battle of the Dogger Bank. This resulted from a sweep undertaken by the German battle-cruiser squadron under Vice Admiral Franz Hipper to raid the English coast and attack the British fishing fleet in the southern part of the North Sea. Warned by radio intercept that elements of Germany's High Seas Fleet were out from their bases on the North Sea coast, the Grand Fleet of Admiral Sir John Jellicoe steamed to meet what the British hoped would be a German attack in strength, which could lead to a decisive fleet engagement.

The British battle-cruiser force, numbering five ships supported by cruisers and destroyers, all under the command of Vice Admiral Sir David Beatty, encountered the German battle-cruiser force of three ships supported by cruisers and destroyers off the Dogger Bank, half-way between the U.K. and Germany. Hipper reversed course for Germany, but Beatty used the greater speed of his force to overhaul the Germans,

The German battle-cruiser Derfflinger *sinking after the German fleet was scuttled at Scapa Flow on 21 June 1919.*

HMS Hood, *a Hood-class battle-cruiser of the Royal Navy during sea trials in January 1920.*

whose ships he engaged with long-range fire, in the process disabling the *Blücher*, a hybrid of battle-cruiser and armoured cruiser features, and damaging Hipper's flagship, the battle-cruiser *Seydlitz*. Then Beatty's flagship, the *Lion*, was damaged and fell out of the line. Through misunderstanding of signals, the remainder of the British squadron contented itself with sinking the disabled *Blücher*, and Hipper's other ships escaped.

The long-awaited fleet engagement finally took place on 31 May and 1 June 1916 in the form of the Battle of Jutland. The High Seas Fleet, under the command of Vice Admiral Reinhard Scheer, had put to sea on 30 May in a leisurely progress toward the Skagerrak. Von Hipper's scouting force, 40 fast vessels centred on five battle-cruisers, were in the van, and well behind was the main fleet of 59 ships, 16 of them Dreadnought battleships and another six pre-Dreadnought battleships. Again learning of the German sortie as a result of radio intercepts, the Grand fleet sailed under the command of Jellicoe. In the van was Beatty's Battle-Cruiser Fleet of 52 ships, including his six battle-cruisers and Rear Admiral Hugh Evan-Thomas's squadron of four Queen Elizabeth-class super-Dreadnought battleships. Jellicoe's main strength, somewhat farther back, comprised 99 ships including 24 Dreadnought battleships. In overall terms, the British had 151 ships including 37 capital ships (28 Dreadnought battleships

The British battleship HMS Barham is seen at sea with one of its destroyer's escorts.

and nine battle-cruisers) while the Germans had 99 ships including 27 capital ships (16 Dreadnought and six pre-Dreadnought battleships as well as five battle-cruisers).

The Battle-Cruiser Fleet, steaming east in two divisions with the super-Dreadnought battleships on the left and the battle-cruisers on the right, sighted Hipper's force at 15.30 hours on the following day as it was heading south, having already spotted the British and turned to lure them onto the guns of Scheer's main force. Beatty turned on a parallel course, signalling Evan-Thomas, whose squadron Hipper had not yet seen, to follow. Both battle-cruiser forces opened fire at a range of some 16,500yds (15100m), the German gunnery soon revealing itself as the more accurate. The *Lion*, Beatty's flagship, took several hits and then followed fatal hits on others of the thin-skinned British battle-cruisers: a salvo from *Von der Tann* tore into the Indefatigable, which blew up; and accurate

fire from the *Derfflinger* sank the *Queen Mary* only 20 minutes later.

With only four ships against the Germans' five vessels and Evan-Thomas still out of range, Beatty signalled his ships to engage the Germans more closely. Soon after this, at 16.42 hours, Beatty saw the German main force moving toward him and immediately turned north toward Jellicoe, emulating Hipper's initial gambit in trying to draw the enemy onto his own main force. Hipper's ships had already turned and were hitting the ships of both Beatty's and Evans-Thomas's squadrons, of which the last was slow in turning and therefore taken under fire by Scheer's main force. For more than 60 minutes the chase to the north continued, much damage being done on both sides. Shortly after 18.00 hours, Beatty sighted Jellicoe's six divisions arriving from the north-west in parallel columns, preceded by Rear Admiral the Hon. H. L. A. Hood's squadron of three battle-cruisers supported by two light cruisers. The main

strength of the Grand Fleet was still over the horizon from the Germans but, still heavily engaged, Beatty turned east, in front of the Germans, to get himself into line in front of Jellicoe, whose six columns now also turned behind Beatty. Both British admirals were hoping to swing entirely around the High Seas Fleet and cut it off from its base.

Shortly before 18.30 hours, Scheer sighted Hood's squadron to his right front, just as the shells of the British Dreadnought battleships began to fall around the German battle line. Within minutes, practically every major ship in both fleets was within range and a furious general engagement began. The German battle-cruisers caught the worst of the British fire: Hipper's flagship, the *Lützow*, was crippled, but on the British side the *Invincible*, Hood's flagship, was hit and sank with all hands by the *Derfflinger's* guns, and the cruisers *Defence* and *Warrior* were also sunk.

The High Seas Fleet was now inside the

ABOVE
The French battleship Richelieu *at Dakar in 1941.*

ABOVE LEFT
The Gneisenau, *a Scharnhorst-class battle-cruiser of the German Kriegsmarine, as built, with straight bow. Autumn 1938.*

Four of Japan's battleships are seen before World War II: from front to rear, these are the Nagato-class Nagato, the Kongo-class Kirishima, and the Ise-class Ise and Hyuga.

converging arc of the Grand Fleet and taking heavy punishment. At 18.35 hours Scheer, under cover of a smoke screen and destroyer attacks, suddenly reversed course in a perfectly executed simultaneous 180° turn, headed west and in a few minutes was out of range. Instead of pursuing, Jellicoe continued south as he knew that the Grand Fleet was now between the Germans and their base. At 18.55 hours, Scheer made another 180° fleet turn back toward the British, apparently thinking Jellicoe had divided his fleet. Suddenly the entire German fleet was again under the guns of

the entire Grand Fleet. This time it seemed that the Germans could not escape destruction in the hail of projectiles.

For a second time Scheer made a simultaneous turn away, while the four surviving German battle-cruisers, under the command of Captain Hartog of the *Derfflinger*, as Hipper was striving to catch up after transferring to a destroyer, most gallantly charged toward the British line to cover the withdrawal. The *Von der Tann*, her guns already out of action, remained in line only to spread the British fire. Both the *Seydlitz* and the *Derfflinger* were on fire but

remained in action as the German battle-cruisers swung past the British battle line at short range. Then German destroyers sped in toward Jellicoe's battleships to make a torpedo attack and spread a smoke screen. Jellicoe, wary of torpedoes, saved Scheer by ordering a turn away from the torpedo attack. By the time he had resumed his battle line, the High Seas Fleet had disappeared westward into the dusk as Scheer made yet another 180° turn. Amazingly, none of the German battle-cruisers had been sunk in this extremely brave death ride.

The battle was not yet over, however. Scheer knew that the Grand Fleet was now between his fleet and its home ports, and that Jellicoe was steaming to cover the entrances to those ports, and also appreciated that the High Seas Fleet could not survive a renewed general engagement. After dark he turned the High Seas Fleet to the south-east, deliberately crashing into the formation of light cruisers at the rear of the Grand Fleet as it headed south. The High Seas Fleet battered its way through in a chaotic midnight battle of gun fire, sinkings and collisions: the cruiser *Black Prince*, suddenly caught in the middle of the German forces, was destroyed in just four minutes and the pre-Dreadnought battleship *Pommern* was cut in two.

By dawn on 1 June the High Seas Fleet was approaching its anchorage in the estuary of the Jade river, and the Grand Fleet turned for home after appreciating that it had lost the Germans. The British had lost three battle-cruisers, three cruisers and eight destroyers, in the process suffering 6,784 casualties, while the Germans had lost one pre-Dreadnought battleship, one battle-cruiser, four light cruisers and five destroyers, in the process suffering 3,039 casualties.

The German battle-cruiser Seydlitz.

Both sides claimed a victory, but though it can be argued that the Germans had fared better at the tactical level and inflicted greater losses, there can be no denial of the fact that the British had scored a major strategic victory as it was the Germans who had retreated and seldom ventured forth from their bases for the rest of the war. In overall terms, Jutland marked the end of an epoch in naval warfare, for it was the last great fleet action in which the opponents fought it out with gun fire controlled by optical means.

World War I ended in November 1918, its conclusion brought about as much by the political, social and economic collapse of Germany and its Central Powers allies, most notably Austria-Hungary and Turkey, as by the increasing military superiority of the Allied powers, most notably France, the U.K. and the U.S.A. As a result, the end of the fighting was an equally blessed relief for

the almost equally exhausted Allied powers.

For a variety of reasons, none of these countries could consider large-scale naval development or construction in the years following World War I, and this left the U.S.A. and Japan to move up in the naval race. The U.S.A. now felt itself compelled to operate a navy second to none as a protector of its world-wide mercantile interests and as the self-appointed main bastion of democracy, while Japan had grown enormously in power across the eastern Pacific during the war and now felt that parity with the U.S.A. was a realizable and indeed worthy objective that was reflected in the so-called 8-8 programme to build eight new battleships and eight battle-cruisers by the end of the 1920s. Despite its exhaustion, the U.K. felt in the early 1920s that it could not allow its naval superiority to be challenged without any British response, and thus it appeared that a new

naval race might be in the making.

Efforts to prevent such a race, which would be financially costly and politically destabilizing, resulted in the Washington Naval Conference of 1921–22, whose concluding treaty attempted to impose limits on the tonnage of the warships that could be built and on the calibre of the weapons that the ships might carry. In qualitative terms the treaty fixed 35,000 tons and 16-in (406-mm) as the maximum displacement and maximum gun calibre, and in quantitative terms it fixed limits so acute that an immediate result was the scrapping of many American, British and Japanese capital ships then under construction or being planned. These types, some of which were converted into aircraft carriers rather than being scrapped in their entirety, included the American's 43,200-ton South Dakota-class battleships with an armament of 12 16-in (406-mm) guns and the 43,500-ton Lexington-class battle-cruisers with an armament of eight 16-in (406-mm) guns; the British 48,400-ton G3-class battle-cruisers with an armament of nine 16-in (406-mm) guns and the 48,500-ton N3-class battleships with an armament of nine 18-in (457-mm) guns; and the Japanese 40,640-ton Amagi-class battle-cruisers with an armament of 10 16-in (406-mm) guns and the 40,570-ton Tosa-class battleships with an armament of 10 16-in (406-mm) guns.

The designers of capital ships now had to cope with a number of changed technical factors as well as the disruption caused by politically-inspired changes and limitations. On the offensive side, these were basically the revision of turrets and their guns to allow firing at higher elevations angle for the type of longer-range engagement that was now increasingly the norm, the replacement of casemated mountings for

107

secondary-armament guns by turrets located at a higher level for greater range and continued operability in a seaway, the adoption of director firing for the secondary armament, and the increased sophistication of the main armament's director firing system with a longer-base rangefinder for the maintenance of accuracy at increased ranges and a gyroscopic platform whose electric output was used to keep the guns in the same position relative to the horizon, despite the ship's roll, thereby much enhancing the accuracy of fire to a given range.

On the defensive side, the designers had to come to grips with the changed protective requirements imposed by the potential arrival of projectiles at higher impact angles: these were both shells fired at longer range and therefore descending at a more acute angle, and aircraft-dropped bombs arriving at a nearly vertical angle. This latter demanded an increase in horizontal protection to resist the penetration of these high-angle weapons, although no loss of vertical protection could be envisaged because of the continued threat of short-range fire, the torpedo and the mine. Early trials with bombs dropped by warplanes had been largely discounted because of their inaccuracy under all but artificial conditions, but the tendency to ignore the air-launched bomb and its effects were rudely shattered in the early days of World War II (1939–45), when the bomb delivered with considerable accuracy by the dive-bomber became a decisive weapon that was matched later in the war by the bomb dropped by the level bomber with a sight of improved capability. The fact that the threat of the warplane was not ignored, however, was showed by modest improvements in horizontal armour and the introduction of

with a longer and less thickly armoured hull containing a considerably more potent propulsion arrangement for significantly higher speed, despite a full-load displacement of 44,600 tons. Four of the class were ordered in April 1916, but the only unit to be completed was the *Hood*, which had a main armament of eight higher-angle 15-in (381-mm) guns in four superfiring twin turrets on the centreline as well as a secondary armament of 12 5.5-in (140-mm) guns, a maximum armour thickness of 12in (305mm), including a measure of inclined armour providing protection against plunging fire, and steam turbines powered by more efficient small-tube boilers for the delivery of 151,280hp (112795kW) to four shafts for a speed of 32.1kt.

Whereas it was generally the British who had led the way with capital ship design up to this period, the Japanese led the way to the adoption of the 16-in (406-mm) gun in the two ships of the Nagato class that entered service in the early 1920s. These were excellent examples of the fast battleship concept, for the adoption of eight 16-in (406-mm) main guns in two pairs of superfiring twin turrets permitted a significant reduction in armament weight by comparison with the ships of the Hyuga class with their primary armament of 12 14-in (356-mm) weapons in six turrets. The broadside weight of the Hyuga class ships was 17,857 lb (8100 kg) by comparison with the Nagato class ships 17,513 lb (7944 kg) fired to a ranger range with more destructive power. The Nagato class was based on the same hull as the Hyuga class, but this was revised with considerably more and better disposed armour, and a propulsion arrangement in which four steam turbines delivered 80,000hp (59650kW) to four shafts for a speed of 26.75kt. Other

LEFT and OPPOSITE
The German pocket battleship Graf Spee, *with Nazi insignia.*

larger numbers of dedicated anti-aircraft guns. The standard in the later part of World War I had generally been two 3-in (76-mm) guns or similar weapons, but during the 1920s the numbers of anti-aircraft guns increased quite dramatically in the form of larger-calibre weapons for the engagement of high-flying attackers at longer ranges, and smaller-calibre weapons, often of the multiple type, for the creation of a barrage through which any low-level attacker would have to fly at shorter ranges.

As the navies of the world and their designers were coming to grips with the limits imposed on them by the Washington Naval Treaty, the last of the World War I

capital ships were being completed. The finest of these, and arguably the most beautiful of all capital ships, was the British battle-cruiser *Hood*, which resulted directly from the revelation in 1915 that the Germans were preparing a battle-cruiser design with 15-in (381-mm) main guns. The Admiralty decided to respond not with larger calibre, but rather with a battle-cruiser that combined the latest thinking in terms of firepower, protection and speed to provide greater firepower than was available in the Renown-class ships and greater protection than was afforded in the splendid cats. The result was a design that was in effect a Queen Elizabeth-class battleship

The ship that ended its life as the Turkish battle-cruiser Yavuz *(originally* Yavuz Sultan Selim*) was built as the German Moltke-class ship* Goeben, *and became a notionally Turkish ship in August 1914 after escaping from British pursuit in the Mediterranean. The ship remained German-manned up to the end of World War I in 1918, and was formally transferred to Turkey in November 1918. The ship was stricken only in 1954.*

improvements over the Hyuga class were a secondary armament of 20 5.5-in (140-mm) guns and a control top located on what came to be called a pagoda foremast, after this highly distinctive feature of the Japanese capital ship.

American battleships completed in this period included the two ships of the Tennessee class that were in essence improved versions of the New Mexico-class ships with turbo-electric drive and the secondary armament of 14 5-in (127-mm) guns located one deck higher: although one-third less than that of the New Mexico class in purely numerical terms, the secondary battery of the Tennessee class was operationally superior because of its higher

siting. There followed the ships of the Maryland class that was basically a repeat of the Tennessee class with the 12 14-in (356-mm) guns replaced by eight 16-in (406-mm) guns. The class was to have totalled four ships, but the completion of the fourth unit was overtaken by the Washington Naval Treaty. The incomplete ship was therefore used for tests into explosions and blast, and as such probably played as important a part in the development of the American battleship as she would have done if completed.

The first country to design a battleship without the constraints of the Washington Navy Treaty was the U.K. with the two-strong Nelson class, which was designed to

provide parity with the Japanese Nagato and American Maryland-class ships. The design was basically a cut-down version of the projected G3-class battle-cruiser with the same primary armament and level of protection, although displacement limitations meant that thick armour was applied to a reduced area and the propulsion arrangement was considerably down-rated. The principal expedient adopted to provide adequate protection over the vital spaces was the grouping of all three triple turrets, each carrying three 16-in (406-mm) guns, ahead of the superstructure block, resulting in a very truncated stern. The propulsion arrangement comprised just two sets of

steam turbines delivering 45,000hp (33550kW) to two shafts for a speed of only 23.5kt.

This was basically the extent of capital ship construction in the 1920s as limited by the Washington Naval Treaty, although considerable effort was additionally expended by the major powers on improvements to the capabilities of their existing ships, especially in terms of their defensive capabilities for which an additional 3,000 tons of displacement were permitted per ship. The defensive improvements included enhanced anti-aircraft capability in the form of additional armour and extra anti-aircraft weapons, and improved anti-torpedo capability in the form of bulges on

and below the waterline. Other changes that were effected were a revitalization of the propulsion arrangement, with oil-fired boilers replacing surviving coal-fired units, and the addition of one or more catapults for the launch of floatplanes that could extend the parent ship's search horizon and also serve in the gunnery spotting role in long-range engagements. Some countries also went to the trouble and expense of virtually gutting their older battleships and battle-cruisers so that they could be revised into altogether more modern and capable warships. The Japanese, for example, rebuilt their Kongo-class ships with a considerably lengthened hull for the improved length/beam ratio that allowed considerably

higher speed, while the Italians revised their Conte di Cavour and Caio Duilio class battleships virtually out of recognition with extended and reshaped bow lines, heavier main armament achieved by boring out the original weapons, a completely new secondary armament arrangement, and a totally rebuilt superstructure. This last was also a feature of Japanese battleships, which all began to sport a pagoda type of superstructure. British battleships were also extensively revised with new superstructures and main batteries in which the guns' maximum elevation angle was increased to 30° from the original figure of 20° as a means of extending their range.

Plans were also laid in the 1930s for more extensive rebuilds of older ships, but these were generally curtailed on the outbreak of World War II, when the ships were required for immediate service, and the combination of dockyard facilities and resources (financial, matériel and manpower) were earmarked for more important programmes such as the construction of new vessels and the rapid repair of damaged ships.

A revitalization of battleship-building programmes resulted from the 1929 decision of Germany, prohibited by the terms of the Treaty of Versailles from building warships with a displacement of more than 10,000 tons, to build a class of armoured ships (Panzerschiffe) that were really cruisers with a main armament of 11-in (280-mm) guns. This led to the 1st and 2nd London Naval Conferences of 1930 and 1935–36, together with the resulting treaties that sought to maintain the basic concept of the Washington Naval Treaty but added a number of provisos allowing individual countries to react in various ways in response to the actions of other countries. The 1st London Naval

The Scharnhorst, *a* Scharnhorst-*class battle-cruiser of the German Kriegsmarine, as built with straight bow. 1939.*

RIGHT
HMS Warspite.

BELOW
The Royal Sovereign-class battleships HMS Revenge, *HMS* Resolution *and HMS* Royal Sovereign *of the Grand Fleet's 1st Battleship Squadron during World War I.*

Conference involved Japan, the U.K. and U.S.A. while the 2nd London Naval Conference involved France, the U.K. and the U.S.A., and both can with hindsight be seen as attempts to re-establish a situation that was already disappearing even if it had not actually disappeared.

The first result of the Germans' decision to built a class of three Deutschland-class Panzerschiffe was the French order for two Dunkerque class of fast battleships with a main armament of eight 13-in (330-mm) guns in two quadruple turrets ahead of the superstructure, and a secondary armament of 16 5.1-in (130-mm) dual-purpose guns in three quadruple turrets aft and two twin turrets amidships. Protection was decidedly on the light side, with a maximum of 13.6in (345mm) on the barbettes and 9.5in (240mm) on the belt, but this allowed the ships to achieve 29.5kt on the 112,500hp (83880kW) delivered to four shafts by four sets of steam turbines.

This was a period of steadily deteriorating relations between France and Italy, and the former's decision to build two ships was soon followed by the latter's order for two more potent Vittorio Veneto-class battleships with a main armament of nine 15-in (381-mm) guns in three triple turrets and a secondary armament of 12 6-in (152-mm) guns in four triple turrets located in a beam pair abreast the superfiring unit of the two forward main-gun turrets and the after main-gun turret. The Italians preferred to rely on speed and manoeuvrability for protection, and the armour of the two Vittorio Veneto-class ships was therefore on the thin and light side by contemporary standards, but this permitted a speed of 31.4kt on the 134,616hp (100370kW) delivered to four shafts by four sets of steam turbines.

The end was put to the pause in battleship construction, which had started with the Washington Naval Treaty of 1922, by the German decision to renounce the terms of the Treaty of Versailles and start a programme of rearmament that included two improved Panzerschiffe, namely the battle-cruisers of the Gneisenau class, and the revelation that Japan had no real intention of abiding by the terms of the 1936 London Naval Treaty, which ordained that signatory countries could build as many battleships as they liked so long as none of these ships exceeded a displacement of 40,000 tons and a main gun calibre of 14in (356mm). The agreement also contained a provision that in the event of a Japanese non-ratification, the signatories could switch to 16-in (406-mm) main guns, but American and British moves in this direction were hampered by their continued attempts to limit battleship displacement to 45,000 and 40,000 tons respectively. In the event, all these negotiations were overtaken by the outbreak of World War II in September 1939.

Another attempt to limit the growth of Europe's fleet of expensive capital ships was the Anglo-German Naval Treaty of 1935, in which the U.K. agreed to a measure of German rearmament in exchange for a German agreement to limit its capital ship programme to the two battleships of the Bismarck class with an armament of eight 15-in (381-mm) guns in four twin turrets against which the British laid down the first of its King George V class of modern battleship with a main armament of 10 14-in (356-mm) guns in two quadruple turrets and

one superfiring twin turret. This British effort was designed to persuade other countries to limit their main gun calibre to 14in (356mm), but the fact that the originating country did not have much confidence in the success of its effort was signalled by the preparation of plans for the Lion-class battleships with an armament of nine 16-in (406-mm) guns in three triple turrets; but these were later cancelled because of the exigencies of the war.

The two Gneisenau-class battle-cruisers were planned as the fourth and fifth units of the Deutschland class of pocket battleships before it was decided to develop them into altogether larger and more powerful ships to give the Germans parity with the French Dunkerque class of fast battleships. Further delay was occasioned by Adolf Hitler's initial insistence that the ships should have the same main armament as the Deutschland-class vessels, namely six 11-in (280-mm) guns in two triple turrets and the German navy's demand that the minimum feasible armament for ships of this type should be nine 11-in (280-mm) weapons in three triple turrets. The navy had really wanted a larger calibre of gun, and was hard pressed to justify its resistance to Hitler's next demand, which was that the ships should be designed and built with provision for subsequent rearmament with 15-in (380-mm) weapons when these became available. The basic design was modelled on that of two uncompleted battle-cruiser designs of World War I, which were the most advanced types of which Germany had direct experience, with a number of improvements to features such as the disposition of the armour, the introduction of considerably more modern fire-control systems, and provision for catapult-launched aircraft. Completed in the second half of the 1930s and later revised with a clipper bow for improved sea-keeping

HMS Nelson, *a Nelson-class battleship.*

ABOVE
The Lützow *(ex-Deutschland), an Admiral Graf Spee-class armoured cruiser behind her anti-torpedo nets in a Norwegian fjord during World War II.*

ABOVE RIGHT
The Japanese battleship Yamato *in 1941.*

capabilities, the two ships were small but nonetheless impressive vessels of their type, and their details included a primary armament of nine 11-in (280-mm) guns in three triple turrets including a superfiring pair forward of the superstructure, a secondary armament of 12 5.9-in (150-mm) guns, a tertiary armament of 14 4.1-in (105-mm) anti-aircraft guns, armour up to a maximum thickness of 13.8in (350mm), and a propulsion arrangement in which three sets of steam turbines delivered 160,000hp (119360kW) to three shafts for a speed of 31kt. A propulsion arrangement based on diesel engines had originally been considered for very long cruising ranges, the ships being designed for extended commerce raiding capability in the Atlantic, but this was rejected in favour of the higher speed provided by steam turbine propulsion.

The two Gneisenau-class battle-cruisers were followed by the two Bismarck-class battleships. These were designed and built with commendable speed on the basis of theoretical work which German naval

architects had completed during the period in which Germany was prohibited from the construction of warships displacing more than 10,000 tons, but reflected the fact that Germany was short of practical experience in the design, construction and use of modern battleships. The most important aspect of this limitation was that the basic hull concept of the World War I Baden class was reused, albeit in a more refined form with a greater length/beam ratio to allow a higher speed. Considerable development of the basic hull allowed the incorporation of much improved underwater protection and a considerably enhanced armament fit, which now comprised a main battery of eight 15-in (380-mm) main guns in two pairs of superfiring twin turrets, a secondary battery of 12 5.9-in (150-mm) guns in six twin turrets, and a tertiary battery of 16 4.1-in (105-mm) anti-aircraft guns in eight twin turrets complemented by large numbers of 37- and 20-mm cannon wherever deck space could be found; but the basic obsolescence of the hull was

evident in the poor protection provided for the rudders and associated steering gear, the location of the main armoured deck toward the bottom edge of the armoured belt at a time when other countries, drawing on experience in the destruction of older battleships (including German ships surrendered at the end of World War I), had moved this to a position farther up the belt to provide better protection for communications and data-transmission systems. Both of these faults played a decisive part in the eventual loss of the *Bismarck.* Three other weak points were the provision of separate low-angle secondary and high-angle tertiary gun batteries, making extensive demands on deck area and displacement, as a result of Germany's failure to keep abreast of the latest developments in dual-purpose ship's armament, the indifferent quality of the armour that was designed to be proof against penetration by 15-in (381-mm) fire in its key areas but was in fact penetrated by 8-in (203-mm) fire, and the poor quality of

Rescue craft move into the battleship USS West Virginia *while USS* Tennessee *lies damaged beyond, following the Japanese air attack on the U.S. fleet at Pearl Harbor on 7 December 1941.*

The U.S. Navy's battleship West Virginia (BB-48) burning and badly damaged at Pearl Harbor on 7 December 1941, when Japanese carrier-based aircraft of Admiral Nagumo's task force struck the American naval and air installations in the Hawaiian Islands. The USS West Virginia was in Battleship Row when the attack started at 07.55 hours. Shortly after 08.00, Nakajima B5N2 'Kate' torpedo bombers attacked the battleships at anchor off Ford Island and, because no torpedo nets were deployed, succeeded in hitting the West Virginia and two other battleships. Further torpedo strikes set her on fire. Here, fire-fighting crews are at work after the attack. USS West Virginia was severely damaged and sunk in her berth, though she was later raised and repaired.

which was the earliest date in which guns and turrets ordered in 1936 could be delivered, the British opted for the smaller calibre of main gun in combination with armour designed to provide survivability against 16-in (406-mm) fire.

The plan was now to install 12 14-in (356-mm) guns in two pairs of superfiring triple turrets, but the need to provide additional horizontal armour meant the sacrifice of two guns to produce a final disposition of 10 14-in (356-mm) guns installed in two quadruple turrets and one twin superfiring turret. The all or nothing protection was based on armour up to 15in (381mm) thick, and the propulsion arrangement allowed for the delivery of 110,000hp (82015kW) to four shafts by four sets of steam turbines for a speed of 29.25kt.

At much the same time France was planning a class of four battleships offering greater capabilities than the two units of the Dunkerque class and thus providing the French navy with a counter to the German Bismarck and Italian Vittorio Veneto-class battleships. These were the Richelieu-class battleships, of which only one was completed in World War II and another in the period immediately after the end of the war. The type retained the basic configuration of the Dunkerque-class ships, with the primary armament grouped in the forward part of the ship, although in this instance the main armament was eight 15-in (380-mm) guns in two quadruple turrets. The secondary armament comprised nine 6-in (152-mm) guns in three triple turrets in the after part of the ship, and the tertiary armament was 12 3.9-in (100-mm) anti-aircraft guns in six twin turrets clustered round the mack, or combined mast and smoke stack. Protection was adequate, and a speed of 32kt was possible on the

The battleship USS Pennsylvania leads a line of American battleships into Lingayen gulf, prior to the landings in the Philippines.

the 15-in (380-mm) shells, which often failed to detonate. All these factors notwithstanding, the two Bismarck-class battleships were magnificent vessels that exercised a horrible fascination on the British, who retained powerful forces in home waters to meet the threat of these two battleships.

The slightly later British contemporaries of the Bismarck class were the five ships of the King George V class, which were originally designed within the constraints of the Washington Naval Treaty with a primary armament of nine 15-in (381-mm) guns in three triple turrets, a secondary armament of 6-in (152-mm) guns, and only modest

speed. Revision of the core design in 1934 resulted in the replacement of the 6-in (152-mm) weapons with 4.7-in (120-mm) guns, but the final selection was the excellent 5.25-in (133-mm) dual-purpose gun mounting introduced on the Dido class of light cruisers. Finally the 15-in (381-mm) main guns were replaced by 14-in (356-mm) weapons ordained as the maximum by the London Naval Treaty: the British felt that Japan might not ratify the treaty, thereby opening the probability that other countries would opt for the 16-in (406-mm) weapons then allowed by the treaty, but as British plans were based on the possibility of war with Germany by 1940,

155,000hp (115570kW) delivered to four shafts by four sets of steam turbines.

The only other countries to complete new classes of battleship in this period were Japan and the U.S.A. The Japanese offering was the extraordinary Yamato class, of which two were completed during World War II as the largest, most strongly defended and most powerfully armed battleships ever placed in service. The result of an evolutionary process that had seen the creation of 23 designs in the period between 1934 and 1937, the Yamato-class design resulted in ships of magnificent appearance with a full-load displacement of 71,660 tons, armour up to a maximum of 25.6in (650mm) thick on the turrets and 16.1in (410mm) thick on the belt, a propulsion arrangement in which steam turbines delivered 150,000hp (111840kW) to four shafts for a speed of 27kt, and a comprehensive armament fit that included a main battery of nine 18.1-in (460-mm) guns in three triple turrets (including a superfiring pair forward), a secondary battery of 12 6.1-in (155-mm) guns in three triple turrets clustered round the superstructure, and a tertiary battery of 12 5-in (127-mm) dual-purpose guns in twin mountings. The two 6.1-in (155-mm) turrets in the wing positions were later replaced by an additional 12 5-in (127-mm) guns for increased anti-aircraft protection at a time when American land-based and carrierborne warplanes were rampant in the Pacific, and by the end of its life in 1945 the Yamato had a specialized anti-aircraft armament of no fewer than 150 25-mm cannon.

There can be no denial of the fact that the two completed ships were obsolete by the time of their service debuts, and saw little effective use in the fact of overwhelming American air power

OPPOSITE
The Atlantic Fleet.

LEFT
Bismarck-class battleship of the Kriegsmarine at sea with her guns trained to port.

BELOW
HMS Queen Elizabeth *immediately after refit in the Norfolk Navy Yard, U.S.A. after damage from an Italian limpet mine in Alexandria. 2 June 1943.*

USS Alaska *(CB-1), an Alaska-class heavy cruiser off Philadelphia Navy Yard, Pennsylvania, 30 July 1942.*

An aerial view of the American cruiser USS Cleveland *(CL-55) in Cape Cod Bay, Massachussetts, U.S.A.*

superiority. Both ships were in fact lost to air attack, the strength of their construction being attested by the fact that the *Musashi* absorbed between 11 and 19 torpedo hits and at least 17 bomb strikes before succumbing, while the *Yamato* took between 11 and 15 torpedo hits and seven bomb strikes before sinking.

The last American battleships were the two ships of the North Carolina class, the four ships of the South Dakota class, and the four ships of the Iowa class. The North Carolina class was the first American battleship type built after the end of the Washington Naval Treaty limitations, but was originally planned round the London Naval Treaty armament of 12 14-in (356-mm) guns in two pairs of superfiring turrets. When the Japanese refused to ratify the treaty, the Americans recast the North Carolina-class ships with a primary armament of nine 16-in (406-mm) guns in three triple turrets and this arrangement, with a superfiring pair of turrets forward and a single turret aft, became standard in the two succeeding classes: this gun fired a 2,700-lb (1225-kg) shell to a range of 36,900yds (33740m) at an elevation of 45°, and was a notably successful weapon. The secondary armament comprised 20 5-in (127-mm) guns around the superstructure. All or nothing protection was based on armour up to 16in (406mm) thick, and a speed of 28kt was provided by four shafts receiving 121,000hp (90220kW) from four sets of steam turbines.

The four ships of the South Dakota class were built to what was a basically an improved version of the South Carolina-class design with reduced habitability, an increased level of blast interference from the 5-in (127-mm) guns, and a hull shortened by 50ft (15.2m) to allow the incorporation of much improved horizontal

respect superb fighting ships, but the obsolescence of the type as the capital ship had been highlighted by World War II operations, including the Japanese air attack on the U.S. Pacific Fleet in Pearl Harbor during December 1941. The American battleships of World War II were, with a few exceptions, generally not used in an effort to bring Japanese battleships to decisive action. The older ships were generally used to provide gunfire support for amphibious operations, while the more modern ships were generally operated as force flagships and/or escorts for aircraft carrier task forces. Most of the American battleships were retired shortly after the end of World War II, but the four Iowa-class ships were recalled to active service in the Korean War (1950–53) and during the Vietnam War (American involvement between 1961 and 1973), and were later upgraded with offensive and defensive missile capability for continued service into the early 1990s in the gunfire support and flagship roles.

In passing, it is worth noting two other capital ship types. The British Vanguard,

and underwater protection.

The four ships of the Iowa class were the last American battleships to be completed, and were designed as successors to the South Dakota class with a longer and finer hull whose additional volume and displacement were used for additional protection and power than greater

armament. This resulted in a type possessing basically the same primary and secondary armaments as carried by the two preceding classes, but armoured to a maximum of 19.7in (495mm) and capable of 33kt on the 212,000hp (158065kW) delivered to four shafts by four sets of steam turbines.

The Iowa-class battleships were in every

The USS New Jersey (BB-62) firing Tomahawk SLCM (Sea Launched Cruise Missiles) during trials off California on 10 May 1983.

completed in 1946 and little used in any meaningful fashion as the day of the battleship was past, was a singleton type resulting from the survival of the four 15-in (381-mm) twin turrets removed from the *Courageous* and *Glorious* after World War I. These were installed in superfiring pairs on a hull that was basically an improved version of that designed for the King George V class. Finally there are the four units of the Kirov class completed by the U.S.S.R. (and succeeding Commonwealth of Independent States) between 1980 and the early 1990s. These are attractive and highly capable major surface combatants often dubbed battle-cruisers. With a full-load displacement of 23,400 tons, the ships have a hybrid propulsion arrangement in which the steam from two pressurized water-cooled nuclear reactors is superheated by two oil-fired burners to power two sets of steam turbines delivering 150,000hp (111840kW) to two shafts for a speed of 30kt. The ships are armoured, although the basis of this armour has not been revealed, and the primary armament is missiles rather than the guns that had been used in all previous capital ship designs: this armament comprises 20 SS-N-19 Shipwreck anti-ship missiles with a conventional or nuclear warhead, and is complemented by three types of surface-to-air missile, a hybrid surface-to-air missile/30-mm cannon system for close-in defence against aircraft and missiles, a twin launcher for SS-N-14 Silex anti-submarine missiles, and a gun armament comprising two main guns (3.9-in/100-mm or 5.1-in/130-mm depending on ship) and eight 30-mm Gatling cannon for close-in defence.

USS Iowa *(BB-61). A fire-fighting party responds to an explosion and a fire in gun turret number two on 19 April 1989.*

Chapter Three
The Destroyer & Escort Vessel

The S77 and S81 were first-class torpedo boats of an Imperial German Navy-class of seven vessels completed in 1894–96. The class details included a displacement of 177 tons, a steam-propulsion arrangement delivering 1,745hp (1300kW) to one shaft for a speed of 22.5kt, and an armament of one 50-mm gun and three 17.7-in (450-mm) torpedo tubes with four torpedoes.

When the locomotive torpedo became a practical weapon from 1868, most navies thought it only sensible to start the process of building flotillas of fast torpedo-armed vessels, whose role was initially seen as the coast defence task, which they were to accomplish by threatening the battle fleets of any potential invader. Such was the perceived threat of the torpedo boat in the minds of many senior naval officers, who feared for the survival of the battleship fleets that were several nations' most important military assets, that a rival and comparable effort was soon launched for the design and

construction of ships possessing the speed and firepower to intercept and destroy torpedo boats before these smaller vessels had closed to torpedo-launch range of their battleship targets. This anti-torpedo boat role demanded a speed at least comparable with that of the torpedo boat as well as a primary armament of quick-firing guns plus a small complement of torpedo tubes (replaceable by additional quick-firing guns as and when required) so that the type could also be used as a torpedo boat.

The first of these torpedo boat catchers, a designation soon changed to torpedo boat destroyers, were launched in the U.K. in 1886. The ships lacked the speed to intercept their prey, however, and it was only in 1892 that the Admiralty took the plunge in a decisive way, ordering no fewer than 42 turtleback torpedo boat catchers from a number of yards that were given considerable discretion about the manner in which they fulfilled the Admiralty's basic requirement for a given armament, triple-expansion steam engines and a speed of 27kt. The first of these generally successful A-class torpedo boat destroyers were ordered from Yarrow as the Havock and Hornet with triple-expansion steam engines powering two shafts for a speed of 26kt with an armament that comprised one 12-pdr and three 6-pdr guns as well as three

18-in (457-mm) torpedo tubes that could be replaced by two more 6-pdr guns.

The two vessels and their successors quickly revealed a superiority over the torpedo boat proper so marked that the earlier type was soon discontinued in favour of rapid development and construction of the torpedo boat destroyer, a designation soon trimmed to destroyer, as a dual-purpose type capable of undertaking torpedo attacks on the enemy's fleet and protecting its own fleet against the torpedo attack of enemy vessels. These early destroyers were capable of speeds in the order of 26 or 27kt, although a lengthening of the hull and the installation of more powerful engines soon allowed the creation of improved destroyers with a speed in the order of 30kt, and 60 of these improved torpedo boat destroyers were ordered for later allocation to the B, C and D classes depending on their use of four, three and two funnels respectively.

Perhaps the single most decisive moment in the development of the early destroyer came in 1897, when the Hon. Charles Parsons produced his Turbinia to prove the capabilities of his steam turbine propulsion arrangement. So impressive was the performance of this privately funded experimental vessel that the Royal Navy switched to the steam turbine for its latest

design matched by a more powerful propulsion arrangement and greater bunkerage for the all-important improvement of seaworthiness and range. The ships were built in a large number of subvariants by different yards to a standard that included a full-load displacement of some 620 tons, a propulsion arrangement of triple-expansion steam engines delivering some 7,000hp (5220kW) for a sustained speed of 25.5kt, and the same armament as the smaller 30-kt vessels, although from 1906 this was increased to four 12-pdr guns and two 18-in (457-mm) torpedo tubes.

With the advent of the River-class vessels, the era of the true destroyer may be said to have started in a meaningful way, for all that was now needed to create the modern destroyer was the combination of the improved size and therefore seaworthiness of the River class with turbine propulsion based on oil- rather than coal-fired boilers. The first move in this direction came in the period between 1907 and 1909, when the 12 units of the Tribal or F class were completed in two major subclasses as five and seven ships as what may be regarded as the destroyer equivalents of the Dreadnought battleship for, by comparison with preceding classes, the displacement was virtually doubled, calibre of the primary armament was

HMS Lightening, *the Royal Navy's first torpedo boat, in 1877.*

destroyers, starting with the Viper that was completed in 1900 with a speed of 33.75kt on a light displacement of 344 tons with a four-shaft steam turbine propulsion arrangement.

Whether powered by triple-expansion or later by turbine engines, these and other early destroyers were capable of reaching their legendry speed only under ideal conditions, however, and higher speeds in anything but a smooth sea made the vessels very wet and rendered the forward guns all but unworkable. By the early 1900s, therefore, the British and other navies had decided that greater size was inevitable and

also desirable: a longer and slightly beamier hull would permit the introduction of more powerful engines so that a high speed could be maintained under adverse conditions, and it would also make possible the adoption of a raised fore castle so that wetness forward would be reduced and the forward guns could be fought under most operational conditions. The way was paved by the German S90 class in which a raised fore castle replaced the turtledeck for improved seaworthiness, and the British responded with the 34 units of the River or E class with considerably greater displacement and a far more seaworthy basic

125

increased to 4in (102mm), and the
propulsion arrangement was based on
turbines using steam from oil-fired boilers.
As such, these ships were the first genuinely
ocean-going rather than sea-going
destroyers, and while the earlier vessels had
a displacement of between 865 and 890
tons, a length of between 250 and 270ft
(76.2 and 82.3m) and a speed of between
33 and 36kt with a propulsion arrangement
in which steam turbines delivered 14,500hp
(10815kW) to three shafts, the later vessels
had a displacement of between 970 and
1,090 tons, a length of 280ft (85.3m) and a
speed of between 33 and 36kt with a
propulsion arrangement in which steam
turbines delivered 15,500hp (11555kW) to
three shafts.

Completed in 1907, the Swift can be
seen as a portent of things to come for the
ship was designed and constructed as a
flotilla leader with a displacement of 1,850
tons, an armament of four 4-in (102-mm)
and one 2-pdr guns as well as two 18-in
(457-mm) torpedo tubes, and a speed of

39kt on the 50,000hp (37280kW) delivered
to four shafts by steam turbines. The Swift's
size not only improved seaworthiness, but
also allowed the provision of room for the
flotilla commander and his staff and their
equipment without intrusion into the
ordinary working of the ship.

All these early destroyers had provided
both builders and the Royal Navy with
considerable experience in the design and
operation of destroyers, and the sensible
decision was now taken to concentrate on
the introduction of classes of identical
ships at the rate of between 16 and 24
ships per year. The first of these groups
was the 16-strong Basilisk or G class
completed in 1909 and 1910 with a
displacement of between 885 and 965
tons, an armament of one 4-in (102-mm)
and three 12-pdr guns as well as two 18-in
(457-mm) torpedo tubes, and a speed of
some 27 to 28kt on the 12,500hp
(9320kW) delivered to three shafts by
steam turbines supplied from coal-fired
boilers, which were adopted in what
initially appeared to be a retrograde move
but in fact reflected British fears that
supplies of oil from the Middle East might
be interrupted in the event of war. As a
result of their propulsion arrangement
these ships were comparatively slow by the
standards now becoming accepted for
destroyers, but on the other side of the
tactical coin the ships were very seaworthy,
which allowed them to maintain a higher
speed in conditions that would have forced
smaller and less seaworthy destroyers to
trim their speed. The following Acorn or
H class, of which 20 were completed in
1910 and 1911, was somewhat smaller
with a displacement of 780 tons, but was
capable of a speed between 27 and 30kt on
the 13,500hp (10065kW) delivered to
three shafts by steam turbines supplied

from oil-fired boilers, which now became a
standard feature of British destroyers. The
armament was two 4-in (102-mm) guns
and, for the first time in British destroyers,
two 21- rather than 18-in (533- rather
than 457-mm) torpedo tubes. Each ship
was built in an average time of 18 months,
a rate considerably faster than earlier types,
and this reflected the German's claim that
they were building large numbers of
destroyers in a unit time of between 12
and 15 months.

Following in 1911 and 1912, the
Acheron or I class totalled 20 ships that
comprised 14 to the standard pattern and
six slightly different ships with a more
powerful propulsion arrangement and a
number of innovatory features for the
exploration of technical avenues that might
lead to the development of superior
destroyers. The standard type had a
displacement of between 750 and 780 tons,
an armament of two 4-in (102-mm) and
two 12-pdr guns as well as two 21-in (533-
mm) torpedo tubes, and a speed of between
27 and 30kt on the 13,500hp (10065kW)
delivered to three shafts by steam turbines,
while the more powerfully engined type had
a speed of between 29 and 31 on the
15,000 to 16,500hp (11185 and 12300kW)
delivered to three shafts by steam turbines.
Another six ships of the same basic type
were delivered to the Royal Australian Navy,
three of them being diverted from original
British contracts and replaced by another
three ships built by Yarrow to an improved
standard with a displacement of 790 tons
and a speed of between 32 and 35kt on the
20,000hp (14910kW) delivered to three
shafts by steam turbines. The last three ships
were in effect the prototypes for the later
Yarrow variants of the Admiralty standard
destroyer design.

The last two destroyer classes

introduced before the outbreak of World War I in 1914 were the Acasta or K class and the L class, the latter pioneering the new British system of naming in which all the ships of a given class had names starting with the same letter. The Acasta class was completed in 1912 and 1913, and comprised 12 standard ships, six ships with a different armament disposition and a two- rather than three-shaft propulsion arrangement, and two prototypes for the two- and three-funnel versions of the following L class. The standard version had a displacement of 780 tons, an armament of two 4-in (102-mm) guns and two 21-in (533-mm) torpedo tubes, and a speed of between 27 and 30kt on the 13,500hp (10065kW) delivered to three shafts by steam turbines.

The L class was the definitive version of the British destroyer in the period leading up to World War I, and totalled six two-funnel and 16 three-funnel ships that introduced a raked rather than vertical stem, twin torpedo tube mountings and a bandstand mounting for the amidships gun. The basic data for these ships included a displacement between 965 and 1,070 tons, an armament of three 4-in (102-mm) and one 2-pdr guns as well as four 21-in (533-mm) torpedo tubes, and a speed of between 29 and 31kt on the 22,500 to 24,500hp (16775 and 18265kW) delivered to two shafts by steam turbines.

As World War I broke out in August 1914, the first of the new M-class destroyers were coming into service as improved versions of the L-class ships with a

displacement in the order of 994 to 1,042 tons, an armament of three 4-in (102-mm) and one 2-pdr guns as well as four 21-in (533-mm) torpedo tubes, and a speed of 34kt (often exceeded by a considerable margin) on the 25,000hp (18640kW) delivered to three shafts by steam turbines. The M class was deemed to be very successful and was also comparatively simple to build and outfit, and was therefore constructed in very large numbers during World War I. The overall total was 112 ships, which was so great that the Admiralty ran out of suitable names beginning with M and therefore gave many of the ships names beginning with N, O and P as well as a few with names starting with R and T.

The M-class ships were followed by 49 R-class ships with names starting with R, S,

*USS Schenck (DD 159), a
Wickes-class destroyer
underway in San Diego
harbour during the early
1930s.*

*RIGHT
HMS Winchelsea, a W-class
destroyer of the Royal Navy
at sea in 1939–1940.*

T and U to a standard that differed from
that of the M class mostly in their
bandstand mounting for the after 4-in (102-
mm) gun and their propulsion arrangement
of 27,000hp (20130kW) delivered to three
shafts by geared rather than direct drive
steam turbines for a speed of 36kt. The final
class of 1,000-ton British destroyers were
the 67 units of the S class with names
starting with S and T, a displacement of
1,075 tons, an armament of three 4-in
(102-mm) and one 2-pdr guns as well as
four 21-in (533-mm) and two 14-in (356-
mm) torpedo tubes of which the latter were
later removed, and a speed of 36kt on the
27,000hp (20130kW) delivered to two
shafts by geared steam turbines.

By the middle of World War I, it was
clear that further improvement of the
destroyer concept could only be provided
on the basis of a larger hull with a greater
displacement, and this led to the
development of the VW class with names
starting with V and W, a longer and beamier
hull, a displacement of between 1,272 and
1,339 tons, and a speed of 34kt on the
27,000hp (20130kW) delivered to two
shafts by geared steam turbines. The ships
fell into two subclasses differentiated
primarily by their armament: the V subclass
had an armament of four 4-in (102-mm)
guns and one 3-in (76-mm) anti-aircraft
gun as well as four 21-in (533-mm) torpedo
tubes, while the W subclass had an
armament of three 4-in (102-mm) guns and
one 3-in (76-mm) anti-aircraft gun as well
as six 21-in (533-mm) torpedo tubes in two
triple mountings.

As evident from the earlier design and
construction of the Swift, the Royal Navy
appreciated that effective control of
destroyer flotillas demanded the use of
flotilla leaders with the additional size to
carry a flotilla commander and his staff, but

HMS Daring *(H16), a D-class destroyer of the Royal Navy, 1932.*

had only the Swift at the beginning of the war. The service was fortunate, however, that four powerful flotilla leader class were under construction in British yards for Chile and Turkey, and these were taken over as the Botha and Talisman classes for completion in 1914–15 and 1916 respectively. In the latter year there appeared the first new leaders built specifically to British specification, and these were the seven and six units of the Marksman and Later Marksman classes respectively, supplemented in 1917 and 1918 by the three ships of the Shakespeare class and the eight ships of the Scott class that were alternatively known as the Thornycroft and Admiralty types respectively.

The British generally led the world in the design and construction of destroyers in this period, other countries following the British lead. Germany's most advanced destroyer class at the beginning of World War I was the S30 class of six ships completed in 1914 and 1915 with a displacement of 970 tons, an armament of three 3.4-in (88-mm) guns and six 19.7-in (500-mm) torpedo tubes, and a speed of between 33 and 36kt on the 23,500 to 25,000hp (17520 to 18650kW) delivered to two shafts by steam turbines. After 1916 Germany's priority was the large-scale construction of submarines rather than surface warships, and this meant that only 22 more destroyers were completed in the period up to the end of the war in November 1918. The last of these to be completed were the three ships of the H145 class, of which two were commissioned in 1918 and the third only in 1920 for the French navy as part of Germany's war reparations. These ships had a displacement of 1,147 tons, an armament of three 4.1-in (105-mm) guns and six 19.7-in (500-mm) torpedo tubes, and a speed of between 34 and 37kt on the 23,500 to 25,500hp

(17520 to 19010kW) delivered to two shafts by steam turbines.

Advanced destroyers were also built in this period by France, Italy, Japan and the U.S.A., and less advanced ships by countries such as Austria-Hungary and Russia. The last destroyers completed for the French navy in World War I were the 12 units of the Tribal class, which were built in Japanese yards to a standard based on that of the Japanese Kaba class. The ships had a displacement of 690 tons, an armament of one 4.7-in (120-mm) and three 12-pdr guns (one of the latter on a high-angle mounting for anti-aircraft use) and four 18-in (457-mm) torpedo tubes in two twin mountings, and a speed of 29kt on the 10,000hp (7455kW) delivered to three shafts by oil- and coal-fired triple-expansion engines. Other French destroyer classes were the Temeraire class of four 950-ton ships completed between 1910 and 1914, the Bory class of 12 780/880-ton ships

HMS Intrepid, *an Intrepid-class destroyer of the Royal Navy, off Iceland in 1941.*

HMS Duncan, *a destroyer-class leader of the Royal Navy entering port in November 1940.*

completed between 1910 and 1915, the Casque class of three 790/820-ton ships completed between 1908 and 1912, the Huzzard class of 11 407/514-ton ships completed between 1906 and 1912, the Claymore class of 21 340/415-ton ships completed between 1903 and 1911, the Mousquet class of 18 310/370-ton ships completed between 1900 and 1904, the Flamberge class of four 310-ton ships completed between 1900 and 1902, the Durandal class of three 305-ton ships completed between 1899 and 1901, and the Pique class of two 310-ton ships completed between 1900 and 1902.

The last destroyers completed for the Italian navy in World War I were the eight units of the La Masa class. These ships had a displacement of between 785 and 850 tons, an armament of four 4-in (102-mm) guns, two 3-in (76-mm) anti-aircraft guns and four 17.7-in (450-mm) torpedo tubes in two twin mountings, and a speed of between 28.5 and 33kt on the 15,000 to 17,500hp (11185 to 13050kW) delivered to two shafts by steam turbines. Other Italian destroyer classes were the Pilo class of eight 770/850-ton ships completed between 1913 and 1916, the Animoso class of two 750/840-ton ships completed in 1914, the Ardito class of two 695/790-ton ships completed between 1913 and 1914, the Indomito class of six 672/770-ton ships completed between 1913 and 1914, the Soldato class of 10 395/425-ton ships completed between 1907 and 1910, the Nembo class of six 330/385-ton ships completed between 1903 and 1905, and the Lampo class of five 320-355-ton ships completed between 1900 and 1910.

The last destroyers completed for the Japanese navy in World War I were the two units of the Tanikaze class. These ships had a displacement of 1,300 tons, an armament

of three 4.7-in (120-mm) and six 21-in (533-mm) torpedo tubes in two triple mountings, and a speed of 34kt on the 28,000hp (20875kW) delivered to its shafts by steam turbines. Other Japanese destroyer classes were the Amatsukaze class of four

1,225-ton ships completed between 1915 and 1917, the Umikaze class of two 1,150-ton ships completed between 1908 and 1911, the Momi class of eight 850-ton ships completed between 1918 and 1919, the Tsubaki class of six 885-ton ships completed

between 1917 and 1918, the Momo class of four 835-ton ships completed between 1915 and 1916, the Kaba class of 10 665-ton ships completed in 1914 and 1915 and the Sakura class of two 605-ton ships completed between 1911 and 1913.

The last destroyers completed for the American navy in World War I were the first units of the Clemson class, which eventually totalled 94 ships completed up to 1920. These flushdecked ships had a displacement of 1,190 tons, an armament of four 4-in (102-mm) guns, one 3-in (76-mm) anti-aircraft gun and 12 21-in (533-mm) torpedo tubes in four triple mountings, and a maximum speed of 35kt on the 27,500hp (20505kW) delivered to two shafts by geared steam turbines. The preceding class, of which 109 units were delivered between 1917 and 1919, was the Wickes class. This had a displacement of 1,090 tons, an armament of four 4-in (102-

mm) guns, two 3-in (76-mm) anti-aircraft guns and 12 21-in (533-mm) torpedo tubes in four triple mountings, and a maximum speed of 35kt on the 26,000hp (19385kW) delivered to two shafts by geared steam turbines. Other significant American destroyer classes built in World War I included the Caldwell class of six 1,020-ton ships completed between 1917 and 1918, the Tucker class of 12 1,110-ton ships completed between 1915 and 1916, and the Cassin class of 14 1,035-ton ships completed between 1913 and 1915.

After World War I, all the British destroyers up to and including the M class were soon discarded as worn out and also obsolescent in the light of destroyer experience in that war. Further development was based on the VW and Marksman classes. Throughout the 1920s and 1930s, the older destroyers were gradually replaced by newer vessels, and on the outbreak of

World War II in September 1939 the only 1918 destroyers still in British service were one R-class ship, 11 S-class ships used mainly in the minelaying role, the majority of the VW-class ships used mostly in the escort role, and eight leaders.

With large numbers of comparatively new ships on strength at the end of World War I, the Royal Navy ordered no new destroyers in the period between 1918 and 1924, and then made the sensible decision to give Thornycroft and Yarrow, the two premier builders of British destroyers, a relatively free hand in the creation of two prototypes, the Amazon and Ambuscade, for the type of comparative evaluation that could lead to the creation of a new standard type providing significant improvements over the VW class in terms of higher speed, longer range and better habitability. Both ships were launched in 1926, and from them were evolved for the Royal Navy and Royal Canadian Navy the 11 ships of the A class with an armament of four or five 4.7-in (119-mm) guns and quadruple mountings

RIGHT
The French destroyer
Fantasque, *built in 1934.*
She was completely refitted
in the U.S.A. in the mid-
1940s to become one of the
fastest destroyers ever, with
an average speed of 40
knots.

BELOW
HMS Westminster, *an*
Admiralty W-class destroyer
of the Royal Navy in
August 1942.

for their eight 21-in (533-mm) torpedo tubes, nine generally improved ships of the B class, 14 ships of the C/D class with a single 3-in (76-mm) anti-aircraft gun in place of the earlier ships and two 2-pdr anti-aircraft guns, 18 ships of the E/F class with provision for rapid conversion to the minelaying task, 18 generally improved ships of the G/H class, and nine ships of the I class with a tripod rather than pole main mast and quintuple rather than quadruple torpedo tube mountings.

The I-class destroyers were launched in 1936 and 1937, and at this stage the British halted further development along this course to produce the Tribal class of an eventual 27 destroyers for the Royal Navy, Royal Australian Navy and Royal Canadian Navy. These ships reflected British concerns that their destroyers were being outstripped technically and operationally by the large destroyers being built in a number of other countries. As a result, the Tribal class destroyer was a highly capable although expensive warship with its gun armament doubled, its torpedo armament halved, and its anti-aircraft and anti-submarine armaments both significantly enhanced. The Tribal-class destroyers thus possessed a displacement between 1,870 and 1,925 tons, an armament in their baseline British form of eight 4.7-in (119-mm) guns in four twin turrets, four 2-pdr anti-aircraft guns in a quadruple mounting and four 21-in (533-mm) torpedo tubes, and a speed of 36kt on the 44,000hp (32805kW) delivered to two shafts by geared steam turbines.

Though offering a very high degree of ability, the destroyers of the Tribal class were too expensive for a similar level of overall capabilities to be repeated in later classes, which therefore dropped one 4.7-in (119-mm) twin turret, reintroduced two quintuple mountings for 21-in (533-mm) torpedoes, and reduced the number of boilers to just two so that a single funnel could be used. This scheme resulted in the nine and eight ships of the generally similar J and K classes launched in 1938 and 1939. The 16 ships of the equally sized L and M classes differed mainly in having dual-purpose guns in fully enclosed twin turrets, which reflected the growing British appreciation of the importance now possessed by aircraft in naval affairs, but perhaps inevitably the additional expense of this arrangement resulted in the eight ships of the N class reverting to the earlier

The lead ships of the two classes were ordered from Hawthorn Leslie on the River Tyne and, as was customary at the time, both were named after notable commanders: the lead ship of the J class was Jervis, in honour of one of the 18th century's ablest admirals, while the lead ship of the K class was named *Kelly* in honour of Admiral of the Fleet Sir John Kelly, once commander-in-chief of the Atlantic Fleet, who had died in 1936. Captain Lord Louis Mountbatten commissioned the ship as leader of the 5th Destroyer Flotilla in August 1939, and the *Kelly* was still working up at Portland when World War II started at the beginning of the following month. One week later, the *Kelly* dashed to Le Havre to pick up the Duke and Duchess of Windsor, bringing them back to Portsmouth, from which the ship steamed

LEFT
Alisma, *a Flower-class corvette, originally built for the French, but taken over by the Royal Navy in 1941.*

BELOW
HMS Pontentilla *(K 214), a Flower-class corvette of the Royal Navy.*

and simpler arrangement.

Something of the nature of British destroyer operations in World War II can be gleaned from the career of HMS *Kelly*, a K- class unit. Although several destroyers achieved more than the *Kelly* and most had longer careers, it became extremely well known largely as a result of the ship's apparent knack of finding naval hot spots. The origins of the closely related J- and K-class destroyers can be found in a general perception in naval circles that the Tribal class was too large and too costly, and as a result the following J- and K-class destroyers were designed to a more austere pattern, with greater emphasis on torpedoes and less on guns. The two virtually identical classes were ordered in March and April 1937 for delivery by July 1939 in reflection of the British perception that war with Germany was now inevitable, and was made possible only by the inclusion of eight shipyards in the programme.

RIGHT
Minekaze, *a Kamikaze-class destroyer of the Imperial Japanese Navy.*

BELOW
HMS Vanoc, *an Admiralty V-class destroyer of the Royal Navy. 1940–1941.*

to Plymouth. A few days later the *Kelly* was involved in the effort of rescuing survivors of the carrier HMS *Courageous*, which had been sunk. The *Kelly* was then detached to Scapa Flow in the Orkney Islands for two months before steaming to the Tyne for a short period of rest, which was interrupted by an emergency trip to a tanker that had been mined. However, as it went alongside the tanker, the *Kelly* hit another mine, the resulting explosion causing great damage aft. The ship regained the Tyne under tow and spent the next two months under repair. The *Kelly* was ready for sea once more in February 1940 and returned to Scapa Flow and, soon after this, she fell foul of the larger HMS *Gurkha* in a snowstorm while escorting a convoy. Collision damage put the *Kelly* back into dock once more, in this instance on the Thames. The repairs had beem completed in time for the destroyer to be involved in the closing days of the disastrous Norwegian campaign.

The *Kelly* was one of six destroyers ordered to Namsos for evacuation of part of the Anglo-French expeditionary force, but

HMS Wanderer, *an Admiralty-modified W class of the Royal Navy at sea in 1943.*

the ships were heavily dive-bombed on 3 May, both HMS *Afridi* and the French *Bison* being sunk. Only a week later, German forces moved into the Low Countries and France, and the *Kelly* was one of seven destroyers escorting the cruiser HMS *Birmingham* when the latter was despatched to intercept a German minelaying force that had been reported west of the Kattegat. The *Kelly* and HMS *Kandahar* were detached en route to investigate a U-boat sighting, but no contact was made and, joined by the older HMS *Bulldog*, the destroyers steamed to

rejoin the main force. Just after nightfall, a torpedo hit the *Kelly*'s port side right on the ship's weakest point, the junction between two boiler spaces. Pouring steam, the *Kelly* immediately lost way with water pouring into the forward boiler room through a huge hole between the keel and the waterline. Even though the badly damaged hull was grinding badly in an uncomfortable sea, the ship's longitudinal framing held: the *Kelly* settled to starboard but, with the bulkheads fore and aft of the boiler room shored thoroughly, seemed safe for the time being. The *Bulldog* came

alongside and passed a tow line, and the *Kelly* then had to use emergency steering to reduce a tendency to yaw. Meanwhile, the crew threw overboard all movable topweight.

Up to this time there had been no indication of the torpedo's source (in fact the S31, one of four E-boats operating in the area), but at about midnight another E-boat appeared out of the night as the Germans attempted to finish the damaged destroyer: the boat sideswiped the *Bulldog* and then screeched down the *Kelly*'s starboard side, which was nearly level with the water: the E-boat then disappeared astern, and not one shot had been fired. On the following day the *Bulldog* continued to tow the *Kelly*, which was now settling further into the water as there was no power to run the pumps. All non-essential members of the crew were taken off, and a tug then arrived to take over the tow. It was only after four days that the *Kelly* reached the Tyne, where the ship was taken over for repair by its builder.

It was in December 1940 before Mountbatten could recommission his ship. In the spring of 1941 the *Kelly* was once again based at Plymouth as leader of the 5th Destroyer Flotilla, which was ordered to Malta in April. The Mediterranean theatre was at this time is a state of very considerable turmoil: the Allies were on the verge of losing Greece as Royal Navy ships were evacuating some 50,000 troops to Crete, Axis forces were taking the islands of the Aegean, and German aircraft based in Sicily were pounding Malta. There was thus the very real possibility that the Allies would lose both Crete and Malta.

Smaller naval vessels were still able to operate from Valletta, the capital and main harbour of Malta, and these included the

ships of the 5th Destroyer Flotilla that was part of Force K, the Malta-based naval element that attempted to intercept and sink Italian ships taking men, equipment and supplies from Italian ports to the Axis forces in North Africa. While returning from one of these night-time forays, on 2 May, the men of the *Kelly* witnessed the mining of a sister ship, HMS *Jersey*, at the entrance to Valletta's Grand Harbour: the *Jersey* was brought in, but was declared a constructive total loss.

From the middle of May it became clear that the time had come for the German assault on Crete. British naval strength was sufficient to prevent a seaborne invasion, but the Germans instead undertook an audacious airborne assault that was to be reinforced by sea. The German airborne troops fought with a grim determination to hold their air-heads as the British committed every available warship to prevent the arrival of seaborne reinforcements. By night, the British ships had great success in sinking large numbers of caiques loaded with German troops, but by day the German air force made life dangerous in the extreme: on 21 May HMS *Juno* sank within two minutes of being hit by a large bomb; and on the next day HMS *Greyhound* succumbed, as too did the cruisers HMS *Fiji* and HMS *Gloucester* after they had exhausted all their anti-aircraft ammunition. On 23 May the *Kelly* reached the area from Malta in company with HMS *Kashmir*, HMS *Kelvin*, HMS *Kipling* and HMS *Jackal*. Together with the *Kashmir* and *Kipling*, the *Kelly* was ordered to undertake a night-time shelling of the German-held airfield at Maleme in Crete. The *Kipling* was prevented from participation in the attack by mechanical problems, but even so the effort began well with the interception and destruction of a pair of heavily laden caiques. The nights at

this time of the year are short, however, and with most surviving British ships pulled back to Alexandria on the Egyptian coast, the *Kelly* and its sisters were out on a limb.

By dawn the ships were only just off Crete, but they evaded a first high-altitude level bombing attack. The level bombers were followed by altogether more dangerous dive-bombers: operating from nearby airfields on the Peloponnese, some 24 Ju 87 dive-bombers attacked the two destroyers. Both British vessels undertook violent evasive manoeuvres and tackled the attackers with a hail of fire from their machine-guns, 20-mm cannon, 2-pdr pom-poms and even 4.7-mm (119-mm) main guns even as the Germans cleverly attacked from every direction. In only a very short time the *Kashmir* was foundering, its back broken, and the Germans now concentrated on the hapless *Kelly*. The ship was turning at full speed and heeling strongly in the process when a bomb struck just aft of amidships. The ship did not recover, rolling onto her beam ends and then capsizing to port: after 30 minutes, and with many of the crew still trapped, the ship slipped under the water.

Fortunately for the survivors, the *Kipling* now arrived and was able to pick up 219 men from the water. The ship was heavily attacked right through this exercise, but completed its task and headed for Alexandria, which it reached on the following day.

By the time that the N-class destroyers were under construction, the U.K. had accepted the inevitability of war with Germany and, as a result of its reluctance in World War I to adopt the convoy system and the consequent merchant shipping losses to submarine attack, had decided to waste no time in the introduction of a convoy system as soon as war did finally break out. This raised the need for large numbers of

specialized escort vessels if the Royal Navys force of fleet destroyers was not to be stripped to the point is could not support major surface forces. The result was a series of dual-role and escort destroyer classes optimized for the escort role with the same basic hull construction and boiler arrangement as the latest fleet destroyers but with an armament of main guns in single mountings, improved anti-submarine weapons, and enhanced anti-aircraft weapons in which the standard arrangement of four 2-pdr guns in a quadruple mounting was supplemented by four single (later twin) mountings for 20-mm cannon that were replaced later in the war by 40-mm weapons in single mountings.

The dual-role destroyer classes comprised the eight ships of the O class fitted for minelaying and with 4-in (102-mm) rather than 4.7-in (119-mm) guns in four of the vessels; the eight ships of the generally similar P class with 4-in (102-mm) rather than 4.7-in (119-mm) guns and, in

OPPOSITE
Welcoming home the HMS Magpie, one of an escort group. The ship was a sloop of the Modified Black Swan-class.

LEFT
An American escort being watched by British sailors from a passing ship as it steams into port.

BELOW LEFT
HMS Spey, one of the first group of River-class frigates, moves past part of the convoy its was escorting across the Atlantic.

ABOVE
La Malouine, *a corvette of the Free French Navy.*

RIGHT
With her fo'c'sle and super-structure covered in ice, the corvette HMS Lotus *nears harbour at the end of a patrol in northern waters.*

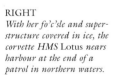

four of the vessels, one 4-in (102-mm) anti-aircraft gun in place of one of the two quintuple mountings for 21-in (533-mm) torpedoes; the eight ships of the Q class with the light anti-aircraft armament increased from four to six 20-mm cannon; the eight ships of the R class with eight 20-mm cannon and surface warning radar; the eight ships of the S class that introduced the 4.5-in (114-mm) dual-purpose gun in one ship, had eight 20-mm cannon in all ships, and in some ships replaced the 2-pdr quadruple mounting with two 40-mm guns or four 20-mm cannon; the eight ships of the T class with 10 and later 12 20-mm cannon; the eight ships of the U class with lattice masts and a diverse arrangement of anti-aircraft guns; the eight ships of the V class with a light anti-aircraft armament of two 40-mm guns in a twin mounting or four 2-pdr guns in a quadruple mounting and eight 20-mm cannon in four twin mountings; the eight ships of the W class with a light anti-aircraft armament of two 40-mm guns in a twin mounting and eight 20-mm cannon in four twin mountings or, in some ships, four or five 40-mm guns in single mountings; and the eight ships of the Z class with 4.5-in (114-mm) dual-purpose guns and a light anti-aircraft armament of two 40-mm guns in a twin mounting and six 20-mm cannon in two twin and two single mountings.

Finally in the first series of this family of dual-role ships came the 32 destroyers of the C class in four eight-ship CA, CH, CO and CR subclasses with a displacement of some 1,720 tons, an armament of four 4.5-in (114-mm) dual-purpose guns in single mountings, four 40-mm anti-aircraft guns in one twin and two single mountings, four 20-mm anti-aircraft cannon in two twin mountings and four 21-in (533-mm) torpedo tubes in a quadruple mounting, and a speed of 36.75kt on the 40,000hp (29825kW) delivered to two shafts by geared steam turbines.

Despite the very difficult time they had endured in the first stages of World War II, British destroyers also achieved considerable offensive results throughout the war, one of the most impressive being the sinking of the Japanese cruiser *Haguro* in May 1945. This resulted from the sighting by the British S- class submarine HMS *Subtle*, operating between Malaya and the island of Sumatra, of a ship which it reported as a Nachi-class cruiser and three escorts (one of them identified as a destroyer) in the late afternoon of 10 May. The Japanese ships were steaming to the north-west, but the *Subtle* and two sister submarines were not

able to close the Japanese force as a result of shallow water and a fast tidal flow in combination with the Japanese ships' zigzag progress.

The cruiser *Haguro*, accompanied by the destroyer *Kamikaze* and two patrol vessels, had sailed from Singapore on the previous day for Port Blair in the Andaman Islands, from which the ships were to evacuate the Japanese garrison. Primed by an earlier intelligence report, an Allied force had already left Colombo in Ceylon to intercept the *Haguro*. Commanded by Vice Admiral H. T. C. Walker, this force was based on the battleships HMS *Queen Elizabeth* and the French *Richelieu*, supported by the Dutch destroyer *Tromp* and four escort carriers. However, on 11

May a Japanese reconnaissance aeroplane spotted this force, and the *Haguro* was instructed to return to Singapore, in the process passing the British submarine line: the *Kamikaze* depth charged the *Subtle*, but did not sink the submarine.

The *Haguro* then slowed as its captain waited for an order to head once more to the Andamans once a planned air attack had destroyed or driven back the Ceylon-based Allied force. The air attack did not take place, but the captain of the *Haguro*, encouraged by the success of an escorted Japanese transport in reaching the Nicobar Islands, a mere 200 miles (320km) to the south of Port Blair, then headed for the Andamans once more on 14 May. All but one of the submarines forming the patrol

BELOW LEFT
Ratings from other ships cheering HMS Hesperus *as she entered harbour with her bows damaged after ramming a U-Boat.*

BELOW
HMS Churchill, *a converted American destroyer in harbour after escorting an Allied troop convoy.*

The destroyer USS Greer *(DD 145) in high seas on convoy escort duties during the Battle of the Atlantic in 1943.*

line between Malaya and Sumatra had now been withdrawn, so the *Haguro*'s force reached the Andaman Sea without detection. Walker felt that this might be the case, and early on 15 May detached Captain Manley Powers of the 26th Destroyer Flotilla to find the *Haguro*.

Leading in the S class, HMS *Saumarez* with the V-class destroyers HMS *Venus, Verulam, Virago* and *Volage* following, Power was off the north-western tip of Sumatra by the break of day, when he was informed that reconnaissance aircraft had found the transport returning from the Nicobars. Power headed for the transport, but later in the same morning received orders from Ceylon instructing him to break off his search for the *Haguro*, which was now not considered a realistic threat to Allied operations in the Bay of Bengal. Power decided to query the order on the grounds that the commander-in-chief was not in full possession of the facts and, pending clarification, maintained his course. A reconnaissance aeroplane then reconfirmed the sighting of the transport and, farther to the north, the *Haguro*'s little flotilla. The Japanese turned back once they had been sighted, but Power held his course even as an air attack failed to sink the *Haguro*.

Early in the afternoon the British destroyers passed the northern tip of Sumatra and entered the strait at a speed of 21kt. Right through the afternoon reconnaissance, aircraft reported that the *Haguro* was heading south-east at modest speed. The tactical situation now demanded that the 26th Destroyer Flotilla make contact just before dark so that a night attack could then be undertaken on the vastly superior heavy cruiser. The destroyers were redeployed from line ahead to line abreast so that the swathe of sea their look-outs could cover was maximised, and the start of heavy rain squalls now started to shift the tactical balance in favour of the destroyers with their more advanced radar. The line of British destroyers was steaming east-south-east when the *Venus* on the northern extremity of the line, at 22.40

hours reported radar contact of a target some 40 miles (64km) to the north-east and heading south-east.

The well trained 26th Destroyer Flotilla knew exactly what to do as Power led his ships past the *Haguro*, which was now some 14 miles (23km) to port of them, and then turned north to pass ahead of the Japanese cruiser before attacking from each side.

The *Haguro*, with the *Kamikaze* on her port quarter, was 10 miles (16km) from the centre of the British line and closing on 16 May when, at 00.45 hours, the cruiser's radar picked up the destroyers. The cruiser manoeuvred as if not certain of the detected ships' identities, for they were approaching from the direction of Singapore, but then reversed course. Only the *Venus* had managed to work its way behind the target by this time, and was now on the cruiser's port bow. While Power's other destroyers increased speed to overtake, the *Venus* crossed the *Haguro*'s bow to attack from ahead and to starboard, but missed its opportunity and had to undertake a rapid 300° pot turn in order to disengage. It would seem that the Japanese assumed that torpedoes had been launched and again reversed course, but still without opening fire. Power's four destroyers were now closing at a relative speed of over 50kt. Any misunderstandings as to identity were resolved as the *Saumarez* passed the *Kamikaze* on a reciprocal course and raked her at close range with both main armament and light weapons fire.

Just after 01.30 hours both sides fired starshell. The *Saumarez* was bathed by the greenish glare at a range of only 3,000yds (2245m) from the *Haguro*, which opened fire. The destroyer was soon hit in a boiler room, but managed a tight turn to port and launched a full salvo of torpedoes. Almost simultaneously the *Verulam* attacked from

sufficiency in the course of protracted operations away from a major base, and a much heavier anti-aircraft armament for the protection not only of itself but of the larger warships (especially the aircraft carriers) it was supporting. Some 44 of the class, including two for the Royal Australian Navy, were ordered but only 28 were completed as 16 units of the second group were cancelled. The Battle-class ships had a displacement of some 2,325 tons and a speed of 35.75kt on the 50,000hp (37280kW) delivered to two shafts by geared steam turbines, and was characterized by two types of armament: in the first group this comprised four 4.5-in (114-mm) dual-purpose guns in two twin turrets, one 4-in (102-mm) anti-aircraft gun, 14 40-mm anti-aircraft guns in four twin and six single mountings or alternatively 12 40-mm anti-aircraft guns in three twin and six single mountings, and eight or 10 21-in

BELOW
USS Butler (DMS-29) is lashed alongside the USS Ute (ATF-76) after being crashed by a Japanese suicide aircraft during support operations in Nakagusuku Wan (Buckner Bay), Okinawa, Ryukyus Islands. On this day , 445 Japanese aircraft, of which nearly one third were kamikaze planes, attacked shipping targets off Okinawa. This photograph was taken from the USS West Virginia on 25 May 1945.

some 90° farther round, profiting from the Japanese concentration on the *Saumarez* to do so without be fired on.

The cruiser, manoeuvring violently by now, was hit forward by three torpedoes. The ships forward armament fell silent and the vessel began to list only to be hit by one or possibly two more torpedoes in the machinery spaces. For the next 10 minutes the *Haguro* was tackled with gun fire from various directions before the *Venus* and *Virago* attacked from opposite directions and fired a total of 11 torpedoes. It is probable that only three of the torpedoes struck home, but by this time the cruiser's fire was limited and under local control. On the bridge most of the cruiser's senior officers had been killed by a direct hit by a 4.7-in (119-mm) shell.

The *Volage* had not yet launched a torpedo attack, and at 01.50 hours Power ordered this destroyer to deliver the coup de grâce against the cruiser, which was lying

deep in the water, listing and burning aft. Despite a range of only 1,500yds (1370m) every torpedo missed, so it was the *Venus*'s last two torpedoes that finished the *Haguro*, which sank at 02.06 hours about 45 miles (72km) south-west of Penang. The British destroyers departed shortly after this, allowing the *Kamikaze* to return and rescue 400 men from the water. The British losses amounted to only two men killed, both of them on the *Saumarez* that was the only British ship to have been hit.

From a time late in World War II, when the defeat of Germany was certain and greater emphasis was then placed on operations against the Japanese in a Pacific campaign calling for a significantly longer range capability, the British designed a new destroyer type as the Battle class on the basis of a larger hull to provide greater seaworthiness, enlarged bunkerage for the required longer range, enhanced self-

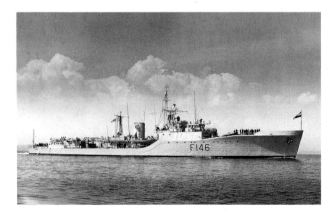

(533-mm) torpedo tubes; in the second group this comprised five 4.5-in (114-mm) dual-purpose guns in two twin and one single turrets, eight 40-mm anti-aircraft guns in three twin and two single mountings, and 10 21-in (533-mm) torpedo tubes.

Another class, designed at a slightly later date but eventually completed to the extent of only two ships, was the Weapon class optimized for the anti-aircraft and anti-submarine roles with anti-ship capability offered only by the low-angle fire of its six 4-in (102-mm) dual-purpose guns, which were installed in three twin turrets, and its 10 21-in (533-mm) torpedo tubes.

The standard type of escort destroyer built by the British was the Hunt class of which 86 units were completed in four subclasses including the Hunt Type IV class of only two ships. These ships were essentially small and simple, and the three main subclasses were the Hunt Type I class of 20 ships generally used in home waters with a displacement of 907 tons, an armament of four 4-in (102-mm) anti-aircraft guns in two twin turrets, four or five 2-pdr anti-aircraft guns in one quadruple and one single mounting and two 20-mm cannon, and a speed of 26kt on the 19,000hp (14165kW) delivered to two shafts by geared steam turbines; the Hunt Type II class of 36 ships generally used in home and Mediterranean waters with a displacement of 1,050 tons, an armament of six or four 4-in (102-mm) anti-aircraft guns in three or two twin turrets, four or five 2-pdr anti-aircraft guns in one quadruple and one single mounting, and two or three 20-mm cannon in single mountings, and a speed of 25kt on the 19,000hp (14165kW) delivered to two shafts by geared steam turbines; and the Hunt Type III class of 28 ships generally used in home and Mediterranean waters with a displacement of 1,085 tons, an armament of four 4-in (102-mm) anti-aircraft guns in two twin turrets, four or five 2-pdr anti-aircraft guns in one quadruple and one single mounting, two or three 20-mm cannon in single mountings and two 21-in (533-mm) torpedo tubes, and a speed of 25kt on the 19,000hp (14165kW) delivered to two shafts by geared steam turbines.

In World War I the Royal Navy received an eventual total of 72 Flower-class ships that were officially designated as fleet minesweeping sloops. These were built in three subclasses as the *Acacia*, *Azalea* and *Arabis* types, and although designed mainly for the fleet minesweeping role soon proved themselves so versatile that they were adapted for other roles such as escort or, in the case of 39 more ships, completed as Q-ships with hidden armament that was designed for the destruction of submarines lured to the surface by the apparently innocuous appearance of these merchant ships. A further 24 ships were built in the 24 class of general-purpose sloops with a central funnel, a dummy bridge aft, and a straight stem and stern to present a double-ended appearance that made it difficult to detect the way the ships were moving at slow speed, especially as effective dazzle painting was employed. These two classes of sloop provided most of the Royal Navy's coastal escort strength in the second half of World War I, and remained in declining service through the 1920s and 1930s.

In the later 1930s, the apparent inevitability of war with Germany, and with

by geared steam turbines.

Experience soon revealed that the Black Swan and Modified Black Swan classes offered very useful escort capabilities, but also that they were not necessarily the most cost-effective way to provide these capabilities as they were fairly large vessels built to full warship standards with a geared steam turbine propulsion arrangement, and this made for an unattractive combination of high cost and slow production. The Admiralty had already sensed that this would in fact be the case, and in 1939 it ordered another Flower class, in this instance of escort corvettes. Eventually 270 of these fine little ships were completed in the U.K. and Canada for service with the navies of the British empire as well as a number of Allied navies. Based on a whale-catcher design, the Flower-class corvette was designed for construction to a mercantile (and therefore cheaper and more quickly constructed) standard with a triple-expansion steam propulsion arrangement. The Flower-class corvettes were produced in two forms. The basic Flower class had a displacement of 950 tons, an armament of one 4-in (102-mm) gun, one 2-pdr anti-aircraft gun or four 0.5-in (12.7-mm) machine-guns in a quadruple mounting and four 0.303-in (7.7-mm) machine-guns in two twin mountings, and a speed of 16kt on the 2,750hp (2050kW) delivered to one shaft by a triple-expansion steam engine, while the Modified Flower class had a displacement of 980 tons, an armament of one 4-in (102-mm) gun, one 2-pdr anti-aircraft gun, six 20-mm cannon in single mountings and one Hedgehog anti-submarine projector, and a speed of 16kt on the 2,880hp (2145kW) delivered to one shaft by a triple-expansion steam engine.

The importance of the two subclasses of the Flower class to the Allied victory

HMS Pelican (U86), an Admiralty 'M' Matchless-class destroyer of the Royal Navy at sea in April 1944.

it the apparent inevitability of a submarine campaign against the merchant navy fleet on which the U.K. was wholly reliant, persuaded the Admiralty to reconsider its capabilities for the escort of merchant ship convoys. This process led to orders for 20 fast escort ships for the oceanic role, orders for 56 whale-catcher type vessels for the coastal role, the conversion of old destroyers to the escort task, and the construction of a new class of oceanic escorts as the sloops of the Black Swan class. These last were launched from mid-1939, and eventually totalled 37 ships including four for the Royal Indian Navy, with the final five (including another two Indian ships) cancelled in the closing stages of the war.

The ships were built in two forms as the Black Swan class with a displacement of 1,250 tons, an armament of six 4-in (102-mm) anti-aircraft guns in three twin turrets, four 2-pdr guns in a quadruple mounting, and four 0.5-in (12.7-mm) machine-guns in a quadruple mounting or 12 20-mm cannon in six twin mountings, and a speed of 19.25kt on the 3,600hp (2685kW) delivered to two shafts by geared steam turbines, and as the Modified Black Swan class with a displacement of 1,350 tons, an armament of six 4-in (102-mm) anti-aircraft guns in three twin turrets and 12 20-mm cannon in six twin mountings, and a speed of 20kt on the 4,300hp (3205kW) delivered to two shafts

ABOVE
The USS James C. Owens
*(DD 776), an Allen M.
Sumner FRAM II-class
destroyer underway off the
coast of Oahu, Hawaii on
31 May 1968.*

ABOVE RIGHT
*Almirante Valdes (D 23),
an ex-U.S. Fletcher-class
destroyer of the Spanish
Navy.*

RIGHT
*Seoul (DD 92), an ex-U.S.
Fletcher-class destroyer of the
navy of the Republic of
Korea entering Pearl
Harbor, Hawaii on 26 June
1968.*

over Germany by May 1945 cannot be
overestimated, but from an early date the
Admiralty realized that the hull of the
Flower-class ship was slightly too small for
the oceanic escort role and therefore
ordered the larger and faster River-class
frigates, which were also built to
mercantile standards but had a two-shaft
propulsion arrangement powered by triple-
expansion steam engines. Some 139 of this
class were completed in the U.K., Australia
and Canada for service with the navies of
the British empire as well as several Allied
navies. The River-class frigate had a
displacement of 1,370 tons, a varied
armament of anti-ship and anti-aircraft
weapons as well as a Hedgehog anti-
submarine projector, and a speed of 20kt on
the 5,500hp (4100kW) delivered to two
shafts by triple-expansion steam engines.
    The River-class frigate was economical to
build and certainly effective in operational

The USS Brooke *(DEG-1) with the auxiliary submarine USS* Bluegill *(AGSS-242) in the Pacific. 15 June 1969.*

terms, but its length precluded its construction in many of the smaller yards that had been able to build the corvettes of the Flower classes. The Admiralty thus exploited this underused construction source with the Castle class of corvettes, which was built from 1943 and totalled 44 units with a large number of others cancelled at the end

of the war. The details of this excellent class included a displacement of 1,010 tons, an armament of one 4-in (102-mm) gun, 10 20-mm cannon in two twin and six single mountings and one Squid anti-submarine projector, and a speed of 16.5kt on the 2,880hp (2145kW) delivered to one shaft by a triple-expansion steam engine.

The River class was followed into production by the Loch and Bay classes of general escort and anti-aircraft frigates, which were built from prefabricated assemblies to speed the construction process. Some 56 units of these two classes were completed, with another 54 cancelled late in the war. The details of the Loch class

ABOVE
The USS Halsey Powell
*(DD-686), a Fletcher-class
destroyer alongside USS*
Ticonderoga *(CVA 14) for
a highline transfer.
23 September 1962.*

ABOVE RIGHT
The USS Perkins *(DD-877),
a Gearing-class FRAM II
destroyer of the U.S. Navy in
the Pacific on 16 April
1969.*

included a displacement of 1,435 tons, an armament of one 4-in (102-mm) gun, four 2-pdr anti-aircraft guns in a single mounting, six 20-mm cannon in two twin and two single mountings, and two Squid anti-submarine projectors, and a speed of 20kt on the 6,500hp (4845kW) delivered to two shafts by geared steam turbines or 5,500hp (4100kW) delivered to two shafts by triple-expansion steam engines. The details of the Bay class included a displacement of 1,580 tons, an armament of four 4-in (102-mm) anti-aircraft guns in two twin turrets, four 40-mm anti-aircraft guns in two twin mountings, four 20-mm cannon in two twin mountings and one Hedgehog anti-submarine projector, and a speed of 20kt on the 6,500hp (4845kW) delivered to two shafts by geared steam turbines or 5,500hp (4100kW) delivered to two shafts by triple-

expansion steam engines.

When the U.S. became embroiled in World War II during December 1941, the U.S. Navy had 171 operational destroyers, including 71 of the two related flushdeck types that had been built to the extent of 272 destroyers in World War I. Some 31 and 40 of these were of the Wickes and Clemson classes. After the completion of ships already under construction at the end of World War I, construction of destroyers had been ended in the U.S.A. until the early 1930s, when destroyer developments in other parts of the world finally persuaded the Americans to undertake the construction of a more advanced type in the form of the Farragut class of seven ships with a displacement of 1,395 tons, an armament of five 5-in (127-mm) guns in single mountings and eight 21-in (533-mm)

torpedo tubes in two quadruple mountings, and a speed of 36.5kt on the 42,800hp (31910kW) delivered to two shafts by geared steam turbines. In the period leading up to World War II, the U.S. Navy developed the conceptual design of the Farragut class via the Mahan class of 18 ships (five 5-in/127-mm guns in single mountings, 12 21-in/533-mm torpedo tubes in three quadruple mountings) to the Craven class of 22 ships (four 5-in/127-mm guns in single mountings, four 1.1-in anti-aircraft guns in single mountings and 16 21-in/533-mm torpedo tubes in four quadruple mountings).

A parallel course of evolution produced the eight and five ships of the Porter and Somers classes respectively for the squadron leader task. The basic design of the Porter class included a displacement of 1,850 tons,

way for the Fletcher-class destroyer that was the U.S. Navy's most important ship of its type in the first part of World War II. Built to the extent of 178 ships that were delivered from 1942 with a beamier, flushdecked hull, a displacement of 2,050 tons, an armament of five 5-in (127-mm) guns in single mountings, between six and 10 40-mm and 20-mm anti-aircraft guns and 10 21-in (533-mm) torpedo tubes in two quintuple mountings, and a speed of 37kt on the 60,000hp (44,870kW) delivered to two shafts by geared steam turbines.

The destroyers of the Fletcher class were supplemented from 1944 by the destroyers of the Allen M. Sumner and Gearing classes, which were bigger and more heavily armed vessels specifically created for the demands of long-range operations in the western Pacific, where they were often exposed to

LEFT
A huge underwater explosion following the launch of an ASROC anti-submarine missile during exercises from the destroyer USS Agerholm (DD-826), in March 1970.

BELOW
An ASROC (RUR-5A) anti-submarine missile is launched from USS Brooke (DEG-1) during fire power demonstrations in the Pacific Ocean on 15 June 1969.

an armament of eight 5-in (127-mm) guns in four twin mountings and eight 21-in (533-mm) torpedo tubes in two quadruple mountings, and a speed of 37kt on the 50,000hp (37280kW) delivered to two shafts by geared steam turbines, and the Somers class differed mainly in its uprated propulsion arrangement with 52,500hp (39145kW) for a speed of 37.5kt.

Further development of the basic fleet destroyer concept in the late 1930s led to the Sims class of 12 ships that proved to be top-heavy, so one of their five 5-in (127-mm) guns and one of their three quadruple 21-in (533-mm) torpedo tube mountings were soon removed. The same fate befell the early units of the Benson class, which was an improved version of the Sims class, and itself later upgraded as the Livermore class. Construction of the Benson and Livermore classes totalled 32 and 64 ships respectively.

Experience with these classes paved the

RIGHT
Forbin *(D 635), a Type T53
air direction destroyer of the
French navy. Forbin differs
from the other two ships in
the class by having a
helicopter pad in place of a
Y-turret. Her forward gun
is a twin 5-inch (127-mm).
1973.*

BELOW
Annapolis, *an Annapolis-
class destroyer escort in
1972. Canadian frigates
are optimized for operations
in the harsh sea and
climatic conditions often
encountered in the North
Atlantic.*

intensive Japanese air attack by kamikaze as
well as conventional aircraft. The 58 Allen
M. Sumner-class destroyers were completed
to a standard that included a displacement
of 2,200 tons, an armament of six 5-in
(127-mm) dual-purpose guns in three twin
turrets, 12 40-mm anti-aircraft guns and 10
21-in (533-mm) torpedo tubes in two
quintuple mountings, and a speed of 36.5kt
on the 60,000hp (44870kW) delivered to
two shafts by geared steam turbines. The 99
Gearing-class destroyers completed in and
immediately after the closing stages of
World War II as a development of the Allen
M. Sumner-class design with a lengthened
hull had a displacement of 2,425 tons, an
armament of six 5-in (127-mm) dual-
purpose guns in three twin turrets, 12 or 16
40-mm anti-aircraft guns and 10 (none in
ships with 16 40-mm guns) 21-in (533-
mm) torpedo tubes in two quintuple
mountings, and a speed of 35kt on the
60,000hp (44870kW) delivered to two
shafts by geared steam turbines.

The U.S. Navy had not initially seen the

need for specialized destroyer escorts, and the type was originally ordered in 1941 by the U.K., which contracted with American yards for an initial 50 destroyer escorts, or escort destroyers as they were called by the British, before increasing this total to 250 in the following year. By this latter date the U.S.A. had entered the war, and soon appreciated the vital nature of the destroyer escort for the protection of troop and equipment convoys in the Pacific, where their faster and more heavily armed destroyer half-brothers were better employed for the protection of carrier and amphibious task forces. Thus only 55 of these American ships were finally transferred to the British, and of the orders placed by 1943 for 1,005 destroyer escorts, 508 were completed as 452 destroyer escorts (29 of them for transfer to Allies other than the U.K.) and the other 56 as high-speed transports.

The ships were completed with two

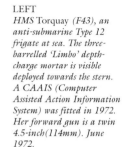

LEFT
HMS Torquay *(F43), an anti-submarine Type 12 frigate at sea. The three-barrelled 'Limbo' depth-charge mortar is visible deployed towards the stern. A CAAIS (Computer Assisted Action Information System) was fitted in 1972. Her forward gun is a twin 4.5-inch(114mm). June 1972.*

LEFT
The British commando carrier HMS Hermes *being shadowed by a Soviet Kanin-class destroyer. On the Kanin's afterdeck can be seen the twin air-to-air SA-N-1 missile launcher. She is also armed with three 12-barrel anti-submarine MBU launchers (one on the foredeck and one on each side of the mainmast), two quadruple 57-mm mountings forward of the bridge and four twin 30mm guns (two each side of the aft funnel) and two sets of quintuple torpedo tubes amidships. October 1973.*

RIGHT
The HMAS Stuart *(48), a River-class frigate of the Royal Australian Navy.*

BELOW
Iskenderun (D343), an ex-U.S. Fletcher-class destroyer of the Turkish navy.

types of hull. The original group of 61 ships was the Evarts class with an overall length of 283ft 4in (86.36m), while the others had an overall length of 306ft 0in (93.27m) and were the Buckley, Rudderow, Cannon, Edsall and John C. Butler classes. The ships of the Evarts class had a displacement of 1,140 tons, an armament of three 3-in (76-mm) guns in single mountings, four 40-mm anti-aircraft guns and five 20-mm cannon, and a speed of 21kt on the 6,000hp (4475kW) delivered to two shafts by a diesel-electric propulsion arrangement. The ships of the Buckley class had a displacement of 1,400 tons, an armament of three 3-in (76-mm) guns in single

mountings, six 40-mm anti-aircraft guns and three 21-in (533-mm) torpedo tubes, and a speed of 23.5kt on the 12,000hp (8950kW) delivered to two shafts by a turbo-electric propulsion arrangement. The following Rudderow class had a displacement of 1,450 tons, an armament of two 5-in (127-mm) guns in single mountings, 10 40-mm anti-aircraft guns and three 21-in (533-mm) torpedo tubes, and a speed of 24kt on the 12,000hp (8950kW) delivered to two shafts by a turbo-electric propulsion arrangement. However, in the Cannon class a diesel-electric propulsion arrangement had to be adopted, as in the Buckley class, because of shortages of turbo-electric equipment, and this resulted in a displacement of 1,240 tons, an armament of three 3-in (76-mm) guns in single mountings, six 40-mm anti-aircraft guns and three 21-in (533-mm) torpedo tubes, and a speed of 21kt on the 6,000hp (4475kW) delivered to two shafts by the diesel-electric propulsion arrangement. The Edsall class was similar, and its details therefore included a displacement of 1,200 tons, an armament of three 3-in (76-mm) guns in single mountings, eight 40-mm anti-aircraft guns and three 21-in (533-mm) torpedo tubes, and a speed of 21kt on the 6,000hp (4475kW) delivered to two shafts by a diesel-electric propulsion arrangement. The ships of the final John C. Butler class were somewhat different, and they were completed to a standard that included a displacement of 1,350 tons, an armament of two 5-in (127-mm) guns in single mountings, 10 40-mm anti-aircraft guns and three 21-in (533-mm) torpedo tubes, and a speed of 24kt on the 12,000hp (8950kW) delivered to two shafts by geared steam turbines.

Of the other Allied powers in World

War II, only France operated a large navy to any effect, and then in any strategically meaningful manner only to the time of the French capitulation of June 1940. The French destroyer force, in order of design, included the six large destroyers of the Jaguar class launched in 1923 and 1924 before being completed to a standard that included a full-load displacement of 3,050 tons and a primary armament of five 5.1-in (130-mm) guns in single mountings, the 24 medium destroyers of the Simoun class launched in two groups between 1924 and 1929 before being completed to a standard that included a full-load displacement of

2,000 tons and a main armament of four 5.1-in (130-mm) guns in single mountings, the 18 large destroyers of the Guépard class launched in four groups between 1928 and 1932 before being completed to a standard that included a full-load displacement of 3,400 tons and a primary armament of five 5.5-in (139-mm) guns in single mountings, the six large destroyers of the Le Fantasque class launched in 1933 and 1934 before completion to a standard that included a full-load displacement of 3,400 tons and a primary armament of five 5.5-in (139-mm) guns in single mountings, the 12 small destroyers of the La Melpomène class

launched between 1935 and 1937 before being completed to a standard that included a full-load displacement of 900 tons and a primary armament of two 3.9-in (100-mm) guns in single mountings, the two ships of the Mogador class that were the last word in large destroyer design and capability after launch in 1936 and 1937 before being completed to a standard that included a full-load displacement of 4,020 tons, a primary armament of eight 5.5-in (139-mm) guns in four twin mountings, and a speed of 39kt on the 92,000hp (75265kW) delivered to two shafts by geared steam turbines, and the eight large destroyers of the Le Hardi class launched between 1938 and 1939 before being completed to a standard that included a full-load displacement of 2,575 tons and a primary armament of six 5.1-in (130-mm)

ABOVE
Zeeland (D809), a Holland-class destroyer of the Royal Netherlands Navy, 1976.

ABOVE LEFT
HMS Antrim (D18), a County-class destroyer of the Royal Navy, executes a turn at speed. Clearly visible is the Wessex anti-submarine helicopter aft and Seaslug missile launcher. April 1975.

RIGHT
Aconit *(D 609), a Type*
C 65 destroyer of the French
navy. 1977.

BELOW
HMS Ariadne *(F 72), a*
broad-beamed Leander-class
frigate of the Royal Navy.
August 1977.

guns in three twin mountings.

Facing the navies of what became the Allied powers were the naval forces of the three nations that constituted the Axis powers, namely Germany, Italy and Japan. The first destroyers to be built in Germany were the 22 ships of the Type 34 or Maass class, which were laid down from 1934 for launch in 1937 and 1938. Despite their attempts to keep abreast of current design trends in the time they had been denied the right to build such ships, the Germans found themselves faced with a number of technical problems, most notably in the propulsion arrangement, and in service the ships soon acquired a reputation for unreliability. Considerable size was chosen for advantages in seaworthiness as well as weapon installation and location, but the use of a short bow section with insufficient flare and freeboard meant that the Type 34 units were very wet ships in any sort of sea.

In an attempt to match the projectile weight of the latest French destroyers, a new 5-in (127-mm) weapon was designed to supersede the well proven 4.1-in (105-mm) gun, but although in itself a successful weapon this gun was installed in an obsolescent mounting that precluded its use as a dual-purpose weapon. The details of the ships included a full-load displacement of 3,160 tons, an armament of five 5-in (127-mm) guns in single mountings, four 37-mm anti-aircraft guns in two twin mountings, six 20-mm cannon in single mountings and eight 21-in (533-mm) torpedo tubes in two quadruple mountings, and a speed of 38kt on the 70,000hp (52200kW) provided to two shafts by geared steam turbines.

The survivors of these ships were complemented from the years in the middle of World War II by the 15 ships of the Type 36A or Narvik class, which was a development of the Type 34 design with greater weight of fire provided by a change to a main-armament calibre of 5.9in (150mm) in a gun that was difficult and slow to work. The details of this class included a full-load displacement of 3,600 tons, an armament of five 5.9-in (150-mm) guns in one twin and three single turrets, four 37-mm anti-aircraft guns in two twin mountings, five 20-mm cannon in single mountings and eight 21-in (533-mm) torpedo tubes in two quadruple mountings, and a speed of 36kt on the 70,000hp (52200kW) delivered to two shafts by geared steam turbines.

The problems with the main armament of the Type 36A class persuaded the German naval high command that the switch to a 5.9-in (150-mm) gun had been wrong, and the German navy's next destroyers were the units of the Type 36B class that reverted to the 5-in (127-mm)

gun. Only three of the ships were completed with a full-load displacement of 3,505 tons, an armament of five 5-in (127-mm) guns in single mountings, four 37-mm anti-aircraft guns in twin mountings, 15 20-mm cannon in three quadruple and three single mountings, and eight 21-in (533-mm) torpedo tubes in two quadruple mountings, and a speed of 36kt on the 70,000hp (52200kW) delivered to two shafts by geared steam turbines.

At the smaller end of the destroyer spectrum, Germany operated a number of ships including the 12 ships of the Albatros and Iltis classes laid down in the 1920s with an armament of three 4.1-in (105-mm) guns in single mountings as well as a useful torpedo armament; 21 ships of the Type 35 and Type 37 classes that were too small for real utility, and then the 15 ships of the Type 39 or Elbing class that were launched between 1942 and 1944. These last were

still comparatively small ships, but had an appearance sufficiently imposing to make them often mistaken for larger fleet destroyers. Their details included a full-load displacement of 1,755 tons, an armament of four 4.1-in (105-mm) guns in single mountings, four 37-mm anti-aircraft guns in two twin mountings, six 20-mm cannon in single mountings and six 21-in (533-mm) torpedo tubes in two triple mountings, and a speed of 33.5kt on the 32,000hp (23860kW) delivered to two shafts by geared steam turbines.

Italy also operated a mixed fleet of small and large (or in American terminology fleet) destroyers, some of them fairly old. The small type of destroyer was epitomized by a basic design originating in World War I with a length of 239ft 6in (73m). The first three of these classes have been mentioned, and comprised the eight Pilo-class ships of 1914–15 with an armament of five 4.1-in

(102-mm) guns in single mountings and four 17.3-in (440-mm) torpedo tubes in two twin mountings, the four Sirtori class ships of 1916–17 with an extra gun, and the eight La Masa-class ships of 1917–19 with the main armament restored to four guns. Then came the six Generale-class ships of 1921–22 with a full-load displacement of 890 tons, an armament of three 4-in (102-mm) guns in single mountings, two 3-in (76-mm) anti-aircraft guns in single mountings and four 17.3-in (440-mm) torpedo tubes in two twin mountings, and a speed of 30kt on the 15,000hp (11185kW) delivered to two shafts by geared steam turbines.

A 269-ft (82-m) hull was used in the four Palestro-class ships of 1919–20 for a nearly 50 per cent increase in power, which offered a higher speed with the same basic armament as the La Masa class, and the same hull was retained for the improved Curtatone class of 1922–23.

ABOVE
A Soviet Krupny-class guided missile destroyer, mid-1970s.

ABOVE LEFT
Alpino (F 580), an Alpino-class frigate of the Italian navy.

HMS Glasgow (D88), a Type 42 destroyer built by Swan Hunter Ltd, Wallsend on Tyne and commissioned in May 1979. She displaces 3,500 tons standard and 4,100 tons full load. Her dimensions are 412ft (125.5m) long overall by 47ft (14.3m) beam by 13.9ft (4.2m) to keel. The ship carries a Lynx helicopter and is armed with Sea Dart missiles.

There followed a long gap in Italian small destroyer design and construction until the advent of the 32 Spica-class ships from 1936. These had their boiler uptakes trunked into one funnel to maximize usable deck area and enhance gun traverse arcs, and their armament was based on three 3.9-in (100-mm) guns in single mountings as well as four 17.7-in (450-mm) torpedo tubes located initially as four single tubes but later as two twin mountings. Further development of the same concept resulted in the Ariete class. Planned in 1941, the class was to have numbered more than 40 ships, but only 16 were laid down: a mere one of these was delivered to the Italian navy before Italy's armistice with the Allies in September 1943, but another 13 were later completed in the shipyards of northern Italy for German use. The type had a full-load displacement of 1,125 tons, an armament of two 3.9-in (100-mm) guns in single mountings, two 37-mm anti-aircraft guns in single mountings and six 17.7-in (450-mm) torpedo tubes in two triple mountings, and a speed of 31kt on the 22,000hp (16405kW) delivered to two shafts by geared steam turbines.

Another stream of Italian destroyer development had become evident in the mid-1920s with the appearance of the first Sauro-class ships and then the closely related Turbine-class ships with the hull lengthened by some 9ft 10in (3.0m) to allow the incorporation of a higher-rated propulsion arrangement. Respective totals of four and eight such destroyers were built in the mid- and late 1920s with details that included, for the definitive Turbine class, a full-load displacement of 1,700 tons, an armament of four 4.7-in (120-mm) guns in two twin mountings, two 40-mm anti-aircraft guns in single mountings and six 21-in (533-mm) torpedo tubes in two triple

Roger de Lauria *(D 42)*, *a Roger de Lauria-class destroyer of the Spanish Navy.*

mountings, and a speed of 36kt on the 40,000hp (29825kW) delivered to two shafts by geared steam turbines.

Between 1928 and 1930 the Italians produced, as successors to the four Sauro-class destroyers, the 12 units of the Navigatore class in which a heavy armament and considerable power were shoehorned into a comparatively small hull for a full-load displacement of 2,580 tons, an armament of six 4.7-in (120-mm) guns in three twin mountings, three 37-mm anti-aircraft guns in single mountings and four or six 21-in (533-mm) torpedo tubes in two twin or triple mountings, and a speed of 38kt on the 50,000hp (37280kW) delivered to two shafts by geared steam turbines.

In 1930–32, the Italian navy introduced the four ships of the Dardo class in which maximum possible use of the deck area was made possible by the trunking of the boiler uptakes into a single funnel. This permitted a main armament of four 4.7-in (120-mm) guns in two twin mountings. Further development of the same concept led to the four destroyers of the improved Folgore class with each gun mounting provided with its own director to make possible the simultaneous engagement of two targets. The main limitation of the Dardo and Folgore classes was their lack of seaworthiness, and in the following 1934 Maestrale class of four ships the hull was lengthened by some 32ft 9in (10m) and also increased in beam. Basically the same hull was used in the 1936 Oriani class of four ships; with the threat of war increasing at this time, the Italian navy in 1937 and 1938 placed orders for another 12 destroyers modelled on the Oriani-class design. These were the Soldato-class destroyers with a full-load displacement of 1,460 tons, and armament of four or five 4.7-in (120-mm) guns in two twin and one

HMS Charybdis *(F 72)*, *a broad-beamed Leander-class frigate of the Royal Navy, armed with 4 MM38 Exocets and a Seawolf.*

The USS Oliver Hazzard Perry.

single mounting, one 37-mm anti-aircraft gun and six 21-in (533-mm) torpedo tubes in two triple mountings, and a speed of 39kt on the 48,000hp (35790kW) delivered to two shafts by geared steam turbines.

In the period up to the later part of World War I in 1918, the Japanese had closely followed the British lead in destroyer concepts, either buying directly from the U.K. or constructing ships based directly on British thinking. This system resulted in two lines of design and construction, leading in large first-class destroyers and smaller second-class destroyers. In the closing stages of World War I, the Japanese decided that there was something to be learned from German destroyer thinking, especially in the matter of a well between the fore castle and the forward part of the superstructure to break the force of water streaming over the bows in any sort of weather. This resulted in the 13 Minekaze- and 21 Momi-class first- and second-class destroyers launched in the years immediately following World War I as what were basically large- and small-scale versions of the same basic design. The Minekaze-class ships had a full-load displacement of 1,650 tons, an armament of four 4.7-in (120-mm) guns in single mountings and six 21-in (533-mm) torpedo tubes in two triple mountings, and a speed of 39kt on the 38,500hp (28685kW) delivered to two shafts by geared steam turbines. The nine Kamikaze-class destroyers that followed were basically similar to the Minekaze-class ships, and further improvement of the same concept came with the 12 Mutsuki-class destroyers that introduced the 24-in (610-mm) torpedo as an exceptionally potent anti-ship weapon.

During 1927 the Japanese launched the first of an eventual 20 Fubuki-class first-class destroyers, and in the process created a type that was a trend-setter in destroyer design as

it switched from British and German design influences to a basically Japanese concept with a higher fore castle, no well between the fore castle and the forward part of the superstructure, and a strengthened superstructure that was thus considerably less prone to damage in heavy seas. These impressive ships had a standard displacement of 2,090 tons, an armament of six 5-in (127-mm) guns in three triple turrets and nine 24-in (610-mm) torpedo tubes in three triple mountings with no fewer than 18 torpedoes, and a speed of 38kt on the 50,000hp (37280kW) delivered to two shafts by geared steam turbines.

In 1931 the Japanese introduced a small destroyer type as the Tomodzura class, whose four units were designed to complete the destroyer tonnage allocated to the Japanese in the Washington Naval Treaty. These ships were designed for coastal operations off Japan and along the shore of

eastern Asia, and were ambitious attempts to install maximum capability into minimum hull: with a standard displacement of only 650 tons, each ship carried an armament of three 5-in (127-mm) guns in one twin and one single mounting as well as four 21-in (533-mm) torpedo tubes in two twin mountings, and was capable of a speed of 30kt on the 11,000hp (8200kW) delivered to two shafts by geared steam turbines. That too much had been attempted on this hull was revealed by the top-heaviness of the class in general and the capsize of the lead ship in particular, and this problem was addressed in the following Ootori class of eight ships launched between 1935 and 1937 with a longer but still very narrow hull but a reduced armament. The details of the Ootori class included a full-load displacement of 1,050 tons, an armament of three 4.7-in (120-mm) guns in single mountings, one 40-mm anti-aircraft gun

and three 21-in (533-mm) torpedo tubes in a triple mounting, and a speed of 30kt on the 19,000hp (14165kW) delivered to two shafts by geared steam turbines.

Although the Fubuki-class destroyers had offered considerable capabilities as the time of their introduction a decade before the capable British J-class destroyers with a slightly inferior specification but a very high reputation, the tend-setting nature of the class had resulted in a number of operational problems that were addressed in succeeding classes. The first of these was the Akatsuki class of four ships launched between 1931 and 1933 with a lightened topside structure on a shorter hull, and there followed the Hatsuhara class of six destroyers with a hull that was shortened still further, resulting in the loss of one 5-in (127-mm) gun mounting and one torpedo tube triple mounting, and a propulsion arrangement of reduced power as Japanese

ABOVE
The USS Aylwin *was completed as one of the large Knox class of destroyer escorts for the oceanic escort role.*

ABOVE LEFT
USS Elliot *(DD-967), a Spruance-class destroyer.*

157

designers sought to comply with the limitations imposed by the first of the London Naval Agreements. Further development of the Hatsuhara-class design led to the Shiratsuyu class of 10 ships with a further shortening of the hull but an improvement in torpedo armament to eight 24-in (610-mm) tubes in two quadruple mountings with reloads.

In 1937 there appeared the first of 10 Asashio-class ships that ignored the London Naval Agreement limitations and were therefore very similar to the original Fubuki-class ships. The excellence of this basic design was further attested by the completion of 18 Kagero-class destroyers that introduced a slightly beamier hull and were launched between 1938 and 1941 before completion to a standard that included a full-load displacement of 2,490 tons, an armament of six 5-in (127-mm) guns in three twin mountings, four 25-mm anti-aircraft guns in two twin mountings and eight 24-in (610-mm) torpedo tubes in two quadruple mountings, and a speed of 35kt on the 52,000hp (38,770kW) delivered to two shafts by geared steam turbines. So successful was the type considered, moreover, that the following 20 Yugumo-class destroyers were basically similar.

The final type of Japanese large destroyer constructed in World War II was the Akitsuki class, of which 12 units were launched between 1941 and 1944. These were planned as anti-aircraft escorts for major surface forces, and were designed to offer the same capabilities as the American Atlanta and British Dido-class cruisers on a smaller hull that would therefore be cheaper and quicker to build. One of the keys to this capability was the adoption of a main gun of somewhat smaller calibre than those used in the Western ships, the loss of projectile weight in the Japanese gun being

OPPOSITE LEFT
The USS Albert David *was built as one of the Garcia class of destroyer escorts for the oceanic escort role.*

OPPOSITE RIGHT
Built in West Germany, the Bayern *was completed as the third of the four Hamburg-class destroyers.*

LEFT
The USS Glover *was completed as a member of the Brooke class of oceanic escorts to a design similar to that of the Garcia class.*

LEFT
The Schleswig-Holstein *was a destroyer of the Hamburg class.*

The ex-U.S. Navy Rio Grande Do Norte *of the Brazilian Navy.*

more than balanced by its considerably higher rate of fire. The details of the class included a full-load displacement of 3,700 tons, an armament of eight 3.9-in (100-mm) dual-purpose guns in two pairs of superfiring turrets, four 25-mm anti-aircraft guns in two twin mountings and four 24-in (610-mm) torpedo tubes in a quadruple mounting, and a speed of 33kt on the 52,000hp (38770kW) delivered to two shafts by geared steam turbines.

It is worth noting that the Japanese, during the course of the Pacific campaign,

came to appreciate that all their warships lacked the firepower to cope with saturation attacks by American warplanes, and in the surviving Akitsuki-class destroyers, the defensive anti-aircraft armament was steadily increased to 50 25-mm guns.

In the first half of the Pacific campaign of World War II, the Japanese proved themselves particularly adept in the art of destroyer combat, for they had long thought about the tactics required for this type of warfare and undertake very considerable training in this type of

engagement, which required quick analysis of the tactical situation and the arrival at tactically astute solutions. The Japanese skills in light surface warfare were nowhere more apparent than in the Solomon Islands. In May 1942 the Japanese were consolidating their hold on the Solomons. From bases in these islands they could threaten not only the New Hebrides and Fiji but also Australia and, perhaps most importantly of all, the American lines of maritime communication between the U.S.A. at their north-eastern end and New

Zealand and Australia at their south-western end. With the strategic initiative wrested from the Japanese by the U.S. Navy's success in the Battle of Midway at the beginning of June 1942, though, the Americans determined that the Solomons would be the point at which Japan's flow of outward expansion would finally be halted. The decisive point in the battle that was therefore about to erupt was the island of Guadalcanal in the south-eastern part of the Solomons. The island was in itself strategically unimportant, but the fighting

for its possession was the focus of American and Japanese efforts for nearly six months.

By a time early in July 1942 the Americans were getting ready to mount their first amphibious operation of World War II, an operation that was brought forward as far and as fast as was possible when aerial photo-reconnaissance revealed that the Japanese were building an airstrip on Guadalcanal and a seaplane base on neighbouring Tulagi. Virtually unopposed, the landing took place on 7 August and two days later it seemed that the Americans had

only to complete the mopping-up process. On the night of 9 August, however, Vice-Admiral Gunichi Mikawa's cruisers swept into the area and savaged an American and Australian cruiser force off Savo Island. In itself, this defeat of part of the forces covering the American landing area on Guadalcanal was only a tactical success, for Mikawa failed to press his advantage and descend on the now poorly protected force of transports lying off the northern shore of Guadalcanal. Even though the American transports were not attacked, the

commander of the assault force felt it only prudent to pull back, and in the process leaving 16,000 U.S. Marines unsupported on the island. Working feverishly in great heat and high humidity, the USMC's engineers had completed the Japanese airstrip by 15 August with the name Henderson Field, and this airstrip was to play a crucial role in the campaign that now followed. The completion of the airstrip allowed small quantities of essential supplies to be flown in, and larger quantities were delivered by destroyers and fast transports that made the run to and from the island under cover of darkness.

During the night of 17/18 August a Japanese force of high-speed transports, escorted by seven large destroyers, landed almost 1,000 troops on Guadalcanal as the start of the Japanese effort to retain Guadalcanal. Its speed was just high enough for the force to get in and out again in darkness, and the night activities of this force soon became so regular that the American nicknamed it the Tokyo Express. For a week the Japanese ran in small numbers of men to build up their strength to the point at which the reconquest of the island could be contemplated, but even at this early stage of the campaign the Japanese had to undertake their movements by night as American air power by day was virtually complete. During the early hours of 22 August the destroyer USS *Blue*, which was one of the radar pickets that had been so ineffective a fortnight previously in the

Battle of Savo Island, was one of two such pickets sent to interdict the Japanese. Again the American ships were surprised and the *Blue* was so badly damaged by torpedoes from the Japanese destroyer *Kawakaze* that it was later scuttled.

On 24 August the Japanese attempted a direct assault. While the inconclusive Battle of the Eastern Solomons was being fought between the main fleets to tie down the U.S. Navy's main strength, a Japanese bombardment force of four destroyers under the redoubtable Rear-Admiral Raizo

Tanaka escorted a group of transports down The Slot, the long channel dividing the double chain of the Solomons. The destroyers shelled Henderson Field but had one transport set on fire and the destroyer *Mutsuki* disabled because it tarried and was overtaken by daylight. The landing was called off, and the *Mutsuki* was scuttled.

By launching his Tokyo Express raids from Shortland Island, just off the south-eastern tip of Bougainville island at the north-western end of the Solomons (therefore closer to Guadalcanal than the

main Japanese base at Rabaul on New Britain island to the north of New Guinea), Tanaka was able to shorten the trip that his ships had to complete in one night but nonetheless remained out of the range of the Douglas SBD Dauntless dive-bombers now based on Henderson Field. Three destroyers landed 350 men on the night of 26–27 August and 130 more men during the following night. Now slightly over-confident, the Japanese left too early on the next round-trip operation and were caught at dusk, losing the *Asagiri* together with the

troops and equipment embarked on this destroyer.

As the Tokyo Express became more firmly established, it became the standard practice for the destroyers to undertake a short bombardment of Henderson Field after they had landed their troops and supplies. On 5–6 September the American destroyer/transport's USS *Gregory* and USS *Little* sought to intervene, and were sunk for their pains.

By mid-September the situation on Guadalcanal had become something of a stalemate as neither side possessed the strength to overwhelm the other. It was at this stage that the Japanese made Guadalcanal a high-priority objective, and rotated the destroyers of the Tokyo Express through a rapid modification that saw a considerable boost in their stowage and

anti-aircraft weapons through the removal of some main-battery weapon; the torpedo armament was left unaltered.

Supplemented by powered barges, the destroyers now built up the Japanese strength on the island for what the Japanese high command anticipated would be the decisive offensive. The Americans had greater strength on the island than the Japanese had estimated, however, and the defeat of the Japanese offensive meant that the Tokyo Express had to ferry in the replacements that were now urgently needed. The Americans meanwhile landed 4,000 more men of the U.S. Marine Corps at the cost of the carrier USS *Wasp* and a destroyer from the covering force.

During October the destroyer force under Tanaka's command achieved a major success, the nightly deliveries by the Tokyo

LEFT
D'Estrées *(D629), lead of the T47-class ships of the French navy.*

OPPOSITE LEFT
USS Robinson *(DDG 12), a Charles F. Adams-class.*

OPPOSITE RIGHT
The Perry-class USS Gallery *(FFG-26).*

USS Spruance *(DDG 963)*.

Express accomplishing the delivery of 20,000 men and considerable quantities of vital equipment. The American warplanes based on Henderson Field were a constant thorn in the side of the Japanese effort, however, and on the night of 11/12 October four Japanese heavy cruisers, under the command of Rear Admiral Goto, swept down The Slot as escort to a convoy and also to undertake a major bombardment of the airstrip and its surrounding area. However, the Japanese cruisers encountered a superior American force, under Rear Admiral Scott, that had been covering one of their own landings. In the resulting Battle of Cape Esperance, the Japanese were taken unawares and the American cruiser line crossed the T of the Japanese cruiser line, the Japanese losing one cruiser and one destroyer in the resulting firefight. Two Tokyo Express

LEFT
USS Wilson *(DD 847) was built as a member of the classic Gearing class of fleet destroyers.*
BELOW LEFT
HMS Ambuscade *(F 172) was completed as a member of the F 21 or Amazon class of frigates designed by private enterprise rather than the Admiralty's design department*
BELOW
The USS Tattnall *(DDG 19) was a unit of the important Charles F. Adams class of guided-missile destroyers for the oceanic escort of major surface forces.*

Bremen, *lead ship of the F 22-class frigates during sea trials in the Baltic in June 1981.*

destroyers were also sunk by aircraft at dawn.

By now the Japanese had decided that the destruction of Henderson Field was essential to any possibility of Japanese success on Guadalcanal. Japanese aircraft bombed the airstrip and undertook two heavy daylight bombing raids during 13 October, hampered repairs to the cratered runways with artillery fire and finally, after the fall of night, steamed in two battle-cruisers which, in the course of a 90-minute bombardment, struck at the airstrip with more than 900 14-in (356-mm) shells: the result of this Japanese effort was the destruction of 48 American aircraft and most of the airstrip's aviation fuel. More bombing on the following day was followed by 150 8-in (203-mm) shells from two heavy cruisers during the night. At the same time the Tokyo Express escorted a transport force that delivered more men and equipment and then, believing that Henderson Field was out of action, lay offshore during the day. Putting into the air everything that they could muster, the Americans sank three transports and forced Tanaka to pull back with his destroyers. On the night of 15–16 October, Tanaka returned with heavy cruisers and hit

*Tromp (F801), a Tromp-
class frigate of the Royal
Netherlands Navy.*

RIGHT
*The Argentine navy's Meko
360-type destroyers, the*
Almirante Brown *and* La
Argentina.

FAR RIGHT
USS Hayler, *a Spruance-
class DD.*

RIGHT
The Aradu *was built by
Blohm und Voss in Germany
as a 'Meko 360' class frigate
for the Nigerian navy.*

Henderson Field with 900 8-in (203-mm)
and 300 5-in (127-mm) shells. Even so, the
defenders of Henderson Field were able to
check the ground assault that the Japanese
launched between 22 and 26 October in
what was later to be proved their final effort
to overwhelm the Americans. The destroyer
force under Tanaka, who believed that it
was now safe to provide fire support for the
army by day, was given a very heavy
battering by American artillery.

All too aware of the drain that was
being imposed on their resources by the
continuing campaign on and around
Guadalcanal, the Japanese now brought in
stronger elements of the Combined Fleet to
tackle the U.S. Navy's forces, now under
the command of Vice-Admiral William F.

USS Kidd (DDG-993) underway in the Persian Gulf, 1987.

HMS Boxer (F 92), a stretched Broadsword-class frigate during sea trials armed with Exocet SSMs and Seawolf SAMs. 29 September 1983.

Halsey. This led to the Battle of Santa Cruz on 26 October. Though suffering a prohibitively expensive toll in aircraft and pilots, the Japanese succeeded in adding the carrier USS *Hornet* to the cost of Guadalcanal to the Americans. During the first 10 days of November, Tanaka ran 65 destroyer sorties to boost the Japanese forces ashore on Guadalcanal. As a result the Japanese then had a 1,000-man advantage over the American force of 29,000 men. In the process the Tokyo Express suffered damage to three destroyers.

On 12 November the Japanese used a convoy of 11 transport vessels, escorted by 11 destroyers and covered by a force including two battleships, to deliver 13,000 more men. Warned by their intelligence service of the Japanese plan, the Americans were ready for the Naval Battle of Guadalcanal: on 13 November the battle degenerated into a confused melee, the Americans losing four destroyers and two cruisers against the Japanese loss of one battleship and two destroyers. Undeterred, the Japanese returned during the following night, Henderson Field being on the receiving end of 1,400 shells from cruisers and destroyers in a mere 30 minutes. However, the break of day found the airstrip still able to launch aircraft, which found the bombardment force and sank one heavy cruiser. The shelling of Henderson Field had achieved its primary objective of diverting attention from the destroyers of the Tokyo Express, which had escorted 10 transport ships to deliver more men and supplies: six of the transports fell victim to air attack and the other four were beached to guarantee that their loads could be delivered.

Cover was provided by another substantial force that penetrated down The Slot: near Savo Island the battle-cruiser

171

HMS Dido.

Kirishima was destroyed by the fire of the battleship USS *Washington* and, with two American and one Japanese destroyer, thus became another wreck on the bed of what was now known as Ironbottom Sound. Only 2,000 of 7,000 Japanese troops got ashore to bolster the Japanese forces, which were now outnumbered by 40,000 men to 25,000.

Only the destroyers of the Tokyo Express could now save the situation for the Japanese. Tanaka's ships, now beginning to suffer from the effects of constant service and high-speed running without proper maintenance, could deliver supplies only by pushing them overboard in rubberized containers for possible recovery by the men on Guadalcanal. During the night of 30 November eight of Tanaka's destroyers, cluttered with supplies and personnel, were surprised by an American force of five cruisers and six destroyers off Tassafaronga in the Battle of Rennells Island. The well trained and now highly experienced Japanese reacted rapidly with salvoes of potent torpedoes, while the less experienced Americans betrayed their positions by reliance on radar-directed gun fire. As a result the Americans had four of their cruisers torpedoed, one of them sinking, while the Japanese lost one destroyer but had turned a potential defeat into victory and still delivered the goods.

The first part of December was characterized by high-speed runs of up to 10 destroyers at a time, the operation on 12 December losing the destroyer *Teruzuki* to torpedo attack by a PT boat. The pace of operations without air superiority was now telling in terms of a massive tiredness of men and ships, and the Japanese therefore suspended their effort until the next moonless period, which was in the early part of January 1943. By this time,

however, the Japanese had decided that their forces could not retake Guadalcanal and therefore opted for an evacuation. On 14 January the Tokyo Express delivered 600 high-grade troops to act as rearguard while the remnants of the forces on Guadalcanal were extricated. Under the command of Rear Admiral Koyanagi, who had replaced Tanaka, the Japanese used one cruiser and 20 destroyers to evacuate the surviving 13,000 men from Guadalcanal in the period between 2 and 7 February. The Americans did not realize what was happening, so the only Japanese loss was a destroyer that fell victim to a mine.

Guadalcanal cost the Americans about 1,600 ground troops and a large number of sailors, while the Japanese lost more than 23,000 men. Each side had lost 24 ships of destroyer size or greater in the course of many skirmishes and seven major actions. The Japanese naval forces, experienced but outnumbered, performed with great skill

and courage, while the Americans were at first very inexperienced but fought with courage and soon learned the required skills to emerge from the Guadalcanal campaign as experienced victors who could look forward to the next campaign with high expectations.

So far as convoy escorts were concerned, the Japanese suffered heavily as a result of the erroneous thinking of their high command, which had persistently based its planning on the concept of a quick victory and therefore ignored the possibility of a protracted war and a long defensive effort in which Japan would be strangled by American submarine and air power unless vital convoys could be protected. The belated realization that such ships were desperately needed resulted in the Matsu class of escorts, of which only 17 of a planned 28 were completed in 1944 and 1945 with a full-load displacement of 1,530 tons, an armament of three 5-in (127-mm)

guns in one twin and one single mountings, 24 25-mm anti-aircraft guns in four triple and 12 single mountings, and four 24-in (610-mm) torpedo tubes in a quadruple mounting, and the speed of 27.5kt on the 19,000hp (14165kW) delivered to two shafts by geared steam turbines. Another and somewhat more austerely equipped escort was planned as the Tachibana-class type of which more than 90 were planned, 27 laid down and only a few completed.

In the period after World War II, it has been the U.S. Navy that has dominated the Western approach to destroyer design. Soon after the end of the war relations between the U.S.A. and U.S.S.R. began to deteriorate rapidly, especially after the Soviet development of nuclear weapons, and as it became clear that the Soviet navy was planning to develop a major submarine capability based on the design of the German Type XXI-class boat, the U.S. Navy decided that a major upgrade of its escort

ABOVE
Warszawa *of the Polish navy, a modified Kashin.*

ABOVE LEFT
HMS Edinburgh *(D 97) was built by Cammell Laird as one of the four guided-missile destroyers of the Royal Navy's Manchester class.*

173

HMS Lancaster *(F 233) is a Type 23-class guided-missile frigate optimized for the hunting and killing of submarines in the North Atlantic.*

This guided-missile frigate of the Soviet navy is identifiable by its pennant number as the Zadornyy, *a unit of the important Krivak I class.*

forces was required to protect the carrier battle groups that were now the core of the service's operational thinking. Many of the surviving Fletcher, Gearing and Allen M. Sumner-class fleet destroyers were therefore revised to oceanic escort standard with a reduced gun armament but much improved anti-submarine capability. This made economic sense as the Americans had large numbers of these ships, which were still almost new, and the Soviet threat was slow to materialize in numbers and also in basic capability. Thus the conversions of World War II fleet destroyers into anti-submarine escorts provided the U.S. Navy's main surface strength with a more than adequate defensive element, and the service could thus use its relatively limited funding to provide more modern escorts for the protection of convoys, which were seen to fall into two basic categories as merchant

ships providing fuel, food and raw materials for the U.S.A.'s allies in Europe, and as amphibious warfare vessels transporting formations of the U.S. Marine Corps and U.S. Army for offensive operations in any part of the world.

These smaller ocean escorts, which were the equivalent of the destroyer escorts of World War II, were the 13 ships of the Dealey class, four units of the Claud Jones class, and two units of the Bronstein class used as prototypes of more advanced types. The first two classes were created in the 1950s and the last in the early 1960s with basically conventional weapons, although the Bronstein class introduced the RUR-5 ASROC weapon which was a rocket used to deliver a homing torpedo or nuclear depth charge to the position of a target submarine detected and localized by sonar.

Further development of this ocean

HMS Gloucester *(D96), a
Batch III Sheffield-class
destroyer of the Royal Navy.*

USS Mahan (DDG 42), a U.S. Navy Coontz-class destroyer.

escort type, now generally reckoned to be a
frigate rather than a destroyer, resulted in
the 10 ships of the Garcia class that were
followed by the seven units of the Brooke
class that suffered in the replacement of one
of the two 5-in (127-mm) dual-purpose
gun mountings by a launcher for 16 RIM-
24 Tartar surface-to-air missiles in
recognition of the growing threat posed
from the early 1960s by Soviet warplanes.
This tendency was continued in the 46 ships
of the Knox class optimized for the anti-
submarine role but offering a useful anti-
aircraft capability with its octuple launcher for
RIM-7 Sea Sparrow short-range SAMs.

The current mainstay of the U.S. Navy's
frigate force is the Oliver Hazard Perry class
of 51 ships commissioned from 1977.
Although small, the type has a fair measure
of electronic sophistication, and its primary

*The U.S.S.R. Kashin-class
Krasny-Kavkaz.*

*The Persian Gulf in October
1987. Iranian command
and control platforms near
Rashadat, in the Persian
Gulf, were shelled by U.S.
Navy ships, in what the U.S.
called a 'measured and
appropriate response' to
Iranian missile attacks on
a U.S.-flagged tanker in
Kuwaiti waters the week
before.*

details include a full-load displacement of
4,100 tons, an armament of one 3-in (76-
mm) dual-purpose gun, one 20-mm Vulcan
six-barrel cannon in a close-in weapon system
mounting, one single-arm launcher for 40
missiles (generally four RGM-84 Harpoon
anti-ship and 36 RIM-66 Standard Missile
surface-to-air missiles), six 12.75-in (324-
mm) torpedo tubes in two triple anti-
submarine mountings and, in some ships,
provision for one anti-submarine helicopter,
and a speed of 29kt on the 41,000hp
(30570kW) delivered to one shaft by two
General Electric LM2500 gas turbines.

In a slow process that started in the
early 1950s, the mantle of fleet escort
destroyer was gradually assumed from World
War II conversions by new ships. The first
of these were the four highly capable but
also highly expensive destroyers of the
Mitscher class optimized for the anti-
submarine role, then the 10 destroyers of
the Farragut class optimized for the dual-
role anti-submarine and anti-aircraft roles
with ASROC missiles, homing torpedoes
and one twin-arm launcher for 40 RIM-2
Terrier SAMs, and finally the 18 destroyers
of the Forrest Sherman class optimized for
the general-purpose role with neither
ASROC nor SAM weapons.

By the 1960s the Soviet threat was
becoming appreciably more acute, and this
led to the introduction of the 23 Charles F.
Adams-class destroyers with ASROC anti-
submarine and RIM-24 anti-aircraft weapons,
and then in the 1970s to the 31 Spruance
and four Kidd-class destroyers with
significant anti-submarine, anti-aircraft and
anti-ship capabilities in the form of missiles,
torpedoes and a multi-role helicopter. The
final expression of this tendency, which
continued throughout the 1980s, is the
Arleigh Burke class, of which 26 are planned
primarily for the anti-aircraft role with a

slightly downgraded version of the AEGIS weapon system (SPY-1 radar and Standard Missile weapons) designed for the Ticonderoga-class cruisers.

These American leads have generally been followed in Western Europe,

particularly in the U.K., France, Italy, Germany and the Netherlands, and in the Far East, where Japan has built up an impressive destroyer and frigate force since the early 1960s.

The U.S.S.R. also developed a major

destroyer and frigate force from the late 1950s, and although the earlier of these classes were intended at the time of their introduction mainly for the destruction of American surface battle groups with large anti-ship missiles, later classes were

completed to a more balanced standard with anti-submarine, anti-aircraft and anti-ship capabilities. The more modern of these classes, in order of introduction, were the 14 destroyers of the two Kashin subclasses, the 22 destroyers of the Sovremenny class and the 12 destroyers of the Udaloy class; and the 40 frigates of the three Krivak subclasses and the three frigates of the Neustrashimy class.

The most impressive of these are the Sovremenny and Udaloy-class destroyers delivered from 1980. The Sovremenny-class design is optimized for the anti-ship and anti-aircraft roles with a full-load displacement of 7,300 tons, an armament of four 5.1-in (130-mm) dual-purpose guns in two twin turrets, four 30-mm six-barrel cannon in single mountings, two quadruple launchers for eight SS-N-22 Sunburn anti-ship missiles, two launchers for 44 SA-N-7 Gadfly SAMs, two 12-tube anti-submarine rocket launchers, four 21-in (533-mm) torpedo tubes in two twin mountings, and one helicopter, and a speed of 32kt on the 110,000hp (82015kW) delivered to two shafts by geared steam turbines. The Udaloy-class design is optimized for the anti-submarine and anti-aircraft roles with a full-load displacement of 8,700 tons, an armament of two 5.1-in (130-mm) dual-purpose guns in single turrets, four 30-mm six-barrel cannon in single mountings, two quadruple launchers for eight SS-N-14 Silex anti-submarine missiles, eight octuple vertical launchers for 64 SA-N-9 SAMs, eight 21-in (533-mm) torpedo tubes in two quadruple mountings, two 12-tube anti-submarine rocket launchers and two multi-role helicopters, and a speed of 30kt on the 110,000hp (82015kW) delivered to two shafts by a COGOG (COmbined Gas turbine Or Gas turbine) arrangement with four gas turbine engines.

Chapter Four
The Cruiser

As a sailing ship in its original guise, the cruiser (sometimes rendered cruizer) was a fourth-rate ship or large frigate that was generally detached from the main fleet to sail independently in search of the enemy, whose position was then reported back to the fleet so that a major engagement could be brought about. The term cruiser was also employed for frigates and smaller vessels operated independently against the enemy's maritime lines of communication in what is generally known as the *guerre de course* role. In both these tasks, the essential requirement of a successful cruiser was its ability to sail better than any prospective enemy, especially in terms of speed and ability to point high into the wind.

All this changed with the advent during the middle part of the 19th century of steam propulsion, and of iron (later steel) construction and protection. At this time cruiser ceased to be a generic name for any warship acting independently of the main fleet and became a type of warship in its own right. The pure cruiser came into existence during the middle and later parts of the 19th century in four basic types, namely the armoured cruiser with a displacement of up to 14,600 tons and a high level of protection matched by an armament of powerful guns, and the

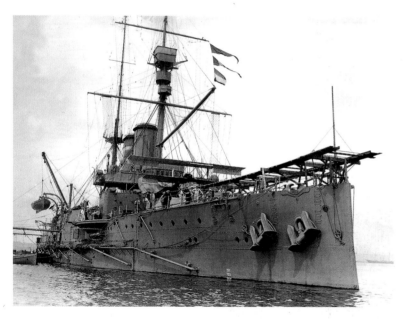

cruisers with maximum displacements of 14,200, 6,000 and 3,000 tons respectively.

The British built a total of 136 cruisers of these pre-Dreadnought types in the form of 35 examples of the armoured cruiser and 21, 51 and 29 examples respectively of the first-, second- and third-class protected cruisers. The armoured cruisers were intended to provide a scouting capability within sight of the Royal Navy fleets to which they were attached, and also to serve as the flagships of overseas squadrons in areas that did not need the combined political and naval power represented by a battleship, while the tasks of the three subclasses of protected cruiser were the protection of British merchant shipping as it plied the seas of the world, the escort of convoys of troopship on their way to and from various parts of the British empire, and the provision of a naval outpost capability in less advanced parts of the world. By the outbreak of World War I in August 1914, 51 of these older ships had been deleted or reduced to non-combatant status, and another seven had been converted into minelayers. It is also worth noting that the Royal Navy also possessed 10 small cruisers with a displacement of up to 1,850 tons.

The evolution of the cruiser through the second half of the 19th century

protected cruiser that was built in three subclasses with horizontal deck armour but no vertical belt armour, as well as the supplementary protection and survivability offered by the arrangement of the coal bunkers on the sides of the ship along the waterline and the compartmentalization of the hull's interior spaces. In descending order of size, these three subclasses were the first-, second- and third-class protected

paralleled that of the battleship. The type
started as a wooden vessel: to this core were
first added both a layer of protective armour
and steam machinery to supplement the
three-masted ship rig with its full
complement of sails; then came a
progression of interim stages in which iron
and then steel became the primary
structural medium and the steam propulsion
system gradually superseded the sailing rig;
and finally the cruiser reached the point at
which the masts survived only in vestigial
form to provide the means of hoisting flags
and carrying control tops, and the main
armament comprised a mixed assortment of
breech-loading weapons in which the
largest-calibre guns were carried in trainable
turrets, the intermediate-calibre guns were
installed in casemates, and the smallest-
calibre weapons were carried on open
mountings with perhaps a shield as the only
protection for the guns' crew. The three
main weapons carried by British cruisers
were the 9.2-in (234-mm) gun firing a 380-
lb (172-kg) shell, the 7.5-in (191-mm) gun
firing a 200-lb (91-kg) shell, and the 6-in
(152-mm) gun firing a 100-lb (45-kg) shell.

Typical of the British cruiser types
before the advent of the Dreadnought era in
1906 were the first-class cruisers of the
Warrior armoured and Diadem protected
classes, the Challenger second-class cruisers,
and the Pelorus third-class cruisers.

The Warrior class, of which four were
launched in 1905, had a full-load
displacement of 13,550 tons, an armament
of six 9.2-in (234-mm) guns, four 7.5-in
(191-mm) and 23 3-pdr quick-firing guns,
armour protection up to a maximum
thickness of 6in (152mm), and a speed of
23kt on the 23,000hp (17150kW) provided
to two shafts by triple-expansion steam
engines. The Diadem class, of which eight
were launched between 1896 and 1898,

had a full-load displacement of 11,000 tons, an armament of 16 6-in (152-mm), 14 12-pdr and three 3-pdr quick-firing guns, armour protection up to a maximum thickness of 4.5in (114mm), and a speed of 20.25kt on the 16,500hp (12300kW) provided to two shafts by triple-expansion steam engines. The Challenger class, of which five were launched in two subclasses between 1898 and 1902, had a full-load displacement of 5,880 tons, an armament of 11 6-in (152-mm), nine 12-pdr and six 3-pdr quick-firing guns, armour protection up to a maximum thickness of 3in (76mm), and a speed of 21kt on the 12,500hp (9320kW) provided to two shafts by triple-expansion steam engines. The Pelorus class, of which 11 were launched between 1896 and 1900, had a full-load displacement of 2,135 tons, an armament of eight 4-in (102-mm) and eight 3-pdr quick-firing guns, armour protection up to a maximum

LEFT
The SMS Breslau *was the name vessel of a four-ship class of German light cruisers completed in 1912. All four of the ships survived World War I. As completed, the ships carried 12 4.1-in (105-mm) guns as their primary armament, but during the course of the war two of the ships, SMS Stralsund and SMS Strassburg, were revised with seven 5.9-in (150-mm) guns and two 3.4-in (88-mm) anti-aircraft guns and well as up to 120 mines.*

thickness of 3in (76mm) on very limited areas, and a speed of 20kt on the 7,000hp (5220kW) provided to two shafts by triple-expansion steam engines.

These ships were rendered obsolete by the development of the Dreadnought type of capital ship and comparable evolution in the warships of smaller types, but were still in extensive service on the outbreak of World War I. The armoured cruisers were generally retained for service in home waters until their losses up to and including the Battle of Jutland in May 1916 revealed their terrible weakness against the longer-ranged and considerably heavier shells of more powerfully armed opponents. The protected cruisers, on the other hand, had already

served a useful function, and continued to do so, in their activities in overseas waters in the pursuit and destruction of Germany's merchant raiding force. The ships of this type were also very useful later in World War I, when they were used for the convoy escort role in the North Atlantic.

A major turning point in the design of cruisers came in 1904–05 with the advent of the River class of light warships, in which the torpedo boat and torpedo boat destroyer finally came of age as a single type offering a genuine ocean-going rather than merely coastal or at best sea-going capability. The new ocean-going destroyer was a far greater threat to major surface forces than the earlier coastal or even sea-

going torpedo boat, and the commanders of major surface forces now had to take into consideration the possibility of massed attacks by torpedo-firing ships using their speed and agility to evade destruction and thus close to torpedo range. The growing threat posed by the destroyer in the early part of the 20th century therefore called for the development of a new type of light cruiser that was light and fast enough to work with destroyer flotillas, for which it provided a command capability, and also fast enough and sufficiently well armed with quick-firing guns to operate in the defensive screen that provided the squadrons of larger warships with a first line of defence against attacks by the enemy's destroyer flotillas.

The French battleship Masséna *was completely obsolete even at the time of its completion in 1898, as indicated by its ram bow and primary armament of two 12-in (305-mm) guns in single turrets fore and aft. With six calibres of gun, poor seaworthiness and only a modest speed, the* Masséna *represented the type of old battleship that was rendered wholly useless by the advent of more modern ships down to the size of the cruiser.*

The first results of this new requirement were the 15 ships of the Scout type that were built between 1904 and 1912 with a displacement in the order of 2,700 to 3,500 tons, and the 21 ships of the Town type that were built between 1909 and 1915 with a displacement in the order of 4,800 to 5,500 tons with a much greater endurance and the ability to operate semi-independently from remote bases. There were in fact six classes of Scout-type light cruisers, of which the last was the three-strong Active class with a displacement of 3,440 tons, an armament of 10 4-in (102-mm) guns and two 21-in (533-mm) torpedo tubes, no protection, and a propulsion arrangement of steam turbines

delivering 18,000hp (13420kW) to two shafts for a maximum speed of 26kt. There were five classes of the Town-type light cruisers, of which the last was the two-strong Birkenhead class with a displacement of 5,200 tons, an armament of 10 5.5-in (140-mm) guns and two 21-in (533-mm) torpedo tubes, protection in the form of a 3-in (76-mm) belt, and a propulsion arrangement of steam turbines delivering 31,000hp (23115kW) to four shafts for a speed of 26.5kt.

Early experience with the Scout and Town types of light cruiser indicated that they were useful types of warships, but that a hybrid type would be best suited to the requirements of working with major surface

forces in the North Sea, which was the area in which the Grand Fleet intended to secure a climactic victory over the German High Seas Fleet in the event of an outbreak of war between the U.K. and Germany. This hybrid type combined features of the Scout and Town types with a more potent propulsion arrangement for the higher speed required for effective use in conjunction with the Grand Fleet and its fast destroyer flotillas. The first of the new classes, which eventually totalled nine including the five ships of the Delhi class completed after the end of World War I, was the Arethusa class of eight ships that started to enter service just before the outbreak of the war. As built, the ships had a

Regensburg, *a light cruiser of the Kaiserliche Marine.*

Stettin, *a light cruiser of the Kaiserliche Marine.*

displacement of 3,512 tons, an armament of two 6-in (152-mm) and six 4-in (102-mm) guns as well as eight 21-in (533-mm) torpedo tubes, protection in the form of a 3-in (76-mm) belt and 1-in (25-mm) deck, and a speed of 30kt on the 40,000hp (29825kW) provided to four shafts by four sets of steam turbines. Wartime changes included a revision of the gun armament to three 6-in (152-mm) and four 4-in (102-mm) guns as well as one 4-in (102-mm) or two 3-in (76-mm) anti-aircraft guns, the latter reflecting the first stage of the aeroplane's developing impact on naval operations; at the same time the original pole foremast was replaced by a tripod foremast. The ships were somewhat cramped but soon proved themselves very well suited to their task, and were therefore used as the basis for steadily improved successor classes whose main changes were a larger number of 6-in (152-mm) guns in replacement of 4-in (102-mm) weapons. The details of the Delhi class included a displacement of 4,650 tons, an armament of six 6-in (152-mm) guns and two 3-in (76-mm) anti-aircraft guns as well as 12 21-in (533-mm) torpedo tubes, protection in the form of a 3-in (76-mm) belt and 1-in (25-mm) deck, and a speed of 29kt on the 40,000hp (29825kW) provided to four shafts by four sets of steam turbines.

As the leading maritime power in the world during the last years of the 19th century, the U.K. was generally followed rather than led in the basic shape of naval developments, although rivals such as Germany sought to offset British numerical superiority with qualitative superiority in matters such as firepower and speed. At the beginning of World War I, the German navy had six armoured cruisers, of which the most advanced were the two ships of the Scharnhorst class with a displacement of

HMS Hardy *leading a flotilla of torpedo-boat destroyers.*

11,600 tons, an armament of eight 8.2-in (210-mm), six 5.9-in (150-mm) and 20 3.4-in (88-mm) guns as well as four 17.7-in (450-mm) torpedo tubes, protection in the form of a 6-in (152-mm) belt and 2-in (51-mm) deck, and a speed of 22.5kt on the 26,000hp (19385kW) provided to three shafts by triple-expansion steam engines.

Germany, it should be noted, also produced just one example of what may be regarded as a heavy armoured cruiser. This was the *Blücher* designed to provide a capability comparable to that of the Invincible class, which were the Royal Navy's first battle-cruisers and originally described for disinformation purposes as being armed with 9.2-in (234-mm) guns. The Germans therefore responded to their first perception of the Invincible-class ships with a design based on that of the Westfalen class of Dreadnought battleships but scaled

down and fitted with a primary armament of 8.2-in (210-mm) guns. This resulted in a vessel characterized by a displacement of 15,500 tons, an armament of 12 8.2-in (210-mm), eight 5.9-in (150-mm) and 16 3.4-in (88-mm) guns as well as four 17.7-in (450-mm) torpedo tubes, protection in the form of a 6.75-in (170-mm) belt and turrets, and a speed of 26kt on the 44,000hp (32805kW) provided to three shafts by triple-expansion steam engines. Inevitably the *Blücher* was too lightly armed and armoured to be a real battle-cruiser, and paid the penalty at the Battle of the Dogger Bank in 1915, when she fought alongside the German battle-cruisers and was completely overwhelmed.

The German navy also operated 17 protected cruisers approximating in overall capabilities to the British second-class protected cruisers, and of these it was the

10 ships of the closely related Gazelle, Nymphe and Frauenlob classes that were the most modern, all having been completed between 1899 and 1903 with a displacement of between 2,645 and 2,715 tons, a primary armament of 10 4.1-in (105-mm) guns and two 17.7-in (450-mm) torpedo tubes, protection in the form of a 2-in (50-mm) deck, and a speed of 21.5kt on the 8,500hp (6340kW) delivered to two shafts by triple-expansion steam engines.

In the first part of the 20th century Germany decided, like the U.K., that the protected cruiser was obsolete in conceptual terms and that the immediate future lay with the light cruiser. Germany therefore undertook a major design and production effort, resulting in the construction of no fewer than 14 light cruiser classes in the period up to the end of World War I. The first of these, completed in 1904, was the

The HMS Venus, *an Eclipse-class cruiser of the Royal Navy.*

Bremen class of five ships typified by a displacement of 3,250 tons, an armament of 10 4.1-in (105-mm) guns and two 17.7-in (450-mm) torpedo tubes, protection in the form of a 2-in (50-mm) deck, and a speed of 23kt on the 11,000hp (8200kW) delivered to two shafts by triple-expansion steam engines. The last, completed in 1918 and therefore reflecting the very considerable changes that had taken place in light cruiser thinking as a result of operations in World War I, was the second Dresden class of two ships typified by a displacement of 6,150 tons, an armament of eight 5.9-in (150-mm) guns, two or three 3.4-in (88-mm) anti-aircraft guns, and four 19.7-in (500-mm) torpedo tubes, protection in the form of a 2.5-in (65-mm)

belt and a 0.75-in (20-mm) deck, and a speed of 28.5kt on the 45,000hp (33550kW) delivered to two shafts by steam turbines. The remarkable thing about these two classes, and this was also evident in comparable British classes, was their conceptual similarity: the ships of the later class were larger, were armed and protected more heavily, and possessed a higher speed as a result of a more powerful propulsion arrangement based on steam turbines rather than triple-expansion engines, but in overall terms the design of the ships was just that of the earlier classs units on a larger scale and incorporating improvements suggested by more extensive operational experience.

The most celebrated cruiser of World War I, and the ship that most successfully

exploited the cruiser's capability in the *guerre de course* role, was the German ship SMS *Emden*, one of the two light cruisers of the Dresden class. The ship had been completed in 1908 after construction at the Danzig Dockyard, and at the beginning of World War I was part of the East Asiatic Squadron commanded by Vice-Admiral Maximilian von Spee at the German treaty port of Tsingtao in China. After considering and then rejecting plans for his whole squadron to undertake a raid into the Indian Ocean before crossing the Pacific Ocean to round Cape Horn before passing north up the Atlantic Ocean to return to Germany, Spee decided to seek the most direct route home via Cape Horn, but detached the *Emden* under Commander Karl von Müller to undertake an independent cruise supported by the collier *Markomannia*. From Pagan island, where Spee had made his decision to split the squadron, the two ships steamed along the eastern side of the Marianas Islands in the Pacific, on 13 August in the direction of the East Indies. Two days later, Müller was unable to raise the German radio station on the island of Yap, north-east of the Palau island group and despatched a cutter to investigate what turned out to be the wreckage of the radio station that had been shelled into total destruction by three British cruisers. Müller next steamed toward Angaur island in the Palau island group, which had been leased by a German phosphate company and where a meeting with the Choising was hoped for. There was no sign of the collier, but the *Emden* did meet the steamer *Prinzessin Alice*. Müller took on extra men from the *Prinzessin Alice* and also the *Markomannia*, and sent a letter to his mother by *Prinzessin Alice*, which he ordered to a port in the neutral Philippines.

Müller then steered the *Emden* towards

any sight of the *Tannenfels*, and Müller therefore took on some 470 tons of coal from the *Markomannia*, seriously denting the collier's reserve.

At this point the *Tromp*, a Dutch battleship, arrived and instructed the two German ships to sail as they were in contravention of international neutrality laws, and it was later established that the same Dutch warship had previously ordered the *Tannenfels* out of the area. The Dutch ship escorted the German vessels to the edge of the 3-mile (4.8-km) limit, where Müller headed west in an effort to persuade the Dutch captain that the Germans were heading toward the Pacific. As soon as the Dutch ship had sunk below the horizon, however, Müller reversed course and headed for Bali and the Lombok Strait into the Indian Ocean. As the German ships waited for the fall of night before trying the strait, Müller's

LEFT
Blücher, *a Blücher-class heavy cruiser of the Imperial German Navy.*

BELOW
HMS Exeter, *a York-class cruiser of the Royal Navy.*

the Moluccas with the idea of entering the Indian Ocean via the eastern side of Mindanao and the Dutch East Indies. On the night of 20 August Müller was trying to radio Tsingtao, when he received a radio message from the old German light cruiser SMS *Geier*. During the British bombardment of Yap, the *Geier*'s captain had hidden his ship and its collier in a cove, and Müller now recommended that the *Geier* and its collier head for internment in Hawaii. The *Emden* then departed to the south-west once more, crossing the equator on 22 August and on the following day establishing radio contact with the German steamer *Tannenfels*, with which Müller agreed a rendezvous at the Dutch and Portuguese island of Timor to take on coal and food. The *Emden* and the *Markomannia* reached the rendezvous and waited half a day on 25 August without

ABOVE
The American cruiser USS
Cincinnati *(CL-6),*
underway in New York
harbour on her way to the
Navy Yard for re-fitting.
9 July 1942.

RIGHT
Trainee seaman of the
Deutsche Kriegsmarine,
with the cruiser
Deutschland *in the*
background.

second-in-command came up with a simple yet effective plan to disguise the *Emden*'s identity: three funnels were the trademark of German light cruisers whereas their British opponents had four funnels, and Mücke recommended that the funnel pattern of HMS *Yarmouth* (three round and one oval funnels) be copied with batten and canvas. With this disguise in place, the *Emden* passed into the Indian Ocean and began looking for trade.

On 3 September the *Emden* was approaching Simalur island off the southern coast of Sumatra when the ship's crew spotted HMS *Hampshire*, a cruiser powerful enough to destroy the German ship at long range. Müller escaped detection, however, and then managed to take on board nearly 1,000 tons of the *Markomannia*'s coal before being warned off by an official yacht of the Dutch East Indies government. On 8 September the *Emden* met the 4,094-ton Greek steamer *Pontoporos* carrying 6,500 tons of coal from Calcutta. After careful consideration of the legal situation (the Greek ship was a neutral but carrying contraband cargo) and an examination of the papers on board the *Pontoporos* that revealed the sailing times and destinations of several ships outward-bound from Calcutta, Müller headed the *Emden*, *Markomannia* and *Pontoporos* toward the shipping route linking Calcutta and Colombo in Ceylon.

On 10 September *Emden* intercepted and boarded the *Indus*, a British passenger-carrying freighter en route from Calcutta to Bombay, sent all on board to the *Markomannia*, and then sank the *Indus*. On the following day the *Emden* encountered the *Lovat*, an English ship bound for Bombay to pick up troops, took off all on board and then sank the ship. The tide of success was still running with Müller, and on the following day the *Emden* came up with the *Kabinga*, an English merchant ship carrying jute to New York. The sinking of this ship would make Germany financially responsible for the cargo, so Müller put the personnel from the *Indus* and *Kabinga* on the ship together with a prize crew. During the night of the same day, the *Emden* captured and sank the *Killin*, a Scottish collier making for Bombay from Calcutta with 6,000 tons of coal. Just a few hours later, the German cruiser intercepted and sank the 7,600-ton liner *Diplomat* carrying 1,000 tons of tea.

During the afternoon of the same year, however, the *Emden*'s position was accurately broadcast by a neutral ship, the Italian vessel *Loredano*. In the late afternoon of 14 September the *Emden* sank the 4,000-ton collier *Trabboch*, and in ballast, was encountered and sunk at 18.00 hours on 14 September. Later that

afternoon Müller ordered the *Kabinga*, now carrying the crews of *Killin*, *Diplomat* and *Trabboch*, to the nearby port of Calcutta. Soon after this, the cruiser seized and sank the Scottish freighter *Clan Matheson* making for Calcutta with a shipment of Rolls-Royce cars, steam locomotives, typewriters and thoroughbred racehorses, the last of which were shot before the ship was sunk. The *Clan Matheson*'s crew were transferred to a neutral Norwegian ship on the following day.

On 15 September the *Emden*, *Markomannia* and *Pontoporos* cruised and coaled south of Calcutta, and the *Pontoporos* was then dispatched to a rendezvous at Simalur island. Two days later the *Emden* searched the upper Bay of Bengal, in the process crossing the shipping lane between Madras and Rangoon and between Calcutta and Singapore, but sighted no ships. It was

clearly time for a change, and a raid on Madras recommended itself to Müller for four reasons: it was a long way from the location given by the *Loredano*; it would disturb the British supremacy in India, which had received no real challenge for more than half a century; the Madras port installations were easily accessible from the sea; and one of the *Emden*'s crew had once worked in Madras and thus knew its geography. Madras harbour was protected by Fort St. George, which mounted a battery of 5.9-in (150-mm) guns at least 30 years old. In the evening of 22 September 125 shells were fired into the port area from a range of some 3,550yds (3250m), scoring hits on the tanks of the Burmah Oil Company, which burned fiercely, as well as other parts of the port. None of the return fire hit the *Emden*, which now headed south past the old French colony of Pondicherry and then south-east round Ceylon to reach the great port of Colombo.

By this time there were 14 major Allied warships looking for the *Emden*: this force included the British ships *Empress of Asia*, *Empress of Russia*, *Gloucester*, *Hampshire*, *Minotaur*, *Weymouth* and *Yarmouth*; the Australian ships *Melbourne* and *Sydney*; the French ship *Montcalm*; the Japanese ships *Chikuma*, *Ibuki* and *Yakagi*; and the Russian ship *Askold*. Despite this search effort, the *Emden* encountered and sank the 3,600-ton *King Lud* and the *Tymeric*, the latter carrying a cargo of sugar, before seizing the 4,000-ton *Gryfevale* to carry their crews. *Emden* now needed good-quality coal to fire its boilers, and discovered more than 6,000 tons of this commodity on board the *Buresk*, destined for the British naval base at Hong Kong but now added to the *Emden*'s little flotilla of supporting ships. Müller now headed south,

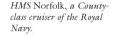

HMS Norfolk, *a County-class cruiser of the Royal Navy.*

*The British flotilla leader
Swift.*

capturing and sinking the *Foyle* and the *Ribera* before the *Emden* reached the Maldive islands and then the Chagos archipelago, where the *Emden*'s crew had the unpleasant task of changing the boiler tubes and overhauling the condensers. Müller now directed his ship's course toward Diego Garcia, where the Germans were welcomed by the French assistant manager of the island's oil company, who had heard no news for three months and therefore did not know of the outbreak of war.

At Diego Garcia the Germans heeled their ship over, cleaned the bottom of barnacles and other growth, and applied a coat of paint. From Diego Garcia the

Emden returned north toward the south-western coast of India, and here its next prizes included the *Clan Grant* on 13 October with a miscellaneous cargo including cattle, the 4,800-ton *Benmohr* carrying machinery, and on 19 October the 7,500-ton *Troilus* carrying valuable metals and rubber. As Müller was gaining these successes, however, the *Markomannia* had been sunk. Coaling from the *Pontoporos* off Pulo Topak, an island off the western coast of Sumatra, during 12 October, the *Markomannia* was surprised by the cruiser *Yarmouth* and sunk with 1,300 tons of coal aboard, while the *Pontoporos* was captured with 5,000 tons of coal in its holds. The *Buresk* was therefore

the *Emden*'s only surviving source of coal.

The *Emden*'s most unusual victim was the 473-ton ocean-going dredger *Ponrabbel*, a British vessel bound for Tasmania but intercepted and sunk on 16 October. The number of prisoners for whom he was responsible was now becoming a burden on Müller's freedom of action, and the German officer solved this problem by capturing the *St. Egbert*, a British ship bound for New York. Two sinking in the same period were the collier *Exford* and the 5,000-ton *Chilkana*.

Early on the morning of 20 October the *Emden* had a close encounter with possible destruction when it came close to the *Hampshire* and the *Empress of Russia*, but was not seen. Six days later the *Emden* and *Buresk* reached Nancowrie in the Nicobar islands to coal in preparation for the dawn raid that Müller was planning against Penang harbour for 28 October.

Entering the harbour on the western side of the Malayan peninsula, the *Emden* saw the Russian light cruiser *Jemtchug* and launched a torpedo that struck the Russian vessel amidships, causing severe damage. There followed heavy and accurate salvoes from the *Emden*'s guns. The *Jemtchug* was on fire and going down fast, but some of her men were returning the *Emden*'s fire. The French destroyer *D'Iberville* also opened fire. The *Emden* put a second torpedo into the *Jemtchug*, which completed the destruction of the Russian ship, and then made for the harbour mouth. A short time later the *Emden* seized the *Glen Turret*, a British ship carrying explosives, but did not sink this wholly legitimate target, instead sending it into Penang with a message from Müller apologizing to the survivors of the *Jemtchug* for not picking them up and to the crew of the pilot boat that the *Emden*

German cruiser's guns. On 30 October the *Emden* seized the 3,000-ton freighter *Newburn* carrying salt to Singapore but then sent it off with the French prisoners for hospital treatment at Khota Raja. During the following day the *Emden* met the *Buresk* near North Pageh island in the Nassau island group, and the next two days were consumed in coaling, cleaning, repairs and recuperation. During this time a Dutch patrol boat arrived on the scene to ensure that *Emden* was outside the 3-mile (4.8-km) limit, and its captain also informed Müller that Portugal had entered the war on the Allied side.

Müller arranged his next rendezvous with the *Buresk*, and steamed for the Sunda Strait dividing Java from Sumatra and thus constituting a natural chokepoint for northbound and southbound traffic. There were no pickings in the area, though, and Müller therefore decided to attack the British telegraph and radio installation on Direction Island in the Cocos (or Keeling) island group, where the Australian, African and Indian cables met. Early on the morning of 9 November the *Emden* anchored off the island, Mücke then taking ashore his landing party of 50 men in a steam launch towing two cutters. The Germans landed at 06.30 hours and encountered no opposition, and after all the people living in the area had been assembled in the square near the telegraph building the German destroyed the installation, using explosives to drop the radio mast but finding it an arduous job to find and cut the undersea cables.

On board the *Emden* a look-out reported a vessel with a single funnel and two masts, a description which fitted the *Buresk*, whose arrival was expected. But the ship was in fact the protected cruiser HMAS *Sydney*, an opponent considerably larger,

LEFT
The French World War II cruiser Montcalm, *photographed in 1935.*

LEFT
Japanese cruisers constructed after World War I were notable for their considerable size, powerful propulsion arrangement for a very high speed, piled-up superstructure and disposition of the main armament in twin or triple turrets, some of them in superfiring positions that were often designed for subsequent replacement by turrets carrying heavier-calibre guns.

had fired on as it was leaving the harbour in the erroneous belief that it was a warship.

Next on the scene was the small French destroyer *Mousquet*, which manoeuvred as though about to launch a torpedo. The *Emden* fired three salvoes, causing the French ship's magazine to explode, but even so the *Mousquet* fired two torpedoes that

the *Emden* evaded without problem even as the French destroyer was sinking. The Germans picked up over 30 survivors, two of whom died during the night of 29 October and were buried at sea. Meanwhile the *Fronde*, sister ship of the *Mousquet*, was following the *Emden* but making sure that it did not come within range of the

The Brooklyn-class USS
Boise *(CL-47) in the New*
Hebrides in 1942.

The Brooklyn-class USS
Boise *(CL-47) in the New*
Hebrides in 1942.

OPPOSITE RIGHT
The Admiral Graf Spee, *a*
Deutschland-class armoured
cruiser of the German
Kriegsmarine.

OPPOSITE LEFT
The Furutaka was the lead
vessel of a two-ship heavy
cruiser class designed to
exploit new constructional
techniques and also to
provide the maximum
firepower possible on a
comparatively low
displacement. As completed
in the later 1920s, at a
displacement of 8,000 tons,
the ships carried six 8-in
(203-mm) guns in single
turrets and six fixed twin
mountings for torpedoes but
were later revised with the
guns in three twin turrets
and eight torpedo tubes in
two trainable quadruple
mountings.

faster and more heavily armed than the
Emden. The arrival of the Australian ship
was no coincidence, for the island's radio
station had broadcast news of the *Emden*'s
arrival before the Germans landed. The
broadcast had been picked up by a convoy
carrying Australian and New Zealand
troops, with the *Sydney* sailing in advance
of the main force of ships. The fate of the
Emden was now in effect sealed. Karl von
Müller was forced to abandon the landing
party as he made for the open sea, and at
09.40 hours the first German salvoes
bracketed the *Sydney* while the fourth salvo
hit the Australian ship and knocked out its
fire-control system. The *Sydney* now pulled
back to a range of 7,000yds (6400m), out
of *Emden*'s range but within the range of
its own 6-in (152-mm) guns, which soon

hit the German cruiser's radio
compartment, bridge, one of the after guns
and the fire-control position. With his ship
increasingly heavily damaged and on fire in
several places, Müller refused to give up
and used the superior agility of his ship to
try to manoeuvre into a position for a
torpedo attack. It was all in vain, and amid
a welter of other shell hits that inflicted yet
more damage and started additional fires
the *Emden* was crippled and its crew were
suffering large numbers of dead, wounded
and injured.
    Müller decided that he must run the
ship aground, and shortly after 11.00
hours the German light cruiser struck the
coral reef south of North Keeling Island.
For the rest of the day the German
survivors suffered the agonies of heat and

thirst, several men being killed as they
tried to swim through the surf. Meanwhile
the *Sydney* had raced off to capture the
Buresk, and on its return opened fire on
the *Emden* once more as the German
ship's colours were still flying. As soon as
Müller had ordered a white flag to be run
up, the Australian ship ceased fire. The
Sydney now freed one of the *Buresk*'s boats,
which it was towing with members of the
collier's German prize crew, who reached
the *Emden* to offer what aid they could.
The *Sydney* turned and headed for
Direction Island to take Mücke's raiding
party, and it was almost 24 hours before
the Australian ship returned and finally
took off the *Emden*'s survivors, of whom
Müller was the last to leave the ship. The
Emden had suffered 141 dead and 65

wounded, and only 117 men were unhurt.

In its three-month independent cruise the *Emden* had covered some 30,000 miles (48280km), sunk or captured 23 merchant ships, destroyed one cruiser and one destroyer, caused £15 million of damage, and caused an Allied naval search involving nearly 80 vessels at one time or another.

France, Italy and Russia followed basically the same course of development at slightly later dates and to smaller overall numbers of ships. The same was basically true of the U.S. Navy, which entered the 20th century with just two armoured cruisers, 15 protected cruisers and three unprotected cruisers, but then began a major programme of development and construction that saw the delivery of more advanced cruisers at an increasing rate. On the outbreak of World War I, when the U.S.A. was still neutral, the most modern type of armoured cruiser was the Tennessee class of four ships launched between 1904

and 1906 with a displacement of 14,500 tons, an armament of four 10-in (254-mm) guns in two twin turrets, 16 6-in (152-mm) guns in casemated mountings, 22 3-in (76-mm) guns, 12 3-pdr guns and four 21-in (533-mm) torpedo tubes, protection in the form of a 5-in (127-mm) belt and 9-in (229-mm) turrets, and a speed of 22kt on the 23,000hp (17150kW) delivered to two shafts by triple-expansion steam engines. Roughly contemporary was the St Louis class of three protected cruisers with a displacement of 9,700 tons, an armament of 14 6-in (152-mm) and 18 3-in (76-mm) guns, protection in the form of a 4-in (102-mm) belt and 5-in (127-mm) conning tower, and a speed of 22kt on the 21,000hp (15660kW) delivered to two shafts by triple-expansion steam engines. The only unprotected cruisers were three wholly obsolete ships of the Montgomery class launched in 1891 and 1892, and the American cruiser force was completed by

the three scout cruisers of the Chester class launched in 1907 with a displacement of 3,750 tons, an armament of two 5-in (127-mm) guns, six 3-in (76-mm) guns and two 21-in (533-mm) torpedo tubes, no protection, and a speed of 24kt on the 16,000hp (11930kW) delivered to two shafts by steam turbines.

Japan followed basically the same course as its Western counterparts, its last armoured cruisers being the two ships of the Kasuga class originally ordered from an Italian yard by Argentina, which sold the two units to Japan in 1903. The ships had a displacement of some 7,650 tons, an

The USS Chester (CA 27) was a heavy cruiser of the Northampton class, an elegant type completed in the early 1930s with a primary armament of nine 8-in (203-mm) guns in three triple turrets.

armament of one 10-in (254-mm) and two 8-in (203-mm) or four 8-in (203-mm) guns in one single and one twin or two twin turrets, 14 6-in (152-mm) guns, 10 3-in (76-mm) guns, six 3-pdr guns and four 18-in (457-mm) torpedo tubes, protection in the form of a 5.9-in (150-mm) belt, barbettes and conning tower, and a speed of 20kt on the 13,500hp (10065kW) delivered to two shafts by triple-expansion steam engines. The equivalent protected cruiser type was the Chikuma class of three ships completed in 1912 with a

displacement of 4,400 tons, an armament of six 6-in (152-mm) guns, eight 12-pdr guns and four 21-in (533-mm) torpedo tubes, protection in the form of a 3-in (76-mm) deck and 4-in (102-mm) conning tower, and a speed of 26kt on the 22,500hp (16775kW) provided to two shafts by steam turbines.

In the course of World War I Japan kept a close watch on warship developments by the U.K., its ally and still the world leader in warship design, and in 1916 felt confident enough of the utility of the new light

cruiser concept to order an initial class of two Tenryu-class light cruisers modelled closely on the British C type that included the closely related Caroline, Cambrian, Centaur, Caledon, Ceres and Carlisle classes. These two Japanese ships were completed only after the end of World War I, but paved the way for future Japanese light cruiser developments.

The main implication of World War I, as far as cruiser design was concerned, was that the naval reconnaissance role was better undertaken by aircraft than by the cruiser,

which was thereafter operated mainly in alternative roles such as escort of major convoys, commerce protection and raiding, and gunfire support of amphibious operations. This had become evident to the British in the later stages of World War I, when they had started to build cruisers somewhat larger than the standard light cruisers that had proved so effective in the earlier part of the war. Many of these latter were still comparatively new ships and were retained in service during the 1920s and 1930s, increasingly for second-line tasks such as the protection of trade routes. The oldest classes to survive into World War II were the Caledon, Carlisle and Ceres classes, which totalled three, five and five ships respectively. The Caledon-class ships were altered little in real terms from the standard in which they fought in World War I, but the three of the Ceres class and all of the Carlisle-class ships were modified

considerably in overall capability by their conversion to an anti-aircraft cruiser standard. The Coventry and Curlew were prototype conversions with a primary armament of 10 4-in (102-mm) anti-aircraft guns in single high-angle mountings and 16 2-pdr anti-aircraft guns in two octuple mountings, but the definitive standard adopted for the other six ships was eight 4-in (102-mm) anti-aircraft guns in four twin high-angle turrets and four 2-pdr anti-aircraft guns in a quadruple mounting.

Four of the five Improved Birmingham-class cruisers survived for limited service in World War II, and in basic terms these larger and generally more effective ships had a displacement of some 9,700 tons, an armament of seven or five 7.5-in (191-mm) guns in single mountings and four or five 4-in (102-mm) anti-aircraft guns in single high-angle mountings and, reflecting the increased threat posed by aircraft in World

War II, eight 2-pdr anti-aircraft guns in two quadruple mountings and 10 20-mm anti-aircraft cannon, protection in the form of a 3-in (76-mm) belt and 1.5-in (38-mm) deck, and a speed of 30.5kt on the 65,000hp (48465kW) delivered to four shafts by steam turbines. Another survivor from World War I and its immediate aftermath was the D class of eight light cruisers originally built in the Danae and Delhi classes, and the two cruisers of the E class completed in the early 1920s with a displacement of some 7,550 tons, an armament of seven 6-in (152-mm) guns and three 4-in (102-mm) anti-aircraft guns, protection in the form of a 2.5-in (64-mm) belt and 1-in (25-mm) deck, and a speed of

ABOVE
Triple 6-in (152-mm) guns aboard HMS Belfast. *1972.*

ABOVE LEFT
HMS Belfast *arriving in London, October 1971.*

The USS Biloxi, *a Cleveland-class cruiser during World War II.*

The USS Newport News *(CA-148), a Salem-class cruiser off the coast of Oahu, Hawaii. 1967.*

33kt on the 80,000hp (59650kW) delivered to four shafts by steam turbines.

The completion of these ships preceded the limitation treaties agreed in the 1920s and 1930s. These treaties placed no limit on the numbers of cruisers that could be built, but did impose qualitative and, later, total tonnage restrictions while at the same time granting the right to replace elderly ships. In combination with analysis of operational experience in World War I, the conditions imposed by the treaties paved the way for the evolution of the cruiser into two forms differentiated primarily by gun calibre: the light cruiser was generally a smaller type with guns of up to 6-in (152-mm) calibre and only limited armour protection, while the heavy cruiser was a larger type with guns of up to 8-in (203-mm) calibre and relatively more effective armour protection.

In British service, the first of these modern cruiser classes was the Kent class of seven heavy cruisers, including two for the Royal Australian Navy, with a displacement

The cruiser Prinz Eugen. *22 May 1945.*

of some 9,800 tons, an armament of eight 8-in (203-mm) gun in four twin turrets, eight 4-in (102-mm) anti-aircraft guns in four twin high-angle turrets, eight 2-pdr anti-aircraft guns in two quadruple mountings, and eight 21-in (533-mm) torpedo tubes, protection in the form of a 5-in (127-mm) belt and 4-in (102-mm) turrets, and a speed of 31.5kt on the 80,000hp (59650kW) supplied to four shafts by steam turbines. The same basic pattern of armament was followed in the London class of three heavy cruisers and the Norfolk class of two heavy cruisers, but the number of 8-in (203-mm) main guns was reduced to six in three twin mountings in the two smaller heavy cruisers of the York class that followed in the late 1920s.

The service life typical of a British heavy cruiser in the first half of World War II is exemplified by that of HMS *Exeter* which, as noted above, had been designed and built in the 1920s as a cheaper counterpart to the high-quality but costly County-class cruisers. In a relatively brief career in world War II, the *Exeter* was a participant in victory against the odds and then catastrophic defeat, but in the process acquired a superb reputation as a fighting ship.

Though successful in its primary aim of preventing expensive and politically destabilizing competition in the construction of capital warships, the Washington Naval Treaty of 1921 had exactly the opposite effect on cruiser construction, for the treaty's limits of a 10,000-ton displacement and an 8-in (203-mm) calibre armament rapidly became the standard into which naval architects crammed as much capability as they could. In the case of the U.K., however, the Admiralty wanted not so much a few very powerful ships but rather a larger number of

The HMS Diadem, *a modified Dido-class cruiser, later PNS* Babur *(84) of the Pakistan navy.*

individually less capable ships possessing the endurance to allow them to patrol British maritime trade routes and show the flag in distant parts of the empire and the world. It was thus with some reluctance that the Admiralty did agree to the production of a class of 8-in (203-mm) heavy cruisers as an answer to such ships in service or under construction for other navies. This agreed type was the A or County class of 13 ships starting with the four vessels of the London subclass in the 1925–26 estimates and following with the seven and two ships of the Kent and Norfolk subclasses respectively. The ships had powerful armament, excellent endurance, high speed and a good standard of habitability, but these features were bought only at the expense of protection. The ships also cost

£2 million each, which was seen as a very high unit price at a time when all national expenditure was being trimmed.

The inevitable result was the creation of the very much smaller B-class cruisers with a standard displacement reduced from about 9,900 tons to less than 8,400 through the reduction in the hull length from 630ft (192m) to 515ft (157m): this meant the trimming of the main battery from eight 8-in (203-mm) guns in four twin turrets to six 8-in (203-mm) guns in three twin turrets, and the reduction of the bunkerage from 3,200 to a mere 1,900 tons resulting in a considerable reduction in range. The three funnels of the A class were reduced to two by the trunking of the two forward uptakes into only one casing, which was therefore thicker than the after unit.

Protection was very light, with a 2-in (51-mm) horizontal deck to protect against long-range plunging fire and a 2/3-in (51/76-mm) vertical belt over the machinery spaces to protect against short-range flat fire. Although a class of seven B-class cruisers was originally planned, financial cutbacks meant that in the event only two were built. The first of the class was HMS *York*, followed into service during 1931 by HMS *Exeter*, the fourth ship to carry that name and constructed, appropriately, at Devonport Dockyard.

On the outbreak of World War II the *Exeter*, the County-class heavy cruiser HMS *Cumberland* and the Leander-class light cruiser HMS *Ajax* constituted the South American Division of the forces available to the Royal Navy's Commander-in-Chief

The USS Canberra *(CA 70), a Canberra-class heavy cruiser of the U.S. Navy underway off Point Loma, California. 1967.*

South Atlantic. This enormous area of water was important mainly for being crossed by several very important trade routes. The German naval high command understood full well the vulnerability of the U.K.'s maritime trade and had constructed ships designed specifically for the decimation of the shipping plying these routes. Among these ships were the three Panzerschiffe or pocket battleships. These were well protected, had diesel engines for great endurance, and possessed a nicely balanced armament including six 11-in (280-mm), eight 5.9-in (150-mm) and six 4.1-in (105-mm) guns. The German rationale was that these ships could outfight what they could not outrun, and outrun what they could not outfight.

Shortly before the outbreak of war, two of the pocket battleships moved into the Atlantic. One of these was the KMS *Admiral Graf Spee* with orders, in the event of hostilities, to disrupt British trade but at the same time to avoid action with warships that could cause damage far from dockyard facilities.

The pocket battleship started work in earnest near the end of September 1939, sinking the liner *Clement* off the Brazilian coast. To catch the *Admiral Graf Spee* the French and British assembled no fewer than eight separate hunting groups. Of these Force G comprised the South American Division reinforced by the Royal New Zealand Navy's HMNZS *Achilles*, a sistership of the *Ajax*. Commanded by

Commodore Henry Harwood, this division had a huge operational area, but despite the *Admiral Graf Spee*'s activities over a large part of the South Atlantic and even the Indian Ocean, Harwood was of the firm belief that the German ship would eventually attempt to disrupt the important shipping routes to and from the estuary of the River Plate between Argentina and Uruguay. That Harwood was right in his assessment was confirmed on 13 December, when the *Admiral Graf Spee* was sighted off the coast of Uruguay. At this time Harwood has only three of his cruisers, the *Cumberland* being near the Falklands.

Harwood had carefully discussed his tactical thinking with his captains, and the British plan to divide the fire of the German

aThe USS Chicago was launched in 1944 as the CA 136, one of the 'Baltimore' class of heavy cruisers with an armament of nine 8-in (203-mm) guns in three triple turrets, but was recommissioned in 1964 as the CG 11 after extensive conversion as a guided-missile cruiser for the escort of major surface forces faced with the threat of air attack. All the 8-in (203-mm) guns were removed, leaving a gun armament of only two 5-in (127-mm) dual-purpose guns in single turrets, and the primary armament became four twin-arm launchers for surface-to-air missiles: two of these were allocated to the Talos long-range system with 104 missiles, and the other two to the Tartar medium-range system with 84 missiles. The ship, one of three such conversions, was decommissioned in 1980 after the arrival of purpose-designed missile cruisers.

ABOVE
The USS Oklahoma City
(CG-5), a converted
Cleveland-class guided
missile cruiser of the U.S.
Navy. 1976.

ABOVE RIGHT
USS Belknap *(DLG-26) in*
Agusta Bay, Sicily as part of
the U.S. 6th Fleet in the
Mediterranean.

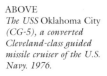

ship went smoothly into operation as the cruisers deployed with the *Exeter* on one side and the two light cruisers on the other side. The action began at a range of more than 19,000yds (11315m) as the *Admiral Graf Spee* initially fired on the two light cruisers, which could put up a greater volume of fire. However, as the *Exeter*'s salvoes began to straddle the *Admiral Graf Spee*, Captain Hans Langsdorff ordered the fire of his ship to be switched to the British heavy cruiser. Turning nearly 180° from its initial south-easterly course, the *Admiral Graf Spee* had the *Exeter* slightly abaft her port beam, with the six 11-in (280-mm) guns of its primary battery bearing, but was able at the same time to engage the two light cruisers with the 5.9-in (150-mm) guns of its secondary battery. The Germans had the advantage of radar which could pass ranges to the gunlayers, and the *Exeter* was soon hit by three 11-in (280-mm) shells, losing a turret and the steering. The heavy

cruiser, now under emergency control, pressed on and launched its starboard torpedoes without effect. Hit again, the *Exeter* started listing to starboard and turned in that direction to fire her port torpedoes, which the *Admiral Graf Spee* again evaded.

By this time the damage was beginning to tell on the *Exeter*'s accuracy and rate of fire. The pocket battleship secured two more hits on the heavy cruiser, this time putting another turret out of action and starting a fire that soon became serious. The *Exeter* was now forced to pull out of the fight, disengaging and steaming to the south.

The two light cruisers, which had not yet suffered any significant damage, now manoeuvred to create the threat that would deter the *Admiral Graf Spee* from pursuing the *Exeter*. But the German ship now seemed unwilling to press home its tactical advantage and tended to the west, with the

Ajax and *Achilles* shadowing, to reach the roads off Montevideo. The *Admiral Graf Spee* had suffered only modest casualties (including 36 killed by comparison with the *Exeter*'s 61 killed), and the physical damage it had suffered from 21 hits was superficial. Nevertheless, in the belief that very much more capable Allied forces were about to reach the area and so prevent any chance of a return to Germany, Langsdorff ordered the scuttling of his ship, after which he committed suicide. Thus the British tactical reverse of the Battle of the River Plate became a major operational victory.

After receiving temporary repairs at Port Stanley in the Falkland Islands, the *Exeter* returned to the U.K. for a considerable time in dockyard hands for major repairs. Once these had been completed, the ship proceeded to the Far East, where the situation was worsening in a most threatening way. In December 1941 the Japanese committed themselves to World

War II, and as part of their initial moves to extend their empire into south-east Asia and defensive perimeter in the Pacific, swept into Malaya and Burma before falling on the Dutch East Indies.

An extemporized assembly of Australian, British, Dutch and American warships made up the so-called ABDA force which, by the end of February 1942, had been badly mauled as it tried without success to check the Japanese amphibious advances. In February 1942 Singapore fell and Java remained the last Allied bastion before Australia, which at the time was thought to be a Japanese objective. On 21 February 1942 it was reported that two Japanese forces were approaching Java: the larger, eastern group comprised 41 merchant ships carrying the main invasion force and covered by four cruisers and 13 destroyers under the command of Rear Admiral Takeo Takagi.

Under a Dutch officer, Rear Admiral

Karel Doorman, a force of five cruisers (including the *Exeter*) and 10 destroyers sailed to intercept this invasion fleet. Measured in terms of firepower, there was little difference between the forces of the Allies and the Japanese, but the latter were superior in the size and armament of their individual cruisers, and in the morale of its men.

Battle was joined on 27 February, and after an opening gunnery duel the Japanese launched a determined torpedo attack at the moment when the *Exeter*, lying second in the Allied cruiser line, was hit in the boiler room by an 8-in (203-mm) shell from the *Nachi*. On fire and its speed reduced to a mere 5kt, the *Exeter* pulled out of line and the ships astern of it were thrown into confusion. Covered by four destroyers making smoke, the *Exeter* turned south, in the process taking the liaison officer and the code books through which the Dutch-speaking Doorman communicated with the

English-speaking remainder of his force.

Successive probes by Doorman's reorganized force against the Japanese transports were successfully parried by the Japanese warships, the Allied ships being driven back to the point at which the crippled *Exeter* once again became embroiled. Harried by Japanese light cruisers and destroyers, the British heavy cruiser was saved only by the spirited defence of the escorting destroyers, of which HMS *Electra* was lost. The battle now moved off to the north once more in a number of short but sharp little engagements. After nightfall, disaster struck the Allies as Doorman was killed when both his Dutch cruisers were sunk, but the *Exeter* and her remaining screen meanwhile reached at least temporary safety at Surabaya.

Patched and partially refuelled, the little group set off during the evening of the following day in an effort to reach Ceylon. The ABDA combined force had ceased to exist, for the Battle of the Java Sea had cost the Allies not only their two Dutch cruisers but also all but five of their destroyers. The *Exeter*'s little flotilla was spotted by Japanese reconnaissance aircraft as it left Surabaya, and even though it was capable of 23kt by daybreak on 1 March, the *Exeter* found itself confronted by a Japanese force of four heavy cruisers and four destroyers. In a wholly unequal battle that lasted for more than two hours and was typified by determined attacks by the destroyers HMS *Encounter* and USS *Pope* before the *Exeter* succumbed to gun and torpedo hits, rolled over to starboard and sank. The two destroyers were also sunk in the following 30 minutes.

Construction during the 1920s gave the Royal Navy a strong force of heavy cruisers, and in the 1930s the services focus switched

The U.S. Navy's guided-missile cruiser USS Long Beach *was also the world's first nuclear-powered warship, being commissioned in 1961. The 14,000-ton warship is fitted with advanced guidance and tracking radars and is armed with two twin-launcher RIM-2 Terrier missile installations forward and one twin-launcher RIM-8 Talos missile installation on the aft deck. Situated directly behind the main superstructure can be just seen the Asroc launchers for deploying nuclear depth-charges against submarines with two conventional guns aft of this. The USS* Long Beach *is here seen entering Pearl Harbor, Hawaii. 17 June 1966.*

*The HMS Blake (C99), a
Tiger-class helicopter cruiser
entering Hong Kong waters.
1974.*

to the replacement of the light cruiser types
surviving from World War I with more
advanced ships designed to complement the
new generation of heavy cruisers. The first
result of this effort was the Leander class of
light cruisers of which eight were
constructed as five for the U.K. and three
for Australia. The British ships had a
displacement of some 7,200 tons, an
armament of eight 6-in (152-mm) guns in
four twin turrets, eight 4-in (102-mm) anti-
aircraft guns in four twin high-angle turrets,
eight 2-pdr anti-aircraft guns in two
quadruple mountings, and eight 21-in
(533-mm) torpedo tubes, protection in the
form of a 4-in (102-mm) belt and 2-in
(51-mm) deck, and a speed of 32.5kt on
the 72,000hp (53685kW) delivered to four
shafts by steam turbines. The three

Australian ships differed in their
displacement of some 6,900 tons and lack
of 2-pdr pom-pom anti-aircraft guns. The
following Arethusa class of four ships was
somewhat smaller with a displacement of
some 5,250 tons, an armament of six 6-in
(152-mm) guns in three triple turrets, eight
4-in (102-mm) anti-aircraft guns in four
twin high-angle turrets, eight 2-pdr anti-
aircraft guns in two quadruple mountings
and six 21-in (533-mm) torpedo tubes,
protection in the form of a 2-in (51-mm)
belt and deck, and a speed of 32.25kt on
the 64,000hp (47720kW) delivered to four
shafts by steam turbines.

The next class to come out of British
yards was a hybrid type combining the size
and most of the protection of the heavy
cruiser with a beefed-up version of the

typical light cruiser armament. This was the
Southampton class of which 10 examples
were built in three subclasses totalling five,
three and two ships respectively. The first
two subclasses had displacements of 9,100
and 9,400 tons respectively, an armament of
12 6-in (152-mm) guns in four triple
turrets, eight 4-in (102-mm) anti-aircraft
guns in four twin high-angle turrets, eight
2-pdr anti-aircraft guns in two quadruple
mountings and six 21-in (533-mm) torpedo
tubes, protection in the form of a 4-in
(102-mm) belt and 2-in (51-mm) deck and
turrets, and a speed of 32 and 32.5kt on the
75,000 or 82,500hp (55920 and 61510kW)
respectively delivered to four shafts by steam
turbines. The ships of the last subclass had a
displacement of 10,000 tons, an armament
of 12 6-in (152-mm) guns in four triple
turrets, 12 4-in (102-mm) anti-aircraft guns
in six twin high-angle turrets, 16 2-pdr anti-
aircraft guns in two octuple mountings and
six 21-in (533-mm) torpedo tubes,
improved protection in the form of a 4.5-in
(114-mm) belt and 2-in (51-mm) deck, and
a speed of 32kt on the 80,000hp
(59650kW) delivered to four shafts by
steam turbines. The ships proved
remarkably resilient in service, and saw very
extensive use.

When the ships of the Southampton
class were being laid down in the mid-
1930s, it had already become clear that the
warplane was rapidly becoming one of the
most potent weapons faced by naval forces,
and the British responded to this increasing
threat with a classic class of dedicated anti-
aircraft cruisers, the Dido class, of which 16
examples were completed in 11- and five-
ship subclasses with a displacement of 5,450
and 5,770 tons respectively and an
armament in the first subclass of 10 5.25-in
(133-mm) dual-purpose guns in five twin
turrets, eight 2-pdr anti-aircraft guns in two

The French cruiser Colbert *(C 611) in 1981.*

quadruple mountings and six 21-in (533-mm) torpedo tubes, or in the second subclass of eight 5.25-in (133-mm) dual-purpose guns in four twin turrets, 12 2-pdr anti-aircraft guns in three quadruple mountings and six 21-in (533-mm) torpedo tubes. Features common to both subclasses were protection in the form of a 3-in (76-mm) belt and 2-in (51-mm) deck, and a speed of 33kt on the 62,000hp (46225kW) delivered to four shafts by steam turbines.

Next in British construction came the Fiji class that reverted to the standard light cruiser concept, and these 11 ships were completed in eight- and three-ship subclasses whose common features included protection in the form of a 3.25-in (83-mm) belt and 2-in (51-mm) deck, and a speed of 33kt on the 72,500hp (54055kW) delivered to four shafts by steam turbines. The first subclass had a displacement of 8,000 tons and an armament of 12 6-in (152-mm) guns in

four triple turrets, eight 4-in (102-mm) anti-aircraft guns in four twin turrets, nine 2-pdr anti-aircraft guns in two quadruple and one single mountings and six 21-in (533-mm) torpedo tubes, while the second subclass had a displacement of 8,800 tons, and an armament of nine 6-in (152-mm) guns in three triple turrets, 20 2-pdr anti-aircraft guns in five quadruple mountings and 20 20-mm anti-aircraft cannon in 10 twin mountings.

The last British cruiser class of World

War II was the Minotaur class, of which six examples were completed in three-ship subclasses during or immediately after the war to a design based on that of the second Fiji subclass. The features that the two types shared were principally the hull and the protection, the latter in the form of a 3.5-in (89-mm) belt and 2-in (51-mm) deck and turrets. The ships of the first Minotaur subclass had a displacement of 8,800 tons, an armament of nine 6-in (152-mm) guns in three triple turrets, 10 4-in (102-mm) anti-aircraft guns in five twin turrets, 16 2-pdr anti-aircraft guns in four quadruple mountings, eight 40-mm anti-aircraft guns in eight single mountings and six 21-in (533-mm) torpedo tubes, and a speed of 32.5kt on the 72,500hp (54,055kW) delivered to four shafts by steam turbines, while the ships of the second Minotaur subclass, whose construction had been suspended at the end of World War II and resumed only at a later time, had a displacement of 9,550 tons, an armament of four 6-in (152-mm) dual-purpose guns in two twin turrets and six 3-in (76-mm) anti-aircraft guns in three twin turrets, and a speed of 31.5kt on the 80,000hp (59650kW) delivered to four shafts by steam turbines. It should be noted, however, that reduction in the number of guns carried by the ships of the second subclass was more than counterbalanced by the incorporation of the latest fire-control methods, which included extensive radar equipment.

In World War II, existing cruisers were extensively modified as they underwent refits or major repairs after suffering battle damage. The major part of this improvement effort was devoted to the upgrading of the ships' anti-aircraft capability by the addition of 20-mm cannon in place of the original machine-guns, the later replacement of these 20-mm cannon by 40-mm weapons, the boosting of fire control by the addition of radar systems to the original fit of optical systems, the removal of aircraft (between one and three depending on the specific class) together with their associated hangar and catapult facilities as long-range warning of ships and aircraft was increasingly and more reliably provided by radar, and in many ships the removal of one of the after main gun turrets to provide additional deck area for anti-aircraft weapons and radar equipment.

The Americans disposed of most of their World War I cruisers during the 1920s and 1930s, but at the time of the U.S.A.'s entry into World War II as a result of the Japanese attack on Pearl Harbor in December 1941, the Americans had a total of 37 cruisers in the form of 18 heavy cruisers and 19 light cruisers. The size of this total was fortunate, for after the Japanese attack on Pearl Harbor and the loss, permanent or temporary, of many of its battleships, the U.S. Navy in general and its Pacific fleet in particular was forced to rely on its cruiser force as its primary surface warfare capability as the surviving battleships were used for the escort of vital troop convoys. The intensity of this surface warfare in the period up to the middle of 1943 is attested by the fact that all of the pre-war cruisers involved in the protracted Solomons campaign were either sunk or damaged, and after the middle of 1943 the surviving cruisers were generally used for the gunfire support of amphibious landing and for the escort of carrier task forces. In common with their British counterparts, the American cruisers exploited every extensive stay in port, either for refit or repair, for enhancement of their fighting capabilities: radar was fitted and the anti-aircraft armament was considerably enhanced by the adoption of both greater firepower and specialized fire-control systems. The former was based on the lighter type of weapons (of 20-mm and 40-mm calibres for the most part) designed to provide a high volume of fire for short-range defence against mass air attacks. The type of enhancement provided in cruisers, which played a key part in American naval thinking in World War II, is exemplified by the revisions to the Northampton-class ships, which each received 16 40-mm guns in four quadruple mountings and about 27 20-mm cannon in single mountings.

The addition of so much additional topweight sometimes led to a severe loss of stability, but even so the ships displayed a remarkable ability to survive battle damage. This was a testament to the ships' excellent construction and basic design, which emphasized extreme sturdiness. Even so, there were some structural failures as a result of poor welding: for example, the *Pittsburgh* lost 90ft (27.4m) of its bows in a typhoon after the failure of a poor weld. In common with most other navies of the period, the U.S. Navy standardized two types of cruiser during the 1920s. These were the heavy cruiser with an armament of 8-in (203-mm) guns and moderately thick armour, and the light cruiser with an armament of 6-in (152-mm) guns and comparatively thin armour.

The oldest class of heavy cruiser to see service during World War II was the Pensacola class, whose two units were launched in 1929. These were built in accordance with the dictates of the Washington Naval Treaty and were flushdecked ships with a low freeboard. The U.S.A. was the last of the treaty signatories to start on the construction of

new heavy cruisers, and was therefore able to capitalize on its perceptions of the heavy cruisers that had already been built by other signatories: the French and Italians had both opted for high speed at the expense of protection in the Duquesne and Trento-class ships respectively. The Japanese had been influenced by initial reports of very heavy gun armament on the proposed American ships and had therefore opted for an additional main gun turret as well as good protection and a high turn of speed in the Myoko class that in fact exceeded the treaty displacement limit by some 1,000 tons. The British had in the Kent class decided for a design that was altogether lighter than its contemporaries in firepower, protection and speed but which, as events were to prove, was extremely robustly built and possessed excellent sea-keeping qualities. After assessing these classes, the Americans opted for an approach similar to that of the Japanese with a main armament of 10 8-in (203-mm) guns located not in five twin turrets, as in the Japanese ships, but in superfiring pairs of triple and twin turrets located fore and aft of the main superstructure block. This primary armament was complemented by eight 5-in (127-mm) dual-purpose guns in single mountings, and the other details of these ships included a full-load displacement of 12,050 tons, protection in the form of a 3-in (76-mm) belt and 2-in (51-mm) deck, and a speed of 32.5kt on the 107,000hp (79780kW) delivered to four shafts by steam turbines. A notable feature of the basic design was the considerable weight saving that the Americans managed to achieve in the design and construction of these fine ships, which had a displacement some 900 tons under the treaty standard displacement limit of 10,000 tons and therefore represented better value than the

A stern view of the Kirov, *a Kirov-class battle-cruiser during running trials in the Baltic. The ship carries a formidable array of armament including SA-N-6 surface-to-air missiles and SS-N-19 anti-ship missiles. Toward the stern are four 23-mm cannon turrets with, further forward, two 3.94-in (100-mm) guns. Hidden behind hull panels are two 21-in (533-mm) torpedo tubes. The stern door for the MF-towed, variable-depth sonar can be clearly seen. 1981.*

The Kresta II-class cruiser
Marshal Voroshilov *passing*
through the English Channel
as seen from an RAF
Nimrod. The quadruple
SS-N-10 missile launch
tubes can be clearly seen
flanking the bridge. 1974.

considerably heavier Japanese ships.

The Pensacola class set the pattern for the following heavy cruiser classes, which began with the six ships of the Northampton class launched in 1929 and 1930. This was in effect a development of the Pensacola class with a raised fore castle for improved seaworthiness and reduced wetness forward, and with further weight-saving effected by the replacement of the Pensacola-class primary armament of ten 8-in (203-mm) guns in four turrets with a primary armament of nine 8-in (203-mm) guns in three triple turrets located as a superfiring pair forward and a single turret aft. The ships initially displayed a tendency toward severe rolling, but this was cured by the installation of deeper bilge keels, and the primary details of these ships included a full-load displacement of some 12,250 tons, an armament of nine 8-in (203-mm) guns and eight 5-in (127-mm) dual-purpose guns, protection in the form of a 3-in (76-mm) belt and 2-in (51-mm) deck, and a speed of 32.5kt on the 107,000hp (79780kW) delivered to four shafts by steam turbines.

The sea battles fought around the Solomon Islands during the second half of 1942, comprised a bloody series of six short, sharp engagements that were often dominated by cruisers. The battles often took place at night as the Japanese believed that they had a decisive advantage in night fighting. The early stages of the fighting for the island of Guadalcanal, on which the Japanese had landed during July 1942, were characterized by serious setbacks for U.S. and Australian naval forces in several stunning blows, particularly in the Battle of Savo Island on the night of 8/9 August 1942.

After the strategic defeat of the Japanese in the Battle of Midway in June 1942, the Americans switched over to the offensive in the Pacific. This resulted, among other operations, in the landing on Guadalcanal and the neighbouring Tulagi islands as a first stage in the reconquest of the Solomons. The 1st Marine Division landed on 7 August, and within hours gained control over the yet poorly established Japanese garrison. This early example of an amphibious assault entailed the presence offshore of a considerable number of transports, which would need an estimated four days to discharge. In addition to local naval cover, the ships of the American invasion force had the distant support of Vice Admiral Frank J. Fletcher's carrier task force. These three carriers comprised virtually all the flightdecks remaining to the U.S.A. in the Pacific theatre and, anxious not to hazard them a moment longer than necessary, Fletcher decided to withdraw after only 36 hours.

Initially off-balance at the time of the American landings, the Japanese reacted swiftly. Vice Admiral Gunichi Mikawa departed from Rabaul within hours of the American landing to cover the 700 miles (1125km) to Guadalcanal with a force centred on his flagship, the heavy cruiser *Chokai*, and including two light cruisers and a destroyer. By 14.00 hours the Japanese squadron had covered 200 miles (320km) and had rendezvoused near Bougainville with a powerful reinforcement of four more heavy cruisers. Pressing on to the south-east, Mikawa used the passage between the double island chain of the Solomons, a passage that was soon to become known as The Slot.

The north-west was the direction from which the Americans expected any Japanese riposte to come, and they had therefore covered this quadrant with reconnaissance flights, which twice spotted the advancing Japanese ships during the morning of 8 August. The reconnaissance reports were poorly worded and took considerable time to trickle though the official system, so Rear Admiral Richmond K. Turner, commanding the amphibious force, learned on between 18.00 and 19.00 hours that a Japanese force was approaching and also that Fletcher's carriers were leaving. The latter was alarming, but the former was not treated with undue concern as the report indicated that the enemy force consisted largely of seaplane tenders: this accorded fully with the type of base that the Japanese had been establishing on Tulagi, and such ships posed no direct threat. With imminent attack not anticipated, no special precautions were taken as the Allied force was thought generally superior as it comprised six heavy cruisers, two light cruisers and four destroyers, a mixed American and Australian force under the command of an Australian officer, Rear Admiral Crutchley. This force could not be concentrated, however, because of the geography of the approaches to the landing area.

Between Guadalcanal and the islands of Florida and Tulagi to the north there is a deep channel between 15 and 25 miles (24 and 40km) wide. At the wider end, to the north-west, which Mikawa was now approaching, the sound is divided by Savo Island, about 5 miles (8km) wide. Between Guadalcanal and Savo, Crutchley had established a southern force comprising his flagship HMAS *Australia*, her sistership HMAS *Canberra* and the USS *Chicago*, and between Savo and Florida/Tulagi was a complementary northern force of three heavy cruisers, the USS *Astoria*, USS *Quincy* and USS *Vincennes*. Across the approaches to the north-west, and serving as pickets to warn of the Japanese approach, were two radar-equipped American

The Slava, *1983.*

destroyers. The south-eastern approach to the area, which was thought a less likely avenue of Japanese advance, was allocated to two light cruisers and two destroyers. In overall terms, Crutchley's disposition of his force was tactically sound, at least in theory.

The evening of 8 August was very dark, with low cloud and periods of heavy rain. Turner was distinctly worried by the withdrawal of Fletcher's carriers, and summoned Crutchley to a meeting. Crutchley covered the 20 miles (32km) to the area off Lunga Point on Guadalcanal's northern shore in the *Australia*, leaving the southern force to his deputy in the *Chicago*. Crutchley arrived off Guadalcanal at 22.30 hours, and at this time the Japanese force was only some 50 miles (80km) distant but closing rapidly and undetected.

At 00.43 hours on 9 August the Japanese, in line ahead with the *Chokai* in the van, sighted an American destroyer at the distance of more than 5 miles (8km) despite the darkness. This was the USS *Blue* which was covering the approach to the southern channel past Savo Island as the USS *Ralph Talbot* was covering the northern approach. Despite its length and approach from the expected direction, the Japanese forces was not detected visually or by radar, and passed between the two ships at about 26kt. Anxious to deliver his attack and withdraw before any air strike from Fletcher's carriers, which he believed still to be present, Mikawa risked the loss of surprise by launching reconnaissance aircraft. These were seen by the Americans but the significance was not appreciated.

By 01.25 hours the Japanese had Savo Island abeam, and soon after this sighted the two remaining cruisers of the southern group. At 01.38 hours the Japanese ships opened their attack with the typical ploy of a salvo of torpedoes and, only minutes later,

the peace of the night was shattered by the impact of two torpedoes on the *Canberra* just as air-dropped flares bloomed overhead. The *Chicago* was equally surprised and, even as the alarm was sounded, a torpedo shattered the ship's bow. The battle was only four minutes old, and the Japanese ships had still not been seen. The two crippled cruisers nonetheless attempted to reply as the Japanese forces swept by them and started a turn to port round the south-eastern side of Savo Island. This disrupted

the Japanese line to the extent that the Japanese now advanced in two parallel columns which, by a chance favourable to the Japanese, nicely enclosed the northern group of cruisers. The Chicago had not alerted them, and they had not responded to the sounds of the first engagement only 5 miles (8km) away.

The three American cruisers, steaming in line ahead at a mere 10kt with their guns unmanned and trained fore-and-aft, now found themselves lit up at close range by

searchlights. At a range of barely 400yds (365m), the Japanese opened fire with every weapon at their disposal. The engagement lasted a mere 10 minutes, and ended with the three American cruisers on fire, mainly as a result of the fuel for their floatplanes leaking from shattered tanks and catching fire.

Nothing stood between Mikawa and his primary target, the transport ships of the American assault forces. Yet at 02.00 hours Mikawa ordered a retirement, in the course

of which the two radar pickets were fired upon. Allied losses were four heavy cruisers sunk and one, the *Chicago*, severely damaged together with more than 1,000 men killed, while the Japanese had lost only 38 men killed when limited damage was inflicted on the *Chokai* and *Aoba*.

By the time the Northampton class was under construction, the other signatories of the Washington Naval Treaty had produced their second generation of heavy cruisers, and the Americans were yet again able to

profit from a survey of these vessels: the primary lesson learned from this survey was that the French and Italians had decided that their first-generation heavy cruisers had sacrificed too much protection in an effort to secure the highest possible speed, and the new Suffren and Zara classes, together with the Canarias class designed for Spain in the U.K., were notable for improved protection at a modest sacrifice in speed. The British and Japanese did not follow the same course as they had already opted for a better

215

balance of protection and speed, and the Americans felt that this was the best option for the Indianapolis class of two ships, which were very similar to the preceding Northampton class except for a redistribution of the armour to provide additional protection amidships. The details of the ships, which were launched in 1931 and 1932, therefore included a full-load displacement of 12,575 tons, an armament of nine 8-in (203-mm) guns and eight 5-in (127-mm) dual-purpose guns, protection in the form of a 4-in (102-mm) belt and 2-in (51-mm) deck, and a speed of 32.75kt on the 107,000hp (79780kW) delivered to four shafts by steam turbines.

The final American heavy cruisers built to the constraints of the Washington Naval Treaty were the seven ships of the Astoria class, which were in every way superlative ships matched in overall combat capability only by the single ship of the French Algérie class and the three ships of the German Admiral Hipper class. The principal changes from the Indianapolis class were the rearward lengthening of the fore castle for improved seaworthiness, pole rather than tripod masts, and improved protection in the form of a longer belt and thicker armour for the decks, turrets and conning tower. The details of the ships, which were launched between 1933 and 1936, therefore included a full-load displacement of 13,500 tons, an armament of nine 8-in (203-mm) guns, eight 5-in (127-mm) dual-purpose guns and 16 1.1-in anti-aircraft guns, protection in the form of a 5-in (127-mm) belt and 3-in (76-mm) deck, and a speed of 32.75kt on the 107,000hp (79780kW) delivered to four shafts by steam turbines.

The one unit of the Wichita class, launched in 1937, had been planned as the eighth Astoria-class ship but in the event

was completed to a standard resembling that of the Brooklyn class of light cruiser except in its armament details. The ship had a full-load displacement of 13,700 tons, an armament of nine 8-in (203-mm) guns and eight 5-in (127-mm) dual-purpose guns, protection in the form of a 5-in (127-mm) belt and 3-in (76-mm) deck, and a speed of 32.5kt on the 100,000hp (74560kW) delivered to four shafts by steam turbines. This similarity between the Wichita and Brooklyn classes provides clear evidence of the gradual merging of American heavy and light cruiser design concepts, the heavy cruiser generally having slightly greater length and the light cruiser having five turrets each carrying three 6-in (152-mm) guns rather than the heavy cruiser's standard arrangement of three turrets each carrying three 8-in (203-mm) guns. The Japanese also followed this concept, although not to so standardized a degree, and were therefore able to upgrade the Mogami-class light cruisers to heavy cruiser standard by the replacement of the triple 6.1-in (155-mm) turrets by twin 8-in (203-mm) turrets.

The tendency towards the use of a conceptually similar design for light and heavy cruisers became fully evident with the Baltimore class of 17 ships launched between 1942 and 1945 (only 14 being completed before the end of World War II) with an 18th following in 1951. The design was derived from that of the Cleveland class of light cruisers with the hull lengthened by 65ft (19.6m) and widened by 4ft (1.2m), and with the main armament revised to heavy cruiser standard. By the time of the earlier ships' completions, all but the German navy had in effect abandoned the heavy cruiser concept, but the U.S. Navy believed that with large oceans off its eastern and western seaboards there was still

OPPOSITE
Although rated as a guided-missile frigate, HMS Beaver of the Broadsword (Batch 2) class is typical of the type of modern frigate that possesses considerably more capability than the cruisers of World War II. The ship's primary armament comprises four launchers for Exocet anti-ship missiles and two sextuple launchers for the extremely capable Sea Wolf surface-to-air missile, while the provision of a hangar and platform for two helicopters permits long-range operations against submarines and lighter surface vessels.

LEFT
The US Navy cruiser Antietam, a member of the Ticonderoga class with its extraordinarily capable AEGIS radar and fire-control system, fires a mix of missiles against surface targets, submarines and aircraft. The launching system can be adapted for a variety of ship classes, such as destroyers and frigates.

Zhdanov, a Russian Sverdlov-class cruiser.

belt and 3-in (76-mm) deck, and a speed of 33kt on the 120,000hp (89470kW) delivered to four shafts by steam turbines.

To complete the story of American heavy cruisers with 8-in (203-mm) guns, it is necessary to mention two classes that were designed during World War II but completed after the end of hostilities and then only in small numbers and in different forms. The Oregon City class was planned as eight ships, but only four of these were completed to an improved Baltimore-class standard with a single rather than twin funnels to give the guns improved arcs of fire. The Des Moines class was planned as 12 ships, but only three of these were completed to an improved Oregon City-class standard with automatic 8-in (203-mm) guns, a tertiary battery of 24 3-in (76-mm) anti-aircraft guns in 12 twin turrets to replace the 40-mm guns of the preceding classes, and a longer and thicker belt of waterline armour.

So far as any account of American heavy cruiser thinking is concerned, mention must also be made of the magnificently elegant Alaska class of large heavy cruisers, often but wrongly called battle-cruisers. The origins of the class are to be found in the report before the U.S.A.'s involvement in World War II that Japan was following the German lead and building a class of pocket battleships. The U.S. Navy responded with the Alaska class projected at six large heavy cruisers of which only three were laid down and two actually completed to what was basically an enlarged version of the Baltimore-class design with a primary armament of nine 12-in (305-mm) rather than 8-in (203-mm) guns in three triple turrets and the protection scaled up to approximately the same extent. With a full-load displacement of 34,250 tons and a length of 808ft 6in (246.4m), the large

a need for heavy cruisers offering a combination of firepower, protection, speed and range that was unrivalled by anything but a capital ship. The Baltimore-class heavy cruisers were superb examples of this concept, which certainly retained a full validity up to and indeed after the end of World War II.

The primary features of the Baltimore-class design were a considerable deck area to allow the siting of large numbers of short-range anti-aircraft weapons in addition to the turrets carrying the primary and secondary armaments, a shorter but thicker

length of belt armour to provide enhanced protection for the ship's citadel region, and the absence of all side scuttles so that all interior spaces had to be artificially ventilated and illuminated. The details of these fine warships included a full-load displacement of 17,070 tons, an armament of nine 8-in (203-mm) guns in three triple turrets, 12 5-in (127-mm) dual-purpose guns in six twin turrets, 48 40-mm anti-aircraft guns in 11 quadruple and two twin mountings, and up to 28 20-mm anti-aircraft cannon in single mountings, protection in the form of a 6-in (152-mm)

heavy cruisers of the Alaska class carried a primary armament of nine 12-in (305-mm) guns in three triple turrets including a superfiring pair forward, a secondary armament of 12 5-in (127-mm) dual-purpose guns in six twin turrets, and a tertiary armament of 56 40-mm guns in 14 quadruple mountings and 34 20-mm anti-aircraft cannon in single mountings. The ships were protected by extensive but only moderately thick armour that included an 8-in (203-mm) belt and 3.75-in (95-mm) deck, and the highly impressive sustained speed of 33kt was attained on the 150,000hp (111840kW) delivered to four shafts by steam turbines.

The oldest class of light cruisers still in service with the U.S. Navy at the time of the American entry into World War II was the Omaha class of 10 ships planned in the aftermath of World War I as the first light cruisers designed in the U.S.A. for more than 10 years. The light cruiser had fully proved its worth in World War I, and as the starting point for its new type the U.S. Navy took the British Danae and Delhi classes as well as the German Dresden class. These classes had a speed of 29 and 28.5kt respectively for the British and German types, which had a main armament of six 6-in (152-mm) and seven 5.9-in (150-mm) guns respectively, so the U.S. Navy decided that its new class should have a speed of 35kt and an armament of eight 6-in (152-mm) guns on a displacement of 7,100 tons. The guns were in casemated mountings fore and aft, and included four guns that could bear on either beam: it was therefore decided to add four more 6-in (152-mm) guns in two twin turrets located fore and aft, although this meant an increase of 400 tons in displacement, a 9-in (0.23-m)

A Russian Kresta-class cruiser.

increase in draught, a 1-kt decrease in speed, and the trimming of the belt to a length on each beam alongside the machinery spaces. It was then decided that the originally planned torpedo armament of two submerged tubes should be replaced by 10 tubes above the waterline, and that two catapults and aircraft should be added, so the further increase in weight resulted in the omission of the after 6-in (152-mm)

casemated guns in half of the class for improved stability. The ships were launched between 1920 and 1924, and during World War II were generally used in the South Atlantic and a few secondary actions in the Pacific as well as for the gunfire support role in a number of secondary amphibious landings. As completed, the ships had a full-load displacement of 9,150 tons, an armament of 12 or 10 6-in (152-mm) guns

including four in twin turrets, eight 3-in (76-mm) anti-aircraft guns in single high-angle mountings and ten 21-in (533-mm) torpedo tubes, protection in the form of a 3-in (76-mm) belt and 1.5-in (38-mm) deck, and a speed of 33.5kt on the 90,000hp (67105kW) delivered to four shafts by steam turbines.

With an arrangement of four tall funnels grouped in two pairs, the Omaha-

details included a full-load displacement of
some 12,700 tons, an armament of 15 6-in
(152-mm) guns in five triple turrets, eight
5-in (127-mm) dual-purpose guns in eight
single mountings or, in the case of the last
two units, four twin turrets, and 16 1.1-in
anti-aircraft guns in four quadruple
mountings, protection in the form of a 5-in
(127-mm) belt and 3-in (76-mm) deck, and
a speed of 32.5kt on the 100,000hp
(74560kW) delivered to four shafts by
steam turbines.

Modifications that were effected to the
ships of the Brooklyn class during World
War II included a strengthening of the anti-
aircraft armament by 16 40-mm guns in
four quadruple mountings and between 20
and 24 20-mm cannon in single mountings.
The Brooklyn-class ships saw very extensive
and successful service in World War II, in
which only one of the vessels was lost, and
in the early 1950s six of the ships were
passed in pairs to three U.S. allies in South
America, where some of the ships survived
in fully serviceable form until the end of the
20th century.

The Atlanta class, which was the U.S.
Navy's next class of light cruisers, was
completely different from the Brooklyn class
and, indeed, from any other type of
American light cruiser. This resulted from
the fact that the ships of the Atlanta class
were intended for service as anti-aircraft and
flotilla leader types, a role which indicated
that their inspiration was the British Dido
class of anti-aircraft cruisers. Although the
four ships of the Atlanta class, launched in
1941, shared a commonality of role with
the ships of the Dido class, they were wholly
American in the way in which their role
should be achieved. The class had the
armament (including two banks of torpedo
tubes) and speed required for co-operation
with destroyer flotillas operating round the

class light cruisers were not visually
attractive, but the same cannot be said of
the Brooklyn class that followed the last
Omaha-class ships after an interval of more
than 10 years. The spur for the
development of this classic class was the
Japanese Mogami class of large light cruisers
that began to appear in 1935 in response to
Japan's completion of its quota of 12 heavy
cruisers permitted under the limitations of
the Washington Naval Treaty. Japan's
answer to this limitation was the Mogami
class, which was planned as a light cruiser
type able to offer heavy cruiser capabilities
through the combination of a large hull and
an armament of no fewer than 15 6.1-in
(155-mm) guns in five centreline turrets
(three forward, including one superfiring
pair, and two aft in a superfiring pair). In
the days before radar, when the maximum
effective firing range was limited by
visibility, the advantage in nocturnal and

indifferent weather operations lay with the
ships that could deliver the higher volume
of aimed fire, and here the Japanese felt that
the advantage would generally lie with the
Mogami-class light cruisers even in
engagements with heavy cruisers.

The Americans responded to the
Mogami-class ships with a type of basically
similar concept but greater displacement,
thicker armour (to the same basic levels as
the Astoria class of heavy cruisers with the
exception of a slightly thinner but longer
belt) and shorter overall length: the hull was
of the flushdecked type, and the main
armament of 15 6-in (152-mm) guns was
carried in five triple turrets arranged in the
same manner as those of the Japanese ships
with the exception that in the American
ships it was B rather than C turret that was
the superfiring unit of the forward trio. The
nine units of the Brooklyn class were
launched between 1936 and 1938, and their

A *Frunze-class cruiser of the Russian navy.*

edges of a carrier task force, but was really too large for this role: wartime experience revealed that more success might have been achieved by a reduction in the number of main-calibre guns to allow the incorporation of more than just two high-angle directors, which limited each ship's ability to the engagement of just two aircraft at any one time. As completed, the ships had a full-load displacement of 8,100 tons, an armament of 16 5-in (127-mm) dual-purpose guns in eight twin turrets, 12 or 16 1.1-in anti-aircraft guns in three or four quadruple mountings, eight 20-mm cannon in single mountings and eight 21-in (533-mm) torpedo tubes, protection in the form of a 3.5-in (89-mm) belt and 2-in (51-mm) deck, and a speed of 33kt on the 75,000hp (55920kW) delivered to four shafts by steam turbines.

Next came the 27 light cruisers of the Cleveland class, which was to have numbered 39 including three ships that were cancelled and nine that were converted into aircraft carriers. The Cleveland class was an improved version of the Brooklyn class with one 6-in (152-mm) triple turret sacrificed to make space for a much improved anti-aircraft armament. Launched between 1941 and 1944, the ships had a full-load displacement of 13,755 tons, an armament of 12 6-in (152-mm) guns in four triple turrets, 12 5-in (127-mm) dual-purpose guns in six twin turrets, between eight and 28 40-mm anti-aircraft guns in four twin to four quadruple and six twin mountings, and between 10 and 21 20-mm cannon in single mountings, protection in the form of a 5-in (127-mm) belt and 2-in (51-mm) deck, and a speed of 33kt on the 100,000hp (74560kW) delivered to four shafts by steam turbines. There followed the seven anti-aircraft light cruisers of the Oakland class, which were completed in two

groups of two ships launched between 1942 and 1944 as well as three ships launched between 1945 and 1946. The Oakland class was a further development of the Atlanta class with a full-load displacement of 8,200 tons, armour protection in the form of a 3.75-in (95-mm) belt and 2-in (51-mm) deck, and a speed of 33kt on the 75,000hp (55920kW) delivered to four shafts by steam turbines. The two groups differed principally in their armament: the four ships of the first group had 12 5-in (127-mm) dual-purpose guns in six twin turrets, 16 40-mm anti-aircraft guns in eight twin mountings, 16 20-mm cannon in single mountings, and eight 21-in (533-mm) torpedo tubes; while the three ships of the

second group had 12 5-in (127-mm) dual-purpose guns in six twin mountings, 32 40-mm anti-aircraft guns in six quadruple and four twin mountings and 20 20-mm cannon in single mountings.

Comprising only two out of a planned 13 ships, the Fargo class was a further development of the Cleveland class with modifications to improve the efficiency of their guns' fire: these changes included a more compact superstructure and the two uptakes trunked into a single funnel to give the guns larger firing arcs. The details of the two ships, which were launched in 1945, included a full-load displacement of 13,755 tons, an armament of 12 6-in (152-mm) guns in four triple turrets, 12 5-in

(127-mm) dual-purpose guns in six twin turrets, 28 40-mm anti-aircraft guns in six quadruple and two twin mountings, and 28 20-mm cannon in 14 twin mountings, protection in the form of a 5-in (127-mm) belt and 3-in (76-mm) deck, and a speed of 33kt on the 100,000hp (74560kW) delivered to four shafts by steam turbines.

The last American light cruiser design created during World War II was the Worcester class, of which only two out of a planned 10 units were completed well after the end of the war. The design was in essence a development of the Oakland class with 6-in (152-mm) guns in fully automatic twin turrets replacing 5-in (127-mm) guns in manually operated twin turrets, resulting

RIGHT
A Chinese sailor secures a line of the *USS* Reeves *(CG-24) in Qingdan, China.*

OPPOSITE
The USS Ticonderoga.

in a longer hull and a larger displacement. The details of the class included a full-load displacement of 18,000 tons, an armament of 12 6-in (152-mm) dual-purpose guns in six twin turrets and 24 3-in (76-mm) dual-purpose guns in 11 twin and two single turrets, protection in the form of a 6-in (152-mm) belt and 3-in (76-mm) deck, and a speed of 32.75kt on the 120,000hp (89470kW) delivered to four shafts by steam turbines.

Two other naval powers involved in World War II on the Allied side were France and the U.S.S.R., neither of which played a major part in naval hostilities. The French cruiser force included the three light cruisers of the Duguay Trouin class launched in 1923 and 1924 with a full-load displacement of 9,350 tons and a main armament of eight 6.1-in (155-mm) guns in four twin turrets, the two heavy cruisers of the Duquesne class launched in 1925 and 1926 with a full-load displacement of 12,200 tons and a main armament of eight 8-in (203-mm) guns in four twin turrets, the four heavy cruisers of the Suffren class launched between 1927 and 1930 with a full-load displacement of 12,780 tons and a main armament of eight 8-in (203-mm) guns in four twin turrets, the single but outstanding heavy cruiser of the Algérie class launched in 1932 with a full-load displacement of 13,900 tons and a main armament of eight 8-in (203-mm) guns in four twin turrets, the single light cruiser of the Émile Bertin class launched in 1933 with a full-load displacement of 8,480 tons and a main armament of nine 6-in (152-mm) guns in three triple turrets, and the six excellent light cruisers of the La Galissonnière class launched between 1933 and 1935 with a full-load displacement of 9,100 tons and a main armament of nine 6-in (152-mm) guns in three triple turrets.

The U.S.S.R. operated a number of obsolete and obsolescent cruisers in the 1920s and 1930s, and the only truly modern type available in World War II was the Kirov class, of which six were completed before and during the war with a full-load displacement of 11,500 tons and a main armament of nine 7.1-in (180-mm) guns in three triple turrets.

Facing the Allied powers in World War II were the nations of the Axis, namely Germany, Italy and Japan, supported by a number of smaller nations none of which made any real naval contribution. Germany planned a class of five Admiral Hipper-class heavy cruisers from the early 1930s, and these were orthodox but large ships of their type. Launched in the second half of the 1930s, only three of the ships were completed: of the other two one was delivered incomplete to the U.S.S.R. as part of the treaty signed between the two countries in 1939, and the other was not completed. The main armament of the Admiral Hipper class was limited to eight 8-in (203-mm) guns in four twin turrets located as superfiring pairs forward and aft, and this allowed a considerable proportion of the displacement to be devoted to a sturdy structure and very good protection. One of the ships was sunk by Norwegian shore batteries in April 1940, but the other two survived the war after playing distinguished roles in its first phases. The basic details of these impressive ships included a full-load displacement of 18,400 tons, an armament of eight 8-in (203-mm) guns in four twin turrets, 12 4.1-in (105-mm) dual-purpose guns in six twin turrets, 12 37-mm anti-aircraft guns in six twin mountings, 24 20-mm cannon and 12 21-in (533-mm) torpedo tubes, protection in the form of a 3.1-in (80-mm) belt and 2-in (50-mm) deck, and a speed of 33.4kt on the

The Arkansas *(CGN 41) is a nuclear-powered fleet escort cruiser of the U.S. Navy's Virginia class, and its primary armament comprises two twin-arm missile launchers located fore and aft, the first with 24 missiles and the latter with 44 missiles.*

132,000hp (98430kW) delivered to three shafts by steam turbines.

Germany's only other cruisers were the six light cruisers of the Köln class, which were relatively modern ships but not particularly notable with their armament of nine 5.9-in (155-mm) guns and six 3.4-in (88-mm) anti-aircraft guns.

Italy was a firm believer in the cruiser, which it saw as tactically efficient for the support of its battle force in the central Mediterranean Sea and also as a cost-effective means of providing powerful warships suited to the tasks of commanding and supporting flotilla operations by light

cruisers and destroyers in more confined waters such as those of the Aegean Sea. In the years after World War I the Italian navy lacked the financial resources to undertake the construction of many new ships, and for this reason retained a number of obsolescent types such as the two San Giorgio-class armoured cruisers, the single Libia and Campania-class protected cruisers, and the one Quarto, two Bixio, three Poerio, three Mirabello, four Aquila and three Leone-class scout cruisers. During the 1920s, however, relations between France and Italy began to worsen, and when the French started work on the

two Duquesne-class heavy cruisers to the limits imposed by the Washington Naval Treaty, Italy responded with the Trento-class ships offering firepower and speed comparable with those of the French class in combination with somewhat better protection.

The Trento-class ships were still under construction when France responded with its four Suffren-class heavy cruisers in which a measure of speed was sacrificed to greater protection. Italy did not undertake an immediate response to these impressive ships, largely as a result of financial and industrial problems, but this gave the Italian

The USS Bainbridge, *the sole example of its type.*

navy the time to assess the qualities of the Suffren-class design before it responded three years later with the four ships of the Zara class. This sacrificed some performance, the propulsion arrangement being reduced to 108,000hp (80535kW) delivered to two shafts by steam turbines for a speed of 32kt, for better protection: this took the form of a 5.9-in (150-mm) belt and 2.75-in (70-mm) deck, and the firepower of these impressive heavy cruisers was provided by a main battery of eight 8-in (203-mm) gun in two pairs of superfiring turrets forward and aft of the superstructure, a secondary battery of 16

3.9-in (100-mm) dual-purpose guns in eight twin mountings, and a tertiary battery of eight 37-mm anti-aircraft guns.

In light cruiser design and construction, the Italians were again content, or rather had to be contented, with replies to French leads. Thus the construction of the three Duguay Trouin light cruisers spurred the construction from 1928 of the first four of an eventual 12 light cruisers of the Condottieri type produced in five subclasses as four Bande Nere, two Diaz, two Montecuccoli, two Aosta and two Garibaldi-class ships. Like their French counterparts, the Bande Nere class ships carried a primary

armament of eight 6-in (152-mm) guns in two pairs of superfiring twin turrets and carried only vestigial armour protection, but were very fast. The four later subclasses of he Condotierri type were a response to the French light cruisers of the La Galissonnière class with improved protection, and successive subclasses introduced greater size and displacement to permit the incorporation of better protection and a more potent propulsion arrangement so that speed did not suffer. The last pair of ships, launched in 1933, were the Garibaldi class with a further enlargement in beam and draught to allow the incorporation of two

227

additional main-calibre guns. The details of these ships therefore included a full-load displacement of 11,260 tons, an armament of 10 6-in (152-mm) guns in superfiring pairs of triple and twin turrets, eight 3.9-in (100-mm) anti-aircraft guns, eight 37-mm anti-aircraft guns, 10 20-mm anti-aircraft cannon and six 21-in (533-mm) torpedo tubes, protection in the form of a 5.1-in (130-mm) belt and 1.6-in (40-mm) deck, and a speed of 32kt on the 102,000hp (76060kW) delivered to two shafts by steam turbines.

Although the concept of the small scout cruiser had generally lapsed after the end of World War I except in Japan, where a number of such ships were built in the 1920s, the French reverted to such a type in the mid-1930s with the Mogador class of ships officially rated as large destroyers but in fact scout cruisers with a full-load displacement of 4,010 tons, an armament of eight 5.5-in (140-mm) guns in two superfiring pairs of twin turrets, four 37-mm anti-aircraft guns in two twin mountings and 10 21.7-in (550-mm) torpedo tubes, and the remarkable speed of 39kt on the 92,000hp (68630kW) delivered to two shafts by steam turbines.

The excellence of these ships, of which only two were built to a standard that effectively outgunned the British Dido-class light cruisers, was seen by the Italians as a major threat that was countered by the Capitani Romani class of fast light cruisers: 12 ships were laid down, but only four were completed. The key to the design was a long and relatively beamy hull able to accommodate a sizeable propulsion arrangement: the machinery of the Italian ships was capable of generating 125,000hp (92,310kW), which was about the same as that of the four times heavier Des Moines-class heavy cruisers, and this was delivered

to two shafts for the truly remarkable speed of 43kt. The ships carried virtually no protection, however, and the armament comprised eight 5.3-in (135-mm) guns in two superfiring pairs of twin turrets, eight 37-mm anti-aircraft guns, eight 20-mm anti-aircraft cannon and eight 21-in (533-mm) torpedo tubes.

Like the Italians, the Japanese saw the cruiser as a cost-effective weapon for a country that lacked a large industrial base and adequate quantities of indigenous raw materials, especially iron ore. In Japanese naval thinking, the cruiser offered the possibility of striking at larger and potentially more threatening warships by using its speed and agility, in combination with daring Japanese tactics, to close to effective torpedo range. The first result of this philosophy after World War I, which had seen the laying down of the two Tenryu-class light cruisers, was the five light cruisers of the Kuma class with a displacement of 5,100 tons, an armament of seven 5.5-in (140-mm) guns in single mounting and eight 21-in (533-mm) torpedo tubes, protection in the form of a 2-in (50-mm) belt and 1.5-in (37-mm) deck, and a speed of 36kt on the 90,000hp (67105kW) delivered to four shafts by steam turbines. Two of the vessels, it is worth noting, were adapted in 1941 into the ultimate torpedo-armed cruisers after the introduction of the 24-in (610-mm) Long Lance torpedo, a weapon that could deliver a devastatingly large warhead over a long range at high speed. The two ships were altered by the change of the gun armament to four 5.5-in (140-mm) weapons in two twin mountings and up to 36 25-mm anti-aircraft guns in six triple and 18 single mountings, and the deck was widened on each beam with sponsons to carry a total of 10 quadruple

mountings for the Long Lance torpedo.

After World War I Japan planned to build its armed forces to the extent that the country would become the most potent military power in the western half of the Pacific as well as in eastern and south-eastern Asia. An early decision was that the Japanese navy was lacking in balance, for construction before and during World War I had been concentrated on capital ships and destroyers. With a major capability in the ocean vastnesses of the western Pacific now required, there was clearly demand for larger numbers of more capable cruisers to provide scouting and ambush capabilities. The first result of this was the Natori class of six light cruisers completed in the period between 1922 and 1925. These were unexceptional ships based on the Nagara class with a displacement of 5,170 tons, an armament of seven 5.5-in (140-mm) guns in seven single turrets and eight 24-in (610-mm) torpedo tubes, protection in the form of a 2-in (50-mm) belt and 1.5-in (37-mm) deck, and a speed of 36kt on the 90,000hp (67105kW) delivered to four shafts by steam turbines. The Japanese navy adhered to the same basic philosophy in the succeeding Sendai class of six light cruisers, of which only three were completed. This class had basically the same dimensions, armament and protection as the two preceding classes, although a change was made in the propulsion arrangement that now included 11 oil- and one mixed-burning boilers by comparison with the eight oil- and four coal-burning boilers of the Nagara class and the 10 oil- and two mixed-burning boilers of the Kuma class.

As the Sendai class was being planned and laid down, the final negotiations of the Washington Naval Conference were being undertaken and the probability of new types of cruiser persuaded the Japanese

USS Truxtun.

The USS Ticonderoga (CG 47) during sea trials on the Gulf of Mexico in 1982.

navy to build the single Yubari-class light cruiser as an experimental type offering the same broadside weight as its predecessors on a displacement of only 2,900 tons. This was achieved by cutting the protection to a 2-in (50-mm) belt, trunking the two uptakes into a single funnel, limiting the torpedo armament to four 24-in (610-mm) tubes, locating the main armament of six 5.5-in (140-mm) guns on the centreline in two twin and two single turrets with the twin turrets in superfiring positions, and revising the propulsion arrangement for a speed of 35.5kt on the 57,900hp (43170kW) delivered to three shafts by steam turbines. The ship was a considerable

success at the technical level, and paved the way for the design and construction of both light and heavy cruisers within the constraints of the Washington Naval Treaty.

The first result of this process was the Kako class of two heavy cruisers completed in 1926. These were impressive ships well within the treaty limits for the new class of heavy cruisers with 8-in (203-mm) guns and a maximum displacement of 10,000 tons as they were armed with six 7.9-in (200-mm) guns in single turrets located equally fore and aft of the superstructure and had a displacement of 8,100 tons. Their other primary details included a secondary armament of four 3-in (76-mm) anti-aircraft

guns in single mountings and 12 24-in (610-mm) torpedo tubes, protection in the form of a 3-in (76-mm) belt and 1.5-in (37-mm) deck, and a speed of 34.5kt on the 102,000hp (76050kW) delivered to three shafts by steam turbines. The overall capabilities of the class were improved in the late 1930s, when the original six single gun turrets were replaced by three twin turrets (a superfiring pair forward and a singleton aft) carrying 8-in (203-mm) weapons. The following two ships of the Aoba class were generally similar with the exception of having their six 7.9-mm (200-mm) guns, later replaced by 8-in (203-mm) weapons, in three twin turrets and the strengthened anti-aircraft armament of four 4.7-in (120-mm) guns in single mountings. With a displacement of 8,300 tons and protection in the form of a 3-in (76-mm) belt and 1.5-in (37-mm) deck, the Aoba-class cruiser attained a speed of 34.5kt on the 102,000hp (76050kW) delivered to four shafts by steam turbines.

These first two classes of Japanese heavy cruiser paved the way in the mid-1920s to the considerably superior Myoko class of four ships. These were completed in 1928 and 1929 to a standard that included a displacement of 10,940 tons, armament of 10 7.9-in (200-mm) guns, later replaced by 8-in (203-mm) weapons, in five twin turrets (three forward and two aft), six 4.7-in (120-mm) anti-aircraft guns in single mountings, 12 24-in (610-mm) torpedo tubes, protection in the form of a 4-in (102-mm) belt and 5-in (127-mm) deck, and a speed of 35.5kt on the 130,000hp (96930kW) delivered to four shafts by steam turbines. The most important features made possible by the additional size and displacement of this class were the considerably heavier main armament, carried as a triplet forward with the central unit as the superfiring turret and as a superfiring pair aft, and the considerably thicker armour that made these vessels particularly resistant to terminal battle damage.

The following four ships of the Takao class were completed to an improved Myoko-class design with a more piled superstructure of streamlined design, welded rather than riveted construction wherever possible, and light alloy in place of steel wherever possible to keep weight to a minimum, increased armour protection for the magazines, and a primary armament of 8-in (203-mm) guns from the beginning of their lives. The details of the ships therefore included a displacement of 11,350 tons, an armament of 10 8-in (203-mm) guns in five twin turrets (three forward and two aft), four 4.7-in (120-mm) anti-aircraft guns in

LEFT
The Harpoon is a capable American long-range anti-ship missile that can be launched from aircraft, or alternatively fired from ships. From surface ships the standard methods are an angled launch from a special container or, alternatively, vertical launch from the new type of multi-cell vertical-launch system. Seen here is a submarine-launched missile launched through a torpedo tube in a sealed capsule to start its booster rocket as the capsule breaks the surface of the water.

LEFT
The primary close-in weapons system of U.S. warships for last-ditch defence against aircraft and missiles is the Phalanx system, which is an autonomous radar-controlled 20-mm cannon with six barrels firing, among other projectiles, depleted uranium rounds.

2008, Guided Missile Cruiser (Ticonderoga class).

USS Ticonderoga transits the Suez Canal en route to the Mediterranean Sea following a deployment in support of Operation Desert Shield.

single mountings and eight 24-in (610-mm) torpedo tubes, protection in the form of a 4-in (102-mm) belt and 1.5-in (37-mm) deck, and a speed of 35.5kt on the 130,000hp (96930kW) delivered to four shafts by steam turbines.

By 1931 Japan had completed the maximum of 12 heavy cruisers permitted under the terms of the Washington Naval Treaty, so further construction was limited to light cruisers carrying guns with a calibre of no more than 6.1in (155mm). The Japanese answer to this dilemma was the creation of the four Mogami-class cruisers with the exceptional armament of 15 6.1-in (155-mm) guns in five triple turrets, and it was the obvious threat of these ships that persuaded the Americans and British to develop more advanced cruisers in the forms

of the Brooklyn and Southampton classes respectively. The Japanese felt that displacement was clearly going to be a critical problem given the number of turrets that were to be shipped, so the use of welding and light alloys, already pioneered in the Takao class, was taken to a greater extreme. This solution was not without its problems, though, and sea trials with the first two ships were hampered by excessive top weight and structural problems as a result of poor welding, resulting in hull deformations that prevented the main turrets from being trained over their full arcs. The two ships were therefore rebuilt with a wider hull carrying external bulges, and this provided greater structural strength as well as improving stability. The latter pair of ships were completed to this revised

standard, and in 1939 all four ships were revised to full heavy cruiser standard with their 15 6.1-in (155-mm) guns in triple turrets replaced by 10 8-in (203-mm) guns in twin turrets. As completed to definitive initial standard, the ships had a displacement of 11,200 tons, armament of 15 6.1-in (155-mm) guns in five triple turrets, eight 5-in (127-mm) anti-aircraft guns in four twin turrets, four 40-mm anti-aircraft guns in single mountings and 12 24-in (610-mm) torpedo tubes, protection in the form of a 4-in (102-mm) belt and 1.5-in (37-mm) deck, and a speed of 35kt on the 152,000hp (113330kW) delivered to four shafts by steam turbines.

The final Japanese heavy cruisers were the two ships of the Tone class, which were completed in 1938 and 1939. The design was an improved version of that developed in the Mogami class with the main armament reduced to 12 6.1-in (155-mm) guns in four triple turrets all located forward with one unit in a superfiring position. This arrangement was adopted as the ships were intended specifically for the scouting role associated with Combined Fleet operations in the Pacific, and allowed the after part of the ship to be dedicated to the floatplane complement of five aircraft (as opposed to the three and two aircraft carried respectively by the preceding two classes) and two beam catapults. The details of the Tone class included a displacement of 11,215 tons, an armament of eight 8-in (203-mm) guns in four twin turrets, eight 5-in (127-mm) anti-aircraft guns in four twin turrets, 12 25-mm anti-aircraft guns in six twin mounting and 12 24-in (610-mm) torpedo tubes, protection in the form of a 4-in (102-mm) belt and 2.5-in (63-mm) deck, and a speed of 35kt on the 152,200hp (113480kW) delivered to four shafts by steam turbines.

Another autonomous close-in weapon system is the Dutch Goalkeeper system with a 30-mm six-barrel cannon and radar fire control.

Late in the 1930s the Japanese navy decided that it should replace its older light cruisers built in the early 1920s with a main armament of 5.5-in (140-mm) guns. The first result of this decision was the completion between 1942 and 1944 of the four ships of the Agano class with a full-load displacement of 8,535 tons, an armament of six 5.9-in (150-mm) guns in three twin turrets (a superfiring pair forward and a singleton unit aft), four 3-in (76-mm) anti-aircraft guns in two twin turrets, up to 59 25-mm anti-aircraft guns in 10 triple and 29 single mountings and eight 24-in (610-mm) torpedo tubes, protection in the form of a 2.25-in (57-mm) belt and 0.75-in (19-mm)

deck, and a speed of 35kt on the 110,000hp (82015kW) delivered to four shafts by steam turbines.

The last cruiser completed by the Japanese in World War II was the single light cruiser of the Oyodo class, which was based in the Agano-class design with revisions suiting it to the somewhat different role of commanding a scouting and hunting group of aircraft and submarines. The primary gun armament of six 6.1-in (155-mm) guns was therefore located forward of the superstructure in a superfiring pair of triple turrets, and this left the after part of the ship clear for the floatplane installation, which comprised two aircraft launched from a single centreline catapult but recovered from the sea at the ends of their missions by a pair of beam cranes. The other details of this ship, which was completed early in 1943, included a displacement of 8,165 tons, a secondary armament of eight 3.9-in (100-mm) anti-aircraft guns in four twin mountings and 12 25-mm anti-aircraft guns in four triple mountings, protection in the form of a 2-in (50-mm) belt and 2-in (50-mm) deck, and a speed of 35kt on the 110,000hp (82015kW) delivered to four shafts by steam turbines.

The Japanese cruisers saw very extensive service in World War II, and in general proved to be excellent and sturdy warships well able to undertake the tasks asked of them. Wartime modification was extensive as the ships were refitted and repaired, most of the modification efforts being concerned with the improvement of the ships' short-range anti-aircraft defences in an effort to provide them with a counter to the overwhelming air superiority that the Americans were able to bring to bear from a time late in 1942. Virtually every spare part of deck area was used for single or multiple

anti-aircraft mountings, and the need for such enhancement often meant the removal of some or all of the aircraft capability, and also some of the torpedo capability.

The end of World War II spelled the effective end of the gun-armed cruiser as a worthwhile naval weapon, for the guided missile was rapidly replacing the gun as the primary weapon carried by major warships. The more modern of existing ships were maintained in service to provide an interim capability, but the way forward was revealed by the U.S.A. in the first half of the 1950s, when two heavy cruisers of the Baltimore class were converted as guided missile cruisers for the fleet escort role: the after end of each ship was revised with a pair of twin-arm launchers (for a total of 144 RIM-2 Terrier medium-range surface-to-air missiles) and their associated surveillance, target acquisition and missile guidance radars together with the fire-control systems. The success of the two conversions, which were recommissioned in 1955 and 1956, paved the way for a similar conversion of six Cleveland-class light cruisers, whose after ends were similarly cleared and adapted for the carriage of one twin-arm launcher for 120 Terrier SAMs and their associated radar and fire-control system. These ships were recommissioned between 1958 and 1960, and were followed between 1962 and 1964 by more elaborate conversions. These were three more Baltimore-class ships that were stripped of all their main gun turrets to permit their modification into two-ended missile ships with a pair of twin-arm launchers for a total of 104 RIM-8 Talos long-range SAMs complemented by another pair of twin-arm launchers abreast of the forward superstructure for 84 Terrier SAMs. These launchers were complemented by the associated radar and fire-control systems, the provision of four target-tracking/missile-

A Harpoon missile being launched from a ship.

While its cruisers provide the U.S. Navy with the means to protect its main surface assets, which are its aircraft carriers, against submarine, ship and air attack, these cruisers themselves need a lower level of escort protection so that they can concentrate on their primary task. Such protection is provided in part by guided-missile destroyers, which also help protect the aircraft carriers, but also in part by small surface vessels such as the guided-missile frigates of the Oliver Hazard Perry class, here epitomized by the USS George Philip (FFG 12), an early unit of this large class.

guidance radars allowing the simultaneous engagement of four targets rather than the maximum of two that was possible with the earlier conversions.

The success of these ships paved the way for the creation of purpose-designed guided-missile cruisers fully optimized for the defence of the carrier battle groups that had become the most important surface warships operated by the U.S. Navy. The first of these new missile cruisers carried the same missiles as their predecessors, but

these were replaced in due course by the superb RIM-66 and RIM-67 medium- and long-range versions of the Standard Missile. The missile cruisers were built in two basic forms with conventional or nuclear propulsion, the latter being designed for the support of nuclear-powered aircraft carriers on extended-duration deployments, but financial considerations generally meant that production of nuclear-powered missile cruisers has lagged behind the totals required for protection of the nuclear-

powered aircraft carriers, which therefore operate with a mix of conventionally and nuclear-powered cruisers.

The force of such cruisers built for the U.S. Navy includes the single nuclear-powered ship of the Long Beach class completed in 1961, the nine conventionally powered ships of the Leahy class completed between 1962 and 1964, the single ship of the Bainbridge class completed in 1962 as a nuclear-powered version of the Leahy-class design, the nine conventionally powered ships of the Belknap class completed between 1963 and 1965, the single ship of the Truxtun class completed in 1964 as a nuclear-powered version of the Belknap-class design, the two nuclear-powered ships of the California class completed in 1974 and 1975, the four nuclear-powered ships of the Virginia class completed between 1976 and 1980, and finally the planned 27 units of the Ticonderoga class completed from 1983 with the extraordinarily complex and capable AEGIS mission system based on the SPY-1A electronically scanned planar-array radar system.

The Long Beach is the largest of these ships with a full-load displacement of 16,600 tons; an armament of two twin-arm launchers for 120 Standard Missiles, one octuple launcher for eight RUR-5 ASROC anti-submarine weapons, one octuple launcher for eight BGM-109 Tomahawk cruise missiles, two quadruple launchers for eight RGM-84 Harpoon anti-ship missiles, two 5-in (127-mm) dual-purpose guns in single turrets, two 20-mm Vulcan six-barrel cannon in two Phalanx close-in weapon system mountings, and two triple tubes for 12.75-in (324-mm) anti-submarine torpedoes; and a speed of 30kt on the 80,000hp (59650kW) delivered to two shafts by steam turbines powered by two Westinghouse C1W pressurized water-cooled reactors. In all, this represents a prodigious capability against targets ranging for aircraft to pinpoint land objectives via submarines, ships and other surface targets on both sea and land.

The later nuclear-powered missile cruisers are somewhat smaller and have reduced, although still very formidable, capabilities, but the most modern of the cruiser classes currently in service is the prolific Ticonderoga class. This is based on a development of the hull designed for the

Spruance-class destroyer, and its details include a full-load displacement of 9,450 tons, an armament of two twin-arm or, in later ships, two vertical-launch systems for a total of 68 or 122 weapons respectively in the form of various mixes of Standard Missile, up to 20 RUR-5 ASROC anti-submarine and 20 BGM-109 Tomahawk cruise missiles, two quadruple launchers for eight BGM-84 Harpoon anti-ship missiles, two 5-in (127-mm) dual-purpose guns in single turrets, two 20-mm Vulcan six-barrel cannon in Phalanx close-in weapon system mountings and two triple tubes for six 12.75-in (324-mm) anti-submarine torpedoes; and a speed of 30 or more knots on the 80,000hp (59650kW) delivered to two shafts by four General Electric LM2500 gas turbines.

Other Western countries that have built cruisers since the end of World War II include France with the single de Grasse-class light cruiser with a main armament of 16 5-in (127-mm) dual-purpose guns in eight twin turrets grouped in superfiring quadruplets forward and aft, and the single Colbert-class light cruiser with a main armament of 16 5-in (127-mm) dual-purpose guns in eight twin turrets grouped in superfiring quadruplets forward and aft but later rebuilt as a guided missile cruiser with an armament of one twin-arm launcher for Masurca SAMs aft and two 3.9-in (100-mm) guns in a pair of superfiring single turrets forward; Italy with the two Andrea Doria-class helicopter cruisers with an armament of one twin-arm launcher for Terrier (later Standard Missile) SAMs forward, eight 3-in (76-mm) dual-purpose guns in single turrets, and up to four anti-submarine helicopters aft; and the single Vittorio Veneto-class helicopter cruiser with an armament of one twin-arm launcher for Terrier (later Standard Missile) SAMs

forward, eight 3-in (76-mm) dual-purpose guns in single turrets, and up to nine anti-submarine helicopters aft; the Netherlands with two de Ruyter-class light cruisers with an armament of eight 6-in (152-mm) guns in two pairs of superfiring twin turrets; and the U.K. with three Tiger-class light cruisers with an armament of two 6-in (152-mm) guns in one twin turret, two launchers for Sea Cat SAMs, and up to four anti-submarine helicopters.

On the other side of the Iron Curtain, politico-military divide that emerged in the period after World War II, the only country of the Warsaw Pact nations to have built cruisers was the U.S.S.R. This country had a strength of 15 cruisers in 1947, this strength comprising two Russian ships from World War I, one American Omaha-class ship, one ex-German Nürnberg-class ship, one ex-Italian Aosta-class ship, two Kirov-class ships, four Maksim Gorky-class ships and four Chapayev-class ships. The U.S.S.R.'s next cruiser type was the Sverdlov class: 24 of these were ordered, 20 were laid down, 17 were launched but only 14 were finally completed between 1951 and 1955 with a full-load displacement of 17,200 tons, an armament of 12 6-in (152-mm) guns in two pairs of superfiring triple turrets, 12 3.9-in (100-mm) dual-purpose guns in six twin turrets, 16 37-mm anti-aircraft guns in eight twin mountings and 10 533-mm (21-in) torpedo tubes, protection in the form of a 4.9-in (125-mm) belt and 3-in (75-mm) deck, and a speed of 32.5kt on the 110,000hp (82015kW) delivered to two shafts by steam turbines.

These ships were obsolete even as they were being built, but in the later 1950s the U.S.S.R. started to create considerably more powerful cruisers of two new types within the context of the Soviet ambition to create

The USS John A. Moore (FFG-19), an Oliver Hazard Perry-class frigate of the U.S. Navy.

a navy with genuine blue-water capability. This might not be able to seize command of the seas from the U.S. Navy, but was schemed to create the strength that could inflict major casualties on any American force attempting an amphibious invasion of the U.S.S.R.

The first of the new types was intended specifically for the engagement and destruction of American aircraft carriers and their supporting warships in operationally vital carrier battle groups, and its first example was the Kynda class of four ships completed between 1962 and 1965 with a full-load displacement of 5,600 tons, an armament of two quadruple launchers for 16 SS-N-3 Shaddock nuclear-armed anti-ship missiles, one launcher for 24 SA-N-1 SAMs, four 3-in (76-mm) dual-purpose guns in two twin turrets, two 12-tube anti-submarine rocket launchers, and six 21-in (533-mm) torpedo tubes, and a speed of 34kt on the 100,000hp (74560kW) delivered to two shafts by steam turbines. The Kynda-class ships provided a very useful initial capability against the American aircraft carrier force, but were complemented in 1967 and 1968 by the four Kresta I-class cruisers that still provided a major offensive punch but were better able to provide their own protection against aircraft and submarine attack. The

ships therefore had a full-load displacement of 7,500 tons, an armament of two twin launchers for just four SS-N-3 Shaddock anti-ship missiles, two twin-arm launchers for 44 SA-N-1 SAMs, four 57-mm anti-aircraft guns in two twin mountings, two 12-tube and two six-tube anti-submarine rocket launchers, 10 21-in (533-mm) torpedo tubes, and one anti-submarine and/or missile-guidance helicopter, and a speed of 34kt on the 100,000hp (74560kW) delivered to two shafts by steam turbines.

The nuclear-powered ballistic missile submarine was beginning to come to the fore as a decisive strategic weapon during

this period, and the threat of the U.S.A.'s growing force of such boats was reflected in the construction of the Kresta II class of 10 cruisers adapted from the Kresta I-class design for the specialized task of hunting and killing American nuclear-powered submarines. In this task the primary sensor was an advanced sonar system located in the forefoot of the lengthened bow section, and the primary weapon the SS-N-14 Silex missile used to deliver a homing torpedo or nuclear depth charge to the area pinpointed by the sonar (either shipborne or helicopter-carried) as the location of the target submarine. From 1971, the Kresta II-class cruisers were complemented by seven Kara-class anti-submarine cruisers, which were the first full-size cruisers to enter service with the Soviet navy after the Sverdlov-class ships. With a full-load displacement of 9,900 tons, the ships of this class carry an armament of two quadruple launchers for eight SS-N-14 Silex anti-submarine weapons, two twin-arm launchers for 72 SA-N-3 Goblet SAMs, two twin-arm launchers for 40 SA-N-4 Gecko SAMs, four 3-in (76-mm) dual-purpose guns in two twin turrets, four 30-mm six-barrel anti-aircraft cannon in single mountings, up to 10 21-in (533-mm) torpedo tubes, and two 12- and two six-tube anti-submarine rocket launchers. Propulsion is based on the delivery of 134,000hp

(91710kW) to two shafts by a COGOG (COmbined Gas turbine Or Gas turbine) arrangement of four large and two small gas turbines for a speed of 34kt.

The Kara-class ships seem to have persuaded the Soviets of the advantage of a full-size cruiser hull for good ocean-going and weapon-carrying capability, and the most recent Soviet class has been the four ships of the Slava class optimized for the dual-role anti-ship and anti-submarine task with a full-load displacement of 11,200 tons for the carriage of a weapons fit that includes eight twin launchers for SS-N-12 Sandbox anti-ship missiles, eight octuple launchers for 64 SA-N-6 Grumble SAMs, two twin-arm launchers for 40 SA-N-4 Gecko SAMs, two 5.1-in (130-mm) dual-purpose guns in a twin turret, six 30-mm six-barrel anti-aircraft guns in single mountings, 10 21-in (533-mm) torpedo tubes, two 12-tube anti-submarine rocket launchers, and one anti-submarine/missile update helicopter. Propulsion is based on the delivery of 120,000hp (89470kW) to two shafts by four gas turbines for a speed of 34kt.

The Soviet cruiser force was completed by the two hybrid helicopter cruisers of the Moskva class that were commissioned in 1967 and 1968 with a full-load displacement of 19,300 tons, an armament of two twin-arm launchers for 48 SA-N-3 Goblet SAMs, one SUW-N-1 twin launcher for 18 FRAS-1 anti-submarine weapons, two 12-tube anti-submarine rocket launchers, four 57-mm anti-aircraft guns in two twin turrets, and 14 anti-submarine helicopters. Further development of the cruiser is in abeyance as the CIS lacks the need and financial resources for further such ships, and in these circumstances the U.S.A. is well equipped with its current types.

LEFT
Area defence against air attack for British ships operating in the North Atlantic was a task that led to the creation of the Sheffield-class of guided-missile destroyers, which are little short of cruisers in terms of their overall capabilities. Completed in the late 1970s and early 1980s, the class numbered 10 ships with the Sea Dart surface-to-air missile system (one twin-arm launcher with 22 missiles) as the primary weapon. The ship illustrated is HMS Nottingham, *the penultimate vessel of the class.*

Chapter Five
The Aircraft Carrier

It was an American who made the first successful take-off from and first successful landing on board a ship, when in November 1909 Eugene Ely flew a Curtiss biplane off the cruiser *Birmingham* and then in January 1911 landed on the cruiser *Pennsylvania*. The push toward the creation of the first primitive shipboard aircraft operations then attracted the interest of the British, who began their development of the concept in 1912 with a take-off from the moored battleship *Hibernia* during January and continued with a take-off from the moving battleship *Africa* in May. This capability was seen at the time as experimental, and more serious consideration was given to the use of aircraft in their flying boat and floatplane forms as a means of supporting naval operations with an eye in the sky reconnaissance capability to extend the horizon to which a search for enemy ships could be undertaken. The first ship completed for this task was the *Ark Royal*, which was converted while building as a collier to be completed as a seaplane carrier. This first aircraft-dedicated British ship had internal accommodation for seaplanes, which were lifted into and out of the water by a crane before and after flight operations, which involved taking off from the water and then an alighting on the same medium

before the seaplane taxied to the *Ark Royal* for recovery. Although successful in basic terms of being able to operate its seaplanes, the *Ark Royal* lacked the speed and range to support fleet operations by squadrons of modern warships, so eight ferries, all of them faster ships for use in rapid crossings of confined waters, were taken in hand for a similar type of conversion. These ships were the *Empress*, *Engadine*, *Riviera*, *Ben-my-Chree*, *Manxman*, *Vindex*, *Pegasus* and *Nairana*, all of which were converted into seaplane carriers and saw valuable service. These first-generation operational seaplane carriers were supplemented by the converted liner *Campania*. It was appreciated from the beginning of such operations, however, that the seaplane carrier concept was cumbersome, involving as it did considerable time between the ships' halt and the completion of the launching process (and vice versa at the end of any mission), and several of the ships were later fitted with a flying-off platform allowing the operation of wheeled aircraft, which were initially converted floatplanes but later standard landplane types.

As World War I (1914–18) continued, the importance of aircraft for all surface operations, over the sea as well as over the land, increased dramatically. One of the reasons for this was the technical

development of aircraft: early aircraft were able to lift only a modest quantity of fuel and their crews, but as the war progressed more effective machines were developed to carry larger quantities of fuel and also an effective payload in terms of armament (bombs and guns for offensive and defensive purposes respectively) or equipment such as radio for the reporting of reconnaissance results. These aircraft were of necessity stronger, heavier and larger than their predecessors, so thought was inevitably given to the creation of larger ships to carry a greater number of more substantial aircraft that could be operated from longer platforms at higher weights. The light battle-cruiser *Furious* was converted into an aircraft carrier for service from March 1918, and was supplemented from October 1918 by the *Vindictive* and *Argus*, which had been laid down as a cruiser and a liner respectively. As the war ended in November 1918, the U.K. was building two more aircraft carriers as the *Eagle*, whose hull had been laid down as that of a sister ship to the battleship *Canada*, and the *Hermes* that was the first ship to be designed as an aircraft carrier rather than converted to this role.

During the 1920s the *Furious* was rebuilt to full aircraft-carrier standard with a flush flightdeck, and her two half-sisters, the light battle-cruisers *Courageous* and

Glorious, were also converted to aircraft-carrier standard, with a starboard-side island, in the period between 1924 and 1930. This gave the British a force of four large aircraft carriers by the mid-1930s. The two Courageous-class ships each had a displacement of 22,500 tons, an armament that by the beginning of World War II had reached 16 4.7-in (119-mm) anti-aircraft guns in single mountings as well as provision for 48 aircraft, protection in the form of a 3-in (76-mm) belt and deck, and a speed of 30.5kt on the 90,000hp (67105kW) delivered to four shafts by geared steam turbines. The *Furious* had a displacement of 22,450 tons, an armament by the beginning of World War II of 12 4-in (102-mm) anti-aircraft guns in six twin mountings and 24 2-pdr anti-aircraft guns in three octuple mountings as well as provision for 33 aircraft, protection in the form of a 3-in (76-mm) belt and deck, and a speed of 30.5kt on the 90,000hp (67,105kW) delivered to four shafts by geared steam turbines. The *Eagle* had a displacement of 22,600 tons, an armament by the beginning of World War II of nine 6-in (152-mm) guns in single mountings, four 4-in (102-mm) anti-aircraft guns in single mountings and eight 2-pdr anti-aircraft guns in an octuple mounting as well as provision for 21 aircraft, protection in the

Given the short take-off and landing runs of early aircraft, such as this Sopwith Pup, early British aircraft carriers could have a centrally mounted hatch for aircraft to be moved by crane between the flightdeck and hangar.

form of a 7-in (178-mm) belt and 4-in (102-mm) deck, and a speed of 24kt on the 50,000hp (37280kW) delivered to four shafts by geared steam turbines.

Experience with these large carriers as well as a few small carriers provided the British with considerable aircraft carriage experience in the period between the world wars, and in the later part of the 1930s they produced a new Ark Royal to embody the lessons of this experience in an altogether larger ship with better protection (passive armour as well as active guns) and a large aircraft complement of which most could be accommodated in a large two-storied hangar under the full-length flightdeck. The ship therefore had a displacement of 22,000 tons, an armament of 16 4.5-in (114-mm) anti-aircraft guns in eight twin mountings, 48 2-pdr anti-aircraft guns in six octuple mountings and 32 0.5-in (12.7-mm) machine guns in eight quadruple mountings as well as 72 aircraft, protection in the form of a 4.5-in (114-mm) belt and 3-in (76-mm) deck, and a speed of 30.75kt on the 102,000hp (76050kW) delivered to four shafts by geared steam turbines.

By the period immediately preceding World War II, the British had decided that the threat posed by aircraft to the aircraft carrier had reached such a level that the demands of survivability could only be met by the adoption of an armoured hangar under an armoured flightdeck, and the greater topweight generated by this change meant that a single-level hangar had to be used with a consequent reduction in aircraft capacity to 36 in the Illustrious-class carriers, which were the first full series-built carriers to reach British service. The class was planned as six ships, but while the first three were completed to the originally planned standard, the last three were delivered to a modified standard with an

additional half-hangar aft even though this meant a reduction in the armouring of the ships' upper sections. The original four Illustrious-class carriers were delivered in the first half of World War II and each had a displacement of 23,000 tons, an armament of 16 4.5-in (114-mm) anti-aircraft guns in eight twin mountings, 48 2-pdr anti-aircraft guns in six octuple mountings and eight 20-mm cannon in single mountings as well as 36 aircraft, protection in the form of a 4.5-in (114-mm) belt, 4.5-in (114-mm) hangar side and 3-in (76-mm) deck, and a speed of 31kt on the 110,000hp (82015kW) delivered to four shafts by geared steam

turbines. The last two carriers of the class were delivered later in World War II and each had a displacement of 26,000 tons, an armament of 16 4.5-in (114-mm) anti-aircraft guns in eight twin mountings, 48 2-pdr anti-aircraft guns in six octuple mountings and 38 20-mm cannon in 17 twin and four single mountings as well as 72 aircraft, protection in the form of a 4.5-in (114-mm) belt, 1.5-in (38-mm) hangar side and 3-in (76-mm) deck, and a speed of 32kt on the 148,000hp (110350kW) delivered to four shafts by geared steam turbines.

The importance that carrierborne air

power would exercise on the course of naval affairs was first revealed to a significant extent on 11 November 1940. On this day British carrierborne aircraft of Admiral Sir Andrew Cunningham's Mediterranean Fleet, operating from the aircraft carrier *Illustrious*, launched an attack on the Italian's major naval base at Taranto in southern Italy. For the loss of only two of the 21 aircraft involved, the British carrierborne aircraft left three Italian battleships in a sinking condition, severely damaged two cruisers, and sank two fleet auxiliaries. The attack firmly re-established British naval supremacy in the

RIGHT
Soryu, *a Soryu-class aircraft carrier of the Imperial Japanese Navy, passing the entrance to Tokyo Bay in January 1938.*

BELOW RIGHT
The Amagi, an aircraft carrier of the Imperial Japanese Navy on her side at Yokosuka following the earthquake of 1923. When she was righted it was found that she was too badly damaged and was therefore scrapped.

OPPOSITE ABOVE LEFT
The British aircraft carrier HMS Hermes, seen in company with a British cruiser.

OPPOSITE BELOW LEFT
The American aircraft carrier USS Enterprise (CV-6) launched in 1934 is here seen with Grumman F4Fs, Devastators and Wildcats on the flight deck.

OPPOSITE RIGHT
HMS Courageous, a Courageous-class aircraft carrier of the Royal Navy after refit. Spring 1934.

Mediterranean, and as well as confirming the overall importance of carrierborne air power to modern warfare, provided the still-neutral Japanese with the germ of an idea for a major carrierborne air attack of their own.

That this was not a flash in the pan success, possibly never to be repeated, had in fact been presaged by other carrierborne air operations within the context of the naval war between the U.K. and Germany up to this time, and was to be further confirmed by carrierborne operations in 1941 before naval air power came truly of age in 1942 in the Pacific campaign.

An event that in a single episode confirmed the decline of the battleship's importance and the rise of the aircraft carrier's star occurred in the middle of 1940. On 18 May the German battleship *Bismarck*, an object of considerable fear to the British naval authorities as a result of its powerful armament and what was believed at the time to be virtually undefeatable

OPPOSITE
HMS Ark Royal, *an Ark Royal-class aircraft of the Royal Navy with Fairey Swordfish flying over. Spring 1939.*

LEFT
The Japanese carrier Hiryu *during her trials. April 1939.*

LEFT
The USS Wasp *aircraft carrier and escort underway from off port bow in 1942.*

ABOVE
HMS Argus, *the world's first flushdeck aircraft carrier, in dazzle paint.*

RIGHT
HMS Illustrious.

protection, sailed from the port of Gdynia in occupied Poland. The new battleship, generally thought to be the largest and most powerful warship in the world at the time, was accompanied by the new heavy cruiser *Prinz Eugen* and sailed to Bergenfjord in Norway under the command of Rear Admiral Günther Lütjens.

On 21 May the *Bismarck* and *Prinz Eugen* were sighted in Bergenfjord by British reconnaissance aircraft, and all available units of the Royal Navy between Scapa Flow and Gibraltar were ordered to concentrate for the destruction of the German squadron. On the same day the *Bismarck* put to sea under cover of foggy conditions to escape British surveillance, and the two-ship squadron headed for the Denmark Strait between Iceland and Greenland. British cruisers sighted the German ships entering the Denmark Strait late on 23 May, and Vice Admiral Launcelot Holland in the battle cruiser *Hood*, together with the new battleship *Prince of Wales*, intercepted the German ships early on the following morning. The British and German ships opened fire on each other at a range of some 25,000yds (22860m), and a 15-in (381-mm) shell from the *Bismarck* plunged into the *Hood*, causing one of its magazines to explode. The magnificent *Hood* sank immediately, and there were only three survivors from its crew of 1,500 men. The *Bismarck*'s superb long-range gunnery then inflicted severe damage on the *Prince of Wales*, forcing the ship to turn out of the fight.

Despite modest damage to his own ship, Lütjens continued south-west into the North Atlantic in search of British convoys that his ship could decimate. The damaged *Prince of Wales* and the light cruisers *Suffolk* and *Norfolk* trailed the German vessels and continued to report on the *Bismarck*'s position as other British warships gathered for a second interception.

Lütjens decided that he should put the *Bismarck* into port at Brest, in the north-western part of occupied France, for repairs, and also ordered the *Prinz Eugen* to slip away for an independent cruise. The British lost contact for more than a day, but finally a reconnaissance flying boat spotted the German battleship once more in the morning of 26 May, 700 miles (1125km) to the west of Brest. On the following day warplanes from the aircraft carrier *Ark Royal*, operating at the very limit of their endurance, found and attacked the *Bismarck*, inflicting moderately severe damage to the battleship's steering gear and slowing the German warship just sufficiently for other British surface vessels to arrive on the scene.

The two most important British vessels in the engagement that followed on 27 May were the battleships *Rodney* and *King George V*, but before their arrival the *Bismarck* was further slowed by a night attack performed by a destroyer flotilla to inflict further torpedo damage. During the next morning the *Rodney* and *King George V* engaged the *Bismarck* in a furious gun battle, finally silencing her. Though battered into a flaming hulk with no guns still in operation, the German battleship was still afloat and had to be sunk by two torpedoes from the cruiser *Dorsetshire*, finally sinking it with the loss of almost 2,300 men; only 110 survivors were rescued.

The importance of the *Ark Royal*'s intervention in this battle may seem small in direct terms, but the damage caused by the torpedoes of its deck-launched warplanes was instrumental in slowing the *Bismarck* and thereby making its interception and destruction all but inevitable.

The Illustrious-class ships were the last fleet carriers to be completed in the U.K. during World War II, although two of four Audacious-class fleet carriers were completed in the period after the end of the war, and further aircraft deliveries were therefore of the light and escort carriers. The light carriers were really scaled-down fleet carriers, and the first of them in British service were the 10 units of the Colossus class, of which only six were operational by the end of World War II as four light carriers and two maintenance carriers. The light carriers were completed to a standard that included a displacement of 13,190 tons, an armament of 24 2-pdr anti-aircraft guns in six quadruple mountings and 19 40-mm anti-aircraft guns in single mountings as well as 48 aircraft, only light

BELOW
The 19,800-ton aircraft carrier USS Hornet *(CV-8) shortly after her launch date in 1941. She was sunk in October 1942, little more than a year after her commissioning.*

The Imperial Japanese Navy's aircraft carrier Shoho, *converted from the submarine deposit ship* Tsurugizaki.

protection, and a speed of 25kt on the 42,000hp (3131 kW) delivered to two shafts by geared steam turbines. The two maintenance carriers had lighter gun armament and no aircraft, and were designed for support of the British naval force operating with the U.S. Pacific Fleet. The other four ships were completed after the war, and four of the class were later transferred to friendly nations (Australia and thence Brazil, Canada and thence Argentina, France, and the Netherlands and thence Argentina).

There followed five of six light carriers of the Majestic class that were launched during the war but completed after it with a displacement of 14,000 tons, an armament of 30 40-mm anti-aircraft guns

in six twin and 18 single mountings as well as 34 aircraft, only light protection, and a speed of 24.5kt on the 42,000hp (31315kW) delivered to two shafts by geared steam turbines. All of these ships were later transferred or sold to friendly nations (two to Australia, two to Canada and one to India).

There should have followed eight units of the slightly larger and more capable Hermes-class intermediate fleet-carrier type with somewhat higher performance as a result of their considerably more powerful propulsion arrangement, but only four of these were laid down for launch and completion after the end of the war with a displacement of 18,300 tons, an armament of 32 40-mm anti-aircraft guns in two

sextuple, eight twin and four single mountings as well as 50 aircraft, protection in the form of a 1-in (25-mm) deck, and a speed of 29.5kt on the 83,000hp (61885kW) delivered to four shafts by geared steam turbines.

The escort carrier was built to a small and less capable standard as it was designed originally for the convoy escort role and later used additionally for the support of amphibious operations. The ships were initially converted from large merchant ships but later built specifically for the task although generally to mercantile standards. Most of the ships were of American origin, and the vessels used by the Royal Navy included the five units of the Archer class, eight units of the Attacker class, 26 units of the Ruler class, and four miscellaneous ships. The Ruler class may be taken as typical of the breed, and its details included a full-length hangar under the flightdeck, a displacement of 11,420 tons, an armament of two 4-in (102-mm) anti-aircraft guns in single mountings, 16 40-mm anti-aircraft guns in eight twin mountings and 20 20-mm cannon in single mountings as well as 24 aircraft, no protection, and a speed of 17kt on the 9,350hp (6970kW) delivered to one shaft by a geared steam turbine.

Following World War II, the U.K. found itself in a severely straitened financial situation and was already beginning its retreat from empire, so no new aircraft carriers were laid down for some time and the Royal Navy made do with its existing

units, albeit in forms that were often upgraded to a significant degree with features such as an angled flightdeck and the mirror landing system, which were both British inventions. The force available by the middle of the 1950s included the three units of the Hermes class revised as the Centaur class, the lead ship of the Audacious class completed as the sole Eagle-class ship with a full-load displacement of 53,390 tons and provision for up to 60 aircraft, the other unit of the Audacious class completed as the sole unit of the Ark Royal class with a full-load displacement of 53,060 tons and provision for up to 36 aircraft, and the *Victorious* of the Illustrious class revised to a more modern standard with a full-load displacement of 35,500 tons

and provision for up to 36 aircraft.

The sole later addition in the 1950s was the sole Hermes-class carrier that was completed from a Hermes-class carrier with a full-load displacement of 28,700 tons and provision for up to 28 aircraft. In the late 1960s the U.K. decided that large aircraft carriers were no longer appropriate to the country's reduced world status and were also too expensive in maintenance (existing ships) and construction (planned new ships), and were gradually phased out of service in the 1970s, although a couple of the units enjoyed a further lease of life into the early 1980s as commando carriers.

The last British aircraft carriers, which are still in useful service after launch between 1977 and 1981, are the three light carriers of the Invincible class, which were designed to carry helicopters and fixed-wing aircraft of the STOVL type, the latter in the form of the British Aerospace Sea Harrier. These carriers each have a full-load displacement of some 23,000 tons, an armament of one twin-arm launcher for Sea Dart surface-to-air missiles and two 20-mm Vulcan six-barrel cannon in Phalanx close-in weapon system mountings as well as 14 aircraft, and a speed of 28kt on the 112,000shp (83505kW) delivered to two shafts by a COGOG (COmbined Gas turbine Or Gas turbine) propulsion arrangement with four Rolls-Royce Olympus gas turbines.

So successful have these ships proved, despite their small size and limited aircraft complement, in a number of campaigns and peacekeeping roles that in the late 1990s the British government decided that the three small carriers would eventually be replaced by two larger aircraft carriers to a somewhat larger and more advanced concept, probably with a displacement in the order of 40,000 tons.

HMS Biter, *an Archer-class escort carrier of the Royal Navy, 1942.*

The USS Enterprise *about to launch Douglas Dauntless dive-bombers during the Battle of the Coral Sea. Though not actively involved in the battle, the* Enterprise *is shown here launching aircraft at the rate of one every 30 seconds. 4 May 1942.*

The American involvement with carrierborne aviation began in 1922 with the conversion of the collier *Jupiter* into the aircraft carrier *Langley*. This ship provided the fledgling naval air arm with initial experience, and this greater facilitated the entry into service late in the same decade of the two fleet carriers of the Saratoga class which, as a result of the Washington Naval Treaty limitation on capital ship construction, were converted while still under construction from battle-cruisers into aircraft carriers. When completed, the ships were the largest and probably the most advanced aircraft carriers in the world with a full-load displacement of 39,000 tons, an armament of eight 8-in (203-mm) guns in four twin turrets and 12 5-in (127-mm) anti-aircraft guns in single mountings as well as 90 aircraft, protection in the form of a 6-in (152-mm) belt and 3-in (76-mm) deck, and a speed of 34kt on the 180,000hp (134210kW) delivered to four shafts by a turbo-electric propulsion arrangement.

The first American aircraft carrier designed as such was the following and very considerably smaller Ranger, which was launched in 1933 and completed to a standard that included a standard displacement of 14,500 tons, an armament of eight 5-in (127-mm) anti-aircraft gun in single mountings as well as 86 aircraft, protection in the form of a 2-in (51-mm) belt and 1-in (25-mm) deck, and a speed of 29.5kt on the 53,500hp (39890kW) delivered to two shafts by geared steam turbines.

Experience indicated that the Ranger, built to treaty limitations and therefore lacking in protection and performance to ensure that a large number of aircraft could be embarked, was inadequate as a first-line aircraft carrier. The two following units of the Yorktown class, both launched in 1936,

LEFT
U.S. Army B-25Bs on board the USS Hornet *(CV-8), en route to their launching point prior to the Doolittle Raid on Tokyo on 18 April 1942.*

BELOW
Sea Hurricanes taking off from HMS Ark Royal, *as seen from HMS* Sheffield *in May 1941.*

USS Yorktown (CV-5) shortly before sinking on the morning of 6 June 1942 after the Battle of Midway. Following dive-bombing and torpedo attack by the Japanese submarine I-168, the ship finally sank.

USS Lexington (CV-16). Flightdeck crewmen push an F6F-3 Hellcat forward in 1944. Note pilot walking away in the foreground.

were therefore completed to a slightly larger and considerably more capable standard with a full-load displacement of 25,500 tons, an armament of eight 5-in (127-mm) anti-aircraft guns in single mountings as well as 100 aircraft, protection in the form of a 4-in (102-mm) belt and 3-in (76-mm) deck, and a speed of 34kt on the 120,000hp (82015kW) delivered to four shafts by geared steam turbines. These two ships were the *Yorktown* and *Enterprise*, and in 1940 a half-sister was launched as the *Hornet* with a slightly larger flightdeck as well as a number of improved features.

The last American aircraft carrier completed before the entry of the U.S.A. into World War II was the *Wasp*, which was a small carrier along the lines of the *Ranger* as she was designed to fill the American quota for aircraft carrier tonnage under the terms of the Washington Naval Treaty. The American philosophy at this time was that all must be subordinated to aircraft-carrying capability. The *Wasp* therefore carried very nearly as many aircraft as the ships of the Yorktown class, and this meant that major sacrifices had to be made in protection and speed. As completed, the ship had details including a full-load displacement of 21,000 tons, an armament of eight 5-in (127-mm) anti-aircraft guns in single mountings as well as 84 aircraft, protection in the form of a 4-in (102-mm) belt and 1.5-in (38-mm) deck, and a speed of 29.5kt on the 75,000hp (55920kW) delivered to two shafts by geared steam turbines.

In the aftermath of Pearl Harbor, which drew the U.S.A. into World War II on the side of the Allies, the U.S.A. was faced with enormous difficulties as the Japanese invaded the U.S. dependency of the Philippines and scythed through South-East Asia before turning their attentions to the Dutch East Indies and Burma before creating their

LEFT
USS Lexington *burning during the Battle of the Coral Sea on 8 May 1942.*

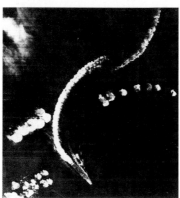

defensive perimeter. At sea all the U.S.A. could undertake were strikes by the aircraft of its three carriers, with *Yorktown* arriving to replace the *Saratoga* damaged by a torpedo attack on 11 January 1942. Carrierborne air attacks were made against Japanese bases in the Gilbert and Marshall Islands on 1 February, in the Wake and Marcus Islands between 24 February and 4 March, and at Lae and Salamaua on 10 March before culminating in the propaganda triumph of the so-called Doolittle Raid of 18 April, when 16 B-25 Mitchell twin-engined bombers of the U.S. Army Air Forces under the command of Colonel James H. Doolittle lifted off from the Hornet to attack Tokyo.

LEFT
The Japanese carrier Hiryu *manoeuvring to avoid bombs from U.S.A.F. B-17s during the Battle of Midway 4–6th June 1942.*

FAR LEFT
A Japanese carrier circling during the Battle of Midway.

A Curtiss SB2C-1C Helldiver on the deck of the USS Bunker Hill *(CV-17) off Saipan.*

W. Nimitz, commander-in-chief of the Pacific Ocean Areas, was able to despatch a task force, under the command of Rear Admiral Frank J. Fletcher, centred on the carriers *Lexington* and *Yorktown* and supported by the British Rear Admiral J. G. Grace's small squadron of American and Australian cruisers and destroyers, to intercept the Japanese.

After it had been detached to attack the Japanese landing on Tulagi, the *Yorktown* rejoined Fletcher's force on 5 May as the Japanese and Allied forces approached each other. At this time Fletcher's force was in the centre of the Coral Sea off the eastern end of New Guinea, and of the two Japanese forces, that of Takagi was steaming into the sea from the north-east and the Port Moresby assault force, supported by the *Shoho*'s squadron, was nearing the Coral Sea from the Solomon Sea to the north.

On 7–8 May there took place the Battle of the Coral Sea. In a series of confused actions, the two carrier forces located and attacked each other. The *Shoho* was sunk by American carrierborne warplanes on 7 May, while a Japanese attempt to attack the American carrier force by night suffered heavy aircraft losses. On the following morning, however, the Japanese sank the *Lexington* (as well as a destroyer and an oiler) and damaged the *Yorktown*, while American aircraft severely damaged the *Shokaku* but failed to hit the *Zuikaku* which was unscathed. Meanwhile, the sinking of the *Shoho* and the threat of Grace's Australian and American force of three cruisers and escorting destroyers, which had survived several Japanese air strikes and an attack by U.S. land-based aircraft without suffering damage, persuaded Inouye to call off the Port Moresby invasion. Fletcher and Takagi almost simultaneously decided to pull back.

These were among the events that prompted the Japanese into a modification of their basic strategic plan to extend the perimeter in the central and southern Pacific. The first step in the revised plan saw Admiral Isoroku Yamamoto, commander-in-chief of the Combined Fleet and the author of the Pearl Harbor plan, order Admiral Shigeyoshi Inouye, commander of the New Guinea theatre, to take and hold base areas in the south-eastern end of the Solomon Islands and to capture Port Moresby on the southern coast of eastern New Guinea. The first task was entrusted to the small carrier

Shoho, four cruisers, and one destroyer as escort for an assault force of several transports destined for Tulagi, a larger force being concentrated at Rabaul for a seaborne attack on Port Moresby.

To provide additional support, the fleet aircraft carriers *Shokaku* and *Zuikaku* were nominated as the core of a support force under the command of Rear Admiral Takeo Takagi, and this force headed south from the Central Pacific to enter the Coral Sea from the east. The Japanese were unaware that U.S. naval intelligence knew of most of these plans, and as a result Admiral Chester

The Battle of the Coral Sea was the first genuine carrier battle as no surface ship of either side saw any of the enemy's ships. The battle was a draw in tactical terms as the Japanese had lost more aircraft and the Americans more ships, but in strategic terms it was an Allied victory as it ended the threat of a seaborne assault on Port Moresby.

Meanwhile, even as he was preparing to implement the revised Japanese strategic plan, Yamamoto discovered that the American carriers *Enterprise* and *Hornet* were in the south Pacific, to which Nimitz had rushed them in a vain attempt to make them available for the Battle of the Coral Sea. Believing that the *Yorktown* and the *Lexington* had each been sunk in the course of the Coral Sea battle, Yamamoto was now sure that the Combined Fleet could strike at Midway Island, at the extreme north-western tip of the Hawaiian chain, without interference from American carrierborne aircraft. Even so, he assembled 165 warships,

the largest force yet seen in the Pacific. Vice Admiral Boshiro Hosogaya's Northern Area Force (two light carriers, seven cruisers and 12 destroyers) was allocated the task of making a diversionary attack against the U.S. bases in Alaska, just before the main blow fell on Midway, and then of seizing bases in the western part of the Aleutian island chain. The rest of the Japanese fleet was divided into three forces for the main part of the Midway operation: these were Nagumo's 1st Air Fleet (less the carriers put out of action at the Coral Sea by damage or loss of aircraft); the Midway Occupation Force under Vice Admiral Nobutake Kondo (the 2nd Fleet with two battleships, one light carrier, two seaplane carriers, seven cruisers and destroyers) to escort 12 transports ferrying 51,000 troops; and the Main Body under Yamamoto himself (seven battleships, one light carrier, four cruisers and 12 destroyers). Moreover, 18 submarines had been despatched into the waters between Midway and Pearl Harbor

to report American movements and to launch attacks on targets of opportunity.

On the other side of the front line Nimitz, alerted by naval intelligence about the Japanese preparations, ordered the task force comprising the *Enterprise* and *Hornet*, under the command of Vice Admiral William F. Halsey, to lose no time in returning from the South Pacific. The Americans preparatory effort was also boosted by the fact that the *Yorktown*, requiring repairs estimated to need three months of dockyard attention, was made ready for sea in a mere three days. The *Enterprise*, *Hornet* and *Yorktown* between them embarked about 250 warplanes, which was a figure similar to that carried by Nagumo's four fleet carriers. Nimitz had only 76 warships available to him, and decided to detach about one-third of these to Alaskan waters to leave his central Pacific force with about 50 ships that would, he planned, be able to rely on air support from the 109 warplanes based on Midway island.

ABOVE
The escort carrier HMS Ruler entering the Grand Harbour at Valetta, Malta during the build-up for the Allied invasion of Southern France on 17 August 1944.

ABOVE LEFT
The aircraft carrier USS Bunker Hill (CV-17) underway in Puget Sound, Washington.

The USS Essex *(CV-9), at Hampton Roads, Virginia, broadside on port bow.*

attack the approaching Japanese attack aircraft. Both these American efforts were repulsed with great loss, the American planes being inferior in speed to the Japanese aircraft. Half of the aircraft attacking the Japanese carriers were shot down by Japanese fighters without inflicting damage on their targets, and at much the same time Nagumo's attack warplanes broke through the American fighter screen and attacked Midway island, though exercising great caution in avoiding the runways that they expected to use at a later time.

Advised that the suppression of Midway's defences would require a second attack, Nagumo ordered that the aircraft held in reserve on his carriers should have their anti-ship loads of armour-piercing bombs and torpedoes replaced by land-attack weapons such as fragmentation bombs and incendiaries. Just after work had begun on this laborious task, a

The HMS Activity *escort carrier at sea on 24 November 1942.*

By a time late in May, some 50 American warships had assembled north of Midway island without detection by the Japanese submarine cordon, which got into position only on 1 June. In the absence of Halsey, who was ill, Rear Admiral Raymond A. Spruance commanded the task force centred on the *Enterprise* and *Hornet*, under the operational command of Fletcher on the *Yorktown*.

The Battle of Midway, little affected by the diversionary operations off Alaska, started on 4 June. In the belief that there were no American carriers in the offing and that the Americans' main strength had been lured away to the north, Nagumo committed 108 aircraft, representing half his attack force, against Midway early in the morning. At the same time, American land-based aircraft lifted off from Midway to attack the Japanese carriers and also to

reconnaissance aircraft reported a force of American warships to the north-east. Now worried, Nagumo reversed his previous order and instructed that the warplanes on his carriers be armed for the anti-ship role even as the aircraft of the Midway strike package was arriving back on the decks of their parent carriers.

Nagumo's force was steaming with its four carriers in a box formation, each escorted by battleships, cruisers and destroyers. He changed course 90° to the east to meet the new threat.

During this period Fletcher had instructed Spruance to launch the aircraft of the *Enterprise* and *Hornet* against the Japanese carriers. The *Yorktown*, several miles to the east, launched half its planes at 07.30 hours: as a result of Nagumo's change of course, Spruance's dive-bombers missed the Japanese carriers in the overcast conditions prevailing, but the torpedo bombers found their targets and attacked without delay at about 09.30 hours even though they lacked fighter cover: almost all of the aircraft were shot down by the Japanese anti-aircraft guns and defensive fighters. The American aircraft had scored not one hit and Nagumo, believing that a major victory was now imminent, was still trying to organize the rearmament and refuelling of the warplanes cluttering his carriers' flightdecks. It was at this moment that the American dive-bombers, representing the squadrons from the *Enterprise*, *Hornet* and *Yorktown* in turn, arrived overhead: by 10.25 hours, the *Akagi*, *Kaga*, and *Soryu* were wrecked ships engulfed in flame, while the fourth Japanese fleet carrier, the undamaged *Hiryu*, was steaming north-east and launching its reserve warplanes to seek out the American carriers responsible for the destruction of the other three carriers.

The Japanese aircraft located the *Yorktown* just after noon and landed three bombs on the American carrier. The *Hiryu*, meanwhile, had completed the rearmament

The aircraft carrier USS Bismark *Casablanca-class at sea in 1944.*

of the aircraft returned from Midway, which now attacked the *Yorktown* to achieve two fatal torpedo hits. Fletcher abandoned his helpless and listing ship at 15.00 hours. American aircraft had found the surviving Japanese carrier, however, and from the *Enterprise* launched 24 dive-bombers to tackle the *Hiryu*, which was fatally damaged and caught fire.

By now it was 17.00 hours and the main part of the Battle of Midway was over: the Imperial Japanese Navy had lost its current force of fleet carriers, while the U.S. Navy still had two operational fleet carriers.

Yamamoto was appalled at the course events were taking, but even so hoped to extract victory from a very unpromising situation. Steaming east during the night with all of his big ships, still vastly more

powerful in surface strength to the Americans, Yamamoto tried to lure the Americans into a surface battle. Fletcher had passed tactical command to Spruance after the abandonment of the *Yorktown*, and Spruance was all too aware of such a danger and had retired to the east in the night. Eventually realizing that he could not trap the American ships and that his own vessels now lacked air defence, Yamamoto ordered his surviving forces to pull back to the west.

For two days the Americans pursued the Japanese by day, but themselves fell back at night. American planes caused additional damage, but no major actions took place. Finally, with his surviving ships' fuel supplies running low, Spruance turned his ships back toward Pearl Harbor. The crippled *Yorktown* was being towed back to Pearl Harbor when

she and an escorting destroyer were torpedoed by a Japanese submarine. These two were the only American ships sunk in the Battle of Midway, in which the Americans had also lost 132 carrierborne and land-based aircraft and 307 men. The Japanese losses were four fleet carriers, one heavy cruiser, 275 aircraft and 3,500 men.

Midway was one of the decisive battles of history, for the loss of its fleet carrier force deprived Japan of the strategic initiative.

By the late 1930s, the radical worsening of international relations combined with the U.S. Navy's now-considerable experience in carrier operations to make both desirable and feasible the design of a completely new type of aircraft carrier. This was the Essex class, which became the mainstay of the U.S. Navy's carrier force in World War II and was built to the final extent of 26 ships. The design included a size comparable with that of the Saratoga-class battle-cruiser conversions with the pure aircraft carrier design features of the Ranger, Yorktown and Wasp classes in a type that was optimized for far-ranging operations against a determined enemy through the incorporation of more ship qualities, much improved protection based not so much on thicker armour as on increased compartmentalization and, for maximum aircraft operating capability including the possibility of upgrade to larger and heavier warplane types, a large flightdeck with an overhanging port side, two catapults and three large elevators (including one deck-edge rather than inset unit) connecting the hangar and flightdeck. The one weak point of the design, certainly relative to British practice at this time, was the installation of the flightdeck as an essentially unarmoured superstructure element rather than as an intrinsic and armoured part of the hull. Even so, the Essex-class carriers were superb warships that possessed the ability to survive considerable combat damage. The details of the Essex-class aircraft carrier included a full-load displacement of 33,000 tons, an armament of 12 5-in (127-mm) anti-aircraft guns in four twin and four single mountings, between 44 and 72 40-mm anti-aircraft guns in 11 to 18 quadruple mountings and 52 20-mm cannon in single mountings as well as 100 aircraft, protection in the form of a 4-in (102-mm) belt and 3-in (76-mm) deck, and a speed of 33kt on the 150,000hp (111840kW) delivered to four shafts by geared steam turbines.

For the rest of 1942 and early in 1943, the U.S. Navy was heavily involved in the campaign to check and then to defeat the Japanese occupation of Guadalcanal in the eastern part of the Solomons, which had been occupied on 7 August 1942 at the same time as Tulagi. There were many naval engagements in the waters north and west of Guadalcanal, but not all of these involved aircraft carriers. The Battle of the Eastern Solomons on 22–25 August involved the Japanese fleet carriers *Shokaku* and *Zuikaku* and the light carrier *Ryujo* against the American fleet carriers *Enterprise* and *Saratoga*, of which the *Ryujo* was sunk and the *Enterprise* was severely damaged. Other elements of the naval fighting around Guadalcanal resulted in severe damage to the *Saratoga* on 31 August and the sinking of the *Wasp* on 15 September, both as a result of torpedo attacks by Japanese submarines. In the Battle of the Santa Cruz Islands on 26–27 October the Japanese deployed the fleet carrier *Shokaku* and the light carrier *Zuiho*, both of which received heavy damage, while the Americans used the *Enterprise* and *Hornet*, of which the former was again badly damaged and the latter so severely hit that it fell prey to Japanese destroyer attack after being abandoned.

The Japanese aircraft carrier Junyo *in Ebisu Bay, Sasebo, Kyushu, Japan. Taken from USS* Mount McKinley.

If in 1942 the Americans first blunted and checked the Japanese military and naval expansion in the South-West Pacific and Pacific Ocean theatres, 1942 was the year in which the Americans went over to the strategic offensive and began the long slog of driving the Japanese back to their home islands. By this time the U.S. front-line forces were growing in size as well as in overall capability as more and more fully trained men became available, and the huge production capacity of American industry was allowing the delivery of ever larger numbers of better weapons, including growing numbers of aircraft carriers as well as light and escort carriers. Not all of these were available for deployment to the Pacific for the war with Japan as U.S. forces were also involved in the war with Germany, but

the bulk of American naval strength was used in the Pacific.

The Pacific Fleet's aircraft carrier strength was involved in several parts of the Pacific, and toward the end of the year eight carriers were part of Spruance's 5th Fleet supporting the landings that wrested the Gilbert Islands from the Japanese in small-scale fighting that was notably bitter on Tarawa. The same 5th Fleet was responsible for the capture of the Marshall Islands in January and February 1944, support being provided by the Fast Carrier Task Force under Vice Admiral Marc A. Mitscher with six fleet and six light carriers.

On 17–18 February the Fast Carrier Task Force attacked Truk, the primary Japanese naval base in the central Pacific. Admiral Mineichi Kogo, commanding the

LEFT
*The aircraft carrier USS
Ranger (CV-4) in the
Pacific.*

OPPOSITE
*The aircraft carrier USS
Oriskany (CV-34) underway
off New York City.*

Combined Fleet since Yamamoto's death when his transport was purposefully intercepted and shot down by American long-range fighters in April 1943, managed to save most of his ships in a rapid dispersal, but the Americans discovered 50 merchant ships in the harbour and 365 aircraft on the island's landing strips: by mid-day the Fast Carrier Task Forces aircraft had sent 200,000 tons of shipping to the bottom and destroyed 275 of the aircraft. The losses of the Combined Fleet were severe rather than fatal, but Kogo appreciated that American carrier strength now made Truk valueless as a fleet base: the Combined Fleet was accordingly withdrawn to bases north of the Caroline and Marianas Islands, while the Americans were content to isolate Truk and its surviving men, which were left to wither on the vine for the rest of the war.

On 1 April Kogo was killed in an air accident and replaced as commander-in-chief of the Combined Fleet by Admiral Soemu Toyoda, who felt that he could still accomplish the destruction of the Pacific Fleet by using land-based air power in combination with a Japanese carrier force that had been swelled in numbers by the advent of new ships and more aircraft. What Toyoda refused to accept, however, was that the aircraft were just new examples of types that had been in service since the beginning of the war and were now obsolete, and that their crews were freshly trained men lacking the acute flying and tactical skills that had characterized the crews of Japan's heady days of success, but were now mostly dead.

In May 1944, therefore, Toyoda ordered Vice Admiral Jisaburo Ozawa, commanding the 1st Mobile Fleet, to draw American naval strength into the area bounded by the Palau, Yap and Woleai islands, where Japanese land-based air power could contribute to its destruction. Ozawa's fleet assembled on 16 May off the southern tip of the Sulu archipelago, where it was harried by American submarines that also kept the high command fully informed of the Japanese carrier force's strength and movements.

In June the Americans launched the major campaign to take the Marianas Islands, for Saipan, Tinian and Guam were large enough for the construction of vast air bases on which could be located the fleets of Boeing B-29 strategic bombers that would decimate Japans war-making capability. The threat to Japan was obvious, and Toyoda responded immediately with a naval offensive that led to the Battle of the Philippine Sea on 19–21 June. Spruance, warned of the advance of Ozawa's fleet immediately after word had been received of the American landing on Saipan, assembled his 5th Fleet, in the form of Task Force 58 under the tactical command of Mitscher, about 160 miles (257km) west of Tinian. The balance of forces pitted the 1st Mobile Fleet's five fleet and four light carriers, five battleships, 11 heavy and two light cruisers, and 28 destroyers against Task Group 58's seven fleet and eight light carriers, seven battleships, eight heavy and 13 light cruisers, and 69 destroyers: the American carriers embarked 956 aircraft whereas the Japanese carriers had only 473 aircraft, but Ozawa felt happier in the knowledge that the battle would be fought within range of the 100 or more aircraft based on Guam, Rota and Yap.

Japanese reconnaissance aircraft found Task Force 58 at the break of day on 19 June, the American forces being 300 miles (483km) from the Japanese advance guard

HMS Hermes *(R12) built by Vickers (Shipbuilding) Ltd., was commissioned on 16 November 1958. Her last refit was in 1980 which included the addition of a ski jump. She carried five Sea Harrier aircraft and nine Sea King helicopters.*

of four light carriers, itself some 500 miles (805km) ahead of the Japanese main body. The opposing fleets were on southerly courses, Task Force 58's carriers some 90 miles (145km) north-west of Guam and 110 miles (177km) south-west of Saipan in Task Groups 58.1 to 58.4 backed by Spruance with the seven battleships, four heavy cruisers and 13 destroyers of Task Group 58.5.

At about this time the land-based Japanese warplanes from the bases in the Marianas and Truk were driven back with heavy losses, although no one informed Ozawa of this fact. Ozawa now launched four waves of attack aircraft and Mitscher, warned of the Japanese onslaught, launched his fighters to intercept and then sent his attack warplanes into the air to keep the flightdecks of his carriers clear.

Even before the carrier battle had been joined, the outcome of the battle for the Japanese was suggested by the attacks of American submarines, which sank the new fleet carrier *Taiho* and also the *Shokaku*, one of the two survivors of the Pearl Harbor operation. Mitscher's fighters inflicted enormous losses on the Japanese attack warplanes, and virtually all of those which broke through the fighter cordon were destroyed by anti-aircraft fire. This was the Great Marianas Turkey Shoot, which cost the Japanese 346 aircraft in addition to the two carriers. American losses were only 30 aircraft and slight damage to a battleship as a result of the one Japanese bomb that found a target.

Meanwhile, Mitscher's attack aircraft had found and effectively neutralized the airfields on Guam and Rota, and the battle was effectively over by 18.45 hours as Ozawa reversed course. Mitscher committed his force to pursuit, but did not regain contact until late in the afternoon of the

The Independencia *(V1), an ex-British Colossus-class aircraft carrier of the Argentine navy during flight operations on 23 September 1964.*

The HMS Albion, *a commando carrier, with Wessex V helicopters of 845 Naval Air Commando Squadron and Sea King helicopters of 826 Naval Anti-Submarine Squadron in a north Norwegian fjord during exercise* Strong Express. *The ship carried 45 Commando RM. September 1972.*

HMS Ark Royal *(R09)
with Buccaneer strike
aircraft and F-4K Phantom
II fighters on the flightdeck.
October 1973.*

following day. At this point Task Force 58
launched 216 aircraft despite the lateness of
the hour. The American warplanes found
and sank the light carrier *Hiyo* as well as two
oilers, and also inflicted severe damage on
several other vessels. The Americans lost 20
aircraft and the Japanese another 65 in this
phase of the battle. As they headed back to
their carriers, the survivors' American pilots
faced major problems in finding their
mothers in the darkness, even though
Mitscher had ordered his ships to be fully
illuminated despite the threat of submarine
attack, and as they ran short of fuel: about
80 aircraft ran out of fuel and ditched in the
sea or crash landed, but destroyers managed
to find some 50 airmen in the water and the
American losses for the day were therefore
only 49 men.

The remnants of the 1st Mobile Fleet
continued to pull back to the west while
Task Force 58 returned to Saipan after the
conclusion of a battle that had seen the
infliction of a fatal blow on Japans carrier
force, whose loss of more than 460 pilots
exhausted its last experienced men as well as
the best of the new crop of pilots. Saipan
fell to the Americans on 13 July, and Tinian
and Guam had been secured by 2 and 10
August respectively.

The U.S. strategy for the next move of
the war in the Pacific was settled in principle
at a conference at Pearl Harbor in July
1944. President Franklin D. Roosevelt
assessed two concepts of approach to the
final objective – an assault on Japan itself:
Nimitz preferred intermediate moves on
Formosa or China, while General Douglas
MacArthur, commanding in the South-West
Pacific theatre, was adamant that an
offensive first be launched to free the
Philippines (for both military and political
reasons), and only then on Japan. Roosevelt
opted for MacArthur's scheme. The staffs of

the U.S. Army and U.S. Navy worked in close collaboration to plan the required moves: first the forces of MacArthur and Nimitz were to take Mindanao and Yap respectively, second a combined invasion of Leyte, third the invasion and capture of Luzon by MacArthur's forces as Nimitz's forces took Iwo Jima and Okinawa, and fourth the invasion of Japan.

As soon as the Marianas operation had ended, Nimitz set Spruance and his 5th Fleet staff to plan the Iwo Jima and Okinawa operations, while Halsey and his 3rd Fleet staff undertook the Yap operation. This was a shift in commanders and staffs only: the ships and men were unchanged as what had been the 5th Fleet became the 3rd Fleet, this including the Fast Carrier Task Force that had been Task Force 58 and now became Task Force 38.

On 15 September, MacArthur's forces landed on Morotai against minimal opposition to establish a forward air base, while in a co-ordinated move, Nimitz's forces attacked Peleliu in the Palau Islands, where the U.S. Marine Corps men of Major General Roy S. Geiger's III Amphibious

HMS Bulwark *on exercise* Deep Express *off Turkey.*

Corps (part of Vice Admiral Theodore S. Wilkinsons III Amphibious Force, later V Amphibious Force) encountered determined resistance. Army units of the III Amphibious Force also took Angaur and occupied Ulithi Atoll, about 100 miles (161km) west of Yap, that became a base for the 3rd Fleet.

On 15 September there was also a change in the strategic plan. In support of the Morotai and Peleliu operations, the carriers of the 3rd Fleet had on 6 September attacked Yap, Ulithi, and the Palaus to neutralize Japanese bases that might otherwise have been able to intervene in the forthcoming operations, and had then

USS Nimitz *CVN-68 making a rendezvous with the oiler USS* Kalamazoo *(AOR-6) in the Caribbean. 13 August 1975.*

267

HMS Eagle *of the Royal Navy.*

swept the Philippine coast in the period 9–13 September. Over the Philippines the 3rd Fleet's aircraft had met so little resistance that Halsey suggested to Nimitz that the intermediate landings on Yap and Mindanao were not longer necessary and that the attack on Leyte should be brought forward. Nimitz agreed, secured basic approval from the Joint Chiefs of Staff, and then with the offer of his III Amphibious Force and the U.S. Army's XXIV Corps currently under his command brought MacArthur on board with agreement that the Leyte landing should take place on 20 October rather than 20 December.

In the period 7–16 October the aircraft of the 5th and 7th Army Air Forces, based in New Guinea and the Marianas respectively, crippled all the Japanese air bases within their range. At the same time the 3rd Fleet's aircraft attacked shipping and shore installations in and around Okinawa, then turned south toward Formosa and Luzon. Between 13 and 16 October there took place the Battle of Formosa. Japanese aircraft from Formosa struck at the 3rd Fleet, severely damaging two heavy cruising and hitting other ships. Japan claimed a great victory, and Halsey felt that this was a good opportunity to lure the Combined

Fleet, whose commanders clearly felt that the Japanese success had been far larger than it really was, to a decisive encounter. Leaving one carrier group to escort the crippled ships, Halsey moved the rest of the 3rd Fleet east into the Philippine Sea and Toyodo took the bait and despatched 600 naval aircraft from Japan to airfields on Formosa for the completion of his destruction of the 3rd Fleet. Halsey then reversed course and struck at Formosa, his aircraft in a two-day period destroying about half these aircraft.

The total score in these operations was more than 650 Japanese warplanes

destroyed, many others crippled, numerous shore installations smashed and, perhaps most importantly off all, the effective destruction of the carrierborne air squadrons that the Japanese had worked so hard to destroy. The 3rd Fleet's aircraft losses were only 75.

Meanwhile, the final preparations for the invasion and reconquest of the Philippine Islands, held by about 350,000 Japanese troops under the command of General Tomoyuki Yamashita, were being completed. Between 14 and 19 October a huge amphibious fleet approached Leyte: some 700 vessels, carrying 200,000 men of General Walter Krueger's 6th Army, comprised Admiral Thomas C. Kinkaid's 7th Fleet. Wilkinson's III and Vice Admiral Daniel E. Barbey's VII Amphibious Forces were supported by Rear Admiral Jesse B.

Oldendorf's gunfire-support group of six old battleships, four heavy and four light cruisers, and 26 destroyers. The air-support group under Rear Admiral Thomas L. Sprague comprised 16 escort carriers, nine destroyers and 11 destroyer escorts. Farther off in the tasks of neutralizing the Japanese air bases on Luzon and guarding the San Bernardino and Surigao Straits was the 3rd Fleet centred on Task Force 38 with eight fleet and eight light carriers with more than 1,000 aircraft, six fast new battleships, three heavy and nine light cruisers, and 58 destroyers.

After the landing area had been pulverized by air attack and bombardment by naval guns, the 6th Army landed its X and XXIV Corps on Leyte. This triggered not only the local defence but also the full implementation of Japan's Sho-1 strategic

plan (already triggered by the U.S. landings on 15 September) to use Japanese land-based air power to neutralize the carrier-based air power of any U.S. invasion force as it closed the Philippines, and so permit the Combined Fleet to destroy the invasion force without hindrance from U.S. aircraft. The task of neutralizing U.S. carrier air power was entrusted to the 1st and 2nd Air Fleets (the former based in the Philippines under Vice Admiral Takujiro Onishi, and the latter training in the Japanese home islands, under the command of Vice Admiral Shigeru Fukodome, until moved to the Philippines at the implementation of SHO-1 to link up with the 1st Air Fleet as Fukodome's 1st Combined Base Air Force) supported by the Imperial Japanese army's 4th Air Army with its 2nd and 4th Air Divisions.

ABOVE
A stern view of USS Nimitz
(CVN-68) in the Atlantic.

ABOVE RIGHT
USS Nimitz *with
ammunition ship USS*
Mount Baker *(AE-34)
alongside during trials in
the Guantanamo area. 31
July 1975.*

RIGHT
The Clemenceau, *a
Clemenceau-class aircraft
carrier of the French navy
in 1979.*

Toyoda launched the naval side of
SHO-1 in all its complexity on 17 October,
with the constituent forces coming under
the control of Vice Admiral Gunichi
Mikawa's South-West Area Fleet as they
approached the Philippines. This naval
portion of SHO-1 called for a four-sided
descent on the U.S. invasion fleet off Leyte.
Vice Admiral Takeo Kurita's 5th Fleet was
ordered to sail from Singapore and other
points before concentrating and refuelling
in Brunei Bay and then dividing into two
parts before approaching the U.S. forces via
the Sibuyan Sea and San Bernardino Strait
(Kurita's Forces A and B, otherwise the 1st
Strike Force, Centre Force) or the Surigao
Strait (Vice Admiral Shoji Nishimuras Force
C, otherwise the 2nd Strike Force, Southern
Force). Vice Admiral Kiyohide Shima's
detachment 2nd Strike Force, Northern
Force, was ordered to sail from the Ryukyus
via the Pescadores Islands to link up with

the Southern Force in the attack through the Surigao Strait. Ozawa's Mobile Force, Strike Force was ordered to sail from the Inland Sea in the Japanese home islands as a decoy for Halsey's main offensive formation, Task Force 38. Toyoda planned that with Halsey and Mitscher lured away to the north by Ozawa, the other three Japanese forces could fall on the American invasion force off Leyte and, unhindered by aircraft from Task Force 38's carriers, destroy its amphibious vessels with gunfire and torpedoes.

The forces involved on each side were prodigious, fully vindicating the description of the Battle of Leyte Gulf as the world's greatest sea battle in numerical as well as strategic terms. On the Japanese side, Forces A and B, otherwise the Centre Force, 1st Strike Force, comprised the super-battleships *Yamato* and *Musashi*, the battleships *Nagato*, *Kongo* and *Haruna*, the heavy cruisers *Atago*, *Takao*, *Chokai*, *Maya*, *Myoko*, *Haguro*, *Kumano*, *Suzuya*, *Chikuma* and *Tone*, the light cruisers *Noshiro* and *Yahagi*, and 15 destroyers. Force C, otherwise the 1st Strike Force, Southern Force, was also a powerful outfit, comprising the battleships *Yamashiro* and *Fuso*, the heavy cruiser *Mogami and four* destroyers, supplemented by Shima's Northern Force of the heavy cruisers *Nachi* and *Ashigara*, the light cruiser *Abukuma* and seven destroyers. And to complete the Japanese offensive disposition there was Ozawa's Mobile Force comprising the fleet carrier *Zuikaku*, the light carriers *Zuiho*, *Chitose* and *Chiyoda*, the hybrid battleship/carriers *Ise* and *Hyuga*, the light cruisers *Oyoda*, *Tama* and *Isuzu*, and eight destroyers; the air strength of the Mobile Force was some 116 aircraft (including 80 fighters) on the four carriers, while the hybrid battleship/carriers had no aircraft.

HMAS Melbourne *(21), a modified Majestic-class aircraft carrier of the Royal Australian Navy in 1977.*

On completion of a seven-month refit, the Royal Navy's HMS Ark Royal leaves Devonport for a seven-day workup before taking part in the Silver Jubilee Review of the Fleet. June 1977.

If the Japanese 68-ship line-up was impressive, that of the Americans was doubly so, their 275 ships and 1,500 aircraft being divided into two fleets. Around Leyte for the escort and protection of the invasion forces was the 7th Fleet which, apart from 600 or more vessels in the vessels in the III and VIII Amphibious Forces (Task Forces 79 and 78 respectively), had Rear Admiral Thomas L. Sprague's 7th Fleet Escort Carrier Group (Task Group 77.4) comprising Task Unit 77.4.1 (six escort carriers, three destroyers and five destroyer escorts), Task Unit 77.4.2 (six escort carriers, three destroyers and five destroyer escorts) and Task Unit 77.4.3 (six escort carriers, three destroyers and four destroyer escorts) with a total of 503 aircraft (304 fighters and 199 attack aircraft). Also part of the 7th Fleet was Oldendorf's Battle Line (Task Group 77.2) comprising six old battleships (including five reconstructed

after their hammering at Pearl Harbor), three heavy cruisers, five light cruisers, 29 destroyers and 45 PT boats for the gunfire support of the invasion and defence of the amphibious fleet and attached escort carriers. The primary offensive capability of the U.S. Navy in the area was the 3rd Fleet, whose major offensive component was Task Force 38: in the Battle of Leyte Gulf, Task Force 38 was only at three-quarter strength as Vice Admiral J. S. McCain's Task Group 38.1 was on its way to Ulithi to refuel and resupply its two fleet carriers, two light carriers, three heavy cruisers and 14 destroyers. For the forthcoming battle Halsey and Mitscher thus deployed Rear Admiral G. F. Bogan's Task Group 38.2 (three fleet carriers, two light carriers, two battleships, four light cruisers and 18 destroyers) off San Bernardino Strait, Rear Admiral Forrest C. Sherman's Task Group 38.3 (two fleet carriers, two light carriers,

four battleships, four light cruisers and 14 destroyers) off Luzon, and Rear Admiral R. E. Davison's Task Group 38.4 (two fleet carriers, two light carriers, one heavy cruiser, one light cruiser and 11 destroyers) off Leyte with a total of 835 aircraft.

SHO-1 got off to a bad start for the Japanese, the 1st Strike Force being spotted by U.S. submarines as it headed north-east on 22 October after concentrating and refuelling in Brunei Bay. Off Palawan Island the submarines reported the position, strength and course of the Centre Force, and then the *Dace* and *Darter* moved into the attack, the former sinking the heavy cruiser *Maya*, and the latter damaging the heavy cruiser *Takao*, which had to turn back to Brunei Bay, and sinking the heavy cruiser *Atago*. Kurita pressed on regardless of the loss of his flagship, the *Atago*, together with most of his signals staff. In the morning of 24 October Kurita moved round the south

ABOVE
USS Forrestal *(CV-59) in Suda Bay, Crete during her 1978 Mediterranean tour of duty.*

ABOVE LEFT
The Minas Gerais, *an ex-British Colossus-class aircraft of the Brazilian navy.*

RIGHT
*The Minsk was completed in
1978 as the second of the
U.S.S.R's Kiev class aircraft
carriers.*

RIGHT
A U.S. carrier off the coast.

OPPOSITE
*Port quarter view of the
USS Kitty Hawk (CV-63)
in the Pacific.*

of Mindoro Island, and the scene was set for
the Battle of the Sibuyan Sea, the first of the
Battle of Leyte Gulf's four component
actions. Halsey appreciated that he could
leave Nishimura and Shima to Kinkaid, and
so concentrated the air efforts of TG 38.2
against the Centre Force, with particular
emphasis on the super-battleship *Musashi*:
between 10.26 and 13.50 hours, TG 38.2
flew 259 sorties to the Sibuyan Sea and, hit
by 19 torpedoes and 17 bombs, the huge
Musashi sank with about half her crew at
18.00 hours. The other casualties in the
Centre Force were the heavy cruiser *Myoko*,
which had to be sent back to Brunei Bay in
a seriously damaged condition, and three
other cruisers were damaged. Kurita broke
away to the west, persuading Halsey that he
was retreating, but then reversed course to
the east again. This caused delay to Kurita's
force, making it impossible for the Centre
Force to co-ordinate its northern attack on
the U.S. 7th Fleet with the southern attack
to be launched by Nishimura and Shima.
Even so, Kurita pressed on, passing through
the San Bernardino Strait at 23.30 hours on
24 October on his way to the third
component action of the Battle of Leyte
Gulf, the Battle of Samar.

But meanwhile the second component,
the Battle of Surigao Strait, was about to
unfold as Nishimura's and Shima's forces
closed on Leyte from the south after
rounding Negros and Bohay Islands. With
the Southern Force some 90 minutes ahead
of the Northern Force, the Japanese began
to penetrate into Surigao Strait early in the
morning of 25 October. The Americans
knew just what was coming and had laid
careful plans for the destruction of the
Southern Force, which would first be
assaulted by torpedo-firing PT boats, then
by 28 torpedo-firing destroyers, and finally
by the Gun Line, especially the six

A low oblique port view of the Soviet Kiev-class aircraft carrier Novorrossiysk *underway during her maiden voyage in the Atlantic.*

battleships of Rear Admiral G. L. Weyler which, with Oldendorf's cruisers, formed a horizontal line across the Japanese axis of advance so that all heavy guns could be brought to bear on the Japanese van. The PT boats attacked between 23.00 hours on 24 October and 03.00 hours on 25 October, but failed to score. Greater success attended the efforts of the destroyers, which sank three of the four Japanese van destroyers (*Michishio*, *Asagumo* and *Yamagumo*) and crippled the

battleship *Fuso*, which broke in two and sank at 04.30 hours. It was now the turn of the Battle Line, which opened fire at 03.53 hours and lobbed 285 14-in (356-mm) and 16-in (406-mm) shells at the Japanese using radar ranging and laying. The *Yamashiro* was hit repeatedly and sank at 04.19 hours, but the badly damaged *Mogami* managed to retire only to collide with Shima's flagship *Nachi* at 04.30 hours as the second Japanese force pressed north into the Surigao Strait even though it had

lost the cruiser *Abukuma* torpedoed by a PT boat at 03.25 hours. At 04.25 hours Shima decided on a prudent withdrawal, later losing the crippled *Mogami*.

But as Kinkaid and his staff were celebrating their victory in Surigao Strait, they received the astounding news that Task Group 77.4's escort carriers had come under gunfire attack off Samar. Kinkaid had not been informed by Halsey that the latter was pulling back from San Bernardino Strait Vice Admiral Willis A. Lee's Task Force 34 (an extemporized force of six battleships, four cruisers and eight destroyers drawn from TF 38) for support of his carriers against the Mobile Force, and through this gap in the U.S. defences Kurita had sailed to engage the dreadfully vulnerable escort carriers of TG 77.4. Closest to the Japanese attack was Rear Admiral Clifton A. F. Sprague's Task Unit 77.4.3 with the escort carriers *Fanshaw Bay*, *St. Lo*, *White Plains*, *Kalinin Bay*, *Kitkun Bay* and *Gambier Bay* escorted by the destroyers and destroyer escorts *Hoel*, *Heermann*, *Johnston*, *Dennis*, *Butler*, *Raymond* and *Roberts*. C. A. F. Sprague was faced by a Japanese force of four battleships, six heavy cruisers and 10 destroyers and, with his aircraft armed for ground-support operations over Leyte, could only run, and this he did most effectively despite the considerably slower speed of his force in comparison with that of the Japanese. The U.S. commander used a rain squall and smoke to break away from the Japanese, and then sent in his destroyers to slow the attackers: it was a confused battle characterized by extreme courage and determination on the part of the Americans, but lack of concerted effort by the Japanese ships. So while the Americans lost the *Gambier Bay*, *Hoel*, *Johnston* and *Roberts*, the Japanese lost the heavy cruisers *Suzuya*, *Chokai* and *Chikuma*. At 09.23 hours Kurita decided to withdraw, wrongly believing that he was up against Task Force 38. The trial of TU 77.4.3 was not yet over, however, for later in the morning the *St. Lo* was hit by a kamikaze aircraft and later sank.

While these events had been unfolding, away to the north Halsey had been pulled in by the deception threat posed by Ozawa and steamed off in pursuit at 23.45 hours on 24 October. By this time Halsey had ordered TG 38.1 back from Ulithi (the group then being diverted to the support of

The sophistication of modern carrierborne aircraft such as these American warplanes, including one Vought A-7 Corsair II attack bomber on the right, requires extensive maintenance. This can be provided only on the enclosed hangar deck under the flightdeck, and exploits the folding wings and other panels of modern aircraft to maximize the utilization of space.

A Boeing (originally McDonnell Douglas) F/A-18 Hornet warplane comes in to land on an American aircraft carrier. This type is very important to the US Navy's current strength as it combines in a single airframe both fighter and attack capabilities that previously required different types of aircraft.

HMS Illustrious *(R06), a carrier of the Royal Navy with a Sea King ASW helicopter and Sea Harriers on the flightdeck. September 1983.*

The Battle of Leyte Gulf had eventually involved 244 ships, of which 32 were sunk. The Japanese had lost three battleships, four carriers, 10 cruisers and nine destroyers totalling 306,000 tons, whereas the American losses had been one carrier, two escort carriers and three destroyers totalling 37,000 tons. The defeat of the Japanese was almost inevitable, and had the monumental effect of stranding Yamashita in the Philippines and so allowing the conquest of these islands, which split the Japanese strategic defence wide open, and also isolated the remnants of the Japanese navy in two groups, that in the south without ammunition and spare parts, and

LEFT
Another view of HMS Illustrious, *an anti-submarine warfare carrier.*

BELOW
HMS Invincible.

the 7th Fleet's escort carriers) and gathered TG 38.2, TG 38.3 (less the *Princeton* sunk by land-based Japanese aircraft earlier in the day) and TG 38.4. Task Force 38 was without its battleships and cruisers, which had been formed into TF 34 under Lee to guard the San Bernardino Strait, but Lee followed some three hours behind Halsey, so letting Kurita through the San Bernardino Strait, before again turning at 11.15 hours on 25 October for a belated attempt to engage Kurita and so protect TU 77.4.3. Halsey's reconnaissance aircraft spotted the Mobile Force at 02.20 hours on 25 October, and at 08.45 hours the first of four U.S. strikes was launched to start the last of the four components of the

Battle of Leyte Gulf, namely the Battle of Cape Engano. Ozawa had turned north late on 24 October to draw Task Force 38 away from Leyte, but was now faced by the overwhelming air strength of his pursuers, who flew 527 sorties to sink the carriers *Chitose*, *Zuikaku* and *Zuiho* plus the destroyer *Akitsuki*. The air strikes also damaged the carrier *Chiyoda*, which with the destroyer *Hatsusuki* was finished off by a force of four cruisers and 10 destroyers under Rear Admiral Du Bose, detached by Halsey at 14.15 hours. The battle came to a close at 24.00 hours on 25 October when Task Force 34 caught the destroyer *Nowaki* in San Bernardino Strait and sank her with gunfire.

BELOW and RIGHT
Two views of HMS
Invincible, *with (below) a*
Sea Harrier being prepared
for take-off and another
(right) coming in to land.

that in the north without fuel. The pitiful remnants of Japan's once-mighty naval air arm had been destroyed at sea and over Luzon to no real effect.

Experience with the Essex-class aircraft carriers showed that while these were excellent ships with considerable offensive and defensive capability, they were hampered by their lack of protection on and below the flightdeck. In the Midway class, of which six were ordered but only three completed in the period after World War II,

the opportunity was therefore taken to increase size and displacement by a very appreciable degree. This allowed much improved horizontal and vertical armour to be worked into the design, which now included an armoured flightdeck even though this and the hangar were still added to the basic structure as superstructure, and also provided for the carriage of a significantly larger complement of current aircraft or a smaller but still considerable number of newer and larger types as these entered service. Other features were the two aircraft-launching catapults, three elevators including one deck-edge unit, and the location of virtually all of the defensive armament in long sponsons along the sides of the hull. The details of this class included a full-load displacement of 60,000 tons, an armament of 18 5-in (127-mm) dual-purpose guns in single turrets, 84 40-mm anti-aircraft guns in 21 quadruple mountings and 82 20-mm cannon as well as

137 aircraft, protection in the form of an 8-in (203-mm) belt and armoured decks, and a speed of 33kt on the 212,000hp (158065kW) delivered to four shafts by geared steam turbines.

Although the U.S. Navy was a firm believer in the overall superiority of the large fleet carrier, the crisis in which it found itself in the days after the Japanese attack on Pearl Harbor persuaded the service to plan for the rapid introduction of a light carrier element based on the hulls of nine incomplete Cleveland-class cruisers. Such was the urgency of the programme that all of these very successful ships entered service in 1943, providing the U.S. Navy with an excellent interim carrier capability until the larger Essex-class carriers could enter service. The details of this class included a full-load displacement of 15,100 tons, an armament of four 5-in (127-mm) dual-purpose guns in single turrets, 26 40-mm anti-aircraft guns in two

quadruple and nine twin mountings and 40 20-mm cannon in single mountings as well as 45 aircraft launched with the aid of two catapults, protection in the form of a 5-in (127-mm) belt and 3-in (76-mm) deck, and speed of 32kt on the 100,000hp (74560kW) delivered to four shafts by geared steam turbines.

The same reasoning that led the British to the concept of the escort carrier was also relevant to the Americans, who saw in this type the possibility of large numbers built in a short time for tasks ranging from convoy escort and anti-submarine warfare to support of amphibious operations via the resupply of larger carriers (both fleet and light) and the reinforcement of island bases in the Pacific. The first of these classes was the Long Island type, of which two were retained by the U.S. Navy and the other four passed to the Royal Navy, and further construction yielded the Bogue class of 11 ships excluding 26 transferred to the Royal

ABOVE
An F/A-18 strike fighter is launched from the deck of the USS Constellation *in the Pacific.*

ABOVE LEFT
British Aerospace Sea Harrier FRS.Mk 1s of the Fleet Air Arm. From top to bottom are aircraft from 801 Squadron, 800 Squadron and 899 Squadron. 1981.

RIGHT
A Clemenceau-class aircraft carrier.

BELOW and BELOW RIGHT
Two views of the USS Saratoga (CV60).

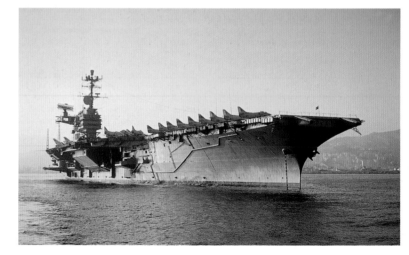

Navy, the Sangamon class of four ships, the Casablanca class of 50 ships that were the first of these type built from the keel up as escort or jeep carriers, and the Commencement Bay class of 19 ships. The details of the Casablanca class, which may be taken as typical of these classes, included a full-load displacement of 10,400 tons, an armament of one 5-in (127-mm) dual-purpose gun, 16 40-mm anti-aircraft guns in eight twin mountings and 24 20-mm cannon in single mountings as well as 28 aircraft launched with the aid of one catapult, no protection, and a speed of 19kt on the 9,000hp (6710kW) delivered to two shafts by triple-expansion steam engines.

The final signal of the eclipse of the battleship by the aircraft carrier, were such a signal still needed, came with the implementation of the Combined Fleet's Kikusai-1 (floating chrysanthemum no. 1)

USS Midway (CV-41)
taken from USS Kitty
Hawk.

plan on 6–7 April 1945. In this senseless operation, which may be regarded as the ultimate kamikaze mission, the super-battleship *Yamato* was expended to no real purpose. The concept behind the operation was that the battleship, accompanied by the light cruiser *Yahagi* and eight destroyers, should make a dash from Tokuyama to Okinawa with the intention of getting in among the invasion fleet that had started to land American forces on the island during 1 April. The battleship was then beached, there being sufficient oil for only a one-way trip to Okinawa, and caused havoc with its massive main armament while the cruiser and destroyers used their extremely potent Long Lance torpedoes. It was anticipated that the American forces would detect the Japanese force before its arrival and would thus try to intercept it before its arrival off Okinawa, this distraction to the north offering the possibility of great success for

the first mass attack by kamikaze aircraft, planned for 6 April. The squadron made for Okinawa in close formation with the battleship ringed by the cruiser and seven destroyers, one having dropped out with engine trouble, and was soon spotted by the Americans, who reacted with a large strike by carrierborne aircraft whose efforts rapidly obliterated the defences. The *Yamato* was hit by many bombs and torpedoes, and sank with 2,488 men, the *Yahagi* went down with 446 men, and four destroyers (including the one that had suffered engine trouble) were sunk with 721 men. The four surviving destroyers were all badly damaged, but got back to base.

In the aftermath of World War II, the U.S. Navy concentrated on the restoration of its war-weary carrier force to full capability and on the completion of those ships in the final stages of construction at the end of the war. The 1947 fleet strength

therefore included 22 Essex, three Midway, three Independence, two Saipan, four Bogue, six Casablanca and 12 Commencement Bay-class carriers. These ships remained in service or were taken in hand for conversion, either to an improved standard or for other roles, as the U.S. Navy analyzed the lessons of World War II. These included the inescapable conclusion that the aircraft carrier had replaced the battleship as the real capital ship, and the development of the U.S. Navy's surface capability was now concentrated even more strongly than in World War II on the operation of carrier battle groups as the core of American naval strength.

Shipbuilding in a major way resumed during the Korean War (1950–53), and included in this first generation of new ships were the four aircraft carriers of the Forrestal class to a design scaled down from that of the United States, a large ship laid down but then cancelled as the carrier of the U.S. Navy's new generation of strategic attack warplanes armed with free-fall nuclear weapons. The Forrestal-class ships were completed between 1955 and 1959 with all the latest aircraft developments including the angled flightdeck and mirror landing system, and its flightdeck carried four deck-edge elevators as well as four catapults. The details of this epoch-making class included a full-load displacement of 78,510 tons, an armament of eight 5-in (127-mm) dual-purpose guns in single turrets as well as 90 aircraft, unspecified protection, and a speed of 33kt on the 280,000hp (208770kW) delivered to four shafts by geared steam turbines.

The next four ships were completed between 1961 and 1968 as the Kitty Hawk class to an improved Forrestal-class design with a full-load displacement of 80,945 tons, an armament of two twin-arm

USS Midway *and Battle Group Alfa in the Makassah Strait.*

The Moskva *and its sister ship* Leningrad *were of a hybrid type that combined a forward part with cruiser capabilities with an after part optimized for the embarkation and operation of helicopters in the anti-submarine role.*

launchers for 80 RIM-2 Terrier surface-to-air missiles as well as 90 aircraft, unspecified protection, and a speed of 33.6kt on the 280,000hp (208,770kW) delivered to four shafts by geared steam turbines. The last of the ships to be completed was the *John F. Kennedy*, which differs from the other ships in its improved underwater protection of the type developed for the first American nuclear-powered carrier.

This is the *Enterprise*, which was completed in 1961 with a full-load displacement of 89,085 tons, an armament of 90 aircraft supplemented by three octuple launchers for RIM-7 Sea Sparrow surface-to-air missiles, unspecified protection, and a speed of 32kt on the 280,000hp (208770kW) delivered to four shafts by the geared steam turbines supplied from eight Westinghouse A2W pressurized water-cooled reactors. The importance of this ship in operational terms was enormous, for it opened the possibility of cruises of extreme range and endurance. The ship has virtually unlimited range without any need for oil fuel, and this leaves all the bunkerage for aviation fuel with consequent advantages in the amount of flying that can be undertaken before the bunkers need replenishment from supply ships: this means that the real limitations to the length of an operational cruise is now crew efficiency and the rate at which consumables (food and other manpower requirements, warplane spares, warplane ammunition and bombs, and warplane fuel) can be replenished.

The success of the *Enterprise* paved the way for the U.S. Navy's current generation of aircraft carriers, which comprise the 10 ships of the Nimitz class completed or scheduled for delivery in the period from 1975 to 2007. The Nimitz-class ships are to an improved Forrestal-class design with a smaller nuclear propulsion arrangement.

LEFT
The Forrestal-class USS Ranger.

the design of the new aircraft carrier will be derived from that of the Nimitz class in terms of its basic configuration and structure, but considerable advances are planned in terms of a new generation of sensors offering greater overall capability but reduced detectability, a comprehensive and fully integrated electronic system to provide a clear and coherent picture of the tactical situation to all relevant members of the crew, a very much higher level of automation to allow a significant decrease in the numbers of the crew from the figure of 5,700 in the Nimitz-class ships, a new generation of propulsion and electric systems offering greater power with superior reliability and maintainability, and a large flightdeck for the launch of embarked warplanes using an electro-magnetic aircraft launching system in place of the now-standard steam catapult.

These huge and extremely capable ships each have a full-load displacement of 102,000 tons, an armament of three octuple launchers for RIM-7 Sea Sparrow surface-to-air missiles and four 20-mm Vulcan six-barrel cannon in Phalanx close-in weapon system mountings as well as an air group of a maximum of 90 but more commonly 70 aircraft launched by a total of four steam catapults (two each on the fore-and-aft and angled sections of the huge flightdeck), unspecified but comprehensive protection, and a speed of 30kt or more on the 260,000hp (193855kW) delivered to four shafts by the geared steam turbines supplied from two Westinghouse A4W or General Electric A1G pressurized water-cooled reactors.

From the late 1990s the U.S.A. was planning the generation of aircraft carriers it will need to succeed the ships of the Nimitz class from about 2013. It is probable that

LEFT
An aerial view of the commando carrier HMS Hermes.

RIGHT
The French navy's aircraft carrier Foch, *whose sister ship is the* Clemenceau, *were completed as conventionally powered ships of middling size, and served capably to the end of the 20th century.*

RIGHT
The flight deck of Foch, *off the coast of Lebanon.*

This much improved standard will be applicable to only one new aircraft carrier, the CVNX-1, which is planned as an interim step between the Nimitz-class units and the first of a new generation of ships whose first unit, currently designated as the CVNX-2, should enter service from 2018. The new class will provide the U.S. Navy with an unmatched capability right through to the end of the 21st century, and will introduce a number of new features in the designation and construction of the hull, the design of the flightdeck with an electro-magnetic aircraft-recovery system to match the electro-magnetic aircraft launching system pioneered in the CVNX-1, and still higher levels of automation and electronic integration.

The only other country to have built aircraft carriers in significant numbers is Japan, which completed its first carrier in 1922 as the *Hosho*. This was a small ship of

limited operational capability, but provided the Japanese navy with the right type of experience to progress to the design and operation of larger and more capable fleet aircraft carriers. The first of these were two conversions from capital ships whose completion was prevented by the Washington Naval Treaty: the *Kaga* and *Akagi* were conversions from related battleship and battle-cruiser designs respectively. The details of the *Kaga* included a displacement of 26,900 tons, an armament of 10 7.9-in (200-mm) guns in two twin and six single turrets and 12 4.7-in (120-mm) guns in six twin mountings as well as 60 aircraft, protection in the form of an 11-in (280-mm) belt, and a speed of 27kt on the 91,000hp (67850kW) delivered to four shafts by geared steam turbines, while the details of the *Akagi* included a displacement of 26,900 tons, an armament

of 10 7.9-in (200-mm) guns in two twin and six single turrets and 12 4.7-in (120-mm) guns in six twin mountings as well as 60 aircraft, protection in the form of a 10-in (255-mm) belt, and a speed of 31kt on the 131,200hp (97825kW) delivered to four shafts by geared steam turbines.

In 1929 Japan laid down its second purpose-designed carrier as the *Ryujo*, which as a result of Washington Naval Treaty limitations had a displacement of less than 10,000 tons as such carriers were not included in Japan's limit of 80,000 tons of carriers. The ship was found to be limited in many operational respects, and after its 1936 refit had details that included a displacement of 10,600 tons, an armament of eight 5-in (127-mm) anti-aircraft guns in four twin mountings and 24 25-mm anti-aircraft guns in 12 twin mountings as well as 48 aircraft (36 operational and 12 spare), unspecified but limited protection, and a speed of 29kt on the 65,000hp (48465kW) delivered to two shafts by geared steam turbines.

In 1934 Japan used its experience with these early carriers to plan its first large fleet carriers designed as such from the keel up. These were the two ships of the Soryu class that were completed in 1937 and 1939 with a displacement of 15,900 and 17,300 tons respectively, an armament of 12 5-in (127-mm) anti-aircraft guns in six twin mountings and between 28 and 31 25-mm anti-aircraft guns in 14 twin mountings or seven triple and five twin mountings as well as 71 aircraft (53 operational and 16 spare), moderate but unspecified protection, and a speed of 34.5kt on the 152,000hp (113330kW) delivered to four shafts by geared steam turbines.

Further improvement of the concept embodied in the Soryu class and the expiry of treaty limitations allowed Japan's next

Representing two of the new breed of light aircraft carrier able to operate fixed-wing aircraft of the STOVL type (currently the Boeing AV-8B Harrier II) as well as helicopters are the Giuseppe Garibaldi *of the Italian navy followed here by the* Principe de Asturias *of the Spanish navy.*

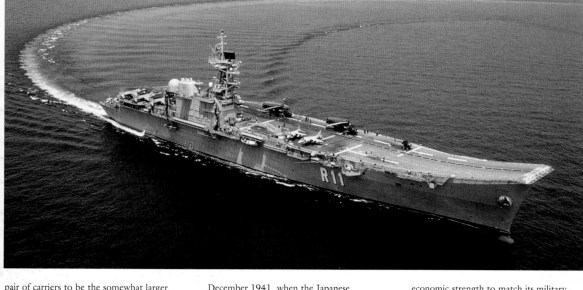

pair of carriers to be the somewhat larger ships of the Shokaku class completed in 1941 with a displacement of 25,675 tons, an armament of 16 5-in (127-mm) anti-aircraft guns in eight twin mountings and 36 25-mm anti-aircraft guns in 12 triple mountings as well as 84 aircraft (72 operational and 12 spare), protection in the form of an 8.5-in (215-mm) belt and 6.75-in (170-mm) deck, and a speed of 34.25kt on the 160,000hp (119135kW) delivered to four shafts by geared steam turbines.

The single event that showed most conclusively that the aircraft carrier had replaced the battleship as the most important type of warship came on 7

December 1941, when the Japanese launched two waves of attack aircraft from six aircraft carriers to inflict what they hoped would be decisive damage on the U.S. Navy's Pacific Fleet at Pearl Harbor in the Hawaiian Islands, and at the same time to strike at all American air power in the area.

Believing that it was intention of the U.S.A. and U.K., supported by countries such as China and the Netherlands East Indies, to strangle its economy by economic means and thus to force them to abandon the conquests they had made in China since 1937, the Japanese had decided earlier in 1941 that war was their only opportunity to turn their country into a major power with

economic strength to match its military capabilities and political ambitions. Japan appreciated that it could not match the resources and industrial strength of the U.S.A. alone, let alone any alliance involving the Americans, but believed that they could successfully use the same offensive/defensive strategic concept that had brought them victory over Russia in the Russo-Japanese War. The Japanese plan was conceived in three phases: firstly, to neutralize the Pacific Fleet and supporting air power, the only strategically significant enemy force in the Pacific and East Asia, by surprise attack while simultaneously seizing the Southern Resources Area (the

OPPOSITE LEFT
The modified Kiev-class
Baku, *of the Russian navy.*

OPPOSITE TOP RIGHT
The USS John F. Kennedy
*(CV-67) and A0188
during Operation Desert
Shield/Storm. 19 February
1991.*

OPPOSITE BELOW
RIGHT
The US Navy's San Jacinto,
Detroit *and the aircraft-carrier* John F. Kennedy
*during Operation Desert
Storm. 1991.*

The core of the US Navy's power-projection capability is the 'Nimitz' class of huge nuclear-powered aircraft carriers, here epitomized by the USS Abraham Lincoln.

LEFT
The Pacific Fleet aircraft carrier USS Ranger *(CV-61) displays a fond farewell to her glorious career as she sails from her last overseas deployment, thus ending a cruise support of Operation Southern Watch and Operation Restore Hope. The* Ranger *was decommissioned in the summer of 1993.*

BELOW
USS Eisenhower *(CVN-69) in the Suez Canal during Operation Desert Storm.*

Philippines, Malaya, Burma and the Dutch East Indies) and also neighbouring areas in which a defensive perimeter could be created; secondly, to consolidate and strengthen the perimeter so that any Allied counter-offensive would be prohibitively expensive; and thirdly, to defeat and destroy all Allied efforts to penetrate the perimeter. The Japanese believed that the strength of their planned defensive perimeter, which could be attacked by the Allies only at the end of very long and therefore highly vulnerable Allied lines of communications, would ensure success.

The second and third phases were wholly dependent on the successful implementation of the first phase, which was the attack by carrierborne aircraft on Pearl Harbor. At this time the balance of naval power in the Pacific pitched 11 Japanese battleships and battle-cruisers against 11 Allied ships (nine American and

two British), 11 aircraft carriers against three, 18 heavy cruisers against 14 (13 American and one British), 23 light cruisers against 21 (11 American, seven British and three Dutch), 129 destroyers against 100 (80 American, 13 British and seven Dutch) and 67 submarines against 69 (56 American and 13 Dutch).

On 26 November 1991 the 1st Air Fleet, under the commanded of Vice Admiral Chuichi Nagumo, sailed from the Kurile Islands, north of the Japanese home islands, with six aircraft carriers, supported by battleships, heavy cruisers and submarines together with supporting vessels such as oilers. Japan's readiness for war was well known to American military and civilian authorities, who expected that the blow would fall on Malaya or the Philippines, and American intelligence, which had broken a key Japanese radio code, knew of the movements and location

HMS Ark Royal.

of most major Japanese army and navy units with the decisive exception of the 1st Air Fleet, which was keeping strict radio silence.

On 7 December a first wave of 183 warplanes launched from a point north of Oahu island, secured complete strategic and tactical surprise as it swept in to the attack, and so disorganized were the defences that the second wave of 180 aircraft also encountered little in the way of effective opposition. The Japanese aircraft attacked ships in the harbour and airfields all over the island, and of the eight U.S. battleships in Pearl Harbor three were sunk, one capsized and the others severely damaged. The Japanese onslaught also sank or severely damaged three light cruisers, three destroyers and a number of other vessels, and on land only 166 of the 231 U.S. Army's aircraft survived or could be repaired, and only 54 out of some 250 U.S. Navy and U.S. Marine Corps aircraft were still usable. The U.S. Navy and U.S. Marine Corps lost more than 3,000 personnel killed and 876 wounded, and the equivalent figures for the U.S. Army were 226 killed and 396 wounded.

It was a blow of huge strategic importance, for the U.S. Navy's Pacific fleet had in effect been neutralized for at least 12 months. The only happy events for the U.S.A. at this time were the absence of the Pacific Fleet's three aircraft carriers (the *Enterprise*, *Lexington* and *Saratoga*) at this time, and the refusal of Nagumo to commit his aircraft to a third attack (to destroy the oil tank farm and repair facilities at Pearl Harbor) lest the aircraft carriers vital to Japan's war plans come under attack. It was also not long before further evidence of the decline of the battleship's importance, resulting from its vulnerability to air attack, was provided by a British disaster. Only a few days after the attack on Pearl Harbor had decimated the Pacific fleet, the Royal Navy lost two capital ships, the battleship *Prince of Wales* and the battle-cruiser *Renown*, to Japanese land-based air attack. On 10 December the two ships were operating off the north-east coast of Malaya and were attacked by warplanes from bases in Indo-China. The Japanese attacked with bombs and torpedoes, and in little more than one hour both British ships had sunk with very heavy loss of life.

The aircraft carriers listed above were the most important aircraft carriers operated by the Japanese navy up to the time of the Battle of Midway (June 1942), when the service lost no fewer than four of the ships together with most of its experienced naval aviators. The Japanese carrierborne arm then went into a decline from which it never re-emerged despite the delivery of new and improved aircraft, fresh aircrews who lacked the experience and therefore skills of their predecessors, as well as a number of new aircraft carriers to supplement the ships surviving from the early operations of World War II. The other ships included the two Shoho-class light carriers completed in 1939 and 1940 with a displacement of 11,260 tons and a capacity of 30 aircraft, the three Taiyo-class escort carriers completed in 1940 and 1941 with a displacement of 17,830 tons and a capacity of between 27 and 30 aircraft, the two Hiyo-class fleet carriers completed in 1942 with a displacement of 24,140 tons and a capacity of 53 aircraft, the single Taiho-class fleet carrier completed in 1944 with a displacement of 29,300 tons and a capacity of 74 aircraft, the single Ryuho-class light carrier completed in 1942 with a displacement of 13,360 tons and a capacity of 31 aircraft, the single Shinano-class fleet carrier converted from a Yamato-class battleship and completed in 1944 with a

The Giuseppe Garibaldi *of the Italian navy.*

Despite the number of aircraft spotted all over spare areas of its flightdeck, which give the impression that the flightdeck is in fact quite small, this primary operating area of the U.S Navy's-'Nimitz' class aircraft carrier is in fact very extensive with a maximum length of some 1,090ft (332m) and maximum width of 257ft 6 in (78.5m). The main fore-and-aft stretch, with two steam-powered catapults at its forward end, is completed by a section angled off to port and carrying two more catapults at its forward end as well as four arrester wires at its after end. The flightdeck and hangar deck are connected by four deck-edge elevators, one on the port side as the after end of the angled section, and the other three on the side as two forward and one aft of the 'island' superstructure.

displacement of 62,000 tons and a capacity of 47 aircraft, the single Shinyo-class light carrier completed in 1943 as a conversion of a German liner with a displacement of 17,500 tons and a capacity of 33 aircraft, the single Kaiyo-class escort carrier completed in 1943 with a displacement of 13,600 tons and a capacity of 24 aircraft, the two Chiyoda-class light carriers completed in 1943 and 1944 with a displacement of 11,190 tons and a capacity of 30 aircraft, and the three Unryu-class light fleet carriers completed in 1944 with a displacement of 17,150 tons and a capacity of 64 aircraft.

Germany and Italy designed and started work on aircraft carriers for service in World War II, but none of these was ever completed. The only other countries that have completed true aircraft carriers are France (the *Béarn* before World War II and the *Foch* and *Clemenceau* after World War II, the latter now replaced by the *Charles de Gaulle*, a nuclear-powered ship that entered service in 2000 and was to have been partnered by the *Richelieu* that was cancelled) and the U.S.S.R. (four Kiev and two Kuznetsov-class ships), although Italy, Spain and Thailand have in recent years each completed one light aircraft carrier suitable for the operation of helicopters and STOVL warplanes.

The *Charles de Gaulle* has a displacement of 40,600 tons, an armament of ASTER 15 medium-range surface-to-air missiles in four eight-round vertical launch systems, Mistral short-range surface-to-air missiles in two six-round launchers and eight 25-mm cannon on four twin mountings as well as an air group of 40 aircraft, unspecified protection, and a speed of 32kt on the 83,000hp (61885kW) delivered to two shafts by two Type 15 nuclear reactor systems.

The first Soviet aircraft carriers were the two helicopter cruisers of the Moskva class, which was a hybrid type somewhat similar in concept to the single ship of the Italian Vittorio Veneto class in being an anti-submarine warfare type combining a cruiser forward end, armed with guns and missiles, and an aircraft carrier after end with hangarage and a comparatively large flightdeck for the operation of a large complement of specialised anti-submarine helicopters. In the case of the Moskva-class ships, this complement was initially 15 Kamov Ka-25 Hormone helicopters, later replaced by Ka-27 Helix helicopters from the same design bureau.

Experience with these two ships was useful, although not wholly relevant, to the overall design of the Kiev class of four aircraft carriers with which the Soviet navy sought to begin the process of creating a carrier force that would eventually be able to challenge the might of the U.S. Navy in deep-water operations. The Kiev-class ships are in fact more akin to the Royal Navy's Invincible-class light carriers, for both classes can operate fixed-wing aircraft of only the STOVL type in addition to helicopters. The Kiev-class aircraft carriers each have a displacement of 40,500 tons, an armament of missiles (three types of surface-to-air missile as well as anti-submarine or, in one ship, anti-ship missiles), torpedoes, four 3-in (76-mm) guns in two twin mountings and eight 30-mm multi-barrel cannon in close-in weapon system mountings as well as 37 aircraft in the form of 12 Yakovlev Yak-38 Forger STOVL warplanes and 21 helicopters, unspecified protection, and a speed of 32kt on the 200,000hp (149120kW) delivered to four shafts by geared steam turbines.

Experience with the Kiev-class aircraft carriers, which were completed between 1975 and 1987, was more directly applicable to what were to become the U.S.S.R.'s first (and indeed only) large aircraft carriers of the true type able to operate a mixed complement of fixed-wing warplanes from a full-length flightdeck that includes an angled portion. The two ships were completed in the early 1990s to a standard that includes a displacement of 67,500 tons, an armament of missiles (one type of surface-to-air missile and one type of anti-ship missile), eight close-in weapons system mountings each carrying eight surface-to-air missiles and two 30-mm multi-barrel cannon, six close-in weapons system mountings each carrying one 30-mm multi-barrel cannon and two anti-submarine mortars as well as an air group of 30 aircraft (12 fixed-wing and 18 rotary-wing machines), unspecified protection, and a speed of 32kt on the 200,000hp (149120kW) delivered to four shafts by geared steam turbines.

Chapter Six
Fast Attack Craft

Large numbers of the world's navies, including many lacking a claim to any long-established naval or even maritime tradition, now possess forces of small but comparatively heavily armed fast combat craft. These craft may be defined as vessels possessing a displacement of up to some 600 tons and a top speed of 25kt or more, and fall into two basic categories: the fast patrol boat and fast attack craft generally abbreviated to FPB and FAC respectively. The FPB is usually fitted with only light armament (most commonly medium and heavy machine-guns of up to 0.5-in/12.7-mm calibre and cannon of up to 40-mm calibre) together with minimal sensor and fire-control suites, while the FAC is a considerably more capable type usually able to attain higher speeds and also to carry a heavier armament of longer-range weapons that can comprise anti-ship guided missiles, guns of up to 3-in (76-mm) calibre, heavyweight anti-ship torpedoes of up to 21-in (533-mm) calibre, and anti-submarine weapons such as lightweight homing torpedoes, rocket-propelled grenades and depth charges, all controlled with the aid of a considerably more sophisticated suite of sensor and fire-control systems. The nature of the primary armament carried by any FAC is usually indicated by a suffixed letter: thus the

FAC(G) carries a medium-calibre gun, the FAC(M) carries anti-ship missiles, the FAC(T) carries anti-ship torpedoes etc.

Recent developments have tended to obscure the fact that the FAC does not represent a wholly new concept, but is a type with more than a century of pedigree behind it under a number of now-discarded designations. The first small warship may be regarded as John I. Thornycroft's torpedo boat *Lightning*, which was built for the Royal Navy in 1876–77. About 10 years earlier Robert Whitehead had demonstrated the capabilities of his new invention, the locomotive torpedo, and since that time Thornycroft had urged the Admiralty for permission to develop a torpedo-armed launch based on his successful series of fast steam launches. Displacing 32.5 tons and possessing an overall length of 87ft (26.5m), the *Lightning* was powered by a compound steam engine delivering 460hp (343kW) to one shaft for a speed of 19kt. The *Lightning* was quickly perceived as opening a new concept in naval warfare, and by the start of the 20th century the Royal Navy alone had received more than 100 such steam-powered boats. The later units were characterized by a displacement of some 200 tons and a maximum speed of 25kt.

By the outbreak of World War I in

August 1914, the concept of the torpedo boat had already seen a split into smaller attack craft (the torpedo boat) and slightly larger defensive craft (the torpedo boat destroyer), and this gap between the two elements of this division widened during the war. The small torpedo boat virtually disappeared, and the torpedo boat destroyer emerged as the multi-role destroyer, a larger and far more capable type offering high speed together with a gun and torpedo armament. The original stream of small attack craft did not disappear entirely, however, for as late as 1918 the Germans were producing such craft. The vessels of the A92 class, for example, displaced 392 tons and had a length of 200ft 9in (61.2m), and their geared steam turbines delivered 6,000hp (4475kW) to two shafts for a maximum speed of 26.7kt. The armament comprised two 3.4-in (88-mm) guns and one 17.7-in (450-mm) torpedo tube.

Wartime operations had meantime confirmed what many critics had already suspected, that such torpedo boats were in reality too small and vulnerable to operate as an adjunct to fleet operations, and at the same time were too large and lacked the manoeuvrability for coastal operations against destroyer-escorted convoys. So the mantle of coastal operations, now firmly established as the primary task of torpedo

The British 55-ft (17-m) Coastal Motor Boat No.65A built by Thornycroft in 1918 and powered by two 375-hp (280-kW) engines. The armament was one or two 18-in (457-mm) torpedoes, up to four depth charges, and four 0.303-in (7.7-mm) Lewis machine-guns.

The Thornycroft 70-ft (21-m) Coastal Motor Boat, (CMB) of which small numbers were built between 1918 and 1922, was intended mainly as a layer of up to four mines, but could operate in the torpedo boat role with up to five such weapons. The gun armament was six 0.303-in (7.7-mm) Lewis machine-guns.

boats, was reallocated to the type of smaller craft made possible by the replacement of the steam powerplant by the internal combustion engine. The main force in the development of such torpedo boats was the German navy. The LM-class units of 1917 and 1918 each displaced between 15 and 17 tons, possessed an overall length of between 48 and 56ft (14.6 and 17.1m), and was powered by three Maybach petrol engines delivering a total of between 630 and 720hp (470 and 535kW) to three shafts for a maximum speed of between 28 and 32kt.

The armament was a single 17.7-in (450-mm) torpedo tube. On the other side, the British developed a similar but somewhat smaller type as the coastal motor boat (CMB) that entered service in 1916. The CMB was evolved from pre-war racing boats with a stepped hydroplaning hull that allowed speeds in excess of 40kt. The type was too small and light to carry a torpedo tube, so the boats were armed with a single torpedo that was launched tail-first over a stern chute, the boat then using its agility to swerve out of the torpedo's path as the

latter accelerated directly along the boat's original course. The boats were built in 40-, 55- and 70-ft (12.2-, 16.8- and 21.3-m) lengths, the 55-ft (16.8-mm) type being most numerous and being manufactured in several forms with differences in their engines and armaments. The typical 55-ft (16.8-m) CMB had a displacement of 11 tons, an overall length of 60ft (18.3m) over the torpedo-launching chute, two petrol engines delivering between 750 and 900hp (560 and 670kW) to two shafts for a speed of between 34 and 42kt, and an armament

of one or two 18-in (457-mm) torpedoes, four 0.303-in (7.7-mm) machine-guns, and up to four depth charges.

The nation which made the greatest use of torpedo craft during World War I was Italy, which built 422 craft of several MAS types. Though completed after the war, a class that typifies such Italian craft is the D group of the SVAN Veloce type. Each unit displaced 28.9 tons and had a length of 72ft 2in (22.0 m), the propulsion arrangement comprised four Isotta-Fraschini petrol engines delivering 1,600hp (1195kW) to four shafts (and two Rognini electric motors delivering 10hp/7.5kW to two shafts were also installed for silent approach), and the speeds of these two arrangements were 30 and 4kt respectively. The armament comprised two 17.7-in (450-mm) torpedoes, two 0.26-in (6.5-mm) machine-guns and up to 20 depth charges. Two of these MAS boats showed the potential of small attack craft by torpedoing and sinking the *Wien*, a pre-Dreadnought battleship of the Austro-Hungarian navy.

After World War I the torpedo craft concept fell into disfavour, and it was only during the later 1930s that it underwent something of a revival. It was Germany that effectively pioneered the renaissance with the S1 of 1929, designed and built by Lürssen of Vegesack as the prototype of the new Schnellboote (fast boats) that were later called E-boats (enemy boats) by the Allies. The craft were based on a hull of the round-bilge rather than hard-chine type for improved seaworthiness. The S1 displaced 51.5 tons and had a length of 88ft 6in (27.0m). The propulsion arrangement comprised three Daimler-Benz petrol engines delivering 3,300hp (2460kW) to three shafts for a speed of 34kt, and the armament included one 20-

mm cannon and two tubes for 19.7-in (500-mm) torpedoes. The S1 proved seaworthy and effective, but serious doubts were raised about its propulsion arrangement, whose petrol engines provided shorter range than the diesel units that were now becoming common for a number of applications, and whose fuel was known to be dangerously flammable by contrast with the higher flash point of the heavier oil burned in diesel engines. This last was appreciated as a matter for particular concern as the craft lacked armour protection and would therefore be highly vulnerable to the fire that might follow hits from conventional rounds, let alone incendiary projectiles.

The S6 therefore introduced the diesel-engined propulsion arrangement that remained standard in all Schnellboote up to the end of World War II. The S7 introduced the distinctive knuckled hull form, and the S18 introduced the Daimler-Benz diesel engine that was used in all subsequent boats. Later craft had a raised fore castle over the torpedo tubes, and reload torpedoes were carried aft. During World War II, gun armament was increased significantly, and the Schnellboote matured as exceptional fast combat craft. Lürssen built 162 of these Schnellboote during World War II, and other yards produced about the same number to the basic Lürssen design. The craft saw extensive service in the North Sea and Baltic Sea, but their undoubted technical merits were not matched by the right type of aggressive leadership and their tactical effect was less than that of the smaller and less capable British craft, which were handled with considerably greater flair.

During the war, the displacement of the average Schnellboote increased from 35 to 105 tons, the length from 91ft 10in

(28.0m) to 114ft 9 in (35.1m), and the speed from 37 to 42kt. Typical of the Schnellboote in fully fledged form was the S186 type built in 1944 and 1945. This had a displacement of 105.5 tons and an overall length of 114ft 9 in (35.1m), and its propulsion arrangement was based on three Daimler-Benz diesel engines delivering 7,500hp (5590kW) to three shafts for a speed of 41kt. The armament included two 21-in (533-mm) tubes for four torpedoes, and two 30-mm cannon (fore and aft) often supplemented by numbers of lighter weapons.

The British returned to the concept of torpedo-armed coastal craft in 1935, when the Admiralty placed orders for motor torpedo boat (MTB) prototypes with the British Power Boat Company. These became the precursors of several important types, most notably the British motor gun boat (MGB) and the American PT (pursuit torpedo) boat, but in the event most British MTBs were built to a baseline Vosper design of hard-chine form. This was enlarged during World War II and fitted with greater power and armament, but remained essentially unchanged. A notable feature of British MTB design in World War II was the frequent replacement of the 21-in (533-mm) heavyweight torpedo, of which only two could be shipped, with the 18-in (457-mm) medium-weight torpedo, of which four could be carried but still provided capability for the destruction of merchant ships and smaller warships. In common with their German foes, the British crews added whatever gun armament they could to their fast combat craft as wartime experience revealed the need for additional cannon and machine-gun armament for use against enemy surface craft and aircraft.

For lack of a suitable British engine,

By comparison with British motor torpedo boats, key features of the German S-boat (known to the British as the E-boat) were a larger hull of different form and the location of the torpedo tubes below deck level to fire over the bow along troughs.

the Italian Isotta-Fraschini petrol engine was used in early craft until the middle of 1940, when Italy's entry into the war on the side of Germany cut off supplies. After a problem with the final drive had been eliminated, Packard engines from the U.S.A. then became the standard type for British craft. It was notable throughout the war, however, that the petrol-engined British craft were considerably more prone to fires than their diesel-engined German opponents.

Typical of the British MTB late in World War II was the Vosper 73-ft (22.25-m) type, which was authorized and built in 1944. This had a displacement of 46.7 tons and a length of 72ft (22m). The propulsion arrangement was three Packard petrol engines delivering 4,050hp (3020kW) to three shafts for a speed of 39.5kt, and the armament comprised four 18-in (457-mm) tubes for

four torpedoes, two 20-mm cannon and four 0.303-in (7.7-mm) machine-guns.

Also built in the later stages of World War II, the Fairmile D class was a larger and more capable craft which could be completed as an MTB or as an MGB. The type had a displacement of 105 tons and a length of 115ft (35.1 m), and the propulsion arrangement comprised four Packard petrol engines delivering 5,000hp (3730kW) to four shafts for a speed of 29kt. The basic armament included one 2-pdr gun, two 20-mm cannon in a twin mounting, four 0.5-in (12.7-mm) machine-guns in two twin mountings, and four 0.303-in (7.7-mm) machine-guns in two twin mountings, although it should be noted that in the last part of the war the 2-pdr gun was replaced by a 6-pdr weapon, and a second gun of the same type was located aft in place of the 20-

mm twin mounting, which was moved farther forward. To this gun armament could be added two 21-in (533-mm) tubes for two torpedoes, although later in the war it was more common to see four 18-in (457-mm) tubes for four torpedoes.

The British also developed dedicated MGBs that complemented the MTBs in providing a balanced offensive capability. Here the primary designer and builder was the British Power Boat Company, which produced five basic classes. The largest of these classes was the MGB-107 type, of which 60 were built from 1942. This type had a displacement of 37 tons and a length of 71ft 9in (21.9m), and the propulsion arrangement comprised three Packard petrol engines delivering 4,050hp (3020kW) to three shafts for a speed of 42kt. The armament included one 2-pdr gun, two 20-mm cannon in a twin mounting and four 0.303-in (7.7-mm) machine-guns in two twin mountings. In 1943 some of the craft were converted into hybrid MTB/MGB types with two 18-in (457-mm) tubes for two torpedoes, and some of the craft were completed to this standard.

Early experience with the MTB and MGB showed the British that a large measure of the tactical surprise could be secured by the type's high speed and small silhouette, but that this element of surprise was often lost because of the two types' high noise signature, a direct consequence of using unsilenced engines. In the longer term, the answer was found to lie in an effective silencing system. In the shorter term, however, the British tried to develop a quieter type with steam propulsion. The resulting steel-hulled steam gun boat (SGB) was a large round-bilge type that was both fast and quiet. On the other side of the coin, however, the SGB's machinery was also extremely vulnerable to damage from

Their extra size and different hull form gave the German S-boats better performance and sea-keeping qualities than their British opponents in heavier sea and weather conditions.

even the lightest of gunfire, and its construction could only be undertaken at the expense of the production of larger warships such as destroyers, frigates, corvettes and sloops. Plans were originally formulated for the construction of 60 SGBs, but in the event only nine were ordered and seven actually built. To provide protection for their vulnerable machinery, the boats were fitted with 0.75-in (19-mm) armour over their machinery spaces, and the weight of this metal reduced speed dramatically. The SGB displaced 165 tons and had a length of 145ft 3 in (44.3 m), and the propulsion arrangement comprised geared steam turbines delivering 8,000hp (5965kW) to two shafts for a speed of 35kt. The armament included two 2-pdr guns in single mountings, four 0.5-in (12.7-mm) machine-guns in two twin mountings, and

two 21-in (533-mm) tubes for two torpedoes. The gun armament was later strengthened to one 3-in (76-mm) gun, two 6-pdr guns in single mountings and six 20-mm cannon in three twin mountings, which required the complement to be increased from 27 to 34. Together with the armour, this raised displacement to 260 tons and reduced speed to 30kt.

A firm believer in the construction of warships suitable for the type of offensive fleet action it thought decisive in naval warfare, the U.S. Navy showed very little interest in fast combat craft of such coastal types until 1939. In this year the U.S. Navy contracted with six yards, including the British Power Boat Company, for prototype craft varying in length between 54 and 80ft (16.5 and 24.4m). The type that found greatest technical favour with the Americans

was that of the British Power Boat Company, and salient features of this design were incorporated in later American designs. Like the British craft, these American boats were of the hard-chine type, and more than 800 such craft had been ordered before the end of World War II. The three main types were the PT 71 class ordered from Higgins Industries of New Orleans, Louisiana, the PT 103 class ordered from Elco (Electric Boat Company) of Bayonne, New Jersey, and the PT 368 class ordered from a number of smaller yards such as R. Jacobs, Herreshoff, the Annapolis Yacht Company, and Canadian Power Boats. The PT 71 class displaced 46 tons and had a length of 78ft (23.8m), and its propulsion arrangement comprised three Packard 4M2500 petrol engines delivering 4,050hp (3020kW) to three shafts for a speed of 40kt or more: the armament comprised two or four 21-in (533-mm) tubes for two or four torpedoes, one 40-mm gun, two 20-mm cannon, varying numbers of 0.5-in (12.7-mm) machine-guns and, in two-tube craft, 12 depth charges or four mine racks. The PT 103 class displaced 45 tons and had a length of 80ft 4in (24.5m), and its propulsion arrangement again comprised three Packard 4M2500 petrol engines delivering 4,050hp (3020kW) to three shafts for a speed of 40kt or more: the armament comprised four 21-in (533-mm) tubes for four torpedoes, two 20-mm cannon and varying numbers of 0.5-in (12.7-mm) machine-guns. The PT 368 class displaced 43 tons and had a length of 70ft (21.3m), and its propulsion arrangement comprised the standard three Packard 4M2500 petrol engines delivering 4,050hp (3,020kW) to three shafts for a maximum speed of 40kt or more: the armament comprised two 21-in (533-mm) tubes for two torpedoes as well as varying numbers of

PT 337 was an 80-ft (24-m) boat of the Elco type built in 1942. The boat had a displacement of 80 tons and a speed of 40kt on the 4,050hp (3020kW) delivered to three shafts by petrol engines, and the armament comprised four 21-in (533-mm) torpedo tubes and two 20-mm cannon.

20-mm cannon and 0.5-in (12.7-mm) machine-guns.

The engagement that perhaps typifies attempts to use the MTB, or rather the PT boat, in a major battle during World War II is the Battle of Surigao Strait, which was fought on 25 October 1944 as the Japanese sought to fight their way north to destroy the American invasion force off the beaches of Luzon in the central part of the Philippine Islands. Launched five days earlier, this invasion possessed two strategic objectives: the reconquest of the Philippines as a precursor to the eventual assault on the Japanese home islands, and the provoking of the Japanese navy into a decisive battle under conditions favourable to the U.S. Navy. U.S. naval intelligence had given the American forces a good idea of how the Japanese reaction, planned under the codename Sho-1, would unfold and the U.S. Navy had planned accordingly.

The aircraft carrier had dominated the campaign in the Pacific to the extent that neither side would consider anything but the destruction of such assets whenever and wherever possible. Thus the Japanese, who had recently wasted their last reserves of adequately trained carrier aircrews in the Battle of the Philippine Sea, planned to use their remaining aircraft carrier strength as a lure to draw the American carriers away to the north, thereby leaving the invasion force proper without the air cover to fight off a concerted attack by three other Japanese naval forces and Japanese air power based in the Philippines.

The American choice of Leyte as the site for their invasion of the Philippines suited the Japanese well, for Leyte Gulf could be approached from the west by two routes of access, namely the San Bernardino Strait in the north and the Surigao Strait in the south. The series of

four major actions resulting from the Japanese attempt to destroy the U.S. Navy forces supporting the invasion became known as the Battle of Leyte Gulf, which was the largest sea battle ever fought.

Launched on 1 October, the Sho-1 plan called on Vice Admiral Jisaburo Ozawa's Carrier Force to approach the Philippines from the north-east and entice Vice Admiral William F. Halsey's 3rd Fleet from a position off the eastern side of Samar island, just to the east of Leyte, and so facilitate simultaneous attacks, from the north and south by forces arriving from the south-west, on the weaker force of Vice Admiral Thomas S. Kinkaid's 7th Fleet that was supporting the landings and following campaign.

The Japanese force heading from Borneo toward the San Bernardino Strait (the Northern Force or Force A under Vice Admiral Takeo Kurita and including the magnificent battleships *Musashi* and *Yamato*), was sighted by submarines, which sank two heavy cruisers, and then mauled by Halsey's carrierborne aircraft on 23–24 October as it passed through the Sibuyan Sea, losing the *Musashi*. Then at 11.00 hours on 24 October, Ozawa's carriers (the Carrier Force or Strike Force) were spotted. Halsey took the bait and led the 3rd Fleet north in pursuit, leaving Kurita's force still advancing and the San Bernardino Strait unguarded. Though his force had fallen behind the Japanese schedule, Kurita duly passed north through the San Bernardino Strait and fell on an American escort carrier group which, much against the odds and in an action of considerable courage and skill, persuaded Kurita to retire in the Battle off Samar.

Meanwhile the Southern Force had also been attacked during its approach to the Philippines, but was now nearing the

southern end of the Surigao Strait. The Southern Force comprised two elements that had arrived from separate directions: Vice Admiral Shoji Nishimura's Force C (part of the 1st Striking Force with Force A) led with the older battleships *Yamashiro* and *Fuse*, the heavy cruiser *Mogami* and four destroyers, and about two hours behind came Vice Admiral Kiyohide Shima's 2nd Striking Force of two heavy cruisers, one light cruiser and seven destroyers.

The divided approach of the two Japanese forces provided Kinkaid, well advised on the Japanese position, course and speed by submarine and aircraft reports, with the time to plan and deploy his defences. The Japanese forces were to be harassed throughout their approaches first by PT boats and then by destroyers, each using the night torpedo attacks, and any Japanese ships that passed through this hail of torpedoes would find themselves steaming in line ahead toward Task Group 77.2 under the command of Rear Admiral Jesse Oldendorf with a Battle Line of six old battleships supported by three heavy and five light cruisers as the left- and right-flank elements as well as 29 destroyers as the forward elements.

Recently delivered by sea and in prime condition, an overall total of some 42 PT boats were available to Kinkaid as the forward element of the channel of fire he had prepared for the Japanese. With little in the way of nocturnal air reconnaissance available, the first task of the PT boat squadrons was to find, track and report the arrival of the Japanese force, and then to attack wherever and whenever an opportunity presented itself. The 39 PT boats available on 24–25 October were organized into 13 three-boat sections covering 70 miles (113km) from Bohol Island, across the eastern part of the

The S.14 was the lead unit of a four-strong class of S-boats built in the late 1930s, and was based on the L11 11-cylinder diesel engine rated at 2,000hp (1490kW). The boats had a displacement of 97 tons on a length of 113ft 6in (34.6m), and attained a maximum speed of 37kt.

Mindanao Sea and up the southern half of the Surigao Strait.

As the dark fell on 24 October, Nishimura sensibly moved the *Mogami* and three destroyers ahead of his heavier ships, which steered a course closer to Bohol, to establish the position and nature of any American naval forces in the area. The Japanese were therefore now arranged in three groups: the *Mogami* force in the van, the rest of Nishimura's force in the centre and Shima's force at the rear, some 40 miles behind Nishimura's main force.

The conditions were ideal for PT boat work: the sea was calm, and the night was dark with a quarter moon that was due to set shortly after 24.00 hours. It was at 22.36 hours that the first PT section detected

Nishimura's larger ships on radar. The PT boats then closed at moderate speed to avoid alerting the Japanese with engine noise and white bow waves, but even so the well trained observers on the Japanese ships quickly detected the small craft. Nishimura responded quickly in text-book fashion, turning his ships toward the PT boats to minimize the target size for torpedo attack, and at the same time using the searchlights of his ships to illuminate the small craft for engagement with the rapid fire of medium-calibre guns. Enthusiastic but with little experience, the crews of the PT boats were very surprised and discommoded to a considerable degree: the PT-152 had its forward part pierced in many places by the detonation of a shell that totally destroyed

the forward gun position; the PT-130 made smoke and continued to close the Japanese but was then holed by a shell that did not detonate. As a result none of these first PT boats got into a position to fire torpedoes, but more importantly none of the boats got off a sighting report.

Even as this was happening, though, the *Mogami*'s van element had passed the second section of PT boats, neither side detecting the other's presence. So it was only after the PT boats had first sighted the advancing Japanese that Oldendorf learned of the fact after the relevant message had been relayed through several intermediaries. Fortunately for Oldendorf, the report indicated that the Japanese were heading into the Surigao Strait as he had expected,

A PT boat patrolling off the
coast of New Guinea.

A PT boat patrolling off the coast of New Guinea.

and he therefore had to make no alterations to his dispositions.

The third section of PT boats meanwhile detected the *Mogami*'s van force and attacked just before 24.00 hours near Limasawa island. The PT-146 and PT-151 boats each managed to get a torpedo away, but neither struck a target. Faced with retaliatory fire their lightly built craft could not hope to survive, the PT boats of the third section therefore pulled back. Yet

again, though, Oldendorf received no sighting report.

Realizing that his progress was faced at this stage by only scattered forces, Nishimura decided to concentrate his ships once more. The Japanese generally held the tactical initiative at this stage of the battle, and this was reflected in the confident message that Nishimura sent to Kurita as the latter was approaching the southern end of the San Bernardino Strait. Shortly before

02.00 hours Nishimura's ships were traversing the strait between Panaon and the northern tip of the larger island of Mindanao, after which Nishimura would order a change of course from north-east to north to reach the southern edge of the Surigao Strait. This narrow strait was only 10 miles (16km) wide, and as such constituted a chokepoint ideal for PT boat operations against heavier warships. As a result there were five sections of PT boats in

This Osa I-class FAC(M) of the Egyptian navy carries the primary armament of four SS-N-2A Styx anti-ship missiles in a quartet of large and very clumsy launchers.

attack, and for the first time the Japanese reaction lacked speed and effective decision. The result was that torpedoes struck both of the battleships and three of their escorting destroyers, one of them blowing up. A second wave of destroyers attacked behind the first wave. The battleship *Yamashiro* was struck by another torpedo but forged on; the battleship *Fuso*, already badly damaged by the first torpedo attack, was torn in two by an explosion; and another destroyer blew up. Force A had effectively ceased to exist as a fighting entity, even though Nishimura's flagship, the heavy cruiser *Mogami*, and one destroyer continued to the north in an increasingly indecisive fashion. These three ships were already coming under fire from Oldendorf's TG 77.2 at the northern end of the Surigao Strait, where the ships had the room to steam backward and forward across Nishimura's course so that each ship could fire on the Japanese van.

It was at this stage that the destroyers made their third attack. Even though there were problems with the presence of friendly fire, the destroyers inflicted two more torpedo hits on the *Yamashiro* but suffered heavy damage to one of their own number. The destruction of the *Yamashiro* was now completed within a period of only nine minutes by the fire of the American battleships, and even as this was happening the *Mogami* and the destroyer *Shigure* reversed course and headed south toward Shima's 2nd Striking Force. In the confusion the *Mogami* collided with the cruiser *Nachi* but was able to maintain its course. The PT-131 boat, still in the area after failing to score any success with two torpedoes against the advance of Force A, now spotted a second opportunity as the remnants of Force A retired and launched one torpedo at a destroyer: the torpedo missed its intended target but travelled on

this area. However, the inexperience of the PT boat skippers and their crew meant that there was no co-ordination in the sections attacks, so while several boats got to within effective torpedo range and in fact launched about 12 torpedoes, they scored no hits. The Japanese again responded with searchlights and medium-calibre gun fire. The PT-490 boat was severely damaged while closing in an effort to launch two torpedoes. The PT-493 boats approached to offer aid under cover of smoke, but was hit by three medium-calibre shells which inflicted severe casualties, blew off most of the boat's superstructure, and holed the hull. The crew managed to beach their boat and scramble ashore, but the boat subsequently slid off the shore and sank.

Having brushed aside this latest small craft attack, Nishimura maintained his course. There were now only two more PT boat sections ahead of the Japanese, and

these received orders to remain well clear of the Japanese ships to leave the way free for torpedo attacks by destroyers. At 02.15 hours on 25 October Shima's 2nd Striking force was closing up astern of Nishimura's Force C, while some two hours earlier and farther to the north Kurita's Force A had transitted the unguarded San Bernardino Strait. The threat to the Americans off Leyte was now reaching a critical point.

Even though the PT boats had failed to inflict any real damage on the Japanese ships, their defeat had served to provide the Japanese with an exaggerated belief in their own superiority in this type of night fighting. Then at 03.30 hours the Japanese position began to unravel, for it was at this time that the American destroyers, operating from the blackness of the land behind them, dashed forward to launch torpedoes. The American ships fired 21 torpedoes before the Japanese realized that they were under

HMS Sabre *(P275), a fast training boat of the Royal Navy at sea in 1972.*

to hit and cripple the light cruiser *Abukuma*.

By this time Shima had decided that a fruitful outcome to the operation was impossible and ordered his 2nd Striking Force to turn back. As the disorganized Japanese pulled back, the PT boats saw the arrival of daylight as an opportunity to harass the enemy's ships as they retired. The PT-491 boat followed the *Mogami* for 20 minutes before dashing in to attack with

two torpedoes that missed even as the heavy cruiser responded with salvoes of shells from its 8-in (203-mm) main armament. The PT-137 boat also tried to attack the damaged cruiser, but the *Mogami* and its escorting destroyer drove off the American boat. At much the same time the PT-190 boat, its skipper showing enthusiasm rather than sense, closed on the ships of the 2nd Striking Force and was lucky to get away

with only moderate damage. The PT-323 boat, which had missed an earlier chance for success by the decision to send in destroyers rather than the last two sections of PT boats, had become separated from its two partner boats in the night and now chanced on the blazing wreck of a ship with the damaged destroyer *Asagumo* standing by: the destroyer drove off the PT boat on each of the three times it tried to attack. Adding apparent insult to injury, American cruisers and destroyers now arrived and finished off both the Japanese ships. The PT-150 and PT-194 boats tackled the heavy cruiser *Nachi* without success, the PT-194 being hit by an 8-in (203-mm) shell.

This was the end of the surface action, and American aircraft now took over the task of attacking the ships of the Southern Force, only two cruisers and five destroyers surviving. In overall terms, the force of PT boats had been faced with an immense test of the boats' technical capabilities and their crews' training and determination. At the technical level the PT boats had performed well but had been beaten by the combination of searchlights and guns, which was the remedy first devised in the 19th century for the threat of the torpedo boat; and at the personal level the crews had been found wanting in certain elements of their training but not in their determination and courage.

Like the Americans, and for the same basic reasons, the Japanese were late into the development of coastal craft. All Japanese craft of this type were developed from two British craft, Thornycroft-built CMBs, including one captured at Canton in 1938. Examination of these two types resulted in a Japanese-designed experimental type built in 1940. This led to the construction of at least 248 MTBs before Japan's defeat in 1945. Typical of these was the Type T-14 class, which had a displacement of 15 tons, a length of 49ft 3in (15.0m), a propulsion arrangement of one Type 91 petrol engine delivering 920hp (685kW) for a maximum speed of 28kt, and an armament of two 18-in (457-mm) tubes for two torpedoes as well as one 25-mm cannon or 0.51-in (13-mm) machine-gun. In parallel with these small and highly limited MTBs, the Japanese also

This Nanuchka-class vessel, designed and built in the U.S.S.R., in on the edge of the boundary separating the fast attack craft from the corvette, and offers considerable operational capabilities.

developed some MGBs. Typical of these was the Type H-2 class with a displacement of 24.5 tons, a length of 59ft 2in (18.0m), a propulsion arrangement of two Type 11 petrol engines delivering 2,100hp (1565kW) to two shafts for a speed of 33.5kt, and an armament of two 20-mm cannon, two 0.303-in (7.7-mm) machine-guns and two depth charges. In overall terms, however, the Japanese MTBs and MGBs were a technical dead end.

As had happened after World War I, the end of World War II in 1945 saw a rapid and almost total end to the development, construction and deployment of fast combat craft among the navies of the victorious western Allies. The U.K. and U.S.A. decided that their fast combat craft had played a comparatively ineffective part in the

naval warfare of World War II, and that they should therefore return to the type of pre-war navies whose large surface combatants had dominated operations in the Atlantic and Pacific Oceans. Large numbers of fast combat craft were therefore deleted or transferred to smaller navies. These latter used the craft mainly for patrol, but the navies of some middle-rank nations used them as stepping stones toward the re-creation of conventional navies out of the ashes of their navies of World War II.

The exception to this general tendency of returning to an orthodox navy was the U.S.S.R. This nation had emerged from World War II as a potential superpower, but the Soviet leadership was sure that this potential could be realized only if the U.S.S.R. developed highly capable air and

The Swedish FAC(T) Spica (T121)-class was the lead unit of a six-strong class based on the TNC 42 design.

naval forces with the strategic capabilities that matched the vast strength of the Red Army. Soon after the end of the war Iosif Stalin, the Soviet dictator, issued orders that the Soviet navy was to be built up to a size and strength that would eventually allow it to compete on at least equal terms with the U.S. Navy. It was clear that several decades would be needed for the plan to reach completion, but in the short term there remained the threat of American attack on the Soviet motherland. The Soviets thought this to be a very real threat, for the position of the U.S.S.R. in the centre of the Soviet strategic map

suggested that the country, though vast, was virtually encircled by the unfriendly territory and bases of the U.S.A. and its allies. The greatest threat was posed by American long-range bombers carrying strategic nuclear weapons, but another significant offensive capability was offered to the Americans by their large and superbly equipped navy, which was centred on modern aircraft carriers and amphibious warfare vessels. Submarines offered the Soviets the possibility of tackling an invasion force some distance from the U.S.S.R., but a way had also to be found to tackle any American warships that

evaded the submarine cordon and approached the shores of the U.S.S.R. Here the Soviets turned once more to the concept of fast combat craft, initially armed with the heavyweight torpedo that offered the best chance of crippling or sinking American warships.

In the period leading up to World War II, the U.S.S.R. had made extensive use of stepped-hull boats derived ultimately from the Thornycroft CMB with elements of the Italian MAS. This provided the Soviets with a technical base for the development of an interim type as they prepared a more ambitious plan based on the hard-chine Elco PT boats they had received from the U.S.A. under Lend-Lease during World War II. In 1946 the first post-war Soviet MTB appeared as the P2 class. This was based on the pre-war D3 class but, probably as a result of experience with the Elco craft, introduced to Soviet service the ahead-firing torpedo tube that had been commonplace in other navies for more than 15 years. The MTB of the P2 class had a displacement of 50 tons and a length of 80ft 1in (24.4m), but displayed its conceptual obsolescence in the propulsion arrangement of three petrol engines delivering 4,930hp (3675kW) to three shafts for a speed which Western estimates put at between 40 and 50kt. The type was thus very powerfully engined, even if only at the expense of high flammability, and could thus carry without degradation of performance the heavy armament of two 21-in (533-mm) tubes for two torpedoes and four 0.5- or 0.57-in (12.7- or 14.5-mm) machine-guns in two twin mountings. Production numbers are uncertain, for while some sources indicate that large numbers were supplied to China, the fact that the type was only rarely seen suggests that comparatively small numbers were produced. The type was deleted in 1966, a last remembrance of an older period in fast combat craft design.

The next Soviet MTB was another descendant of the pre-war concept, for though the P4 class switched from a wooden to an aluminium alloy hull, it retained the stepped planing bottom: this hull form is very useful for outright speed, but is also tactically inhibiting as its low stability means that tight turns require considerable slowing. The P4 class entered production in 1950 or 1951, and about 200 units had been completed when production ended in 1956; most of these were later transferred to the navies of Soviet client and allied states. The type was made possible by the advent of the U.S.S.R.'s first effective marine diesel engine, the M 503 rated at

1,210hp (900kW). The P4 class thus had a displacement of 25 tons and a length of 72ft 3in (22.0m), and the propulsion arrangement of two M 503 diesels delivered 2,415hp (1800kW) to two shafts for a speed of 42kt. The P4-class design had a hull/beam ratio of 4.7/1 compared with the 3.65/1 of the P2-class design, and this meant only a slight reduction in speed from the predecessor class despite less than half the installed power. What the P4 class had to sacrifice, however, was some of its predecessor's armament: thus the heavyweight firepower of the P2 class was exchanged for the medium-weight punch from two smaller 18-in (457-mm) torpedoes supplemented by two 0.5- or 0.57-in (12.7- or 14.5-mm) machine-guns

in a twin turret, and between four and eight depth charges. The last P6-class craft were deleted from Soviet service in the mid-1970s, but the type remained in declining service with several smaller navies up to the later stages of the 20th century.

As it was gaining an interim coastal defence capability through the introduction of these two classes, the Soviet navy completed its evaluation of the Elco 80-ft (24.4-m) type of PT boat and finished the design of a new type of MTB. This was the P6 class that entered production in 1953 for the completion of the first units in about 1955 at the beginning of a programme that ran through the 1960s and saw the construction of about 500 craft including some 200 transferred to client and allied navies. the type adopted the hard-chine hull used in the Elco boats supplied under Lend-Lease but reverted to wooden construction, possibly as a result of salt-water corrosion problems with the aluminium-hulled P4 class. The type proved most successful in service. It was reliable and, by comparison with its predecessors, offered higher levels of seaworthiness and manoeuvrability. The greater power available in this type not only improved performance, but also made possible a reversion to the heavyweight 21-in (533-mm) torpedo and the installation of heavier gun armament, the latter comprising four 25-mm cannon in two twin mountings. The forward unit gave the class a distinctive appearance for it was offset to port, probably to give the bridge crew a better field of vision straight ahead. The propulsion that gave the P6 class its high performance was the quadruple arrangement of M 503 high-speed diesel engines, providing twice the power of the twin-engined installation in the P4 class.

About mid-way through the construction programme of the P6 class,

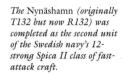

The Nynäshamn *(originally T132 but now R132) was completed as the second unit of the Swedish navy's 12-strong Spica II class of fast-attack craft.*

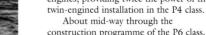

new technologies were reaching the stage where benefit could be gained from a measure of practical experience under operational conditions. One of these technologies was propulsion, where the gas turbine was beginning to mature as a power unit of exceptional capability in terms of an attractive combination of high power and low installed weight and volume. From about 1958, therefore, some 20 P6-class

craft were modified into two new configurations with a CODAG (COmbined Diesel And Gas turbine) propulsion arrangement. At the price of an increase in displacement to 90 tons, the hull was lengthened by some 6ft 7in (2.0m), a small funnel was added abaft the bridge for the considerable quantity of exhaust gases produced by the gas turbine, and an air inlet was installed between the bridge and the

funnel, offset slightly to starboard and facing to port. The propulsion arrangement was one gas turbine delivering 5,095hp (3800kW) to a central shaft and two diesel engines delivering 2,415hp (1800kW) to the two wing shafts.

The P8-class derivative of the P6 class had another addition in the form of a pair of semi-submerged hydrofoils forward, and these were designed to lift and stabilize the bow as the boat planed a high speed on the very flat bottom of its after part. The result was extended cruising endurance and a maximum speed of 45kt with the gas turbine delivering its full power. The slightly later P10-class conversions, produced from about 1960, had no hydrofoils and featured Pot Head surface-search radar instead of the Skin Head radar of the P8 and P6 classes.

Throughout this period the Soviets had been undertaking a high-priority programme of missile development with the intention of creating a range of weapons right across the tactical and strategic spectrum. In the late 1950s, this programme began to yield useful results in the field of surface-to-surface missiles that could be used in the anti-ship role. The first Soviet experiments had been made in the immediate aftermath of World War II on the basis of captured Fieseler Fi 103 (otherwise V-1) missiles, and led to spectacular success in the development of Soviet cruise missiles, which were placed in service some four years before the first of their Western equivalents. The first weapon of this type to attain operational status was the SS-N-1 Scrubber, which entered service in 1958 as a large ship-launched missile carrying a conventional or nuclear warhead to a maximum range of 115 miles (185km) with radar or infra-red homing for the terminal stage of its attack after cruise under the control of an autopilot. Although the SS-N-1 was a great technical achievement and boded well for future Soviet developments, there could be no disguising of the fact that the missile was too large for practical use, and its deployment was limited to Kildin and Krupny-class destroyers.

The SS-N-1 opened the way for more practical weapons of the same aeroplane-type layout, and the first of these more effective weapons was the considerably

smaller SS-N-2 Styx, a missile that can truly be regarded as one of the weapons that revolutionized naval warfare. The Styx weighed 6,614lb (3000kg) and a 1,102-lb (500-kg) high explosive warhead, and its combination of a jettisonable solid-propellant rocket booster and a storable liquid-propellant sustainer rocket provided a theoretical maximum range of 53miles (85km). The full range could only be usefully employed if mid-course updating of the guidance package was provided by a supporting helicopter (an extremely unlikely contingency in this period), so the effective range of the missile was 23 miles (37km) under the control of an autopilot with an active radar taking over for the terminal phase of the attack. The missile entered production in the late 1950s and entered full service late in 1958 or early in 1959.

By this time the process of designing a specialist fast combat craft for the type was well advanced, but as an interim measure it was decided to convert a number of P6-class torpedo craft into simple missile-launch platforms. This resulted in a total of about 100 Komar-class craft that entered service probably in late 1958, though the Western powers became aware of the type only in 1960. The Soviets classified this type of craft as the RK, standing for Raketnyy Kater (rocket cutter), and this designation has been retained for all later Soviet FAC(M)s. Of the 100 or so Komar-class craft completed in the U.S.S.R. by 1961, some 78 were later transferred to the navies of satellite and client countries, and about another 40 of the modified steel-hulled Hegu class were built in China. The Komar class was intended only as an interim type, and the last craft had been retired from Soviet service by about 1981.

Topweight was clearly a problem in the converted craft, for each Komar-class craft

was armed with only two Styx missiles in open-ended but often tarpaulin-sealed launchers that provided only minimal protection against the elements. The missile installation was wider than the hull, so wedge-shaped sponsons, supported by struts braced against the hull, were fitted as outboard projections that helped to protect the missile installation against spray. In an effort to lighten the load on the bow, the bridge and the twin 25-mm cannon mounting were moved aft. The longer range of missiles by comparison with the torpedoes of the P6 class called for the introduction of improved radar, and this was the type designated Square Tie by NATO. The equipment can see to a maximum range of about 50 miles (80km), but its effective range in the acquisition of surface targets is only about 17.5 miles (28km), and it was this that limited the effective range of the Styx in the absence of any mid-course targeting update. The Komar class had a full-load displacement of some 80 tons by comparison with the 73 tons of the P6 class, and this reduced maximum speed from 43 to 40kt on the same power.

The use of hulls that existed or were in production greatly hastened the process of getting the Komar-class craft into service as the pioneer platform for the Styx missile. By the mid-1960s there were a number of theoretically superior types in service, but the utility of the basic system was conformed on 21 October 1967 when SS-N-2 missiles, fired from two Komar-class craft of the Egyptian navy lying in Alexandria harbour, hit and sank the Israeli destroyer *Eilat*: this was the first sinking of a ship by a ship-launched anti-ship missile.

It was immediately apparent that a new factor had entered into the equation of naval power. A similar effect had been

The Vega (T125) was the fifth of the six Spica I-class FAC(T)s to be built. Note the location of the superstructure well aft, leaving the foredeck clear for the 2.2-in (57-mm) Bofors automatic guns. The vessel is seen here with only four of the six possible tubes for 21-in (533-mm) wire-guided torpedoes.

anticipated in the third quarter of the 19th century for the torpedo, which many believed would provide the navies of small and comparatively impoverished countries with the means to tackle and defeat the major warships of the navies operated by larger and more affluent nations. This had not eventuated, however, because partial solutions to the torpedo and torpedo boat were provided by improved protection of larger warships and by the development of torpedo boat destroyers and quick-firing guns respectively. Even so, the threat of the torpedo remained, and this greatly conditioned the tactics of surface warfare right to the end of World War II.

The anti-ship missile now seemed to

offer the same type of threat that had been promised by the torpedo. The SS-N-2 had proved itself an effective weapon, and it was appreciated that technical developments would soon result in the creation of smaller but more potent weapons of the same type. This opened the possibility that the navies of smaller countries could adopt swarms of FAC(M)s to overwhelm the larger and more conventional warships of theoretically more powerful navies. As always, though, it was not long before countermeasures and counter-tactics were evolved to limit the capability of a new weapon type. Thus another first involving a Komar-class craft occurred in April 1972, when a North

Vietnamese vessel of this type launched an SS-N-2 against the USS *Sterett*, a guided missile cruiser that was bombarding coastal targets in North Vietnam. The *Sterett* launched a RIM-2 Terrier surface-to-air missile that intercepted the SS-N-2 in the first successful destruction of an anti-ship missile by another missile under combat conditions.

The Soviets were soon constructing a successor to the Komar-class craft as the units of the Osa class with considerably improved overall capabilities. The Osa class was designed for excellent sea-keeping qualities and full capability in coastal operations, especially in European waters. The type was therefore based on a larger

hull of the displacement rather than planing variety, and was built of steel with a steel and aluminium alloy superstructure providing citadel-type protection against the effects of nuclear, biological and chemical warfare. The gun armament of the Osa-class craft comprises four 30-mm cannon in two remotely controlled mountings on the centreline forward and aft of the superstructure: these mountings are intended for use against attacking aircraft, but also possess a capability against light surface attackers. The sensor fit also reflected the greater capability of the Osa class by comparison with the Komar class, and included the standard Square Tie search radar on the mast and Drum Tilt fire-

control radar for the 30-mm mountings on a small pedestal mounting above the rear of the superstructure between the two after anti-ship missile launchers. The design was fully optimized for the carriage and launching of the SS-N-2 missile, of which four are carried in launchers arranged as two on each side of the deck abaft the bridge. The launchers themselves are fully enclosed to provide their missiles with full protection against atmospheric and water conditions: the front of each launcher is hinged along its upper edge to open, forward and upward, before missile launch, and abaft each launcher is a shield for the outward deflection of the booster rocket's exhaust.

The first of the Osa-class craft was laid

down in 1959 or 1960, and the type entered service in 1961. Production continued up to 1966, and amounted to some 175 craft excluding more than 100 built in China as the Huangfeng class. The Soviet craft served with all four of the U.S.S.R.'s main surface forces (the Northern, Baltic, Black Sea and Pacific Fleets), but over a period of years many of them were transferred to the navies of satellite, allied and client states as more modern craft entered Soviet service.

The first of these more modern types was the improved Osa II class, which entered service in 1966 and resulted in the NATO redesignation of the initial type as the Osa I class. The Osa II class is notably different from the Osa I class in its revised missile arrangement. This comprises four cylindrical launchers, with their rear edges supported just above deck level by short brackets and their front sections raised on twin legs, in place of the original slab-sided launchers. The new arrangement is considerably lighter than its predecessor, also offers less windage, and is associated with an improved variant of the Styx missile. Succeeding what became the SS-N-2A, this was dubbed SS-N-2B by the Americans and is a more compact weapon with folding wings and probably infra-red terminal homing as an alternative to the original active radar homing. The revised guidance package allows the missile to home on the heat signature of the target, and this passive terminal mode offers considerable tactical advantages over the original active system, whose emissions could be detected by the target in time for countermeasures to be implemented.

Production of the Osa II class continued up to 1970 and amounted to perhaps 115 craft. Both Osa classes have a three-shaft propulsion arrangement, but

The number T138 identifies this Swedish fast attack craft as the Pitea, *eighth of the* Spica II *class to be completed. The 2.2-in (57-mm) Bofors automatic gun on the foredeck in a potent dual-purpose weapon, and the rest of the deck is laid out for a primary armament of eight RBS 15M anti-ship missiles or four tubes for 21-in (533-mm) wire-guided torpedoes, the latter evident in this photograph.*

whereas the Osa I class has three 4,025-hp (3000-kW) M 503A diesel engines for a speed of 38kt at a full-load displacement of 210 tons, the Osa II class uses three 5,030-hp (3750-kW) M 504 diesel engines for a speed of 40kt at a full-load displacement of 245 tons. Many of the Osa II-class craft were later upgraded with superior weapons, most notably the SS-N-2C longer-range version of the Styx and the SA-N-5 naval version of the SA-7 Grail man-portable surface-to-air missile.

Craft of the Osa I class have been used in combat by the navies of several countries including India in 1971, when such a missile sank the Pakistani destroyer *Khaibar*, Egypt in 1973 against Israel, Syria in 1973 against Israel, and Iraq between 1980 and 1990 against Iran. The only navy which has

used Osa II-class craft in combat is that of Iraq in the same 10-year Persian Gulf war with Iran. The failure of Arab-operated Osa-class craft against the Israeli navy during the Yom Kippur War of October 1973 highlighted the fact that the type was obsolete not so much in its basic hull but in its primary weapon. On several occasions, SS-N-2 missiles were launched at Israeli targets, but were defeated by Israeli electronic countermeasures. Though a pioneering weapon of its type, the SS-N-2 was obviously obsolescent if not actually obsolete, but the Soviets had appreciated this fact and already placed in service a replacement anti-ship missile carried by a new class.

The new missile was the SS-N-9 Siren, a weapon delivered from the factory in a

sealed container that doubles as the launcher. This greatly improved the unserviced shelf life of the weapon, which weighs some 6,614lb (3000kg) and is another aeroplane-configured weapon powered by a solid-propellant rocket for a high subsonic speed and a range of 40.5 miles (65km) increased to 81 miles (130km) with the aid of mid-course update to the guidance. The missile carries either a 1,102-lb (500-kg) high explosive or 200-kiloton nuclear warhead, the former being installed for general use and the latter if there is the possibility of a major target such as an aircraft carrier, battleship or cruiser.

It is clear that the Soviets now decided that while their previous FAC(M) classes had been useful, these had been based on hulls too small to offer a fully practical seaward defence capability. In the new type, therefore, they opted for a displacement more than three times greater than that of the Osa classes. This allowed the installation of a larger and more varied armament (including a significantly improved anti-aircraft capability) in a hull that could accept greater power for improved performance, greater stability and better general seaworthiness in coastal rather than inshore applications. There are indications that the Soviets did not achieve all their objectives, however, for some reports suggest that the hull has not displayed the required seaworthiness characteristics, and that the engines are somewhat unreliable.

This surface vessel designed as the platform for the SS-N-9 was the Nanuchka class FAC(M), a type large and capable enough to be considered virtually a missile-armed corvette as it has a full-load displacement of 660 tons on a displacement-type hull able to reach the speed of 36kt on the 30,175hp (22500kW) generated by six M 504 diesel engines

Virgo *(T 126), a Spica I-class FAC of the Royal Swedish Navy.*

coupled to three shafts. The greater size and increased capabilities of the Nanuchka class were recognized by the Soviet designation of the new type as an MRK (Malyy Raketnyy Korabl, or small rocket ship) rather than RK. The type that entered service in 1969 was subsequently designated Nanuchka I by NATO, and carries a primary armament of six SS-N-9 missiles used in conjunction with the Band Stand air/surface-search radar located in a large radome above and behind the bridge. The missiles are located in two

triple arrangements flanking the forward superstructure, whose lower parts aft of the bridge are angled out toward the sides of the craft to deflect the exhaust plumes of the missiles as they are fired. The gun armament comprises two 57-mm dual-purpose weapons in a twin mounting, and this is located at the stern. Here it has excellent fields of fire under the control of its associated Muff Cob radar, located above the aftermost part of the superstructure just forward of the gun mounting. The location

of the gun mounting was dictated by the decision to give the new design a greater air-defence capability than preceding classes, in this instance with an inbuilt surface-to-air missile system, the SA-N-4 Gecko medium-weight system. This missile is associated with a twin-arm launcher fed by a 20-round magazine, and is a retractable system covered by a lid when lowered into its circular bin, which is located just forward of the bridge behind a breakwater that helps to keep the area at least partially free from

LEFT
The Spica I-class Castor.

OPPOSITE
*These are Spica II-class
torpedo-armed fast attack
craft of the Swedish navy at
speed. In the foreground of
this photograph is the
Nynäshamn (T132), with
Vasterås (T135) and
Norrtälje (T133) behind.*

water. The associated Pop Group fire-control radar is another retractable system, in this instance located just aft of the launcher in the forward part of the superstructure above and between the forward edges of the SS-N-9 missile installations.

The Soviets built 17 Nanuchka I-class units for their own use, and also exported the type in downgraded form as the Nanuchka II with two triple launcher installations for the SS-N-2C version of the Styx supported by Square Tie radar. Construction for Soviet use then switched to an improved model, the Nanuchka III with the aft-mounted 57-mm guns replaced

by a single 3-in (76-mm) dual-purpose gun and a 30-mm close-in weapon mounting added. Construction of the Nanuchka III class totalled 15 units.

Just 10 years after they introduced the Nanuchka class, the Soviets followed with the Tarantul class, which is a slightly smaller type but still verging on corvette capability and, as such, classified as an MRK. It is still difficult to determine the origins of this class, for its design and other features are in many respects not as advanced as those of the Nanuchka class when the first Tarantul I-class unit was commissioned in 1978. The design is based on that of the

Pauk class of anti-submarine corvettes, and may have been conceived for export. Exports of the Tarantul I class were indeed made to four countries, but the Soviet navy also received two of the type, which has a full-load displacement of 580 tons on a hull possessing an overall length of 183ft 9in (56.0m). One feature in which the Tarantul I class is more modern that that of the Nanuchka class, however, is the propulsion arrangement. This is of either the CODOG (COmbined Diesel Or Gas turbine) or COGOG (COmbined Gas turbine Or Gas turbine) variety in which the two shafts are driven either by two diesel engines or two

A Lürssen FPB-36-class torpedo boat of the Chilean navy.

gas turbines delivering up to 6,035hp (4500kW) for an economical cruising speed of 20kt, or by two NK-12M gas turbines delivering 24,140hp (18000kW) for a maximum speed of 36kt. The armament of the Tarantul class is somewhat strange. The gun armament is a potent variant of the combination of what had now become the standard for Soviet fast combat craft: one 3-in (76-mm) dual-purpose gun and two 30-mm rotary six-barrel cannon in close-in weapon system mountings for short-range air defence. In this task the guns are supplemented by one SA-N-5 quadruple launcher for a maximum of 16 short-range surface-to-air missiles. There is no medium surface-to-air missile system, and the anti-ship missile system is limited to two twin launchers for

the SS-N-2C version of the venerable Styx. Some 20 Tarantul II-class units were delivered between 1980 and 1986.

The basic design might have been conceived for a more powerful anti-ship armament whose missile then suffered development delays. Certainly the Tarantul III class that appeared in 1986 is far more powerfully armed in this respect than its predecessors, with one or two twin launchers for SS-N-22 Sunburn missiles in place of the earlier variant's SS-N-2C missiles. Little is known about the SS-N-22, but this is probably a development of the SS-N-9 with considerably improved electronics. These provide a home-on-jam capability in conditions where the target is using electronic countermeasures, and also allow a true sea-skimming approach to the

target in place of the SS-N-9s 245-ft (75-m) approach height, with all its tactical advantages of low optical and electro-magnetic visibility.

The Soviets did not altogether lose interest in the RK and during the early and mid-1970s developed a design that retained the SS-N-2C missile but was based on a higher-performance hull. The result is the Matka class that started to enter service in 1978 as another classic example of the Soviet predilection for producing hybrids combining the best features of existing craft. Thus the new class retains the basic hull and propulsion arrangement of the Osa II class married to the hydrofoil system developed for the Turya class of torpedo craft. Complete with armament, this results in a full-load displacement of 260 tons and,

The Lürssen-type fast torpedo attack craft Quidora, Tequalda, Guacolda *and* Fresia *of the Chilean navy in 1976.*

on the power of three 5,030-hp (3,750-kW) M 504 diesel engines, a speed of 40kt. The hydrofoil is located just forward of the bridge, and was designed for the dual purposes of lifting the bow and improving seaworthiness. The weapon fit of this hybrid type is also interesting, for it combines just two launchers for SS-N-2C missiles with the fast combat craft gun armament of one 3-in (76-mm) dual-purpose gun and one 30-mm rotary six-barrel cannon in a close-in weapon system mounting. The Matka class was built in Leningrad between 1977 and 1983, but reached a total of just 16 units, probably in reflection of the fact that it is limited in real operational terms by its obsolete missile armament.

Even though it had been responsible

for the introduction of the anti-ship missile with the Komar class in 1960, the U.S.S.R. did not lose its earlier enthusiasm for the torpedo-armed fast combat craft. Yet it was clear that the day of the MTB, a small craft of high speed and considerable agility but little else, was now past and that what was needed under current conditions was the type that matured as the FAC(T) comparable in size with early FAC(M)s and as such a larger torpedo-armed craft offering other attributes in addition to speed and agility. In Soviet terminology, the FAC(T) is designated TK (Torpednyy Kater, or torpedo cutter). The concept for Soviet FAC(T)s was possibly the West German Jaguar class, but the type was derived physically from the Osa class FAC(M). The craft of the resulting Shershen class share

the propulsion arrangement and gun armament of the Osa class, and use what is essentially a scaled-down version of the same hull with overall length reduced from 127ft 11in (39.0m) to 113ft 10in (34.7m). The propulsion arrangement comprises three M 503A diesel engines driving three propellers, and the primary armament is four 21-in (533-mm) torpedoes in four separate tubes located two on each side of the deck outboard of the superstructure.

The close relationship between the Osa and Shershen classes offered clear logistical benefits in terms of production and maintenance. The type remained in construction from 1962 to 1974, and some 85 units were completed. After only a comparatively short period of Soviet service, most of these craft were transferred

The Federal German Navy's Falke (P6112), *a Type 142-class fast attack craft.*

The Federal German Navy's P6117, a Type 142-class fast attack craft at speed.

A Saar-class fast missile attack craft of the Israeli navy.

to the navies of satellite, client and allied states. Constructed specifically for the export market was the Mol class, which was based on the standard Osa-class hull, but only a few such craft were built.

Further development and indeed expansion of the concept embodied in the Shershen class led to the Turya class. This is a FAH(T) or fast attack hydrofoil (torpedo) type analogous to the Matka-class hydrofoil derivative of the Osa class. The type is based on the hull of the Osa II-class FAC(M), but fitted with a single set of continuous half-submerged foils heavily braced in their centre to the hull. These fixed surface-piercing foils are relatively ineffective in

rough water, and were installed mainly to lift the bow and improve stability when the boat is planing on the after portion of its hull, which is trimmed by an adjustable flap located on the transom. Later units of the class have semi-retractable foils to reduce the span of these units and so ease the problem of coming alongside. The foil system was also responsible for the precise nature and disposition of the gun armament. As it was important to keep the bow light, it was decided to install on the fore castle only a small-calibre weapon, in this instance the elderly mounting with a superimposed pair of 25-mm anti-aircraft cannon. With weight over the stern less of a

critical factor, the main armament was located here in the form of two modern 57-mm dual-purpose guns in a twin mounting. It was at first assumed that the type had been conceived for the anti-ship role, but it later became clear that the Turya class was in fact an anti-submarine type, with acoustic homing heavyweight anti-submarine torpedoes and a sensor suite that includes, on the starboard quarter, a dipping sonar of the same basic type as carried by the Kamov Ka-25 Hormone anti-submarine helicopter. This makes the craft particularly useful in the Baltic Sea and the coastal waters of the Pacific Ocean, where the sonar can be lowered to listen for submarines lurking underneath the acoustically insulating thermal layers of these waters.

During the later 1940s the so-called Iron Curtain settled across Europe, dividing the continent between the Soviet-dominated Eastern bloc and the American-led Western grouping, which later became the Warsaw Pact and North Atlantic Treaty Organizations respectively. On the Western side there was initially little enthusiasm for the FAC. The major powers reasoned that Soviet strategic aggression would be met and eliminated by American nuclear power, and that at the operational level any Soviet-led offensive would take place on land with the support of massive conventional air power, and would be countered by the conventional forces and possibly the nuclear weapons of the American-dominated alliance. The Soviet navy was known at this time to be a negligible factor, and it was generally agreed that this navy could only launch and support minor amphibious operations against the allied nations' coastal flanks. Allied air and conventional naval power was more than adequate to meet this threat, so there seemed little purpose in developing fast combat craft specifically to

Puma *(P6122), a Type 143A-class fast attack craft of the German navy.*

protect the allied coast or to carry the coastal war into Soviet territory, where there would be only few and unimportant targets.

The one exception to this general rule was Sweden, which wished to preserve its neutral position through armed strength: this would deter aggression or, failing this, defeat an invasion that could realistically come only from across the Baltic Sea. The Swedish navy was therefore the country's first line of defence, initially with a conventional but obsolescent or even obsolete force of coast-defence battleships,

cruisers and destroyers as the core of three task forces. It soon became clear that the real utility of these forces was non-existent and that far better value for money could be obtained from lighter forces that would also be more effective. Thus there emerged from 1958 the concept of the light navy of perhaps two major surface warships, small but powerfully armed submarines, two flotillas of torpedo-armed fast combat craft, and a larger number of coast-defence flotillas equipped with MTBs.

In the early 1950s, Sweden built 10

T32-class MTBs with a standard displacement of 38.5 tons, an armament of one 40-mm Bofors gun and two 21-in (533-mm) torpedoes, and a maximum speed of 45kt on the power of three 1,500-hp (1118-kW) Isotta-Fraschini 184C petrol engines. These craft were deleted in the early 1970s, but had already been supplemented and effectively supplanted by the 15 slightly larger MTBs of the T42 class built between 1955 and 1957 with a 40-ton standard displacement but basically the same armament and performance as the preceding boats. By the late 1940s, though, the Swedish navy had already come to appreciate that such boats were useful only for inshore defence. For true coastal defence, a larger type was necessary and here the Swedish navy turned to the acknowledged leader in this field, Lürssen of Vegesack, the World War II designer of Germany's Schnellboote. A prototype was built in 1950 as the Perseus with a CODAG propulsion arrangement of one gas turbine and two diesel engines, and this paved the way for the Plejad class of diesel-engined FAC(T)s that eventually totalled 12 craft built in two batches as six craft between 1954 and 1955, and another six craft between 1956 and 1958. Eight of the craft were deleted in July 1977, and the last three in July 1981.

This class may be regarded as the Western starting point for the design of modern FACs. The hull had a length of 157ft 6in (48.0m) for a full-load displacement of 170 tons. The propulsion arrangement comprised three 3,020-hp (2250-kW) MTU 20V 672 diesel engines powering three propellers for a speed of 37.5kt. The armament comprised two guns and six 21-in (533-mm) tubes for heavyweight torpedoes. The barrelled weapons were remotely controlled 40-mm Bofors guns in mountings on the fore castle and on the after deck midway between the bridge and the stern, and the torpedo tubes were located three on each side of the deck to fire wire guided torpedoes.

In the circumstances, it was inevitable that the Swedish navy should capitalize on the advantages provided by this pioneering FAC and develop a series of improved types. The first step was the commissioning, between 1966 and 1968, of the six Spica- (later Spica I-) class

FAC(T)s. The design of these craft was not merely a further developed version of the Plejad-class design, but a major reworking of the original FAC(T) concept to take full advantage of technical developments of the late 1950s and early 1960s in fields such as propulsion, weapons and sensors. The Spica I class therefore switched to gas turbine propulsion, using three 4,240-hp (3160-kW) Rolls-Royce Proteus 1274 gas turbines powering three shafts for a speed of 40kt. The armament comprised a significantly improved gun, the 57-mm Bofors SAK 57 Mk 1 automatic weapon, and a torpedo armament basically similar

to that of the Plejad class, with two tubes flanking the gun (in a location where they had to be swung out through several degrees before torpedoes could be launched) and the other four in side-by-side pairs flanking the rear part of the superstructure, and could be unshipped to allow the craft to serve as minelayers.

Further evolution of the same basic design concept resulted in the 12 units of the Spica II class that were commissioned between 1973 and 1976. These each have a full-load displacement of 230 tons on a modified hull, and the same propulsion arrangement as in the Spica II class results

The Storch (P6152), a Type 148-class fast missile attack craft of the Federal German Navy.

in a maximum speed of 41kt. The original weapon fit included the same arrangement of six torpedo tubes matched with the significantly enhanced SAK 57 Mk 2 gun, and provision was also made for the four after torpedo tubes to be replaced by up to eight launchers for RBS 15M anti-ship missiles. The success of the type was attested by the development of two export variants, the Malaysian Spica-M class and the Danish Willemoes class.

The line-up of Swedish fast combat craft is completed by two units of the remarkable Spica III class that was redesignated the Stockholm class before

the craft were commissioned in 1985. This type may be taken as a current high point in FAC design, for many advanced features are combined in a most compact fashion on a hull that is large but only modestly so. The type was schemed as a flotilla leader with weapons and sensors giving it equal capabilities against surface vessels and submarines and only a slightly lesser capability against close-range attack aircraft. The missile armament comprises four twin launchers for the powerful and long-ranged RBS 15M anti-ship missile. As shorter-range backing for these missiles, each craft carries two wire-guided

heavyweight torpedoes. Further capability against ships, and also against aircraft, is provided by two Bofors guns, one of them the potent 57-mm SAK 57 Mk 2 weapon and the other a modern development of the legendary 40-mm L/70 weapon, and anti-submarine capability is provided by wire-guided lightweight torpedoes, the ahead-throwing Elma rocket system that creates a pattern of high explosive grenades sinking through the water believed to contain the target, and depth charges released from two racks.

In 1956 permission was granted for West Germany to start rearming as a key

Operated by the French navy as a patrol type, La Combattante was the prototype for the highly successful La Combattante II and III classes of FACs.

component of the Western alliance. Its first surface ships were ex-allied types, but it was clear from the beginning that Germany's World War II experience in the design and construction of advanced submarines and Schnellboote would soon result in the indigenous production of coastal submarine and fast combat craft. A head-start with the latter had been provided by Lürssen's design of the Swedish Perseus and the company's part in the construction of the resulting Plejad FAC(T) class, and this was reflected in Lürssen's TNC-42 design for the Jaguar FAC(T) that entered service as the Type 141 class with great similarities to the Swedish Spica I class. Such coastal warfare types were needed for the protection of West Germany's maritime frontiers on the Baltic and North Seas. The 40 Jaguar-class craft were delivered in the late 1950s and early 1960s as orthodox but effective vessels with a full-load displacement of 220 tons on a typical Lürssen non-magnetic hull that had a length of 139ft 9 in (42.6m) under an aluminium alloy superstructure. The hull was of wooden construction, and revealed its Schnellboote ancestry in the raised turtledeck fore castle with a semi-well for the forward gun. The propulsion arrangement was also typical of its time, with four MTU diesel engines delivering 11,990hp (8940kW) to four shafts for a speed of 35kt or more, and the armament was a mix of the standard and slightly unusual: the standard part was the gun armament of two 40-mm Bofors guns located forward and aft in open mountings, while the more unusual part was the torpedo armament of two aft-facing tubes for the launch of Seal wire-guided torpedoes over the stern.

The type has disappeared from German service, which finally designated the upgraded survivors as the Type 142 or Zobel class. The type's relegation from German

A TNC 45-class FAC(M) of the Bahraini navy.

service was made possible by the advent of more capable craft, but coincided the need of some of Germany's NATO allies for improved coastal forces. Thus Greece and Turkey each received seven operational craft as well as three craft to be cannibalized for spares, and another three craft were later transferred to Saudi Arabia. Additional construction resulted in eight craft for Indonesia and nine revised craft for Turkey. The Indonesian craft were completed as

FAC(T)s, four of them with steel hulls and the other four with wooden hulls. The wooden-hulled type proved to have the greater survivability in tropical waters, and the two surviving craft are of this type. The craft built for Turkey comprised the Kartal class of FAC(M/T)s, and these in fact preceded the transfer of ex-West German Jaguar-class FAC(T)s. The Turkish Kartal class is a distinct improvement over the Jaguar class, however, in its impressive

armament. This retains the two 40-mm Bofors guns and two 21-in (533-mm) tubes of the Jaguar class, and makes additional provision either for two more 21-in (533-mm) tubes for a total of four heavyweight torpedoes in the FAC(T) mode or for four launchers for Penguin Mk II anti-ship missiles in the FAC(M/T) mode.

The TNC-42 design marked the appearance of a family of Lürssen designs that have dominated the Western market for

The Achimota (P28) is one of two PB 57-class craft operated mainly in the patrol task by the Ghanaian navy.

fast combat craft since the mid-1960s. These craft have been produced with aluminium alloy superstructures on hulls of different construction (steel for the export market and wood over steel frames for the domestic market), and among their most characteristic features are a high length/beam ratio, a flush deck without the turtledeck fore castle of the TNC-42 design, and the bridge structure located just forward of the amidships position with a

deckhouse generally located farther aft on the units of the larger classes. This layout allows the installation of guns forward and aft, with the room for torpedo tubes on each side of the deck and/or missiles between the bridge and after deckhouse. The machinery space and after portion of the hull are arranged in such a fashion that different propulsion arrangements are possible, with different numbers of diesel engines powering two, three or four shafts

as demanded by the purchaser's operational needs and financial resources.

The smallest of Lürssen's FAC designs is the FPB-36 type dating from the early 1960s. Some 19 of the type have been delivered to five customers in various forms as comparatively simple FACs with two or three shafts and gun, torpedo and missile armaments. Typical of them is the Spanish Barcelo class, whose lead unit was built by Lürssen and the other four under licence in

Spain by Bazan. These five craft were delivered, and are currently used, as simple FAC(G)s with an armament of one 40-mm Bofors gun, two 20-mm Oerlikon cannon in single mountings and two 0.5-in (12.7-mm) machine-guns also in single mountings. The Spanish navy recognized, however, that the basic combination of hull and propulsion arrangement offered the possibility of greater combat capability, and therefore made provision for this in case it was

required at a later date. The craft are thus fitted for but not with two 21-in (533-mm) tubes for heavyweight torpedoes in the FAC(T) role, while the omission of tubes and the removal of the 20-mm cannon allow the installation of four launchers for anti-ship missiles in the FAC(M) role.

The FPB-38 class may be regarded as the larger half-brother of the FPB-36 class with slightly greater size and displacement allowing the installation of heavier

armament. Four such craft are in service as FAC(G)s with the navies of two Persian Gulf states, their most notable feature being a main armament of two 40-mm Bofors guns built under licence in Italy by Breda and installed in a Breda twin mounting. Malaysia requires 18 of the type, but these are to be used mainly in the high-speed patrol role with armament limited to two 20-mm Oerlikon cannon and two 0.3-in (7.62-mm) machine-guns.

LEFT
*The use of a planing hull
allows even small craft to
offer high performance, even
carrying substantial
armament such as the fit
seen here of one medium-
calibre gun and two anti-
ship missiles.*

OPPOSITE
*A broadside view of the
Ipoploiarhos Troupakis
(P 53), a La Combattante
III-class fast missile attack
craft of the Greek navy.*

Next up in size from the FPB-38 class is the TNC-42 design with which this important family of fast combat craft started. A general modernization and slight enlargement of the design, to a length of some 147ft 8in (45.0m) for a full-load displacement of about 260 tons, resulted in the remarkably successful FPB/TNC-45 type with provision for a two-, three- or four-shaft propulsion arrangement. The country responsible for the design was Israel, which had already turned to the

concept of large fast combat craft after a reappraisal of the balance of naval power in the eastern Mediterranean during the first half of the 1960s. The correctness of this change of emphasis from medium-sized surface warships, such as destroyers and frigates, to a mix of small submarines and smaller surface combatants, such as the larger types of FACs, was then confirmed during the 1967 Six-Day War by the shocking loss to anti-ship missiles of the Israeli navy's flagship, the elderly destroyer

Eilat, resulting in the deaths of 47 men and the wounding of another 99 out of a complement of 199. Israel now decided to press ahead with all speed toward the creation of a navy based primarily on FACs armed with guns and missiles for both offensive and defensive purposes.

In the late 1940s Israel had bought at least three and possibly as many as nine Vosper 70-ft (21.3-m) MTBs from the U.K., supplementing these between 1951 and 1952 with six French-built Ayah-class

MTBs. These latter were delivered with four 1,140-hp (850-kW) Arsenal-Marine Otto petrol engines powering two shafts for a speed of 42kt, and were armed with two 18-in (457-mm) tubes for medium-weight torpedoes as well as light gun armament. These 62-ton craft were generally operated as MGBs with the torpedo tubes removed, but in the early 1960s they were revised as MTBs with the two 18-in (457-mm) tubes and a new propulsion arrangement of two 2,500-hp (1865-kW) Napier Deltic lightweight diesel engines. In 1967 the

Vosper MTBs were reported to be unserviceable, but it is estimated that Israel could call on eight MTBs during the 1967 Six-Day War with its Arab neighbours. At the naval level, the war showed conclusively that such boats were too small to be effective, and that missile-armed fast combat craft offered considerable advantages over torpedo-armed boats.

The tactical importance of the anti-ship missile had been appreciated by Israel as early as the late 1950s, and the development of an all-Israeli missile of this type was put

in hand during the early 1960s by MBT, a subsidiary of Israel Aircraft Industries and later known as Israel Military Industries. The resulting weapon is the Gabriel, which proved itself temperamental during its development testing in the late 1960s but soon matured into a highly capable tactical missile by the early 1970s. The weapon has a 220-lb (100-kg) high explosive warhead and is carried on a launch rail inside a launcher that can be located on a turntable on the FAC's deck. This allows the missile to be fired on the target's bearing, launch

data being provided by the FAC's fire-control system using data provided by search radar. The Gabriel I missile had a range of only 13 miles (21km), but the Gabriel II introduced wider-span wings and a longer body for a larger sustainer rocket, and could reach a range of 22.5 miles (36km). Further development yielded the Gabriel III with a larger 331-lb (150-kg) warhead, a longer body for a larger motor producing a range of more than 37 miles (60km), and another seeker option in the form of active radar to supplement the standard semi-active radar.

This was still in the future as Israel launched a large-scale programme to develop its navy along new lines after the 1967 war. For technical and tactical reasons, it made sense for the Israelis to turn to the Western world's leading designer and producer of fast combat craft, namely Lürssen. For emotional and political reasons it was impossible for Israel to undertake the open procurement of weapons from Germany, however, so the order was handled through a French intermediary.

The resulting design was that now known as the FPB/TNC-45 type, and in 1965 and 1966 Israel ordered two batches of six such craft as the Saar class. The first six craft were completed in Israel with three 40-mm Bofors guns as FAC(G)s that also possessed a useful anti-submarine capability through the installation of four 12.75-in (324-mm) tubes for lightweight anti-submarine torpedoes. The second six craft were completed to a more powerful FAC(G) standard with a 3-in (76-mm) OTO Melara Compact gun mounting in place of the

The USS Taurus *(PHM3) was completed as the second of six Pegasus-class fast attack hydrofoils for the U.S. Navy.*

An essential feature of any fast attack craft or hydrofoil fitted with medium- or long-range anti-ship missiles is the ability to locate targets at beyond visual ranges. For this, the preferred option is radar with an antenna located as high as possible, as here, to provide the maximum possible horizon.

The USS Aquila *(PHM4) is
a member of the Pegasus class
of fast attack hydrofoils.*

The USS Aquila *(PHM4) is
a member of the Pegasus class
of fast attack hydrofoils.*

single 40-mm weapon located forward of the bridge; for reasons of weight, this installation meant that anti-submarine capability had to be omitted.

Useful though it was, this FAC(G) standard was only an interim step on the way to the creation of a FAC(M) using the Gabriel missile. The first and last six craft were thus developed respectively to Saar 2 and Saar 3 missile-armed standards. In the Saar 2 this involved the installation of two single launchers for Gabriel missiles toward the edges of the deck between the bridge and the fore castle-mounted 40-mm gun, and the replacement of the two after 40-mm guns with trainable triple launchers for

the same missile type. It was possible to omit the triple launchers and instead fit over the stern two twin 12.75-in (324-mm) tubes for lightweight anti-submarine torpedoes. The Saar 3 standard is comparable but limited to six rather than eight Gabriel missiles in two triple launchers replacing the two 40-mm guns.

The obvious capabilities of the Saar 2 and Saar 3 class FAC(M)s were confirmed in Israel's 1973 Yom Kippur War with Egypt and Syria, when 13 Israeli fast combat craft with 63 Gabriel missile launchers were pitted against 27 Arab Komar and Osa class fast combat craft with 84 launchers for the longer-ranged Styx. On

the first night of the war, five Israeli craft operating off the Syrian port of Latakia, some 200 miles (320km) from their home base, encountered three Syrian Osa-class craft in history's first missile-versus-missile surface action. The Israeli craft defeated 12 Styx missiles fired in two six-missile salvoes, shooting one of them down with 3-in (76-mm) gun fire and evading the rest with the use of electronic countermeasures, and then closed the range during the next 18 minutes to fire a salvo of Gabriel missiles that struck all three Syrian craft: two of these sank immediately, and the Israelis used 40-mm gun fire to finish off the crippled third unit. Two nights later, six Israeli craft were operating off the Egyptian port of Dumyat when they encountered a force of four Egyptian navy Osa-class craft. The Israeli craft evaded 12 Styx missiles fired in four salvoes, and then destroyed three of the Egyptian craft, two of them with Gabriel missiles and the third with gunfire. During actions later in this short war, Arab craft fired another 28 Styx missiles at Israeli vessels, again without scoring a single hit. The success rate of the Gabriel, on the other hand, was 85 per cent to the Arab forces, 0 per cent with the Styx.

Even before the Yom Kippur War proved the utility of the anti-ship missile, the obvious capability of the basic Saar-class craft had attracted an order for similar FPB/TNC-45-type craft from Argentina, which in 1970 ordered two West German-built FPB/TNC-45-class craft, and these were commissioned during 1974 in the FAC(G/T) role. Argentina's possession of these two craft gave it a decided superiority in the southern region of South America, but this superiority was overturned in 1988 when Chile bought two of its Saar 3-class FAC(M)s from Israel. The next order came from South-East Asia, where in 1970 Singapore ordered six FPB/TNC-45-class FAC(M/G)s as two from Lürssen and four locally constructed craft. The armament of these craft is a powerful and interesting combination of Swedish and Israeli weapons. The gun armament is Swedish, and comprises one 57-mm Bofors SAK 57 weapon on the fore castle and one Bofors 40-mm weapon aft. The missile armament initially comprised the first export installation of the Israeli Gabriel weapon, and consisted of five missiles in two fixed single launchers and one trainable triple launcher, though the latter can now be replaced by two twin launchers for an American weapon, the RGM-84 Harpoon.

The Royal Norwegian Navy Hauk-class Terne *firing a Penguin missile.*

The Singapore order was followed by two other contracts from the same region. The first was placed by Malaysia for six licence-constructed craft completed to a less formidable FAC(G) standard with the same gun armament as the Singapore craft but less capable electronics and reduced performance based on a three- rather than four-shaft propulsion arrangement, and the second came from Thailand in the form of a contract for three licence-constructed units essentially similar to the Singapore craft. Other orders were received from Ecuador for three FAC(M/G)s with a notably useful armament that includes the 3-in (76-mm) OTO Melara Compact gun

as well as the MM38 early version of the French Exocet anti-ship missile, from three Persian Gulf states for a total of 17 FAC(M/G)s all carrying the OTO Melara Compact gun and the later MM40 version of the Exocet missile, and from Ghana for two FAC(G)s with the OTO Melara Compact gun but only a modest two-shaft propulsion arrangement.

Despite the manifest seaworthiness and endurance of its original Saar-class craft, Israel decided in the late 1960s that a new type of FAC(M) was needed for longer-range operations in the Mediterranean and, to a lesser extent, the Red Sea. A major factor in this decision was the emergence as a potential

Gorz (P228), a Kaman-class missile fast attack craft of the Iranian navy.

major enemy of Libya, which was using a large proportion of its oil revenues to develop potent armed forces. These included a navy with a considerable missile capability in vessels up to the size of corvettes. The result of the Israeli concern about Libya was the Saar 4 class of FAC(M)s derived by the Israelis from 1968 on the basis of their experience with the earlier Saars. At a length of 190ft 3in (58.0m) and a full-load displacement of 450 tons, the type is somewhat larger than the Saar 2 and Saar 3-class craft, but as range rather than speed was the prime performance requisite, the four-shaft propulsion arrangement remained essentially unaltered for a speed of 32kt but a range of 4,600 miles (7400km) instead of a speed of 40kt or more and a range of 2,890 miles (4650km). The Saar 4 proved its exceptional seaworthiness and range when

four of the class made the passage from Israel's Mediterranean coast to the port of Eilat on Israel's Red Sea coast right round Africa via the Strait of Gibraltar and the Cape of Good Hope, relying exclusively on refuelling at sea. Apart from additional fuel bunkerage, the greater volume and deck area of the Saar 4-class units are used for greater habitability, improved electronics, a superior weapons layout, and significantly upgraded capabilities in terms of sensors and countermeasures. In their original form, the Saar 4-class craft each carried two 3-in (76-mm) OTO Melara Compact guns, two 20-mm Oerlikon cannon in single mountings and/or a maximum of six 0.5-in (12.7-mm) machine-guns in twin mountings, and six launchers for Gabriel missiles. The after gun mounting was later replaced by a 20-mm six-barrel cannon in an American-supplied

Phalanx close-in weapon system mounting for improved last-ditch defence against sea-skimming anti-ship missiles, and from 1978 the missile armament was revised after Israel began to receive the RGM-84 Harpoon anti-ship missile, which can be installed in one or two twin or quadruple launchers replacing a similar number of Gabriel launchers.

Israel constructed 10 Saar 4-class craft for its own use, but subsequently sold two of them to Chile. Another three units of the original configuration were built in the same Israeli yard for South Africa, where another nine were built under licence. The commissioning of Saar 4-class units gave the Israeli navy an impressive force of modern and sophisticated FACs. Early experience in the 1967 war, confirmed by operations in the 1973 war, indicated that these forces could be deployed more effectively in flotillas led by a still more sophisticated flotilla leader with specialized equipment and accommodation for the flotilla commander and his staff. This resulted in the Saar 4.5 class based on the hull, propulsion arrangement, armament (in upgraded form) and electronics of the Saar 4 class. The hull was lengthened to allow the incorporation in two units, at the expense of part of the missile armament, of a hangar and deck pad for a single light helicopter used in the surveillance and missile targeting-update roles. The Israeli's later decided that despite its longer hull, the Saar 4.5-class design was not ideally suited to helicopter operations, and this was one of the primary reasons for the design of the Saar 5-class guided-missile corvette.

Success for the Saar 2 and Saar 3 classes in Israeli service was an advertisement for the quality of Lürssen FAC designs, leading to a steady stream of orders for craft based on the FPB/TNC-45 design. Lürssen also took a further step up the size ladder, for

the company recognized that the type of weapon and electronic fit demanded by its customers was on the verge of overburdening the basic design of the FPB/TNC-45 class. Lürssen appreciated that greater size would simplify the problems of installing current weapons and sensors as well as a new generation of these items, and also accord with the procurement plans of many of the world's smaller navies. Having gained a measure of operational if not combat experience with FACs, these services were now beginning to feel themselves capable of expansion into a larger type of warship. Many of these navies belonged to third-world countries comparatively newly emerged from colonial rule into independence, and for cost as well as technical reasons opted for expansion

programmes not into major warships optimized for a single role but rather into a type one step up from the medium-sized FAC, namely the large FAC offering multi-role capability through a combination of hull and propulsion arrangements that would support later upgrading with more and/or better weapons and sensors.

The result was the versatile FPB/PB-57 design with a full-load displacement of some 400 tons on a hull 190ft 7in (58.1m) long and capable of accepting two-, three- and four-shaft propulsion arrangements. The lead customer was not a third-world country but Spain, whose navy was in the throes of a major modernization including the local construction of fast combat craft initially fitted with limited armament for the patrol role but capable of rapid

development into powerful FAC(M)s in times of crisis. The first of Spain's six Lazaga-class twin-shaft craft was commissioned from Lürssen, but the other five were produced under licence by Bazan. In their present form, the craft are simple FAC(G)s with capable electronics but useful mainly for patrol and training. However, provision was made in the design for the retrofit of potent anti-ship and anti-submarine armament so that the present 3-in (76-mm) OTO Melara Compact and 40-mm Bofors guns would be supplemented by two twin launchers for RGM-84 Harpoon anti-ship missiles and/or two 12.75-in (324-mm) triple tubes for lightweight anti-submarine torpedoes. Bazan also produced for Morocco four units of a FAC(M/G)

Barcelo (P-11), a Barcelo-class fast attack craft of the Spanish navy.

variant with the same comparatively low-powered propulsion arrangement, and developed its own Cormoran class as an export derivative that has been supplied to Morocco as a two-shaft FAC(G) of low performance and indifferent armament, and to Venezuela as a three-shaft FAC(M/G) with higher performance and a combined missile and gun armament.

Lürssen itself has constructed craft for Ghana, Indonesia and Kuwait, and also supplied the lead craft for the Dogan class for Turkey, where another seven of this very powerful FAC(M/G) class were built under licence. The largest operator of the type, however, is Germany with 20 craft in service. These last were ordered in two batches each of ten craft. The first batch was the Type 143 class with the type of composite hull construction favoured by the West German navy, and these highly impressive FAC(M/G/T)s were ordered in

1972 to replace the earliest of the Type 141 FAC(T)s. The new craft were commissioned in 1976 and 1977 with a four-shaft propulsion arrangement for a maximum speed of 40kt. As delivered, the craft each carried the balanced and highly effective armament of two 3-in (76-mm) OTO Melara Compact gun mountings located on the fore castle and over the stern, two twin launchers for the MM38 Exocet, and two 21-in (533-mm) tubes for Seal wire-guided torpedoes. The increasing threat of Soviet tactical air power demanded that steps be taken for improved air-defence capability, however, and this resulted in the modification of the Type 143-class craft to the Type 143B standard by the replacement of the after 3-in (76-mm) gun by the RAM (Rolling Airframe Missile) surface-to-air-missile system using the EX-31 launcher for 24 RIM-116 missiles.

The intermediate Type 143A-class

designation applies to 10 craft that were ordered in 1978 as replacements for the Type 142 FAC(T)s, upgraded Zobel-class survivors of the obsolete Type 141 or Jaguar class. These craft were commissioned between 1982 and 1984, and each carried a single 3-in (76-mm) gun mounting removed from the Type 143-class craft as they were prepared for improvement to Type 143B standard. In other respects the craft are similar to the Type 143B-class units, and like them were only later retrofitted with the RAM surface-to-air missile system. The major differences between the two current Type 143-class standards is the propulsion arrangement, for the Type 143A-class units have less power than their Type 143B-class near-sisters. This does not reduce the maximum speed, but helps to increase the cruising range.

The rationale for producing the larger and heavier FPB/PB-57 design as successor to the FPB/TNC-45 design continued into the 1980s, and the result was Lürssen's largest type to date, namely the FPB/MGB-62 design that verges on corvette size as it has a full-load displacement of over 600 tons and a length of 206ft 6in (62.95m). The first customer for the type was Bahrain, which ordered two craft to an impressive FAC(M/G) standard with powerful armament and comprehensive electronics, the latter including full electronic support measures and countermeasures capabilities. Particularly notable in this variant is the provision for an embarked helicopter carrying anti-ship missiles, for this considerably enhances the vessel's ability to strike at remoter targets. The variants for the other two current operators lack the helicopter of the Bahraini model, but possess exceptional armament. That of the Singapore vessels includes powerful guns and missiles as well as an advanced anti-

RIGHT
The Justice *(P72) is one of the Singapore navy's three Vosper Thornycroft Type A-class FAC(G)s.*

OPPOSITE
Using the same hull design as the Storm-class craft, the Snogg *(P980) was built as the name vessel of a Norwegian navy FAC(M/T) class with one 40-mm Bofors gun, four launchers for Penguin anti-ship missiles and four tubes for 21-in (533-mm) wire-guided torpedoes.*

submarine capability, while that of the Abu Dhabi vessels is notable for the two-layer air defence capability provided by different surface-to-air missile systems backed by a potent dual-purpose gun.

Both FPB/MGB-62 variants for Arab countries carry the MM40 Exocet anti-ship missile. This is the later version of a missile that has been one of the most important Western naval weapons since its service debut in 1974. The missile was developed by Aérospatiale to meet a French navy requirement for a fire-and-forget weapon capable of defeating targets such as major warships. The initial missiles were used for manufacturers' trials in mid-1972, and an important improvement programme was undertaken in 1973 with the first production rounds fired in the following

year. The missile is based on a cylindrical body containing the 364-lb (165-kg) high explosive warhead, the electronics and the solid-propellant booster and sustainer rockets. The missile is accommodated in a boxlike launcher, and before launch its onboard guidance package is primed with data about the target's bearing and range from the launch vessel's fire-control system. The missile is then launched with the aid of its booster rocket before flying on the power of its long-burning sustainer rocket under control of its inertial navigation system. The cruise phase of the flight is undertaken at low level, and at a point some 6.2 miles (10km) from the target's anticipated position the missile's active radar seeker is switched on. Once the seeker had locked onto the target, the missile descends

to sea-skimming height and impacts with the target. The two main versions of the Exocet in its ship-launched form are the MM38 with a range of 28 miles (45km), and the longer and heavier MM40 with a range of 43.5 miles (70km) and the improved seeker introduced on late-production MM38 missiles.

The only Western missile to rival the Exocet in terms of numbers produced and operational flexibility has been an American weapon, the McDonnell Douglas (now Boeing) Harpoon resulting from a U.S. Navy interest in such weapons after the 1967 sinking of the *Eilat*. The programme began in 1968 with the intention of producing an AGM-84 air-launched weapon with a range of 57.5 miles (92.5km), but a ship-launched RGM-84 version was added

The Canadian Bras d'Or
*anti-submarine patrol
hydrofoil vessel was used only
for experimental purposes.*

from 1970, and an encapsulated UGM-84 version for submarine launch was incorporated in the programme from 1972. The Harpoon was planned as a low-risk development, so no completely novel technology was incorporated in a type intended as a capable yet affordable weapon that emphasized reliability rather than outright performance in everything except electronic performance and range. The last was provided by the propulsion arrangement of one solid-propellant booster rocket and one liquid-propellant sustainer turbojet. In layout the Harpoon is similar to the Exocet, and the body of the Harpoon is also used in much the same way as that of the Exocet, with the active radar seeker in the nose with the guidance electronics behind it, the 500-lb (227-kg) warhead between the electronics and the wings, and the rest of the body occupied by the

sustainer engine, which in the case of the Harpoon is a 680-lb st (3.02-kN) turbojet aspirated via a flush inlet between the two lower wings. Production started in 1976, and since that time the Harpoon has been a great technical and commercial success in the American and export markets.

France has developed two important types of fast combat craft as the La Combattante and PR 72 classes. The more important of these types in commercial as well as operational terms is the La Combattante class, itself derived from a West German design by Lürssen. As it was producing the Type 141 FAC(T)s for the West German navy on the basis of its TNC-42 design, Lürssen was also developing a general-purpose hull that could be fitted with different numbers and types of engines and weapons according to the requirements and purse of the purchaser. For a variety of

political reasons this design was transferred to France, where Constructions Mécaniques de Normandie lengthened and modified it for construction as La Combattante, the sole unit of the La Combattante I class, a twin-shaft type that was used mainly as a trials vessel, though provision was made for the type to carry up to 80 commandos for a short passage. The hull was of the composite type favoured by the Germans for its anti-magnetic properties, and the armament comprised two 40-mm Bofors guns located forward and aft as well as a quadruple launcher for the SS.12 missile, a wire-guided type of too little range and striking power for worthwhile use by a FAC.

It soon became clear that the hull lines were excellent, an important factor in the unit's good seakeeping qualities, but also that overall performance capability was limited by the two-shaft propulsion arrangement. With the support of Lürssen, therefore, CMN refined the hull in a steel-built form and lengthened it slightly to produce the multi-role La Combattante II design with considerably higher performance provided by a four-shaft propulsion arrangement using diesel engines of West German rather than French manufacture. The type was offered with a host of electronic and weapon options, though the French exercised considerable pressure on potential customers to adopt French electronics and the Exocet missile. The largest single order was placed by the West German navy, which contracted for 20 Type 148-class craft. CMN and Lürssen built 12 and eight hulls respectively, and these were then delivered to the Lorient Naval Dockyard for completion with a basically French electronic suite, French missiles, and Italian and Swedish guns. Other customers for the La Combattante II class have been Greece, Iran, Libya and Malaysia.

The La Combattante II class proved most successful in service, but several potential customers expressed the desire for a slightly larger derivative providing better seakeeping qualities and the ability to support heavier armament, as well as offering greater endurance through increased fuel bunkerage and improved habitability, and also a much enhanced command facility through the additional volume that allowed a flotilla commander and his small staff to be embarked. The resulting La Combattante III class is 30ft 2in (9.2m) longer than the La Combattante II design, which results in a full-load displacement of some 430 tons by comparison with the earlier design's 275 tons. Much the same absolute performance can be provided by a more powerful four-shaft propulsion arrangement, and range is

either maintained or improved by the provision of additional fuel bunkerage. The major operator of the type is the Greek navy, which ordered four craft from CMN and then built another six craft under licence. The main difference between the French- and Greek-built craft is the latter's less powerful propulsion arrangement, a sacrifice that the Greeks had to make for economic reasons. As in the earlier class, the electronic suite is largely of French origin, but the armament combines French missiles with Italian and Swiss guns, and in some craft German torpedoes. All the craft have two 3-in (76-mm) OTO Melara Compact guns located forward and aft, and four 30-mm Oerlikon cannon in two twin anti-aircraft mountings located on each side of the superstructure's rear portion. The French-built craft have Exocet missiles in two twin launchers, but the Greek-built craft have Penguin Mk II missiles in six single launchers. The French-built craft also possess two 21-in (533-mm) aft-firing tubes for SST-4 wire-guided torpedoes. Smaller numbers of La Combattante III-class craft have been procured by the Nigerian, Qatari and Tunisian navies.

In purely commercial terms, the PR 72 class has not proved as successful as the two La Combattante classes, but is large enough to serve as a flotilla leader. The lead customer was Morocco, which took two units in a FAC(G) configuration that has provision for upgrading to FAC(M/G) standard. Thus the Moroccan craft are each armed with the fairly standard large fast combat craft combination of one 3-in (76-mm) OTO Melara Compact gun on the fore castle and one 40-mm Bofors gun at the stern, but have provision for the retrofit of two twin launchers for MM38 Exocet missiles. Peru placed a more significant order for six more potent FAC(M/G)s with

a more powerful propulsion arrangement of the same four-shaft type for higher performance with an armament that includes two twin launchers for MM38 Exocet missiles, one 3-in (76-mm) OTO Melara Compact gun on the fore castle, two 40-mm Bofors guns in a twin mounting over the stern, and two 20-mm cannon in single mountings.

The two main British designers of fast combat craft are Brooke Marine and Vosper Thornycroft. In general terms, Brooke Marine specializes in robust craft well suited to the demands of third-world navies with difficulties in finding adequate numbers of trained personnel, while Vosper Thornycroft specializes in the more sophisticated end of the market where an advanced hull and propulsion arrangement are combined with an integrated suite of modern weapons and capable electronics.

Within the spectrum of fast craft, the smallest of Brooke Marine's standard hull types are the 80- and 95-ft (24.5- and 29-m) designs, and these have proved successful in securing considerable export orders. These are mostly patrol craft of limited performance and light armament, however, and thus fall outside the fast combat craft category. Next up in size, however, is the 107-ft (32.6-m) design that has formed the basis for two types of fast combat craft, both delivered to African nations and featuring a two-shaft propulsion arrangement for low purchase cost but also low performance. For example, the three units for Kenya were delivered as patrol craft, but as the Kenyan navy became better trained and more experienced it recognized the latent capabilities of the design, and contracted for the craft to be upgraded to limited FAC(M) standard. The original gun armament of two 40-mm Bofors guns in single mountings was replaced by the

HMS Peacock *was built as one of a class of offshore patrol vessels for tasks such as fishery protection, and as such fell into the upper end of the size and performance bracket for large FACs, although without the weight of armament.*

The Hammer (P542) was completed as the fourth unit of the Danish navy's 10-strong Willemoes class of FAC(G/M/T)s to a design very similar to that of the Swedish navy's Spica II class. The vessel has one 3-in (76-mm) OTO Melara Compact automatic gun, two single or twin launchers for Harpoon anti-ship missiles, and two or four tubes for 21-in (533-mm) wire-guided torpedoes.

*Willemoes (P549), a
Willemoes-class FAC of the
Royal Danish Navy firing a
Harpoon missile.*

considerably more modern fit of two 30-
mm Oerlikon cannon in a twin mounting
under control of an optronic director, and
this core armament was supplemented by
four launchers for Gabriel II anti-ship
missiles. Next up in size among Brooke
Marine's core designs is the 123-ft (37.5-m)
type. This retains a low-powered two-shaft
propulsion arrangement similar in concept
to that of the Brooke Marine 32.6-m
design, although with engines that are
higher powered in comparative terms for
better performance. The greater size of the

hull provides better sea-keeping qualities,
and also offers the right combination of
larger area and great volume needed for a
more effective armament layout. Placed by
Oman, the first order covered three
examples of the Al Bushra class of FAC(G)s
armed with two 40-mm Bofors guns in
single mountings forward and aft. These
were commissioned in 1973, and were
revised between 1977 and 1978 as
FAC(M/G)s with two launchers for MM38
Exocet missiles. Another four units were
delivered in 1977 as FAC(G)s with a 3-in

(76-mm) OTO Melara Compact gun on the
fore castle under control of an optical
director, this useful main gun being
supplemented by one 20-mm cannon and
two medium machine-guns. The other main
operator of the Brooke Marine 37.5-m
design is Algeria, which has two British- and
seven Algerian-built craft of the Kebir class.
This is a FAC(G) type of modest
performance, and the armament comprises
one 3-in (76-mm) OTO Melara Compact
on the fore castle as well as two 23-mm
Soviet cannon in a twin mounting aft,

where they replace a single 20-mm Oerlikon cannon. The largest of Brooke Marine's designs currently in service is the 137-ft (41.8-m) type, which is used by Australia in the form of the Fremantle class. This comprises 15 simple FAC(G)s with limited armament, and the craft are used mainly for patrol.

The U.K. has only toyed with the FAC concept since the end of World War II. In the second half of the 1960s, however, the Royal Navy became sufficiently concerned with the threat posed by fast combat craft to order a class of three FACs to train the crews of its major warships in the tactics to counter their attacks. The Scimitar class was designed and built by Vosper Thornycroft, and the three craft were delivered in 1969 and 1970. With a full-load displacement of 102 tons on a laminated wooden hull measuring 100ft 0in (30.5m), the Scimitar- class craft were each fitted with a CODOG propulsion arrangement whose two shafts were powered by two 90-hp (67-kW) Foden diesel engines for cruising or two 4,500-hp (3355-kW) Rolls-Royce Proteus gas turbines for a maximum speed of 40kt. At much the same time, Vosper Thornycroft evolved its Tenacity-class design and built a single craft as a private venture. This had a full-load displacement of 220 tons on a hull that measured 144ft 8 in (44.1m) in length. The propulsion arrangement was of the CODOG type with the three shafts powered by two 600-hp (445-kW) Paxman diesel engines for cruising or three 4,250-hp (3170-kW) Rolls-Royce Proteus gas turbines for a maximum speed of 39kt. This design experience is reflected in a number of types which Vosper Thornycroft evolved for the export market during the 1960s and early 1970s. Typical of these are the Vosper Thornycroft 103-ft, Vosper

Thornycroft 110-ft and Vosper Thornycroft 121-ft classes. The first was built as the 24-strong Kris FAC(G) class for Malaysia, the second was produced in three related FAC(G) forms for Abu Dhabi and Singapore, and the third appeared in three forms including a dedicated FAC(M) type for Brunei and related FAC(G) and FAC(M) variants for Venezuela.

Brooke Marine's and Vosper Thornycroft's different approaches to the FAC concept is highlighted by the altogether superior combat potential of Vosper Thornycroft's Tenacity design to Brooke Marine's less powerful types. This superiority received concrete expression in 1977, when Egypt ordered six FAC(M)s to a design which Vosper Thornycroft extrapolated from that of the Tenacity type. The design of the Ramadan class is a good example of the way in which careful design thinking can pack maximum offensive capability into a comparatively small hull, in this instance possessing a full-load displacement of 310 tons on a length of 170ft 7in (52.0m). The armament is impressive and of Italian origins, and comprises two twin launchers for Otomat Mk 1 missiles between the superstructure and the deck house, one 3-in (76-mm) OTO Melara Compact gun on the fore castle, and two 40-mm Bofors guns in a Breda Compact twin mounting over the stern. The propulsion arrangement is based on West German diesel engines powering four shafts for a maximum speed of 40kt. From the design of the Ramadan class, Vosper Thornycroft developed the Province FAC(M/G) design for Oman, which ordered three craft in the early 1980s and followed with a contract for the fourth in 1986. The design of the Province class provides slightly greater dimensions for a hull of proportionately finer line and,

despite the greater displacement, this ensures high performance with a four-shaft propulsion arrangement with basically the same power as that in the Ramadan class. The craft were delivered in two slightly differing standards, for while all have the same barrelled armament of one 3-in (76-mm) OTO Melara Compact gun and two 40-mm Bofors guns in a Breda Compact twin mounting, the first and last three units have respectively two triple and quadruple launchers for the MM40 variant of the Exocet. The same basic type was ordered by Kenya, which thus received two craft with a nicely balanced weapon fit with lighter missile armament than the Omani units.

Italy is the only other European country that operates a significant force of FACs and also builds such craft. In the period following World War II, the Italian navy made do with a small number of ex-wartime craft, but in 1951 received ex-American PT boats in the form of 11 Higgins 78-ft (23.8-m) craft, and these bridged the operational gap until the advent of Italy's first modern fast combat craft starting with the single Folgore-class prototype that paved the way for the two Lampo-class craft that entered service in the first half of the 1960s. These each had a full-load displacement of 210 tons, a length of 141ft 1in (43.0m), and a speed of 39kt on the CODOG propulsion arrangement of two 3,620-hp (2700-kW) Fiat diesel engines and one 11,700-hp (8725-kW) Nuove Reggiane-built Metrovick gas turbine. The craft could be configured to FAC(T) or FAC(M) standard, each carrying one 40-mm Bofors gun and two 21-in (533-mm) tubes in the former role, and two or three 40-mm Bofors guns plus one missile launcher in the latter role. Further evolution produced the two units of the Freccia class that entered service in 1965 with an upgraded version of the same

These fast attack hydrofoils are the Nibbio *(P421) and* Falcone *(P422) of the Italian navy's Sparviero class.*

propulsion arrangement. This comprised two 4,260-hp (3175-kW) Fiat diesel engines and one 11,870-hp (8850-kW) Nuove Reggiane-built Metrovick gas turbine for a speed of 40kt on a hull 151ft 3in (46.1m) long and having a full-load displacement of 205 tons. The armament was basically similar to that of the Lampo class in FAC(T) and FAC(M) options, although the torpedo fit was

strengthened to four 21-in (533-mm) tubes.

Further Italian interest in the FAC was based on the hydrofoil concept for high speeds, and in 1964 the Italian government joined an Italian builder of commercial hydrofoils (Carlo Rodriguez of Messina in Sicily) and the American company Boeing to establish Alinavi. Through the rest of the 1960s, this organization examined the

potential of the Boeing-designed Tucumcari design and finalized details of the all-aluminium Sparviero that was built between 1971 and 1974. This prototype was based on the Boeing jetfoil system with three retractable foils (one unit forward and two aft). The CODOG propulsion arrangement comprised one diesel delivering 180hp (134kW) to one propeller for hullborne operation and one Rolls-Royce Proteus gas turbine delivering 4,500hp (3360kW) to a waterjet system for foilborne operation up to a maximum speed of 42kt in heavy seas or 50kt in calm water. The Sparviero was commissioned in 1974, proved to have good overall performance, and was evaluated exhaustively before the Italian navy ordered six examples of the Sparviero-class production model with superior radar and the longer-range Otomat Mk 2 missiles.

This is the current limit of the Italian navy's interest in fast combat craft, but Italian industry has been a successful exporter of such craft in the form of medium-sized craft to the Thai navy and larger craft to the navies of Ecuador, Iraq and Libya. The smaller and earlier of the two types for Thailand is the Ratcharit FAC(M/G) class, whose three units offer a modest but locally useful combination of typical armament, with four MM38 Exocet missiles backed by a 3-in (76-mm) OTO Melara Compact gun and a 40-mm Bofors gun. The same yard was responsible for the larger MV 400 class, again of three units. This is a FAC(G) type with two 3-in (76-mm) OTO Melara Compact guns and two 40-mm Bofors guns in a Breda Compact twin mounting, but has the deck area and electronic sophistication for comparatively straightforward retrofit to FAC(M/G) standard should the Thai navy decide that this would provide additional capability in time of crisis.

The country that paved the way for Fincantieri's type of large fast combat craft was Libya, which made strenuous efforts from the early 1970s to create more substantial armed forces including not just greater numbers of men but also more advanced weapons with a capability that included offensive operations. So far as the Libyan navy was concerned, this effort meant a considerable development programme that

centred largely on fast combat craft, and in 1974 the Libyan navy ordered four fast combat craft of the Wadi class, renamed the Assad class in 1981. In this type, the Italian design team produced a multi-capable type that was in effect a light corvette capable of accepting a number of weapon and sensor options. The variant ordered by the Libyans has little more than FAC(M/G) armament, but the larger hull offers better habitability plus an attractive combination of greater range and improved sea-keeping even though speed is reduced by comparison with FACs using a comparable four-shaft propulsion arrangement. Notable features of the basic design are thus a 15-day endurance, full NBC protection, and a multi-role armament that includes four single launchers for Otomat Mk 1 missiles, one 3-in (76-mm) OTO Melara Compact gun, two 35-mm Oerlikon cannon in a twin mounting, two triple 12.75-in (324-mm) tubes for lightweight anti-submarine torpedoes, and provision for 16 mines. Libya was well pleased with the type, which could double as a multi-role combat type in its own right or serve as a fast combat craft flotilla leader, and in May 1980 ordered four more of the class. Before work could begin, however, Libya had fallen under an international cloud for its sponsorship of international terrorism and the order was embargoed.

In the early 1980s, the Iraqi navy ordered six of a similar type in two subvariants. The first two units to be delivered comprise one of these distinct subvariants, and have an armament comparable with that of the Libyan units, though the secondary gun armament is two 40-mm Bofors guns in a Breda Compact twin mounting. The main difference between the Libyan craft and these two Iraqi units, however, is the helicopter capability of the latter, in the form of a telescopic hangar

accommodating an Agusta (Bell) AB.212ASV/ASW helicopter. This is a sophisticated type that can be used in the anti-ship and anti-submarine roles, and its operating platform is revealed by the forward retraction of the hangar. The four other units lack the helicopter capability, and were thus completed with heavier armament in the form of two additional launchers for Otomat anti-ship missiles (giving a total of six) and an Albatros quadruple launcher for Aspide surface-to-air missiles.

Between these two types for Arab customers, the Italian team had produced an upgraded version for Ecuador, which needed a small but powerful fast combat craft type as the spearhead of its surface warfare capability. The resulting Esmeraldas class, of which six were delivered, can be regarded as a derivative of the Libyan design with features of the Iraqi class and a more powerful version of the same four-shaft propulsion arrangement. Each of the Ecuadorian craft therefore has one 3-in (76-mm) OTO Melara Compact gun and two 40-mm Bofors guns in a Breda Compact twin mounting, the latter controlled by the radar-directed Dardo system, two triple launchers for six MM40 Exocet missiles, one Albatros launcher for Aspide surface-to-air missiles, two triple 12.75-in (324-mm) tubes for lightweight anti-submarine torpedoes, and a platform allowing a Bell Model 206B helicopter to be embarked. These weapons are used with an advanced electronic system to turn each member of the class into what is in effect a multi-role corvette or perhaps even a light frigate.

In the 15 years after World War II, the U.S.A. had produced or funded for overseas construction a considerable number of motor gun boats (PGM 33–83, PGM 91 and PGM 102–124), but these were for allied rather than American use. In the

*The nine Al Siddiq-class
FAC(G/M)s of the Saudi
Arabian navy were built to
an American design
offering little short of
corvette-type capabilities.*

early 1960s, however, the Cuban missile
crisis highlighted the U.S. Navy's lack of
fast combat craft for use in confined
waters such as the Gulf of Mexico. It was
therefore decided to built a 22-strong
class of motor gun boats, though the
classification was altered to patrol
combatant during 1967. The resulting
Asheville class was developed for coastal
patrol and blockade, but in the event only

17 of the class were completed between
1966 and 1971 by Tacoma Boatbuilding
and Peterson Builders. The type has a
CODOG propulsion arrangement for long
range at a modest cruising speed and high
speed for combat, and the armament is
based on a 3-in (76-mm) gun in an
enclosed mounting forward of the bridge
and a 40-mm Bofors gun in an open
mounting over the stern. Most of these

craft saw extensive patrol service in the
Vietnam War, and in the mid-1970s four
of them were adapted as FAC(M)s with an
armament of four Standard Missiles (in its
anti-radar form) for service in the
Mediterranean as counters to Soviet spy
vessels. The craft had a very good
reputation for seaworthiness, but were
decidedly uncomfortable in any sort of sea
and suffered propeller cavitation problems

that prevented them from attaining their theoretical maximum speed of 40kt or more.

In the late 1950s, the U.S. Navy also began to acquire an interest in hydrofoil craft for very high speeds, but the sole class to emerge from this interest has been the Pegasus class of six high-speed hydrofoils each armed with a single 3-in (76-mm) Mk 75 gun forward of the bridge structure and two quadruple launchers for eight RGM-84 Harpoon missiles above the stern. As such, the craft are the U.S. Navy's most potent combatants on the basis of firepower per displacement ton. The craft can be highly effective in the right conditions, but they lack the range, endurance and versatility of larger warships. The Pegasus class FAH(M/G)s thus fall outside the main tactical organization of their operating service, which is concerned primarily with deep-water operations.

Even though the Asheville class failed to find any real favour with the U.S. Navy, Tacoma Boatbuilding was confident that the basic type had an export potential, especially among East and South-East Asian nations. The company therefore used the Asheville design as the basis of its Patrol Ship Multi-Mission Mk 5 (PSMM Mk 5) type with a two-shaft COGOG propulsion arrangement using no fewer than six gas turbines. The first customer for the type was South Korea, which operates a large force of fast combat craft against the constant threat of North Korean aggression. The parent company built the first four of the eight craft, the initial three of them reflecting the type's ancestry in a missile armament of four Standard Missiles (each carrying a seeker designed to home on the target vessel's radar emissions) and an American 3-in (76-mm) gun. The last American-built unit switched to the definitive armament of two

twin launchers for the RGM-84 Harpoon missile and the 3-in (76-mm) OTO Melara Compact gun. Construction of the last four units was undertaken by a South Korean subsidiary, and this has also built four somewhat different Dagger class FAC(M)s for Indonesia with a CODOG propulsion arrangement and the revised armament of two twin launchers for four MM38 Exocet missiles, one 57-mm Bofors SAK 57 Mk 1 gun, one 40-mm Bofors gun and two 20-mm cannon. Another customer for the PSMM Mk 5 class was Taiwan, the island nation that until very recently regarded itself as being at war with the communist regime on the Chinese mainland. Clearly the main Chinese threat to Taiwan's continued independence was a seaborne invasion, and against this threat Taiwan maintains powerful naval defences including a powerful force of fast attack craft for the destruction of any elements of the invading force that break though the main offshore defences. Tacoma Boatbuilding thus produced the first unit of the Taiwanese Lung Chiang class, a type similar to the South Korean class with a two-shaft CODOG propulsion arrangement and a barrelled armament of one 3-in (76-mm) OTO Melara Compact gun backed by two 30-mm Oerlikon cannon in an Emerson Electric twin mounting. The missile armament comprises four launchers for the Hsiung Feng I (licence-built version of the Israeli Gabriel) missile. The second unit was licence-built in Taiwan, which planned a large class with the RGM-84 Harpoon missile and an American fire-control system. Under Chinese pressure, the Americans refused to export the Harpoon to Taiwan, which then dropped its plan for a major Lung Chiang class. The only other operator of the PSMM Mk 5 type is Thailand, which has six Sattahip-class craft that are FAC(G)s

useful mainly for patrol and training with their low-powered propulsion arrangement and comparatively light gun armament.

Peterson Builders also have construction capability for a range of ship types and sizes, and this is reflected in the company's main export success in the field of fast combat craft, the nine units of the Al Siddiq class of FAC(M/G)s for Saudi Arabia. These feature toward the upper end of the fast combat craft size scale, but have a two-shaft CODOG propulsion arrangement for high gas turbine-engined speed and good diesel-engined range. The craft were designed specifically for the anti-ship role, and the armament of each unit is thus centred on one 3-in (76-mm) OTO Melara Compact gun, located on the fore castle forward of the superstructure, and the modest anti-ship missile fit of two twin launchers for the RGM-84 Harpoon weapon, located near the stern. Aft of the missile installation is the Phalanx close-in weapon system mounting, whose 20-mm six-barrel rotary cannon has excellent fields of fire for its primary task of destroying incoming anti-ship missiles.

China is, by a very considerable margin, the world's largest operator of FACs. The Chinese navy has been confined almost exclusively to the coast defence role until very recent times, when deeper strategic thinking combined with the possibility of natural resources in the South China Sea to persuade the Chinese to begin development of a technologically more advanced navy possessing offshore capability. China has a long coast whose many good harbours are supplemented by even larger numbers of well positioned smaller harbours. With no real naval threat but the posturing and nuisance raids of Taiwan to fear, China rightly decided that the best way to ensure coastal security and at the same time build the nucleus of a strong navy lay with the creation of a large force of fast combat craft that could become technologically more sophisticated as Chinese industry and service personnel evolved the necessary skills. The core of this operational philosophy evolved in the very early 1950s, when the Chinese navy used armed examples of local craft. On this basis, and with considerable technical and material assistance from the Soviets, the Chinese began to develop a more advanced fast combat craft capability toward the middle of the 1950s. Precise details are still lacking, but it seems that from 1952, more than 70 P4 class MTBs were transferred from the U.S.S.R. to China. It is probable that a comparatively small number of improved P6-class MTBs were transferred at a slightly later date, and that these were used as pattern craft for Chinese construction of about 80 boats. This experience allowed the Chinese to begin development of their own types, starting with the Huchuan class FAH(T) that entered production in 1966 as the world's first foil-equipped naval vessel. Despite the fact that the type was only of the semi-foil variety, with the forward part of the hull lifted by the foil and the rear part planing, the design was clearly successful in meeting Chinese expectations, and production totalled just under 200 units.

Like the Soviets, however, the Chinese had by now seen the virtue of combining torpedo- and missile-armed FACs for the type of two-handed punch that could take an enemy force off balance and inflict severe losses. In the early 1960s, the Chinese navy had received from the U.S.S.R. some seven or eight Komar-class FAC(M)s, and from this simple type the Chinese evolved the Hegu design with a steel rather than wooden hull of slightly modified form and the position of the missile launchers moved slightly inboard by comparison with the

Soviet original. In their time these were limited but effective FAC(M)s, but the Chinese have maintained the type in service long past the time when simple electronic countermeasures have made it easy for any modestly sophisticated navy to defeat the missile carried by the Hegu-class craft.

As in the pattern established earlier with the MTBs, the Soviets followed deliveries of the Komar-class craft with some four examples of the two improved Osa I class (in this instance with four 30-mm rather than 25-mm cannon in two twin mountings) as well as the technical information that allowed the Chinese to build this type as the Huangfen class. The Chinese-built craft differ in detail from the Soviet original, and for an unexplained reason the class is credited with a maximum speed of 41kt to the Soviet type's 35kt. The Huangfen class is still the backbone of the Chinese fast combat craft force but, as with the Hegu class operating the same missile, its combat capability has been virtually removed in recent years by the widespread adoption of electronic countermeasures in potentially hostile navies. This fact has been recognized by China, which is now retrofitting a more modern type of anti-ship missile, which had the additional advantages of smaller size and reduced weight so that a greater number of missiles can be installed. In recent years, the Chinese have made considerable but largely unsuccessful attempts to upgrade their fast combat craft capability, often with the aid of Western companies. Older missiles have been supplemented and largely replaced by more modern weapons, but the Chinese government's suppression of the emergent democracy movement led to the effective halt on all programmes of Western technical support for types such as the H3 class.

So the FAC concept is important in

many parts of the world. Many emerging countries find such craft an ideal way to begin development of their navies, with larger and more sophisticated craft bought to match their developing skills and increased operational ambitions. Many less affluent countries have discovered that such craft are a cost-effective method of maintaining a national presence in territorial waters and offshore zones of possible great commercial importance. But in general the countries that make the greatest and potentially most effective use of fast combat craft are those with confined coastal waters or chokepoints where major maritime routes are constricted by geographical factors. It is therefore no accident that areas where concentrations of fast combat craft are to be found include the Baltic Sea and its exit into the North Sea; the Mediterranean (especially at its western end near the Strait of Gibraltar, its centre near the Sicilian Narrows, its north offshoot in the Adriatic Sea, its north-eastern corner in the Aegean Sea, and its eastern end where Israel and several Arab nations vie with each other); the Persian Gulf; South-East Asia where there are several chokepoints such as the Malacca Strait; the eastern coast of Asia; and various parts of South America where limited finance and confined waters combine with nationalistic and economic rivalries.

LEFT
With its three-point hydrofoil system, the craft of the Italian navy's Sparviero class offer very high performance in terms of speed, but only in calm conditions.

OPPOSITE
The Bille *was the second Willemoes-class FAC completed for the Danish navy.*

Chapter Seven
The Submarine

A Confederate Navy David aground in Charleston harbour, South Carolina at the end of the American Civil War. Though virtually suicidal, a number of these craft were used to attack blockading ships of the Union Navy. Circa 1865.

The submarine is a vessel designed to operate below the surface of the sea so that it can avoid the comparatively easy detection that is the fate of surface vessels. This offers the advantages of allowing the undetected submarine to avoid the interception that can swiftly lead to destruction, and to approach the enemy ship without warning and thus attack before the enemy can start evasive manoeuvres. Concealed attack has long been an object of armed forces, and the concept of a submarine vessel was therefore attractive from early times. There were almost certainly designs (if not prototypes) in the period up to the end of the 16th century, but no known records of these efforts survive.

In the years between 1575 and 1765 many submarines were designed, and the designs of at least 17 survive today. The four men who made the greatest strides in this difficult field were the Englishman William Bourne, the Dutchman Cornelius van Drebbel, and the Americans David Bushnell and Robert Fulton. Of these, it was the two Americans who made the most far-sighted contributions.

Bushnell was born in 1742 and graduated from Yale in 1775, just before the beginning of the American War of Independence (1776–83). Bushnell was bitter in his opposition to the British, and

designed a small submarine as the means for the Americans, lacking a navy, to attack the fleet on which the British relied for the shipment of men, equipment and supplies from England, and also for transport along the coast of the original 13 colonies. Bushnell's Turtle was shaped like an egg, and the flooding of two small internal tanks allowed it to be trimmed right down in the water so that its conning tower was awash. The boat was propelled by a propeller turned by hand, and offensive capability rested with a 150-lb (68-kg) gunpowder charge that was designed for attachment to the underside of the target ship by a screw. In 1776, the Bushnell submarine was launched against the British fleet off New York. Manned by Sergeant Ezra Lee, the submarine reached the *Eagle*, flagship of Admiral Lord Howe, but could not deposit its charge as Bushnell had forgotten that British warships were plated with copper that resisted the penetration of the screw. Two other unsuccessful efforts were made later in the war.

Fulton was born in 1765 and, after an

prototype, the Nautilus. The submarine was of ellipsoid shape, 21ft (6.40m) in length and 7ft (2.13m) in maximum diameter, and could be submerged by opening cocks to flood internal tanks. Surface propulsion was provided by a collapsible mast and sail, and underwater propulsion by hand-cranked propeller. A first test in Brest was successful when the Nautilus placed an external charge under a schooner anchored in the harbour, but the French navy did not pursue the concept and Fulton then tried with equal lack of success to convince the British to take up his submarine. Back in the U.S.A. by 1812, Fulton devised his turtle-boat as a semi-submersible for operations against the British in the War of 1812: this boat was yet again propelled by a hand-cranked propeller and designed to flood down to a freeboard of only 6in (0.15m) so that the craft could, at night, be mistaken for a floating log. The weapon carried by the turtle-boat was a towed train of floating charges which could be swung against the target vessel and detonated from a safe distance with a lanyard. The first trial was not successful, and the turtle-boat was then destroyed by a British raiding party before its trials could be undertaken.

The semi-submersible was also used in the American Civil War (1861–1865). The

The experimental U.S. Navy submarine, the Intelligent Whale, built in 1863–64 and unsuccessfully evaluated in 1872, here on display at Willard Park, Washington Navy Yard in 1975.

early working life as a jeweller's apprentice and portrait painter, decided to become an engineer. In 1794 Fulton travelled to England and became involved in canal engineering, but in 1797 moved to France

and sought to persuade the French that they needed submarines to defeat the British at sea. In 1801, Fulton managed to persuade Napoleon of his concept's validity and was contracted to design and build a

type used by the Confederate navy carried the name David. The Davids, of which some 20 were built, were intended to redress the considerable numerical superiority of the Federal navy and came in two basic forms, using steam or hand power. The best known exploit of a steam-powered David was the attack on the USS *New Ironsides* in Charleston harbour during October 1863. Commanded by Lieutenant Glassel, the David did not get its spar torpedo (a 132-lb/60-kg explosive charge at the end of a long pole) deep enough under the water before the charge was exploded by its impact fuses, and the resulting waves swamped and sank the David without causing more than limited damage to its target. More success attended a hand-propelled David, the *H. L. Hunley*, committed against the USS *Housatonic* just as she was about to get under way in February 1864: the *Housatonic* was holed and opened to the sea. She sank, taking down with her the successful David, whose crew of nine was found inside the sunken vessel when divers went down to the wrecks some years later.

For success, the submarine clearly depended on several features: a hull of circular section to withstand the pressure of the water when submerged, ballast tanks that could be filled with water to make the submarine sink and then refilled with air to restore the buoyancy to bring the boat back to the surface once more, a powerplant able to function without a constantly replenished supply of air when the submarine was submerged, a rudder to provide directional control, and horizontal rudders (hydroplanes) to provide longitudinal control. It was the development of metal construction that opened the possibility of ships and also of submarines with a watertight hull of considerable strength

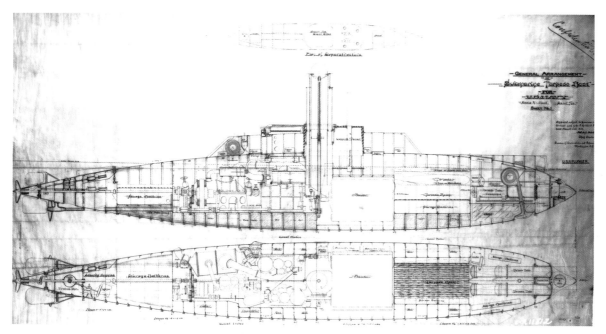

LEFT
*Plans of Simon Lake's
submarine USS* Plunger.
1895.

OPPOSITE
*SS-1, the first of the
Holland-class boats, at the
U.S. Naval Academy with
members of the class of 1902
aboard. They are (in
conning tower) H.G.
Wallace, (by mast) J.H.
Blackburn, (by the
lieutenant) J.W. Woodruff,
(by flag) J.W. Moses. A
lieutenant is instructing
them while ordinary seaman
stand at the bow. 1902.*

without excessive thickness and, during the
second half of the 19th century, American
and French inventors developed a number
of designs up to model form although none
of these secured the backing that could have
allowed their development as full-size boats.

This was perhaps just as well, for the
major problems yet to be overcome were
underwater propulsion and an effective
underwater weapon. Steam power could be
used for surface propulsion, of course, but
was impractical because of the time needed
to damp down the boilers before
submerging and to get up a head of steam
after surfacing. The practical solution

LEFT
*The Resurgam submarine
designed and built in 1879
by the Rev. George Garrett
of Liverpool, England. She
was powered by steam stored
in pressure tanks and could
move at 2 or 3kt for 10
miles (16km).*

RIGHT
Launch of the Royal Navy's first Holland submarine, No.1, from the yards of Vickers, Sons and Maxim at Barrow-in-Furness. 2 October 1901.

OPPOSITE
An A-class submarine building for the Royal Navy. 1904.

appeared in 1885 with the invention of the internal combustion engine by Gottlieb Daimler, although some years passed before this new type of engine had been made powerful and reliable enough for shipboard use, but its very concept was exciting as it offered the possibility of instant shut-down and start-up. However, such an engine cannot be used under water, since it needs a supply of air so large that the engine would exhaust the submarine's supply of compressed air (required for breathing and ballast-blowing) in a very short time.

The combination of electric engines and batteries provided one solution to the problem of underwater running. This combination had its limitations, however,

for though surface running could be entrusted to the internal combustion engine, which could also be used to power the generators that charged the batteries of the underwater system, it required the submarine to surface periodically so that the batteries could be recharged. This meant that the submarine with combined internal combustion and electrical propulsion should be considered a submersible rather than a true submarine as the type could not be genuinely independent of the surface.

The right weapon was found in the locomotive torpedo, a free-running weapon developed into an effective type by Robert Whitehead, a British engineer working at Fiume in Austria-Hungary. The torpedo

used compressed air for motive power and had a hydrostatic valve (later a pendulum system) for stability of depth. The first trials were undertaken in 1867, and by 1869 the locomotive torpedo was a practical weapon that was rapidly adopted by most of the world's more advanced navies. The type was still limited, but progress was made steadily in improving the torpedo's range, speed and course-keeping, the last with the aid of a gyroscopic system invented in Trieste by L. Obry in 1881. The first production torpedo emerged for the Royal Laboratory at Woolwich, England, in the early 1870s. This had a diameter of 16in (406mm) and a contra-rotating assembly of two propellers so that the torque reaction of each unit

cancelled that of the other and therefore removed the tendency of single-propeller torpedoes to roll and thus change course in the direction of the roll; this torpedo had a range of 1,000yds (915m) at 7kt or 300yds (275m) at 12.5kt. Torpedo development was rapid, its pace being indicated by the fact that in 1909 the standard Whitehead torpedo was an 18-in (457-mm) weapon with a range of 2,000yds (1830m) at 35kt or 4,000yds (3660m) at 29kt. Further development was imminent though the enrichment of the torpedo's air oxidant: the British developed a steam/gas engine in which water was evaporated and super-heated by a shale-oil jet, while the Americans produced the Bliss-Leavitt type

with a turbine driven by steam heated by an alcohol torch. By 1914, torpedoes were generally of 18- or 21-in (457- or 533-mm) diameter, with lengths of 17ft 6in and 22ft 0in (5.33 and 6.71m) respectively and ranges of 3,750yds (3430m) at 44kt or 10,000yds (9145m) at 28kt. The torpedo was the ideal weapon for the submarine: it was designed to run below the surface of the water, and in submarines it could be launched by either of two methods: in the drop-collar method the torpedoes were carried externally and merely released from their mountings, and in the tube-launched method the torpedoes were fired by compressed air out of flooded tubes that could then be purged of water by the

closing of the bow doors and reloaded from inside the submarine if the latter was large enough to carry a reserve supply. The latter soon became standard.

These features were first combined by John P. Holland, an Irish-born American. The first Holland submarine was the *Plunger*, a design commissioned by the U.S. Navy and built by the Columbian Iron Works in 1896. The type was too complex for its small size, however, and was not successful. The contract was cancelled in 1900, the year in which the U.S. Navy bought the sole example of Holland's next design, which had been designed as a private venture and built by Crescent. This seven-man vessel had surfaced and

British C-class submarines during World War I.

submerged displacements of 64 and 74 tons on a length of 53ft 9in (16.38m), and with 50hp (37.3kW) available from its petrol or electric engines had surfaced and submerged speeds of 8 and 5kt respectively. The armament included one 18-in (457-mm) torpedo tube and one 8-in (203-mm) dynamite gun, the latter operated by compressed air. The concept clearly held promise, and there followed a group of seven A-class submarines to a design that was slightly enlarged and provided better underwater performance.

Several other countries began to develop submarines in the period around 1900. Germany was an exception, as its navy preferred to wait for the perfection of the considerably safer and more economical compression (rather than spark) ignition engine invented by Rudolf Diesel in 1892 and which ran on comparatively heavy

instead of volatile petrol, which made for considerably greater safety in the confined spaces inside a submarine and which, incidentally, offered much superior fuel economy. This latter factor gradually came to assume major importance as the greater range possible, on a given volume of fuel, for a diesel-engined submarine by comparison with a petrol-powered boat allowed the development of the diesel-engined boat as an independent long-range weapon for commerce raiding rather than a subordinate medium-range weapon associated with battle fleet evolutions on the surface. The first diesel-engined submarine was the French Aigrette, which was launched in January 1904, and this was followed in 1906, May 1910 and May 1911 by the Russian Minoga, British D2 and American Skipjack.

Up to this time the Germans had played

only an insignificant part in the development of the submarine. The first German Unterseeboot (underwater boat, otherwise submarine) was the U1 that appeared in 1906 as a 19-man vessel that was 139ft (42.4m) long. At surfaced and underwater displacements of 238 and 283 tons, it was capable of 10.7 and 7kt respectively on its petrol or electric motors, each developing 400hp. The armament was still limited, made up of just one 17.7-in (450-mm) torpedo tube. This was a traditional boat with the generally unsuccessful combination of a petrol engine for surfaced running and battery charging, and an electric motor for submerged running. The progress made in the next few years is indicated by the size and capabilities of the four boats of the U19 class that were all delivered in 1913 from Danzig Dockyard as the Imperial German navy's first four diesel-engined submarines. These boats were each manned by 39 men, were 210ft 6in (64.15m) long, possessed surfaced and submerged displacements of 650 and 837 tons respectively, were capable of surfaced and submerged speeds of 15.5 and 9.5kt respectively on their powerplant of 1,700-hp (1268-kW) diesel engines or 1,200-hp (895-kW) electric motors, and carried an armament of one 88- or 105-mm (3.4- or 4.1-in) deck gun and four 17.7-in (450-mm) torpedo tubes.

The installation of the deck gun marked a gradual shift in emphasis in the role of the submarine. The torpedo was still seen as the primary weapon for the destruction of larger warships and merchant vessels at medium range, but was an expensive and bulky weapon of which only a relatively few could be carried. The deck gun, on the other hand, could be added without too much sacrifice of internal volume except for an ammunition magazine, and offered the

An E.20 submarine of the Royal Navy, the first of the true ocean-going classes built by Britain. E.20 was part of the third batch of boats being built between 1915 and 1917.

possibility of comparatively cheap shell fire for the destruction of smaller naval vessels and larger merchant vessels. The rules of war dictated that the latter had to be stopped, searched and permitted to evacuate their crews and passengers before being sunk, and this was effectively impossible without the submarine surfacing, when the deck gun became a more cost-effective weapon that the torpedo.

Rapid technical progress was made in the years before World War I, and by the start of that war in August 1914 there were about 400 submarines in service in 16 navies. The British and French had about half of this total, but whereas these vessels

were generally of the small coastal type with a displacement of about 300 tons, the Germans used the larger type suitable for open-sea operations on a displacement between 550 and 850 tons. The Royal Navy had 71 operational submarines with another 31 in construction, and the Germans had 33 boats with another 28 in construction. Most navies saw their submarines as companions to their large surface fleets for use in tasks such as scouting and ambushing the enemy's warships, but the Germans soon came to the conclusion that the submarine could and should be used as a deep-sea raider independent of the surface forces.

The first submarine operations of World War I were very limited, for none of the combatants had any experience in the use of such vessels under wartime conditions. The majority of navies saw the submarine arm as an adjunct to their surface forces. Thus the submarine was seen primarily as a covert reconnaissance machine, and in the first days of the war the Germans sent some of their boats north through the North Sea to watch for the activities of the Grand Fleet, which was based on Rosyth and Scapa Flow in Scotland, while the British despatched some of their submarines into the south-east part of the North Sea in the Heligoland Bight to watch for any sortie of the High Seas Fleet from its base at Wilhelmshaven. In the course of these initial operations the Germans lost two of the 10 boats they sent out.

Striking evidence of what might be achieved was soon provided by U9, which on one day sank the obsolete British armoured cruisers HMS *Hogue*, *Aboukir* and *Cressy*, and then only three weeks later sank the cruiser *Hawke*. Such was the fear of the submarine now instilled in the British that henceforward the major units of the Royal Navy ventured from port only when screened by destroyers. Here the British, and indeed all who sought to counter the threat of the submarine, were severely hampered by the lack of any means to detect a submerged submarine: only the sighting of a raised periscope, or the conning tower of a poorly trimmed boat breaking through the surface, could provide advance warning of an event otherwise signalled by the explosion of a torpedo's warhead against the side of a ship. Moreover, even when they sighted a submarine the crew of a surface warship could achieve little in the way of destroying the boat as there were no specialist anti-submarine weapons.

The typical submarine of 1914–15 was fast enough on the surface to provide a scouting capability for forces of cruising warships but could not match the maximum speed of these ships, and also lacked the underwater endurance and speed to serve as adjuncts to surface forces except by lurking off the enemy's ports to report the departure of such forces and perhaps torpedo a ship if the opportunity offered after the report had been made. Moreover, after a few brief flurries in 1914 and the first part of 1915, the British and German major fleets seemed content to remain in harbour and await the opportunity for a single

climactic battle that would decide the outcome of World War I. So there seemed little part for the submarine to play in conventional naval warfare, so the submarine was turned to other tasks in which it might profitably be employed. Small numbers of submarines were detached to the confined waters such as the south-western corner of the North Sea, the Strait of Otranto, the Dardanelles and other such natural chokepoints, where there was a chance of picking off single warships. Greater possibilities were offered by attacks on the enemy's merchant shipping, for the average ship of the mercantile marine was considerably slower than any warship and therefore easier to intercept, and was not escorted. Such a concept appealed to Germany, which was not reliant on maritime commerce routes for necessities such as food and raw materials, but appreciated that the U.K. and to a lesser extent France would be vulnerable to the interdiction of their maritime trade routes. The problem was how to achieve the disruption of these routes, for as noted above, international law dictated that merchant ships could not merely be sunk, but had first to be halted, have their papers examined, and have their crews either interned or sent to safety before the raider could put a prize crew aboard the vessel or sink her.

This was clearly impractical for a small submarine with no space for prize crews or captured seamen, although as early as October 1914 the U17 had indeed complied with the letter of the law in dealing with the *Glitra*, which was stopped, searched and scuttled off Norway once her crew had been sent to safety in the lifeboats. This is the first instance of the interception and destruction of a merchant vessel by a submarine, but served mainly to highlight both the strategic advantages and practical

difficulties of such a task. Soon after this there occurred the unwarned sinking of the steamship *Amiral Ganteume* off Cape Gris Nez by the U24, which probably thought that the ship, in fact loaded with Belgian refugees, was a troopship and therefore a legitimate target. The Allies saw the sinking of the *Amiral Ganteume* as an atrocity, but the event was in fact a pointer to the submarine's future as World War I descended to the level of total war in which the whole of the nation and not just its armed forces was involved. In February 1915 Germany announced that the waters round the U.K. were now a war zone and that any British of French ship in it was liable to summary sinking without warning, and that as a result of the submarine's limitations (indifferent periscope quality, etc.) it was also impossible to guarantee the safety of neutral ships in the zone. The effect of this change soon made itself apparent: in January 1915 the British and French had lost 47,900 tons of merchant shipping, but after the declaration of the German war zone this total soon rose to 185,400 tons (including 148,000 tons British) per month.

The only threat to Germany and its submarine campaign at this time was not British and French countermeasures, which were wholly ineffective, but world opinion with that of the U.S.A. well to the fore as its commercial interests were threatened. This initial financially inspired response to the German submarine offensive was strengthened by the weight of American public opinion in May 1915, when the U20 torpedoed the large liner *Lusitania*, which sank with the loss of 1,201 passengers including 128 Americans. This was not the first time in which civilians, or even American civilians, had died as a result of submarine attack, but the scale of the losses navies of the Austro-Hungarian and Turkish empires. It was therefore left to the Austro-Hungarians, who initially possessed only seven submarines, to take the offensive in a bold attempt to redress the Mediterranean balance of naval power. During January 1915 the XII torpedoed and severely damaged the French battleship *Jean Bart*, and four months later the V torpedoed and sank the French armoured cruiser *Léon Gambetta*. By this time Turkey had entered the war, and after reinforcing its ally with the U21 sent into the Mediterranean via the Strait of Gibraltar, Germany decided that it would be more cost effective to move six dismantled UB-type coastal submarines by rail to the Austro-Hungarian port of Cattaro (now Kotor), where they would be reassembled for operations under the German flag.

Three of the boats were then sent to Turkey, one disappearing en route and the

June 1944. The capture of U-507 off the Cape Verde Islands.

combined with an astute British propaganda effort to swing American public opinion firmly behind the Allies from this time, and it can be argued that the sinking of the *Lusitania* thus paved the way for the U.S.A.'s April 1917 entry into World War I on the Allied side.

Even as the submarine campaign around the British and French coasts was increasing in the last months of 1914 and the first months of 1915, and also as the Germans were preparing to shift toward unrestricted submarine warfare in these areas and also in the North Atlantic, there was a relatively intense period of submarine warfare in the Mediterranean. Most of France's submarines were based here at Toulon, but in the first months of the war there was little submarine activity as the British and French surface forces were sufficient to bottle up in their harbours the considerably smaller

The 1st U-Boat Flotilla, the Weddigen Flotilla at Kiel during the summer manoeuvres of 1937.

A one-man guided torpedo with crew member aboard during German navy tests in Spring 1944.

continuing its run of success in the Black Sea and the Sea of Marmora. It was not all one-way traffic, however, for the British and French sent three and two obsolescent boats respectively to blockade the mouth of the Dardanelles in case the Germans attempted to unleash their two most powerful ships in the area, the battle-cruiser *Goeben* and the light cruiser *Breslau*, which had reached Constantinople just before Turkey's entry into the war on the side of the Central Powers. The British then felt that it would be worth the effort to force their way past the Turkish anti-submarine defences and against the stream in an effort to reach the Sea of Marmora, where they might find unwary Turkish targets. This proved to be the case, and the B11 there sank the old Turkish warship *Messudieh*. The Turkish ship was of no real operational value, but the fact that it had been destroyed encouraged the British to send seven of the newer E-class boats to reinforce their submarine strength off Turkey. There followed a small but extremely brave and classic submarine campaign as these limited boats, complemented by a small number of French submarines, got through to the Sea of Marmora on several occasions despite the strength of the current flowing south from the Black Sea into the Mediterranean and scored several successes. Some of this havoc was wrought with torpedoes against larger ships, but much useful work was achieved with the submarines' newly provided deck guns against smaller ships and also on Turkish trains on the railway line along the coast. The Allied submarines continued to operate into the Sea of Marmora up to January 1916, when the Allies finally conceded the failure of their land campaign on each side of the Dardanelles and completed a superb amphibious evacuation.

The captains who had developed such

other two reaching Constantinople (now Istanbul), where they joined forces with the U21, which in May 1915 sank the British battleships HMS *Triumph* and *Majestic* off the Dardanelles. These elderly battleships had virtually no anti-submarine protection, but such was the fear of submarine attack put into the British naval forces off the Dardanelles that the local commander ordered all his larger warships back to the harbour of the Greek island of Mudros, thereby leaving the Allied land forces on Gallipoli with virtually no naval gunfire support.

By this time, Italy had entered the war on the Allied side, and soon came to feel the effect of the new type of warfare as the submarines *Medusa* and *Nereide* and the cruisers *Amalfi* and *Giuseppe Garibaldi* were lost to submarine attack. Meanwhile, the squadron of six German boats in Turkey was

skills were returned to the U.K. to continue their efforts in the North Sea, but the surviving submarines were used to strengthen the Allied force watching the mine barrage across the Strait of Otranto, which the Austro-Hungarian navy would have to penetrate in the course of any effort to break out into the Mediterranean proper. The submarine campaign in the confined waters of the Strait of Otranto and around the Dardanelles was mirrored by a somewhat different campaign in the close, shallow and very heavily mined waters of the Baltic Sea, where the Germans faced the Russians, who were supported by a small number of British submarines. The first two out of three British boats arrived at the Russian base of Lapvik in the Gulf of Finland during October 1914. Here the task of the British, and to a lesser extent the Russians who were generally short of new submarines as the engines for their latest craft had been ordered from Germany, was firstly to sink German ships and secondly by the threat they posed to the western end of the Baltic, upset German fleet dispositions and training, of which the latter was habitually carried out in the safe waters off the eastern end of the Kiel Canal and along the German Baltic coast. The British boats at first enjoyed only limited success, but this was sufficient to persuade the German naval commander-in-chief that the British had deployed at least a flotilla of submarines to the Baltic and that the two squadrons of large warships had to be retired to harbour until the flotilla's imagined depot ship had been located and destroyed.

This had a major effect on German naval planning, but more important was the success, from the unfreezing of the Baltic in the spring of 1915, of British boats against the merchant shipping transporting high-grade iron ore from Sweden to Germany.

Several German warships were also attacked by Russian as well as the two British boats, and the success of the campaign in the Baltic soon persuaded the Admiralty to send additional boats into the Baltic. Four more E-class boats made the dangerous run through the Kattegat between Denmark and Norway/Sweden, one being lost in transit after running aground, while four older C-class boats sailed to the Arctic port on Arkhangyelsk, from which they were moved to Lapvik by rail and barge. By the late summer of 1915 the British and Russian submarine force was making a real impact, sinking several German merchant ships as well as four German cruisers, of which two fell to British and the other two to Russian attack. This success could be maintained only as long as the Baltic remained unfrozen, and was resumed in the spring of 1916 until the German land advances

threatened the bases from which the boats operated. Thus the Allied effort was at a very low ebb when the advent of winter in 1916 ended operations for the year, and the full resumption of submarine activities in the spring of 1917 was made all but impossible by the effect of the first Russian revolution in March of that year. More concerned with internal matters and the continued land advances of the Germans, the Russians were unable to provide the technical support required by the British boats. There followed the second Russian revolution in November 1917 and the establishment of the Red (communist) regime, which reached a settlement with the Germans at Brest-Litovsk in the early part of the following year. As part of this settlement, the Soviets agreed to surrender the British submarines to the Germans, but before this condition could be exercised an

icebreaker manned by White Russians opened a path into the Baltic from the base at Helsingfors (now Helsinki) so that the surviving submarines could be taken to deeper water and scuttled.

So far as the British and German naval commanders were concerned, however, the Mediterranean and Baltic were side-show theatres compared with the North Sea, in which the two main protagonists, the British Grand Fleet and the German High Seas Fleet, confronted each other directly in a region that was generally accepted as being that in which the decisive naval engagement would be fought. In was for this theatre, therefore, that each side reserved its best boats and successively introduced its latest classes. At the beginning of the war, the Germans had a modest number of boats in service in this theatre, and were building another 19 (U31 to U41 and U43 to U50), with another six (U51 to U56) soon ordered. All these boats were generally similar, with a displacement in the order of 720 tons, armament of four 19.7-in (500-mm) torpedo tubes located equally in the bow and stern, and a propulsion arrangement that combined two 1,100-hp (820-kW) diesel engines for surfaced running and two 550-hp (410-kW) electric motors for submerged running. It soon became clear that the torpedo was hardly a cost-effective weapon against the small coastal shipping that became the German submarines' main target and the original 37-mm gun, located on a retractable mounting, was rapidly replaced by a 3.4- or 4.1-in (88- or 105-mm) deck gun, as noted above.

There followed the six, three and five boats of the U57, U63 and U66 classes with a submerged displacement in the order of 830 tons, an armament of two or four bow and one or two stern tubes, all firing

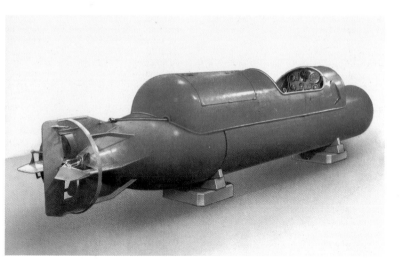

The Italian human torpedo or 'chariot', capable of carrying divers into enemy harbours to attach explosive charges to the bottom of enemy shipping. This type was used with remarkable success against the British battleships Queen Elizabeth *and* Valiant *in December 1941.*

The S-class USS Swordfish was built in the late 1930s and served in the conflict with Japan until lost in January 1945.

the 19.7-in (500-mm) torpedo, as well as a deck gun, and paired diesel and electric motors for surfaced and submerged speeds in the order of 15.5 to 17.5kt and 8 to 9kt respectively. These boats were known as the Mittel-U types, and were the workhorses of the German submarine effort during 1915 and 1916. This was not the limit of Germany's submarine construction effort, for in November 1914 it became clear that there would be no immediate victory on land and, faced with the prospect of a long war, the German naval high command decided to increase its submarine capabilities with two new types of boat, namely the UB and UC types optimized respectively for the coastal and minelaying roles. Both types were originally small, but they were highly successful and were therefore developed in

later classes to considerably greater size and in these improved forms were generally superior in all operational respects to the Mittel-U boats: the UB I class, for example had a submerged displacement of only 142 tons and carried an armament of two 17.7-in (450-mm) torpedo tubes, while the final UB 133 class had a submerged displacement of 656 tons and carried an armament of five 19.7-in (500-mm) torpedo tubes and one 4.1-in (105-mm) gun. The UC I class had a submerged displacement of 183 tons and carried an armament of 12 mines without any torpedo tubes, while the final UC III class had a submerged displacement of 571 tons and carried an armament of three 19.7-in (500-mm) torpedo tubes, one 4.1-in (105-mm) gun and 14 mines. The UB boats proved very successful against coastal

shipping and light warships in the waters round the coasts of the U.K. and northern France as well as in the central Mediterranean, while the UC boats had an inauspicious start but then developed into highly successful types whose ability to lay new minefields quickly and accurately resulted in several spates of Allied losses.

The British followed a course similar to that pursued by the Germans, but their construction programmes were generally a response to German leads rather than original thinking. Unlike the Germans, however, the British had started the war with a number of experimental types for the evaluation of new ideas: the three S-class boats were to an Italian design by Laurenti with diesel engines by Fiat, the four W-class boats were to a French design by Schneider-Lauboeuf, and the four V-class boats were to a Vickers design, while there were also the *Nautilus* and *Swordfish*, the former a large ocean-going boat and the latter a steam-powered boat designed to achieve greater surface speeds than was possible with current diesel-powered boats. After the outbreak of war, the Admiralty decided that there was no time for experimentation, and between October 1915 and August 1916 all seven units of the S and W classes were transferred to Italy.

The first response of the Admiralty to the outbreak of war was an order for an additional 38 boats of the successful E class, supplemented by contracts to Canadian Vickers and the American yard at Fore River for a total of 20 H-class boats using steel bought from the Bethlehem Steel Company. The boats were basically similar to the U.S. Navy's H and Russian navy's AG-class boats, and a further eight boats were ordered from Canadian Vickers by Italy. The group of 10 American-built boats was finally released to the U.K. only after the U.S.A.'s entry into

Submariners relax during World War II in the forward torpedo room of a U.S. submarine, situated in the Pacific war zone. November 1943.

arrangement for surfaced propulsion at 24kt. The fleet task planned for these boats was further reflected in the armament, which included four fixed 18-in (457-mm) torpedo tubes in the bows, two trainable 18-in (457-mm) torpedo tubes on each beam to allow the engagement of targets off the submarines' high-speed surface course, and up to three guns including one anti-aircraft weapon. The K-class boats were designed for entirely the wrong role, for the submarine had no place in close proximity to surface warships as it lacked the manoeuvrability and strength of its surface brethren. This conceptual fault was compounded by the complexity of the K-class design's propulsion arrangement, which was based on two steam boiler units, each with its own funnel and air inlet: before the boat could dive, therefore, the boiler had to be damped down, the funnels retracted, and all openings sealed against water ingress. The 2,650-ton K-class boats were thus unsuccessful, as confirmed most unfortunately by the Battle of May Island in January 1918 when K22 (the renamed K13 after the boat had foundered on its maiden voyage and been raised) suffered a jammed helm while two flotillas of K boats were exercising the battle-cruiser force: the K4 rammed and sank the K6, and the K17 was sunk by a cruiser.

The German influence was also found in two other types of British submarine. After they had captured and examined a UC-type minelayer, the British modified six E-class boats to a similar capability with five mine chutes, each containing two mines, externally in each of the two ballast tanks, the weight of the mine installation requiring that the two beam torpedo tubes, otherwise standard in the E-class boats, be removed. The other British development was a response to the Germans' submarine

the war in April 1917, and even then six of them were transferred to Chile to balance out the British impressment of Chilean warships under construction in British yards earlier in the war.

As work on the H-class boats was starting, the Admiralty received reports, erroneous as it turned out, that the Germans were building a class of high-speed submarines and decided to respond with its own class, which was to be capable of a surfaced speed of 20kt and possess long-range radio so that the boats could be used to create a reconnaissance line deep in the Heligoland Bight to watch for the emergence of the High Seas Fleet and instantly radio this information to the U.K. The result was the seven-strong J class, whose design included a length more than

100ft (30.5m) greater than that of the D and E classes and a surfaced powerplant of three 1,200-hp (895-kW) Vickers diesel engines for a speed of 19.5kt, which made them the fastest boats in the world. The most unfortunate effect of the success of the J class was the fact that it persuaded the Admiralty of the feasibility of using high-speed submarines as part of the main surface force. This led to the design and construction of the 17-strong K class. This extraordinary type of fleet submarine, intended to scout for the Grand Fleet, was designed to exceed the maximum 21-kt speed of current battleships. Such a speed was clearly impossible with the current or even foreseeable generation of diesel engines, so Vickers designed the boat with a 10,000-hp (7455-kW) geared steam turbine cruisers, which were armed with 5.9-in (150-mm) guns for the destruction of small warships and merchant ships in deep ocean areas. The Admiralty responded with an order for four M-class submarines, each armed with one 12-in (305-mm) gun in a turret in addition to four 18-in (457-mm) torpedo tubes in the bows. In the event, only three of these extraordinary boats were completed, only one of them in World War I, and of these two were lost in peacetime accidents.

During this period the large E class (55 boats in three subvariants) had been proving its continued worth, and was followed by 36 units of the L class, which was also produced in three subvariants as an enlargement of the E-class design with a number of detail improvements. The last class of British submarines built in World War I was something of a departure from previous design concepts, for it was planned specifically for the hunter/killer role, seeking and destroying German submarines. Twelve units of this R class were ordered and 10 were completed to a very far-sighted design with a streamlined hull of high length/beam ratio, single-shaft propulsion and enlarged battery capacity. This gave the boats the very high submerged speed of 14kt, which was not exceeded by any submarine class until the closing stages of World War II, as well as longer submerged endurance at high speed: if a submarine detection system more effective than the hydrophone had been available, the R-class boats might very well have proved highly effective.

During this period, German submarine construction had been proceeding apace. The well established UB, UC and Mittel-U classes remained in production right to the end of the war, but further developments were increasing the capabilities of the

German submarine force. The first of these developments, ordered in January 1915, was the UE I class of ocean minelayers, of which 10 were built with two longitudinal tubes (for 32 mines) rather than the vertically inclined tubes of the coastal minelayers. The class also possessed a lower length/beam ratio to allow a significant increase in bunkerage for much greater range. Although five of their number were lost during the war, the boats of the UE I class provided moderately effective and were followed by a further 10 boats of the considerably improved UE II class with the capability to operate off the eastern coast of the U.S.A. These boats were considerably larger than their predecessors, and could carry 48 mines, no fewer than 24 torpedoes

(12 internally and 12 externally) for the four 19.7-in (500-mm) tubes in the bows, and a gun armament of one 5.9-in (150-mm) or two 4.1-in (105-mm) weapons. Another eight of the class were scrapped late in the war before being completed, and it is possible to see in these boats the origins of the German submarines that were so effective in World War II.

Although the success of the minelaying submarines was considerable, it was a success that did not catch the imagination of the naval authorities, so greater attention was paid to the U-Kreuzer types designed as submarine cruisers for long-range offensive operations against Allied shipping. This class resulted from the German realization late in 1915 that it was often wasteful to use a torpedo against a target that could just as effectively be destroyed by surface gunfire, and the result was an initial order placed in May 1916 for the four boats of the U135 class and then complemented in August of the same year for three boats of the generally similar but considerably larger U139 class. The U135 class had a submerged displacement of 1,535 tons and carried an armament of four 19.7-in (500-mm) bow torpedo tubes complemented, according to some sources, by two stern tubes of the same calibre, and also one 5.9-in (150-mm) deck gun, while the U139 class had a submerged displacement of 2,485 tons and an armament of six 19.7-in (500-mm) torpedo tubes (one bow and two stern) as well as two 5.9-in (150-mm) deck guns. An order was later placed for nine of the even larger U142 class with a submerged displacement of 2,785 tons and the same armament as the U139 class, but only one of these boats was completed at about the time of Germany's defeat in November 1918.

The problem with these submarine cruisers was the fact that their greater size and armament were not really needed, for smaller submarines armed with a 3.4- or 4.1-in (88- or 105-mm) gun could achieve basically the same results on a hull that could be constructed more quickly and cheaply, and also provided a higher level of manoeuvrability. It might have been different if the additional size of the submarine cruisers had been used for significantly increased bunkerage for considerably greater range, but the extra size was used for the larger numbers of heavier guns together with their associated ammunition magazines.

As a result of the ever tightening British naval blockade of its ports, which effectively halted all maritime trade, Germany turned to the concept of the cargo-carrying submarine as a means of maintaining a trade in high-value freight. The first of these mercantile submarines was the *Deutschland*, which sailed from Kiel in June 1916 with a cargo of dyes, precious stones and mail. The submarine reached Baltimore in the American state of Maryland just over two weeks later, and as it was entirely unarmed had to be treated as an otherwise conventional merchant vessel. After discharging its outward-bound load, the submarine took on a cargo of nickel, silver and zinc for the return voyage, which was achieved without incident. The *Bremen*, a second vessel of the type, left on a similar voyage to Norfolk in the American state of Virginia, but was lost without trace. It had been planned that the *Bremen*'s voyage would be undertaken alongside a sortie by the U53, which reached Newport in Rhode Island in October 1916. The submarine later departed, as demanded by the rules of war, and after leaving U.S. territorial waters but within sight of an American lightship started to attack Allied shipping. The Americans were extremely angry, but were powerless to intervene before the submarine, after sinking five ships, headed back to Germany. The whole operation had been designed to frighten the U.S.A. into a strict neutrality, but wholly failed to achieve this object. The plan had been conceived within the concept of an all-out submarine offensive along the U.S.A.'s east coast, but Kaiser Wilhelm II had refused to allow the implementation of the plan and the whole concept of the mercantile submarine was therefore reduced to nothing. As a result, the German navy ordered the conversion of the *Deutschland* into a submarine cruiser, and in February 1917 contracted for another six boats with the standard armament of two 19.7-in (500-mm) bow torpedo tubes and two 5.9-in (150-mm) and two 3.4-in (88-mm) deck guns.

German submarine developments in World War I were completed by the small UF- and vast UD-class designs. The UF class was designed for coastal operations in the Strait of Dover. With a submerged displacement of slightly under 300 tons and an armament of two 19.7-in (500-mm) bow torpedo tubes, the type was ordered to the extent of 92 units between December 1917 and July 1918, but none had been completed before Germany's defeat. The UD class had a displacement of 4,000 tons and was intended for the submarine cruiser role with the same armament as the U151 class of converted mercantile submarines, but the type was cancelled as impractical. The only other type of submarine to enter service in World War I was the UA class, which comprised a single small boat originally ordered by Norway.

Before the end of world War I in November 1918, Germany had ordered 811 submarines, 768 of this total resulting from orders placed during the war. More than

*The I-400 (I-400-class)
submarine of the Imperial
Japanese Navy comes
alongside USS Proteus (AS-
19) after the surrender in
1945.*

Japanese Koryu-type submarines at the Imperial Naval Base at Kure. Developed during the later part of the war in the Pacific during World War II, these submarines carried a crew of five and were armed with two torpedoes.

Crewmen of a Japanese Koryu-type five-man submarine during World War II.

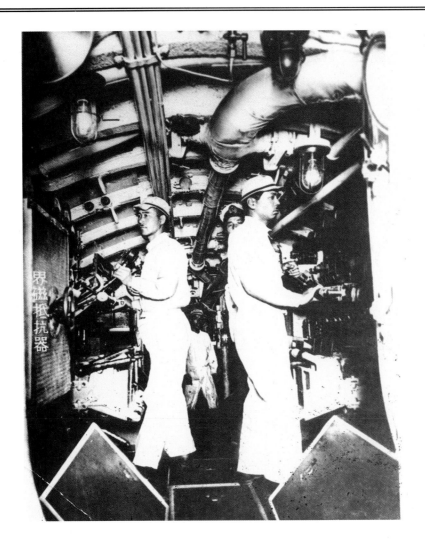

界磁抵抗器

400 of this total were cancelled or scrapped while still incomplete, and 178 of the other boats were lost. This represented some 47 per cent of the submarine arm's boats, and with the boats were killed 515 officers and 4,849 other ranks (40 per cent of the submarine arm's personnel strength) in return for the sinking of more than 11 million of Allied shipping, of which the British share was more than 2,000 ships with more than 14,000 merchant mariners.

The critical point in the submarine campaign came in February 1917, when the Kaiser very reluctantly agreed to the launch of a campaign of unrestricted submarine warfare against Allied merchant shipping. This came as an enormous blow to the Allies in general and the U.K. in particular: during April 1917 merchant shipping losses to submarine attack increased to 881,000 tons, which included one of every four ships bound for a British port. The effect of the campaign was so strong that it was calculated at this time that the British had food reserves for only another six weeks, and the country therefore faced the prospect of starvation or an accommodation with the Germans.

However, it was the launch of its unrestricted submarine warfare campaign that finally sealed the defeat of Germany. Long exasperated by Germany's attitude, which apparently included an effort to foment an anti-American revolution in Mexico followed by a Mexican invasion of the southern U.S.A., the start of the new campaign was the final straw for the Americans, who declared war on Germany in April 1917. There was little that the U.S.A. could achieve in the short term to aid the European Allies except to increase the flow of food and other supplies across the Atlantic, and to undertake limited anti-submarine measures in the western half of

The effect of these losses on Allied thinking were enormous, and a clause of the Armistice agreement with Germany stipulated that all seaworthy German submarines were to be surrendered at designated Allied ports, while unseaworthy boats were to be immobilized and disarmed in German ports pending the arrival of Allied inspection teams. Germany thus surrendered 176 boats, with others preferring internment in neutral ports, and the Allies quickly set about an evaluation of the weapon that had nearly defeated them. Germany surrendered 105 boats to the British, who operated at least three of them for evaluation purposes, 46 to the French who took 10 of them into their own service, seven to the Japanese who took them all into service, 10 to the Italian, and six to the Americans. The Belgians received two boats originally surrendered to the British. With the exception of the French boats, all of these surrendered craft were destroyed by inter-Allied agreement in 1922 and 1923, but by this time all possible implications of German design thinking had been gleaned.

Strangely, the major Allied powers decided that the German submarine cruiser, despite its obvious clumsiness and overgunning, possessed great merit and therefore started on the development of such boats for their own submarine arms. This tendency was exacerbated by the fact that the American and Japanese navies, which received proportionally the largest parts of the German spoils, were expanding rapidly and saw the submarine cruiser as ideal for operations in the ocean vastnesses that were their primary operating theatres. The Americans incorporated many features of the U140 in their V-class boats, which comprised the three boats of the Barracuda subclass and the six other boats that constituted four subclasses. All these boats

The USS Tang *(SS-567) was the name boat of a six-strong class of conventionally powered submarines based on the concept of the German Type XXI class of World War II, and the boats constituted the last non-nuclear class that the U.S. Navy took into service.*

the Atlantic; but this coincided with the belated British introduction of the convoy system, which rapidly proved itself the best method of defence against submarine attack. Although the Admiralty had long argued against the system, on the grounds that it concentrated targets for submarine attack, it soon became clear that the concentration of defence provided by the escort warships was greater than the concentration of opportunity offered to the German submarines, and sinkings soon declined to a significant degree (257 out of 84,000 convoyed ships, or 0.4 per cent, compared with 2,616 ships sailing independently), especially after the Americans were able to provide a measure of protection on their side of the Atlantic.

The failure of the unrestricted submarine warfare campaign coincided with the threatened arrival of vast American armies in France to bolster the steadily

growing Allied offensive capability. This persuaded the German armies to launch their final desperate offensives during the spring of 1918, just before the main weight of the American forces began to make its presence felt, and the failure of these offensives sealed Germany's ultimate defeat in November of the same year.

As the major powers emerged from World War I in the last two months of 1918, most of them were exhausted and determined to ensure that nothing like World War I could take place again. One of the major factors the victorious Allies had to take into consideration was the submarine, and evidence of its importance in World War I was provided by the revelation that the U.K., the world's major maritime power, had lost more than 9 million tons of merchant shipping, representing some 90 per cent of its pre-war tonnage, out of total Allied losses of more than 13 millions tons.

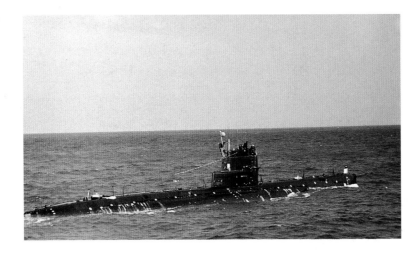

A Whiskey-class of the Soviet navy.

were notable for their very long range, considerable complements of 21-in (533-mm) torpedoes, and large-calibre deck gun comprising one 5-in (127-mm) weapon in all but the *Narwhal* and *Nautilus*, which each carried two 6-in (152-mm) weapons. Among the last six boats was the *Argonaut*, which was a further development incorporating the type of minelaying capability (60 mines) of which the Americans learned from another German submarine, the U117 of the UE II class. The first Japanese cruiser submarine was the I-52, which was derived from the U125, a UE II-class boat which the Japanese had placed in service as the O-1. The Japanese then constructed the four submarines of the Type J1 class, which each had a submerged displacement of 2,790 tons, a range of 24,400 miles (39265km), and an armament of six 21-in (533-mm) tubes with 20 torpedoes, and

two 5.5-in (140-mm) deck guns. Although derived from the UE II class, these boats had no minelaying capability, which was then incorporated in the succeeding but somewhat smaller Type KRS class, of which four were built with provision for 42 mines as well as a standard armament of four 21-in (533-mm) tubes with 12 torpedoes, and one 5.5-in (140-mm) deck gun.

The British also acquired an interest in the submarine cruiser as reflected by the construction of the X1, a development of the uncompleted U173 class of very large submarine cruisers and armed with four 5.2-in (132-mm) guns in two paired mountings as well as six 21-in (533-mm) tubes for 12 torpedoes. The British even used two diesel engines of German manufacture for surfaced running, but these were beset by reliability and other problems and the X1 was scrapped after only five years, ending British interest in

the submarine cruiser.

Of other European nations, only France was the only other nation to adopt the submarine cruiser concept. The French opted for a boat built with guns of 8-in (203-mm) calibre, the largest allowed by the Washington Naval Treaty of 1922. The result was the *Surcouf*, which carried two 8-in (203-mm) guns in a trainable turret, eight 21.7-in (550-mm) tubes for 18 torpedoes, and a mounting for four 15.7-in (400-mm) tubes for eight specialized anti-ship torpedoes. The boat also had provision for a small scouting floatplane, which could be dismantled for carriage in a small watertight hangar, and provision for 40 prisoners.

In the early 1920s serious consideration was given to the outright banning of the submarine by the Washington Naval Treaty, and this was something that the British wanted. The French and Italians, on the other hand, saw the submarine as a comparatively cheap yet effective weapon with which they could rival the larger powers, and therefore pressed for the type's retention. So too did the Japanese, who saw in the type a means of offsetting the Americans' superiority in large surface warships. The result of these machinations was that the submarine was not banned, but merely limited to the same 8-in (203-mm) main gun calibre as the heavy cruiser. And as a result of French pressure, no limit was fixed on the numbers of submarines that each of the powers was allowed to build, and unrestricted submarine warfare was not outlawed. An immediate result was that the world's major navies, restricted by treaty in the numbers and sizes of the major warships they might build, turned their attentions to the large-scale manufacture of submarines, and that the world's smaller navies also stepped up the

HS Triaina *(S 86), an ex-U.S. Balao-class submarine of the Hellenic Navy.*

pace of their submarine programmes. Of these latter, the most adventurous were the Danish, Dutch, Norwegian, Polish and Swedish navies, of which all but the Norwegians opted for indigenous as well as imported designs.

The most far-sighted of these countries, so far as technical innovation was concerned, were the Dutch. In 1937 their O21 class introduced a breathing mast so that the diesel engines could be run when the submarine was just below the surface of the water, thereby allowing the batteries to be charged. This important development went virtually unremarked, and indeed the masts were removed by the British when some of the boats escaped the defeat of the Netherlands in May 1940 and reached the U.K. It was only after they had discovered parts of such a mast in a Dutch shipyard, that its full value was appreciated by the Germans, who developed the concept into the Schnorchel that allowed their boats to travel just under the surface for protracted

A Soviet Whiskey twin-cylinder missile submarine during Soviet Navy Day in Sevastopol, 1967.

periods and therefore receive less attention from Allied anti-submarine aircraft.

The exaggerated significance of the submarine was reflected in the suggestion put to the French parliament in 1920 that the French navy procure a fleet of between 250 and 300 submarines not only to replace the navy's current force of battleships and cruisers, but also to expand France's overall naval capabilities. The French navy countered with the argument that the submarine had recently suffered a severe reverse, and what was needed was a balanced force of surface vessels and submarines. This view prevailed, and the French navy therefore started a programme of submarine construction based on two core types, namely the first-class submarine with a displacement of 1,000 tons or so for

ocean and overseas offensive/defensive use, and the second-class submarine with a displacement of some 600 tons or so for home-based defensive use. The first-class submarines comprised the nine units of the Requin class and the 29 units of the 1,500-tonne class in several subvariants that were to have been replaced in the early 1940s by the 14 units of the Roland Morillot class. The second-class submarines comprised the 10 units of the Ariane class in three subvariants and the 22 units of the Amazone class in five subvariants. Finally, there were the six submarine minelayers of the Saphir class.

The only major state omitted from the naval limitations of the 1920s was the U.S.S.R., which had evolved out of Russia with a fairly large fleet of submarines even

though only 16 were still serviceable in the early 1920s. Soviet military development during the 1920s was restricted principally to the army, in both its ground and air forms. Limited refurbishment of existing naval units was undertaken, however, and it was 1931 before the navy started to receive new submarines in the form of the six D-class units based on an Italian design and then 24 L-class units based ultimately on the British L class of World War I. An example of the L class had been sunk during the Allied intervention of 1919, but was raised in 1928 and commissioned into the Soviet navy during 1931. The last of the resulting L-class boats was not commissioned until 1942. These two types were of moderately large size, and further capability was provided by smaller boats for coast defence. These boats included 90 Shch-class boats commissioned between 1933 and 1942, 33 Stalinets-class boats commissioned from 1936, and three Pravda-class boats also commissioned from 1936. The last were not notably successful, but the Pravda-class boats were very good, possibly because the design was based on the German Type IA class created by one of the clandestine teams that Germany established in the Netherlands, Spain and the U.S.S.R. to maintain an uninterrupted submarine-designing capability despite the ban on such activities imposed by the Treaty of Versailles in 1919.

These boats were the most important elements in the Soviet submarine fleet and the medium-size niche. The U.S.S.R. also went in for both smaller and larger submarines. The former was represented by the Malyutka class with a displacement of only 160 tons and an armament of two 21-in (533-mm) torpedo tubes, and the latter by the Katyusha-class cruiser boats with a displacement of 1,390 tons and an

USS Growler *(SSG-577), a Greyback-class cruise-missile submarine of the U.S. Navy. November 1958.*

armament of 10 21-in (533-mm) torpedo tubes plus two 3.9-in (100-mm) and two 45-mm deck guns. Construction of the Malyutka class amounted to more than 50 boats in the period between 1933 and 1937, more units of two later subvariants being added between 1938 and 1944, and deliveries of the Katyusha class amounted to at least 13 boats between 1940 and 1942.

After failing to have submarines banned by the Washington Naval Treaty, the British came to the conclusion that they had no option but to design submarines possessing capabilities at least equal to those of potential enemies, and during 1923 started to design and construct boats derived from the L class of 1917. This resulted in the O class to a design characterized by greater length and beam than the L-class design but

retaining essentially the same armament in the form of the eight 21-in (533-mm) tubes located as six in the bows and two in the stern with a total of 16 torpedoes. The propulsion arrangement was essentially the same even though the size and displacement were both greater, so the maximum surfaced and submerged speeds were reduced, a fact offset by the enhanced range provided by greater bunkerage. Further development of the same basic design resulted in the modestly larger boasts of the P and R classes.

The next British development was the River class, of which six were built from 1929 with a surfaced speed of 22kt. This was made possible only by the introduction of more powerful diesel engines in a change that necessitated the omission of the stern

torpedo tubes, but it was soon obvious that these boats were successful in the technical sense but had been designed to an invalid operational notion as there was really little need for a submarine with a high surfaced speed except for commerce-raiding sorties in the Pacific Ocean, in which the Royal Navy then had little interest. During the same basic period, the British commissioned six Porpoise-class submarine minelayers each carrying 50 mines in an external casing. Yet once more, these boats were successful at the technical level, but in this instance the boats were made superfluous to requirement by the British development of the type of mine which could be laid through a torpedo tube, allowing conventional submarines to operate as minelayers. The boats of the Porpoise class

The pennant number on the sail of this Oberon-class submarine of the Royal Navy identifies the boat as HMS *Opportune.*

nonetheless proved their worth during 1941 and 1942, when they served successfully to ferry essential supplies into the beleaguered island of Malta.

The British had decided by the late 1920s that its current patrol submarine classes were too large for successful employment in European and Mediterranean waters, and thus started the design of a new and smaller type of submarine as the S class. Some 60 examples of this class were eventually constructed to a standard that included an armament of six 21-in (533-mm) torpedo tubes in the bows. The most important improvement in the S class over the preceding classes, other than its smaller size, was bunkerage wholly inside the pressure hull, thereby removing the type

of telltale oil leaks that had hampered the boats of earlier classes with external bunkerage. The S-class submarine was too small for long patrols, however, and to provide a world-wide capability the British designed the larger but otherwise basically similar T class with 10 21-in (533-mm) torpedo tubes located as eight in the bows (including two in the bulbous bow casing) and two amidships in the casing.

During this period of technical improvement, Germany had been banned by the Treaty of Versailles from any involvement in submarine development. Determined to keep abreast of matters, though, Germany created a clandestine method of keeping current with developments through the establishment of

design offices in neutral countries such as the Netherlands, Spain and the U.S.S.R., where submarines were designed and built for local use and also for the export market. The result of this process was that when the Nazi party came to power in 1933, Germany lacked submarines but was generally knowledgeable about the latest thinking in submarine design and construction. As a result, when the Nazi government decided in 1934 that the construction of submarines in Germany should be resumed, there was a fair measure of knowledge on which the designers and constructors could draw for the rapid creation of indigenous submarines. At this time the German navy was considering five basic types of boat: these were a coastal type with a displacement of up to 500 tons, a coastal minelayer type with a displacement of up to 500 tons, a sea-going type with a displacement of up to 750 tons, an ocean-going type with a displacement of 1,000 tons, and a submarine cruiser type with a displacement of 1,500 tons. The origins of the sea-going type were to be found in the Gür, which had been designed as the Type IA class by a German team and built in Spain for Turkey in the earlier 1930s (the design was also the basis of the Soviet Stalinets class). The origins of three of the other types were to be found, somewhat more loosely, in the best German designs of World War I: the Type II coastal type was derived from the UB II class, the Type VII sea-going type was derived from the UB III class with a number of improvements developed for the Finnish Vetehinen class, and the Type IX ocean-going type was derived from the UE II class. All three were successful, and were therefore built in large numbers through a succession of steadily improved subvariants which each benefited from operational experience with its predecessor.

The most important of the types developed before World War II, which started in September 1939, was possibly the Type VIIB class, which was a slightly enlarged version of the Type VIIA class with higher-powered diesel engines and modified saddle tanks for improved seaworthiness and enlarged bunkerage ensuring increased range despite the higher surfaced speed. The Type VIIB class had surfaced and submerged displacements of 753 and 857 tons respectively, a length of 218ft 3in (66.5m) and beam of 20ft 3in (6.2m), a two-shaft propulsion arrangement with 2,800hp (2088kW) diesel engines and 750-hp (559-kW) electric engines for surfaced and

USS Nautilus *(SSN-571), the world's first nuclear-powered submarine being launched at Groton, Connecticut on 21 January 1954.*

submerged speeds of 17.25 and 8kt respectively, surfaced and submerged ranges of 6,500 and 80 miles (10460 and 129km) respectively at speeds of 12 and 4kt, a crew of 44, and an armament of five 21-in (533-mm) tubes (four in the bows and one in the stern) for 12 torpedoes or 14 mines, plus one 3.4-in (88-mm) deck gun supplemented by one 20-mm cannon for anti-aircraft use. The Type VII submarine was easy to build and, by submarine standards, was decidedly handy. However, as experience was soon to reveal, the Type VIIB class was not perfectly suited to the type of operations that Germany launched in World War II as its surfaced range was limited and its volume too small for protracted patrols, which required that the submarine's interior had to be packed with extra food and spare equipment: this reduced habitability and, as a result, capability on long missions.

By September 1939 Germany had 56 operational submarines and five more in the final stages of construction. This was really too small a number with which to start effective operations, and resulted from the fact that the German navy, on the basis of Nazi estimates, had planned for a war starting in 1944. Even so, 40 U-boats were already off the U.K., sinking the liner *Athenia* on the first day of hostilities despite Hitler's instructions that, to avoid international opprobrium, such targets were not to be attacked. In general, though, the U-boats skippers were very careful in target choice, and up to the time of Germany's May 1940 offensive against the Low Countries and France, the Germans had sunk only 199 merchant ships and in the process lost 18 of their own submarines. The Germans had also sunk several warships including the aircraft carrier HMS *Courageous* and the elderly

battleship HMS *Royal Oak*.

The British had only 38 submarines in home waters at the beginning of the war, and used their boats in what was in effect a World War I manner for reconnaissance of German ports to warn of any movement by Germany's major surface units. This was not an effective way to use a limited resource, for the Germans undertook little in the way of such movements and were able to eliminate several British submarines that they knew must be in these areas as targets for air as well as ship attack with the improved sensors (including ASDIC, later known as sonar) and the more capable weapons that had begun to enter service during the 1930s.

The first real opportunity for the British boats arrived with the German invasion of Norway in April 1940, when they began to lay major minefields off the Norwegian coast and to attack the ships carrying German troops into Norway and then supplying them. HMS *Spearfish* damaged the pocket battleship KMS Lützow and HMS *Clyde* seriously hurt the battle-cruiser KMS *Gneisenau*. In overall terms, the successes of British naval forces (surface as well as submarine) and air forces affected the German navy so badly that this latter lacked the strength for the invasion of the U.K. planned for later in the same year. The whole balance of the submarine war changed in June 1940, when France was defeated and Italy entered the war on the side of Germany. The Royal Navy, now without the aid of the French navy, now had to carry the weight of the naval war against an opponent whose strength had been considerably enlarged. Just as important, or perhaps more so, was the shift in the strategic balance resulting from the fact that Germany could now use captured French bases with direct access to the

South-Western Approaches and the North Atlantic. This extended the radius of U-boats that no longer had to operate from bases in Germany, requiring the boats to pass north and west round the British Isles and all their anti-submarine capabilities before reaching their operational areas. A number of bases were also established for the U-boats in Norway. This paved the way for one of the decisive submarine/anti-submarine campaigns of World War II, for by the end of 1940 no fewer than 12 U-boat flotillas had moved to the French bases of Brest, La Rochelle, La Pallice, St. Nazaire, Lorient and Bordeaux. This last was also home to flotillas for a maximum of 27 Italian submarines, which proved generally inferior to their German counterparts as a result of their large conning towers and relatively low surfaced speed but nevertheless managed to sink nearly 1 million tons of Allied shipping up to the middle of 1943 in their primary operational area off the Azores.

The French bases were close to the U-boats' major operational areas, which were the Atlantic regions through which the convoys carrying the U.K.'s raw materials, food supplies and oil steamed. Though the British had instituted a convoy system from the outbreak of hostilities, the system and the tactics of its escorts were still close to the bottom of their learning curves and thus provided the U-boats with great opportunities.

It was only in August 1940 that Adolf Hitler, the German dictator, finally authorized unrestricted submarine warfare, but the U-boats did not initially score great successes. The British anti-submarine forces in the South-Western Approaches had now developed considerable skill, so it was not until they had moved their operational areas deeper into the Atlantic, largely out of reach

of British aircraft and short-range escorts, that the Germans started to notch up important successes: between June and November 1940 the U-boats sent to the bottom 1.6 million tons of British shipping, most of it during the second half of the period. Even so, the Germans realized the difficulty of their situation. The U.S.A. had exchanged 50 old flushdeck destroyers, which could be easily adapted as effective anti-submarine vessels, for 99-year leases on

British bases in the Caribbean, and in the process revealed that it was going to support the U.K. in the same way that it had in World War I; and the German navy, having been told that this would be a short war, now had to overcome the hurdle of inadequate numbers of U-boats for sustained North Atlantic operations. The construction of new boats was accelerated: four new boats were delivered between September and December 1939, but 60

more came off the slips between January and December 1940 at an increasing rate. Even so, this rate was still not adequate for the replacement of losses and the implementation of a major expansion of the submarine campaign at a time that the Germans had suffered the loss of 34 boats including 32 to Allied attack.

The Germans benefited from the British reaction to the threat of German invasion after the May/June 1940 Dunkirk

HMAS Otama *(62), an Oxley-class (British Oberon-class) submarine of the Royal Australian Navy leaving the Clyde Naval Base, Faslane, Scotland for a work-up cruise. May 1978.*

evacuation, when most destroyers had been withdrawn from convoy escort duties, but as they could put only some 30 U-boats into action at any one time the Germans were still unable to inflict a decisive blow. Even so, the great submarine aces such as Otto Kretschmer and Günther Prien were able to exploit their skills to the maximum, and each sank more than 200,000 tons of shipping in this period. The tactic evolved by men such as Kretschmer and Prien was the surface night attack: here the U-boats could not be detected by the ASDIC of the British escorts, and their very low silhouettes were virtually impossible to spot. Kretschmer took the concept to its ultimate limit by penetrating into the heart of the convoy before starting his attack, making it all but impossible for the escorts, generally operating in a ring outside the columns of the convoy, to launch a counterattack. Admiral Karl Dönitz, commanding the submarine arm, took the concept of the night attack a step further by adding to it the wolf pack concept. In this, as many submarines as possible were vectored into position to ambush a convoy discovered by any one submarine or maritime reconnaissance aeroplane such as the Focke-Wulf Fw 200 Condor: only when a large number of U-boats had been assembled did the boats start a concentrated night attack to swamp the escorts (generally converted trawlers, corvettes and sloops that could not match the 17-kt surface speed of the U-boats) and decimating the convoy in a tactic that was repeated on as many successive nights as possible as long as the pack could keep in contact. The wolf pack night attack system was introduced between October 1940 and March 1941, and was devastating.

Even so, the U-boats were still greatly hampered by their lack of range and their relatively small number of reload torpedoes,

aided the British was their ability to read much of the ciphered German signal traffic. Thus March 1941 was a disaster for the Germans, who achieved some successes but also lost five boats including those of the aces Kretschmer, Prien and Schepke.

To partner their improved methods of detecting U-boats, the British also created and shipped more effective anti-submarine weapons. Though the first of these (the Hawker Hurricane fighter launched on a one-way mission from adapted merchant ships to intercept and destroy German reconnaissance aircraft before themselves ditching in the sea close to a ship that could rescue the pilot) was an expedient, three other weapons held greater long-term promise. The first of these to reach service was a more effective depth charge for use by anti-submarine aircraft instead of the anti-submarine bomb that had not proved successful. In the longer term, greater capability was offered by two weapons that were not yet fully ready for service. These were the escort or jeep aircraft carrier, which was a simple and fairly cheap conversion of a medium-sized merchant ship so that each major convoy could be provided with its own fighter and anti-submarine aircraft in the mid-Atlantic regions that could not be covered by land-based aircraft, and the projector type of weapon that could fire its bombs ahead of the ship against a target submarine still held in the ASDIC's beam. The first of these projector weapons appeared during 1941 as the Hedgehog, which was a spigot mortar firing a pattern of 24 small impact-fused bombs each carrying a 32-lb (14.5-kg) explosive warhead sufficient to penetrate the hull of any submarine. Further development led to the 1943 appearance of the altogether more powerful Squid, which fired three full-sized depth charges each

which was a factor that most affected the Type VII and Type IX boats that formed the bulk of the German submarine strength. A partial remedy was the introduction of the Type XIV or milch cow submarines, which were produced in modest numbers to supply submarines at sea. Each of these boats carried a cargo of 432 tons of oil fuel and four reload torpedoes. Ten of these boats were completed during 1941 and 1942, and all were sunk as the Allies rightly considered them to be a greater threat than the operational U-boats they supported. Despite the importance of the type, another ten such boats were cancelled because of their increasing vulnerability as they transferred fuel on the surface.

Meanwhile the British had responded to the threat of the U-boat operating on the

surface with the introduction of Type 271 radar, which could detect the conning tower of a surfaced submarine at a range of 2.5 miles (4km) and allow the start of an attack while the U-boat was still out of effective torpedo range of the convoy. At almost the same time, high-frequency direction-finding, or Huff-Duff, equipment was pioneered to detect the radio transmissions of U-boats and also to fix their location to a distance of less than 440yds (400m). The combination of these two electronic systems immediately shifted the balance in favour of the British, for the ability of the enemy to locate them in the dark meant that U-boat commanders had ever more frequently to crash dive after gaining contact and reporting the fact, with the result that the contact was then lost. Another factor that

OPPOSITE
*U 29 (S178), a Type 206
submarine of the Federal
German Navy during trials
in 1974.*

RIGHT
*Huancavilca (S11), a Type
209 submarine of the
Ecuadorian navy during
trials in 1977.*

containing 300lb (136kg) of explosive and therefore possessing the ability to cause catastrophic damage with a near miss as well as a direct hit. The advantage of both these weapons was that they were fired at a target that was still being tracked, whereas the standard depth charge, fired from or dropped over the stern of an escort, was released against a target that might well have manoeuvred out of the way or to a different depth after the attacking escort ship's forward-facing ASDIC could no longer track it as the attack was committed.

During December 1941 the U.S.A. entered the war on the Allied side after the Japanese attack on Pearl Harbor and Germany's subsequent declaration of war. This rapidly eased the British task as the

U.S. Navy was now able to play a more active part than its previous patrolling on the western side of the Atlantic, and as American construction facilities became more readily available to meet British needs. In the early part of 1942, therefore, six merchant hulls were converted into escort carriers and of these five were delivered to the U.K., which had pioneered the escort carrier with great success with the *Audacity* that had proved its worth in 1941 before being sunk after a one-month career. However, it should not be ignored that the U.S. entry into the war was initially a disaster for what were now the Allied powers as the U.S. Navy was poorly equipped for the modern anti-submarine role and the U.S. merchant marine offered a

large and tempting number of targets for the German submarine arm, which therefore enjoyed one of its happy times: during the first six months of 1942, a force of only 21 U-boats sank more than 500 American ships, most of them off the eastern seaboard of the U.S.A. and in the Caribbean.

Despite its previous practice of patrolling to the middle of the Atlantic, where the British assumed operational responsibility, the American lack of initial capability resulted directly from the continued U.S. Navy disbelief in the effectiveness of the convoy system by comparison with offensive use of hunter/killer groups of destroyers to search out and destroy U-boats. It was soon clear that this was a completely inefficient way to operate ships optimized for fleet tasks especially, as was soon proved by events, as the environs of a convoy were the best place to find U-boats. This persuaded the Americans to adopt a different tactic: the British had already ordered 50 escort destroyers from U.S. yards, and the U.S. Navy then gladly adopted this slower but more capable dedicated anti-submarine warship. The U.S. Navy initially ordered 200 of the ships for its own use, and by 1943 orders had increased to more than 1,000.

During 1942 the Allied situation in the Atlantic was critical. In 1941 the Germans had sunk 4.328 million tons of British shipping, about half to U-boats and the other half to mines, aircraft and surface raiders. In 1942, the U-boats were responsible for more than 6 million of the 7.79 million tons of shipping lost. And while the U-boat strength had been 91 boats at the beginning of the year it amounted to 212 operational boats by the end of the year despite the loss of 87 boats during this 12-month period. The German war effort was now based largely on the need to secure victory in Europe before the

Americans could bring their huge resources of manpower and industry into play against Germany, and the Germans calculated that they would have to sink at least 800,000 tons of shipping per month to achieve their object of starving the British into submission and preventing the arrival of substantial U.S. forces: during 1942 the Germans seemed to be well on target, for the Allied loss rate was running at 650,000 tons per month. In this decidedly dangerous grand strategic situation, the Allies survived by the replacement of the sunk merchant tonnage (the Liberty and Victory class of standardized ships that could be built quickly and economically) and through the fact that the British escort building programmes were beginning to bear fruit in this period with the delivery of an increasing number of River-class frigates and other ships, all equipped with increasingly sophisticated electronic systems and weapons.

LEFT
The Indonesian submarine
Cakra, *ex-yard No.135,*
during sea trials in the
Baltic Sea.

OPPOSITE
Pijao *(SS28), a Type 209/1-*
class patrol submarine of the
Colombian navy.

The Nazario Sauro *(S 518) is the lead unit of a four-submarine class of notably small Italian boats optimized for operations in the particular conditions of the Mediterranean.*

Exaggerated claims for tonnages sunk persuaded the U-boat arm's command that the increased target of 800,000 tons per month was almost being reached, and the campaign against Allied merchant shipping was therefore maintained at as high a pitch as possible. The Germans anticipated that two developments would tip the tactical balance strongly in the U-boat's favour: these were the acoustically homing torpedo to increase the likelihood of securing a decisive hit, and the radar detector to reduce the likelihood of U-boats being caught unawares on the surface by radar-fitted Allied warships and, increasingly, specialized anti-submarine aircraft that could swoop down for the kill with little or no warning. The appearance of these two new devices came at about the same time as two Allied failures. First, in June 1942, came the general shift of U.S. escort forces from the Atlantic to Pacific that was currently believed to be the more dangerous theatre, and second was the reduction in the proportion of available escort forces allocated to North Atlantic convoys so that there could be a strengthening of the escort forces for the military convoys preparing for the Allied invasion of French North-West Africa scheduled for November 1942. The effect of the German technical developments and the thinning of the Allied defences was a severe swing of the balance toward the Germans that was offset, at first only partially, by the advent of the first Allied support groups. Made possible by the moderately large numbers of new escort vessels coming into service under increasingly experienced commanders, these groups were designed to hunt and kill U-boats drawn to convoys. The convoys' own close escort forces concentrated on the immediate protection of their convoys, leaving the support groups to operate at a longer radius to detect U-boats as they approached and then to prosecute their contacts over a protracted period without having to worry about convoy protection.

By the start of 1943 the two sides were nicely balanced except for the edge provided to the Allies by the availability of long-range aircraft fitted with increasingly sophisticated radar. Despite this fact, it was the Germans who achieved the first major success of the year when, in March, they used intelligence information to ensure the interception by 39 submarines of 77 ships (52 in a slow convoy and 25 in a fast convoy): for the loss of only three of their own number, the U-boats sank 21 ships totalling 140,000 tons. This was without doubt the high point of the German effort in the Battle of the Atlantic. However, the German success in the March 1943 battle was soon overturned as the escort carriers and support groups diverted to the landings in French North-West Africa returned to the role of hunting and killing U-boats, and as the British introduced centimetric-wavelength radar for the ASV (Air-to-Surface Vessel) role: this radar possessed good performance and, perhaps more importantly, could not be detected by the Germans' current generation of radar warning systems. The result was a sharp increase in the number of U-boats lost to British air attack, especially as they transited to and from their operational areas on the surface and under the supposed cover of darkness.

The change in fortune became evident in May 1943, when another great convoy battle occurred but resulted this time in the loss of only a few merchant ships for the sinking of eight out of 12 attacking submarines as the result of the intervention of aircraft and two support groups. This disaster forced the German submarine command into two errors. Still believing that ample warning of a radar-assisted air attack was provided by its radar warning systems, the command ordered that the submarines should be fitted with increasingly heavy anti-aircraft armament (single 37-mm and/or twin or quadruple 20-mm cannon installations) so that they could fight it out with Allied anti-submarine aircraft, which carried only machine-guns that were outranged by the cannon and had also to undertake a vulnerable overflight of any target to release their bombs. This was the Germans' first mistake, for it ignored the possibility of surprise attacks before the anti-aircraft guns could be manned or brought to bear, and also the fact that any warplane that failed to achieve surprise could merely circle out of cannon range and radio for warship support: the U-boat had then to await the probability of surface attack by a specialized ship, or try to escape by undertaking a crash dive that gave the attacking warplane every opportunity to attack without interference in the time between the AA gunner's departure below deck and the U-boats disappearance under the water. The Germans' second mistake resulted from their belief in their own technical superiority: German scientists initially refused to believe that the British had introduced centimetric-wavelength radar, and therefore did not develop a radar warning system. This gave the British a decisive edge in making undetected radar-aided attacks at night and under adverse weather conditions.

These two German faults combined with the continued development of more effective anti-submarine warships and techniques by the British and Canadians, responsible for 98 per cent of oceanic escort, to tip the balance toward the Allies. In April 1943, the Germans had sunk 245,000 tons for the loss of 15 U-boats, but

Arica *(S 46), a Type 209
submarine of the Peruvian
Navy leaving Kiel after
building. 1974.*

in May the trend was reversed by the sinking of 165,000 tons for the loss of 40 U-boats, and in the following two months the trend was continued by the sinking of 18,000 tons for the loss of 17 U-boats during June and by the sinking of 123,000 tons for the loss of 37 U-boats during July. Dönitz now admitted that the U-boats had been bested, and called a temporary halt to the German offensive until better submarines and new weapons became available. The devices now adopted as standard features for Germany's new submarines and as retrofits on existing boats included the Schnorchel to allow the U-boat to replenish its air supply and run its battery-charging engines as it ran just below the surface, the Pillenwerfer ASDIC-spoofing chemical compound that could be fired into the water off the submarine, and the coating of periscopes and even the hull in rubberized compounds in the hope that these would absorb rather than reflect electro-magnetic and acoustic energy.

However, Germany's greatest hope was the successful development and production of the Walter propulsion system, which was basically a closed-cycle turbine system burning diesel oil and oxygen from the breakdown of concentrated hydrogen peroxide to provide high power levels independent of atmospheric oxygen. This opened the possibility of true submarine rather than submersible operations, freeing the submarine from the chance of detection by radar and offering, when the system was installed in a streamlined hull, submerged speeds at least equal to surfaced speeds. The Walter propulsion system had first been tested in 1940, and made its production debut on the Type XVIIA coastal U-boat, of which four examples were completed in 1943 with a propulsion arrangement that geared two Walter turbine systems to one shaft for a submerged speed of 26kt on 5,000hp (3730kW), which was by far the highest underwater speed attained by any

submarine up to that time. This type of true submarine performance created the possibility of a revitalized capability against Allied convoys, and in an effort to introduce the new technology as rapidly as possible, design teams revised the Type XVIIA design into the Type XVIIB and Type XVIIG designs with only one Walter turbine for the still very remarkable submerged speed of 21.5kt on 2,500hp (1865kW).

Germany's main problem was now that which typified many of the country's other very advanced weapons introduced in this and later stages of World War II: firstly these weapons were very expensive (in terms of money, time and resources) to develop and secondly they were pressed into production before all their teething problems had been overcome. So far as the Walter-powered U-boat was concerned, the main teething problems yet to be solved were the production and storage of the concentrated hydrogen peroxide: this was about eight times more expensive to manufacture than diesel oil, and for storage required a very high level of cleanliness to prevent rapid decomposition and spontaneous combustion. This problem was exacerbated by the Walter system's prodigious thirst for concentrated hydrogen peroxide, which was known to the German navy as Ingolin: the Type XVIIB-class U-boat carried 55 tons of Ingolin, which provided a range of 114 miles (183km) at a speed of 20kt. The submarine also possessed a secondary diesel and electric propulsion arrangement rated at 210 and 77hp (156.5 and 57.5kW) respectively for surfaced and submerged speeds of 8.5 and 5kt as well as surfaced and submerged ranges of 3,000 and 40 miles (4828 and 64km).

These problems made it dangerous to rely on the large-scale use of Walter-powered U-boats, and in July 1943 Dönitz

Launch of the Leonardo da Vinci *(S 520), a Sauro-class submarine for the Italian navy. November 1974.*

16kt, surfaced and submerged ranges of 11,150 and 285 miles (17945 and 460km) respectively at speeds of 12 and 6kt, and an armament of six 21-in (533-mm) tubes in the bows for 23 torpedoes (or 12 torpedoes and 12 mines) complemented by four 30-mm anti-aircraft cannon in two remotely controlled twin mountings nicely faired into the front and rear upper corners of the conning tower. Other major improvements were all-welded construction from eight prefabricated sections, an upgraded Schnorchel system that allowed unlimited submerged running of the diesel engines for a speed of 12kt, provision of two 113-hp (84.25-kW) creeper electric motors for silent running at a maximum of 5kt, and a powered torpedo reload system to speed this all-important process.

Dönitz told Hitler that German yards could deliver these improved U-boats from November 1944, but Hitler demanded earlier delivery through the adoption of Nazi rather than standard German shipbuilding methods. As a result, construction of the Type XXI-class U-boats became the responsibility of a system that paralleled construction of the obsolete Type VIIC class with that of the Type XXI by teams combining one-third skilled personnel with two-thirds unskilled labour. Even if it had worked, this system could not have succeeded in its primary objective as the German air force had priority for many of the strategic materials that were needed and the German army for the men who would have been required to crew the new U-boats that, Dönitz estimated, would be completed at the rate of 27 boats per month in the second half of 1943, rising to 30 boats per month in 1945.

These changes further diminished the U-boat arm's overall efficiency, and even the Schnorchel was in many ways unfortunate as

suggested to Hitler that it would be better to concentrate on an interim type known as the Electro boat that could bridge the gap between the standard Schnorchel-equipped U-boat and the planned Walter-powered U-boats. The first of this interim series was the Type XXI class, which was a conventionally powered ocean-going U-boat with a number of improved features including a well streamlined hull and conning tower to reduce submerged drag, and treble battery capacity for greater underwater endurance at higher speed. In theory, such a development had been available for some time, and the deployment of such U-boats during 1944 would have given the Germans enormous tactical advantages.

The Type XXI-class U-boat had surfaced and submerged displacements of 1,621 and 1,819 tons, a crew of 57, a propulsion arrangement that combined two 2,000-hp (1490-kW) diesel engines and 2,500-hp (1865-kW) electric motors for surfaced and submerged speeds of 15.5 and its ability to provide comparatively safe underwater movement removed the chance for the high-speed surface manoeuvring that had often given the German submarines an edge in their battles with convoys and their escorts. Further Allied developments also resulted in radar that could detect a Schnorchel in smooth conditions, and the Foxer towed decoy for acoustic homing torpedoes.

From the middle of 1943 the invasion of Italy by the Allies, and then their slow progress northward along the peninsula, gradually deprived the Germans of the bases they needed for submarine operations in the eastern Mediterranean, and then the July and August 1944 invasions of north-west and southern France removed the bases that were most favourable for operations in the Atlantic and western Mediterranean respectively. As a result, the Mediterranean became an Allied lake, and in northern waters the U-boats were forced back to their original German bases, requiring them once more to undertake the long and dangerous trip round the north of Scotland. Thus the only areas in which the U-boats were still dangerous foes were the Norwegian Sea and Arctic Ocean, in which they continued to achieve a measure of success against the Allied convoys plying the route to the ports of the northern U.S.S.R. The Germans were therefore compelled to turn their attention increasingly to a number of midget submarine classes that could only operate in sheltered waters, but although built in large numbers these Molch, Hecht, Seehund, Biber, Marder and Neger types proved almost wholly ineffective in real terms. The Type XXIII coastal and Type XXI ocean submarines with Walter propulsion began to reach service only in the last weeks of the war, so despite their

technical sophistication they became available too late and in numbers too small to have any effect on the outcome of the U-boat war.

The U-boat effort had been so close to success in May 1943 but then ended in total decline during May 1945, when the German surrender at the end of World War II compelled all submarines at sea to surface, fly a black flag, and then search out the Allied warships that would accept their surrender.

The Mediterranean was vital to British war plans, and Italy's declaration of war in June 1941 led the British to fear a German and Italian submarine campaign on their naval units and convoy routes all along the Mediterranean. Fortunately for the British, the Italians instead sent the best of their submarines and commanders through the Strait of Gibraltar to operate in the central Atlantic from a base at Bordeaux, and the Germans decided not to weaken their North Atlantic offensive by diverting boats to the Mediterranean. This left the British to use their own submarines for the interdiction of Italian shipping moving men, equipment and supplies from Italy to North Africa. Despite the operational difficulties of the theatre, in which aircraft were seldom far for the scene of any naval activity and could spot a submarine down to about 50ft (15m) in virtually all conditions compared with only periscope depth in the North Sea, and 30ft (9m) in the north Atlantic, in both cases under ideal conditions, the British submarines exacted a very high toll from the Italians.

The British submarines initially used in the Mediterranean were the boats of the O, P and R classes, which were easy to spot not only because of their comparatively large size but also by the fact that their external bunkerage tended to leak oil. Even

so, the success rate of the boats was high despite these factors and also the fact that up to February 1941 it remained British policy not to sink merchant shipping without a warning. By May 1941 British submarines operating from Gibraltar, Malta and Alexandria had sunk more than 100,000 tons of Italian shipping, and in the middle months of the same year the boats sank another 150,000 tons. The British success rate imposed a very severe strain on Germano-Italian relations, the Germans accusing the Italians of delivering wholly inadequate quantities of equipment and supplies to their joint forces in North Africa. It was at this point that the Germans decided to intervene more forcefully by introducing some of their own submarines into the theatre.

The effects of this change were soon evident: in November 1941 U-boats sank the aircraft carrier HMS *Ark Royal* and the battleship HMS *Barham*, and in the following month sank the cruiser HMS *Galatea*. Further misery was added by the activities of Italian human torpedoes, which were known to their originators as maiale (pigs) and used with great courage and imagination: in December 1941 two of these craft penetrated into Alexandria harbour and inflicted severe damage on the battleships HMS *Queen Elizabeth* and HMS *Valiant*.

The events of late 1941 in the Mediterranean coincided with the beginning of the Japanese onslaught through the Pacific and into South-East Asia, and an immediate British response was the despatch to this theatre of most of the surviving surface warships from the Mediterranean, leaving the initiative in the Mediterranean to the Germans and Italians. British strength in the theatre now rested almost entirely with the surviving

submarines, which continued to decimate Axis supply convoys and occasional surface warships despite the activities of large numbers of German warplanes. Even so, the British boats achieved notable offensive successes and also performed wonders in running essential supplies into Malta, which was now under Axis blockade. By the middle of 1942 the submarines had delivered 65,000 tons of fuel, food, equipment and medical supplies in to the island. Thereafter the situation eased as the Axis forces in North Africa finally went over to the strategic defensive after September 1942 and were defeated in May 1943.

When Japan entered World War II with virtually simultaneous attacks against the Americans in Hawaii and the Philippines and against the British in Hong Kong and Malaya, its main naval effort was launched against the ships of the U.S. Pacific Fleet in Pearl Harbor. This attack wrought such devastation on the Pacific Fleet's primary surface warships that the Americans were forced to revise their strategic thinking to exploit the capabilities of their surviving assets, namely three large aircraft carriers and most of the U.S. Navy's current strength of 113 submarines. Some 64 of these were obsolete World War I boats and therefore capable of little more than training in coastal waters, while nine other boats were large submarine cruisers whose mechanical unreliability prevented Pacific operations. This left the U.S. Navy with 40 modern boats, pending the arrival of more modern boats, of which 73 had already been authorized and 32 were already under construction. There was little scope for American submarine operations in the Atlantic, so the majority of the available and forthcoming boats was available for Pacific fleet service. The number of American yards able to construct submarines had shrunk to

Mochishio (SS 274), a Yuushio-class patrol submarine of the Japanese Maritime Self-Defense Force. 1981.

Najad, a Nacken-class submarine of the Swedish navy.

The USS Haddo *was a unit of the U.S. Navy's Permit class of nuclear-powered attack submarines. The class was thus named after the loss of the vessel bearing the name of the original class, USS Thresher.*

three between the world wars, but this number was rapidly doubled as two commercial builders and one navy yard developed a submarine-building capability, and the possibility of slowed delivery of boats as a result of delays in diesel engine and/or electric motor manufacture was avoided by the general strength of American industry, which could deliver the

required engines and motors without any major difficulty.

The decision that the Pacific was to be the primary area for American submarine operations made it feasible to standardize a number of features for the new boats, which needed good habitability, considerable surface range, and a large volume for the carriage of considerable stores and as many reload torpedoes so that the least possible time need be wasted in transits between bases and operational areas in the huge expanses of the Pacific. This philosophy had been foreshadowed in the 1920s and 1930s in the construction of the 10 P-class boats that were launched between 1935 and 1937, the 16 S-class boats launched between 1937 and 1939, and the 12 T-class boats launched between 1939 and 1941. The last of these classes included the *Tautog*, which was the most successful American submarine of World War II with a record that included the sinking of no fewer than 26 Japanese ships, and its general specification included a crew of 85, a submerged displacement of 2,370 tons, a propulsion arrangement that paired two 2,700-hp (2015-kW) diesel engines and two 1,370-hp (1021.5-kW) electric motors for surfaced and submerged speeds of 20 and 8.75kt respectively, and an armament of 10 21-in (533-mm) torpedo tubes (six bow and four stern) for 24 torpedoes complemented by one 5-in (127-mm) deck gun and four machine guns.

Existing experience with modern ocean-going submarines permitted the U.S. Navy to agree early in 1941 the basically standardized design of a submarine for large-scale production. This concept was based on a diesel-electric propulsion arrangement (diesel generators driving electric motors coupled to the two shafts through reduction gearing) and a hull of all-

welded construction allowing a maximum diving depth of 300ft (91m), and was produced in three closely related subvariants as the Gato, Balao and Tench classes of 73, 132 and 30 boats respectively, some of the last being completed after the end of the war. The design was based on a double hull (strengthened in the Balao and Tench classes for a maximum diving depth of 400ft/122m) divided into eight watertight compartments, and had four fuel tanks and eight ballast tanks. The primary data for the Balao class included a submerged displacement of 2,425 tons, length of 311ft 9in (95.0m) with a beam of 27ft 3in (8.3m) and draught of 15ft 3in (4.65m), a two-shaft propulsion arrangement that combined General Motors or Fairbanks Morse diesel engines for 5,400hp (4025kW) and two General Electric or Elliot Motor electric motors for 2,740hp (2045kW), surfaced and submerged speeds of 20.25 and 8.75kt respectively, a crew of 85, and an armament of 10 21-in (533-mm) tubes (six forward and four aft) for 24 torpedoes complemented by one deck gun, which was variously a 5-in (127-m) weapon, 4-in (102-mm) weapon or 3-in (76-mm) AA weapon supplemented during the course of the war by AA weapons up to 40-mm calibre.

The submarine strength eventually offered by the later pre-war boats and the units of the Gato, Balao, and Tench classes was very considerable, but was offset in the first two years of the Pacific war by defects in the magnetic fuses of their torpedoes, the same difficulty that had been encountered by the Germans earlier in the war.

The single most characteristic feature of American submarine construction in World War II was virtually complete standardization. This simplified training and the equipping of the boats as well as the

boats' construction on a production-line basis. This was most certainly not true of the Japanese, who had devoted much of their pre-war construction capacity to several submarine cruiser classes. In the late 1930s, though, the Japanese navy finally appreciated that it lacked adequate medium-sized submarines for oceanic duties, and addressed this failing in 1940 with an order for the first nine of an eventually planned 88 but actual 18 Type K6-class boats. Although comparatively small and therefore lacking in habitability, even by Japanese standards that were considerably more austere than those of the Americans, the boats were considered very successful, and may be likened to the first units of the Gato class in range capability. The basic designs for the Type K6 design included a crew of 62, surfaced and submerged displacements of 1,115 and 1,447 tons, a length of 264ft 1in (80.5m) with a beam of 22ft 11.5in (7.0m) and a draught of 13ft 1.5in (4.0m), a two-shaft propulsion arrangement that paired diesel engines for 4,200hp (3131.5kW) and electric motors for 1,200hp (895kW) for surfaced and submerged speeds of 19.75 and 8kt respectively, surfaced and submerged ranges of 11,000 miles (17700km) at 12kt and 45 miles (52km) at 5kt respectively, and an armament of four 21-in (533-mm) torpedo tubes (all bow) for 10 torpedoes and complemented by one 3-in (76-mm) anti-aircraft gun and two 25-mm cannon.

In the same year the Japanese ordered the first nine of a planned 27 but actual 18 boats of the Type KS class, which was a somewhat smaller scouting submarine with a submerged displacement of 782 tons and an armament of four 21-in (533-mm) torpedo tubes for eight torpedoes. It is hard to see how these small submarines could ever have been of any real utility except for

The USS Bremerton *(SSN-698), a Los Angeles-class nuclear-powered attack submarine of the U.S. Navy, underway during sea trials in 1980.*

USS Providence *(SSN-719),*
a Los Angeles-class submarine
of the U.S. Navy.

patrol around Japanese-held islands, for
their surfaced range was only 3,500 miles
(5635km) at 12kt.

The boats of these two classes, one
possessing a genuine ocean-going capability
and the other little more than a coastal
capability, were perhaps considered as
oddities in the Japanese thinking of this
time, for during 1941 the Japanese
returned to the very large ocean-going

submarine with considerable range and
endurance, heavy armament and, in most
cases, provision for a small
reconnaissance/spotter floatplane that
could be dismantled for accommodation in
a watertight hangar. These classes
comprised the planned 14 but actual six
boats of the Type B2 class with a
submerged displacement of 3,700 tons and
an armament of six 21-in (533-mm)

torpedo tubes for 17 torpedoes, the
planned 10 but actual three boats of the
Type C2 class with a submerged
displacement of 3,564 tons and armament
of eight 21-in (533-mm) torpedo tubes for
20 torpedoes but no seaplane, the single
Type A2-class boat that was a virtual copy
of the three Type A1-class boats of 1937
with a submerged displacement of 4,172
tons and an armament of six 21-in (533-

FAR LEFT
*Hatches for Tomahawk
missiles aboard USS*
Oklahoma City *(SSN-723),
a Los Angeles-class
submarine.*

LEFT
The USS Oklahoma City.

mm) torpedo tubes for 18 torpedoes, the
planned 32 but actual three boats of the
Type B3 class with a submerged
displacement of 3,688 tons and an
armament of six 21-in (533-mm) torpedo
tubes for 19 torpedoes, and the planned
45 but actual three boats of the generally
similar Type C3 class with a submerged
displacement of 3,644 tons and an
armament of six 21-in (533-mm) torpedo
tubes for 19 torpedoes. The raison dêtre
for these classes can be found in the
Japanese belief that the outcome of any
Pacific war would be decided by a fleet
action between the Japanese and American
surface fleets. The task of the large
submarines was therefore to reconnoitre for
the Combined Fleet and then, after
reporting fleet strength, position and
course, attack with the intention of sinking
as many American warships as possible.

The Japanese also saw that they might

not be able to create the opportunity for the decisive surface battle, and therefore planned an alternative means to tackle the American ships in harbour. This led to the construction of several midget submarine classes that could be carried by large submarines or seaplane carriers to points off the major American bases, where they would be launched to penetrate the harbour defences and attack the American warships lying at anchor. The first of these midget submarine designs was the Type A class that appeared in 1936 with a two-man crew, a submerged displacement of 46 tons, a 600-hp (447-kW) electric motor for surfaced and submerged speeds of 23 and 19kt respectively, a range of 160 miles (257km) at 6kt submerged, and an armament of two 18-in (457-mm) torpedo tubes for two torpedoes. Some 41 such boats were completed, but after their failure in the Pearl Harbor operation, in which one boat was lost before the main attack was launched, the surviving boats were used only for harbour defence. Further development led in 1942 to just one Type B-class boat to an improved Type A-class design, and then to the 15 Type C-class boats with slightly greater length and displacement to allow the incorporation of a 40-hp (29.8-kW) diesel engine that provided surfaced propulsion as well as battery recharging capability for surfaced and submerged ranges of 300 and 120 miles (485 and 195km) respectively. The Type C- class boats were no more successful than the Type A-class units.

Rather than their technical features, it was their tactical use that was the main problem for Japanese submarines. The overriding desire to bring about the decisive fleet battle led the Japanese navy to ignore the submarine's potential for a campaign against targets other than

warships, which rapidly swelled to numbers far greater than those of U.S. warships and were vital to the long-range amphibious warfare with which the Americans finally checked and pushed the Japanese back. The Japanese also compounded this error in offensive planning with the reciprocal error in defensive thinking: as they saw little purpose in attacking anything but targets, they imagined that the Americans would target Japanese warships to the exclusion of all other shipping.

The Americans saw right from the beginning, though, that transport ships, which were initially unescorted and then only indifferently escorted, were the weakest point in Japan's attempt to create and then hold a strategic perimeter inside which normal mercantile operations could continue. Japan's war-making capability was almost completely reliant on the transmission of raw materials and oil to the Japanese home islands, and on the despatch from Japan of men, weapons, ammunition, equipment and supplies. Thus the Americans decided on the earliest possible severing of Japan's maritime lines of communication to starve its war industries in the home islands and to isolate its island bastions from reinforcement and resupply. The very real nature of the American threat is evident in the fact that Japan relied on sea transport for 20 per cent of its food, 24 per cent of its coal, 88 per cent of its iron ore, 90 per cent of its oil, and 100 per cent of commodities such as rubber, tin and other materials required by industry and transport.

The American campaign to sever Japan's maritime lines of communication was so successful that it is arguable that Japan had been effectively beaten but refused to concede the fact before the dropping of the atomic bombs on Hiroshima and Nagasaki in August 1945.

In 1939 Japan had possessed 2,337 merchant ships but by August 1945 had only 231. Many of the ships within the Japanese total of 4 million tons were lost to air attack, but the majority were sunk primarily by American, but to a lesser extent British and Dutch, submarine attack, directly with torpedoes or indirectly with mines. The Americans lost 60 submarines during the war, although the Japanese had claimed 486, but the loss of these boats and their crews represents a relatively small price for a huge victory that was achieved for the loss of comparatively small numbers of men.

It should not be imagined, though, that the U.S. Navy's submarines confined their attacks to the Japanese merchant navy. American submarines operated scouting and aircrew recovery lines for the major offensive operations of the Pacific Fleet, and also played a major part in sinking Japanese warships, including eight aircraft carriers and 12 cruisers. The most striking example of the former was the sinking of the huge *Shinano* by the USS *Archerfish* in November 1944, and a fine example of the latter was the destruction of the heavy cruisers *Atago* and *Maya* in October 1944 in an ambush by the USS *Dace* and USS *Darter*, which also severely damaged a third cruiser in the same action.

The Americans introduced the wolf pack concept to their Pacific submarine operations during 1943, but by this time were so rampant that a three-boat group was thought sufficient to defeat a convoy supported by the poor escort vessels that the Japanese had started to construct too late.

Although the American submarine arm came to be the complete master of the Pacific, this should not hide the fact that the Japanese boats did achieve some notable successes: in August 1942 the I-26 severely

A Kilo-class diesel-powered attack submarine of the Soviet navy at sea in 1986.

damaged the aircraft carrier USS *Saratoga*; in September 1942 the I-15 severely damaged the battleship USS *North Carolina*; and in September 1942 the I-19 sank the aircraft carrier USS *Wasp*. Such instances were few and far between, for in overall terms the considerable size of the Japanese submarines and the guileless tactics of their commanders greatly eased the task of American escort forces. Arguably the most successful of such warships was the destroyer escort USS *England*, which achieved the destruction of six Japanese submarines in just 12 days during May 1944.

Not all Japanese naval officers were as tactically blind to the capabilities of the submarine as the naval high command. Many Japanese submariners urged attacks on targets other that the Pacific Fleet's large warships. However, it was not until late in 1942, when the significance of the first American amphibious assaults on island groups in the Central Pacific began at last to pierce the confidence of the naval high command, that a change was finally

considered. Yet even then the revised tactical plan for submarine operations was misconceived: the naval high command, appreciating the importance of American amphibious assaults, ordered the submarines to undertake what would have been virtually suicidal attacks on the very well protected ships of the landing forces, and also to transport men and equipment into bases that might become the next targets for American attack. The use of standard submarines for transport was not cost-effective, so the Japanese started to construct specialized transport submarines. The first of these were the 12 out of a projected 104 units of the Type D1 class with surfaced and submerged displacements of 1,779 and 2,215 tons respectively, considerable range, armament limited to one 5.5-in (140-mm) deck gun and two 25-mm cannon, and provision for a payload that could comprise 82 tons of freight or 110 men landed with the aid of two 14.5-ft (4.4-m) boats. Given the intense rivalry between the Japanese navy and the Japanese army, which believed that the navy never provided adequate support for its

forces, the army also decided to construct transport submarines. This led to the creation of the Yu 1 class, of which 12 were built. These were smaller boats than their naval counterparts, with a submerged displacement of 370 tons including 40 tons of freight.

The Japanese navy operated several other submarine classes in the later stages of World War II. The two most extreme of these were the Type STo and Kaiten types. Ordered in 1942 as the largest submarines planned up to that time, the Type STo class was proposed as more than 18 units of which only three were completed with a crew of 144 men, a submerged displacement of 6,560 tons, the enormous surfaced range of 37,500 miles (60350km) at 14kt, and an armament that included eight 21-in (533-mm) torpedo tubes for 20 torpedoes, one 5.5-in (140-mm) deck gun, 10 25-mm anti-aircraft cannon in two triple and four single mountings, and most impressively of all three special attack seaplanes (four torpedoes and 15 bombs were carried for these) designed for attacks on high-value

targets such as American capital ships and the lock gates of the Panama Canal.

The Kaiten types, of which four classes were constructed, were intended for the kamikaze role, and were therefore suicide craft based on the design of the Japanese torpedo. The only operational model was the Kaiten 4 class, of which 419 were completed with a conventional torpedo motor rather than the hydrogen peroxide motors of the experimental Kaiten 2 and Kaiten 3 classes. Major design and construction resources were expended on these essentially defensive craft, which

achieved no successes.

In World War II the Japanese lost 149 of their 245 major boats excluding midget types and the German and Italian boats that were taken over in very small numbers.

Even as the last stages of the war in the Pacific were taking place, Allied technical officers were examining German ports, research centres and construction facilities for information about the last generation of U-boats, and in particular the conventionally powered Type XXI class and the Walter-powered Type XVII and Type XXIII classes. The Allied nations

teams first concentrated on the Type XXI-class design that was currently the most advanced submarine of its type anywhere in the world. The main improvements embodied in these boats were a streamlined hull with the minimum number of excrescences (including the deck gun), the streamlining of the conning tower (including its platforms, periscope standards and various antennae) into a long sail, and the Schnorchel that became known to the Americans as a snorkel and the British as a snort.

The introduction of these fruits of

German research and development allowed the design and construction of new submarine classes with underwater performance characterized by higher speed, quieter running and greater endurance/range. The introduction of the new classes bought time for the primary submarine-minded countries (the U.K., the U.S.A. and now the U.S.S.R.) to plan further developments. These included a practical investigation of the Walter propulsion arrangement. The U.S.A. soon dropped the concept because of the dangers inherent in the system, and by the mid-1950s both the U.K. and the U.S.S.R. had also decided that the adoption of the Walter system was not a satisfactory solution to the question of how to produce true surface-independent submarines. The solution already under active development by the U.S.A. was a nuclear propulsion arrangement in place of the diesel and electric or diesel-electric systems used in most recent submarines. Such an arrangement was based on a heavily shielded nuclear reactor whose controllable heat output was used within a closed-cycle system to generate the steam powering turbines for propulsion and/or the generation of electricity before being condensed back into water for return to the heat exchanger attached to the reactor.

As this longer-term solution to submarine propulsion was being developed, design teams pressed on with the further evolution of conventionally powered boats. The U.S. Navy's response to German developments in World War II was the GUPPY (Greater Underwater Propulsive Power) programme, which led to the revision of most Gato, Balao and Tench-class boats with a lengthened and more streamlined hull and sail, larger batteries, and a snorkel. Others of these boats were revised for use in experimental programmes such as underway replenishment of oil and supplies at sea, and as the launch platform for guided missiles.

This last was of great significance, and began with the 1948–49 conversions of the USS *Carbonero* and USS *Cusk* to carry the Loon surface-to-surface missile developed from the Germans' Fieseler Fi 103 (V-1) flying bomb weapon. The trials confirmed the basic practicality of the concept and the U.S. Navy then undertook the development of the Regulus I, which was a substantial turbojet-powered missile intended for the anti-ship role, and the USS *Barbero* and USS *Tunny* were later adapted to carry two of these missiles in cylindrical hangars. Further development of the Regulus concept resulted in the considerably larger Regulus II with strategic capability, and as this more massive weapon could only be carried by larger submarines the U.S. Navy ordered the USS *Grayback* and USS *Growler*, which were constructed between 1952 and 1958 with two large cylindrical hangars in the forward casing. The Regulus II system was abandoned after only five years, but its submarines were retained for conversion as special forces transports.

The U.S.A.'s last conventionally powered submarines were the six Tang-class units constructed between 1949 and 1952, and finally the three Barbel-class units built between 1956 and 1959. The Tang-class design was modelled on that of the Type XXI class, and as such may be compared with that of the Soviet Whiskey class, which was built in considerably larger numbers although it was in no way as sophisticated a type as the American design. Although obsolescent by American standards at the time of its appearance, the Barbel-class design was interesting as it was the first design for an operational U.S. Navy boat combining several hitherto experimental features: these included the type of low-drag

The power and accuracy of modern wire-guided torpedoes is revealed by this aerial shot taken during trials of the British Spearfish torpedo, fired from the submerged submarine HMS Splendid. The torpedo had struck the obsolete destroyer Devonshire on the starboard quarter in line with the ship's machinery spaces.

LEFT
*A Tigerfish torpedo in the
racks in the torpedo-room
aboard a Royal Navy
nuclear-powered attack
submarine.*

OPPOSITE
*An Upholder-class
submarine of the Royal
Navy.*

The French nuclear-powered strategic missile submarine Le Redoutable *(S 611) cruising on the surface in 1969.*

teardrop hull first tested in the U.S. Navy's experimental USS *Albacore* launched in 1953, a single large propeller turning comparatively slowly for reduced operating noise, all the control systems centralized in an attack centre for greater optimization of operational capability and, as a retrofit, the diving planes on the bows replaced by planes on the sides of the sail.

The period following World War II was marked by a rapid decline in the level of cordiality between the U.S.A. and the U.S.S.R., which were the modern world's only superpowers, and the accompanying emergence of a cold war between the superpowers and their allies. The U.S.S.R. had rapidly followed the U.S.A.'s lead into nuclear weapons capability, and the U.S.A. feared a major air assault with such weapons. Early warning was therefore of paramount importance for defence, and the U.S.A. made extensive use of ships and submarines fitted with long-range surveillance radar for timely warning of any imminent Soviet attack on the continental U.S.A. One of the most fascinating of these boats, most of

which were converted from conventionally powered attack submarines, was the USS *Triton*, which was built in 1959 as one of the first nuclear-powered boats and was for its time the largest submarine in the world with a submerged displacement of 7,773 tons and a two-shaft nuclear propulsion arrangement for surfaced and submerged speeds of 27 and 20kt respectively.

In the U.S.S.R., submarine developments from 1944 (revised from 1945 with information about the Type XXI class) led to the delivery from the early

The Western world's primary designers and manufacturers of torpedoes are, in addition to the U.K. and the U.S.A., France, Germany, Italy and Sweden. This is an example of a modern Italian weapon, the Whitehead A 184 torpedo.

1950s of the very large Whiskey class of conventionally powered submarines for the attack role, to which were later added the radar picket role and, from 1961, the missile launch role in four and 12 boats respectively. Production of this class eventually amounted to 236 boats, and from 1961 moderately large numbers of the boats were transferred to friendly nations.

The next major type to appear in Soviet service was the Zulu class, whose operational capability with a conventional propulsion arrangement was confirmed in 1952 after early efforts to create a version of the Walter propulsion system. Some 26 of the type were built as longer-ranged equivalents of the medium-range Whiskey class, and of these boats six were completed or converted as strategic missile submarines, with the rear part of their sails adapted with vertical launchers for two ballistic missiles. Built at about the same time to a total of 22 units, the Golf class was basically an enlarged version of the Zulu-class design with a longer sail carrying three vertical-launch missiles.

The development of Soviet conventionally powered submarines continued with the Romeo class of which 17 were built between 1958 and 1961 as successors to the Whiskey class with two more torpedo tubes together with greater range and diving depth, the Quebec class of which 30 were built between 1954 and 1957 to replace the pre-war M-class boats in the coastal role and fitted with a closed-cycle propulsion arrangement, and the Foxtrot class of which 76 were built between 1958 and 1967 as successors to the Zulu class with reduced surface range but significantly improved underwater speed. The U.S.S.R. also moved into the development and construction of nuclear-powered submarines, but did not entirely abandon the conventionally powered submarine. Between the early 1970s and 1982, therefore, the Soviet navy received 18 Kilo-class submarines as successors to the Foxtrot-class boats with greater volume for improved habitability, larger battery capacity, and more reload weapons. The final development of Soviet conventional

submarine thinking was the Kilo class, which entered production in 1978 or 1979 with a considerably better hull form that the Tango class for significantly improved underwater speed.

Though the U.S.A. and the U.S.S.R. dominated the technological and constructional aspects of submarine development in the period after World War II, several other countries have also contributed. At the end of World War II, the U.K.'s most important submarines were those of the S and T classes, complemented during the late 1940s by a number of A-class boats designed in World War II for long-range operations in the Pacific but completed too late for this campaign. The S and earlier T-class boats were of riveted rather than welded construction, and were therefore deemed unsuitable for major development after the war even though five T-class boats were given a more streamlined casing, but eight of the later T-class boats and 14 of the 18 A-class boats were taken in hand during the 1950s for modernization along the lines of the American GUPPY

This is the French navy's Rubis (S 601), lead boat of the class that comprises the world's smallest nuclear-powered attack submarines.

system with a lengthened and more streamlined hull containing an uprated propulsion arrangement and more battery cells for a doubled submerged speed. This provided the Royal Navy with a useful attack submarine capability into the late 1950s. Further development was based on new construction in the form of the eight boats of the Porpoise class built between 1956 and 1961 to make full use of the lessons learned from captured German data and British post-war developments in the creation of a type notable for its generally good performance and exceptional quietness. Further development of the concepts embodied in the Porpoise class, individually small but collectively large, resulted in the Oberon class, of which 13 were built for the Royal Navy between 1957 and 1967, and another 14 completed for export customers. To complete the story of British conventional submarine design, mention must be made of the superb Upholder class ordered in the early 1980s to replace the Oberon class. Notably quiet and equipped with submarine-launched anti-ship missiles as well as advanced torpedoes, all controlled for a high-quality fire-control system, the boats have been truncated in production and operational service as a result of the peace dividend resulting from the collapse of the U.S.S.R. in the late 1980s and the effective end of the cold war.

At the end of World War II France was faced with the task of rebuilding not only the country's armed forces but also the industrial base necessary to equip these forces with weapons of indigenous design and manufacture. So far as its navy's submarine arm was concerned, a start was made with the receipt of four British S-class boats for training purposes and the completion to a modernized standard of five La Créole-class submarines from incomplete L'Aurore-class hulls that had survived the war. This bought time for French designers to assess the latest thinking in submarine theory, resulting in the six Narval-class ocean-going submarines completed in the period between 1957 and 1960, and the four Aréthuse-class sea-going submarines completed between 1957 and 1958 after design as the world's first dedicated hunter-killer submarines. Between 1964 and 1970, the Aréthuse class was supplemented and finally supplanted by the slightly large Daphné class, of which 11 were constructed as smaller counterparts to the Narval-class boats. Ten more Daphné-class boats were built in France for Pakistan (three), Portugal (four) and South Africa (three), and another four were produced under licence in Spain as S 61-class boats.

The three other northern European countries that have designed and built their own submarines are the Netherlands, Sweden and, inevitably, Germany. Dutch design and construction have been responsible for the four Dolfijn-class submarines with a unique triple hull design, the two Zwaardvis-class attack submarines, and the four Walrus-class boats of an improved attack type. Swedish design and construction have yielded the six boats of the Hajen class based on the Type XXI design, the six boats of the Draken class, the five boats of the Sjöormen class of teardrop-hulled attack submarine with an X-shaped arrangement of surfaces at the stern, the three boats of the smaller Näcken class of attack submarines, and the four advanced boats of the Västergötland class of attack submarines.

Once permitted from the mid-1950s, West Germany started to rebuild its armed forces with emphasis on the ground and air elements that would have to play a key part in the defence of West Germany, the most likely avenue for any Soviet-led communist offensive. The navy was not neglected, though, and plans were laid for the creation of small but high-quality elements responsible for operations in the western end of the Baltic Sea and in the southern part of the North Sea. Part of this capability was inevitably vested in a new submarine arm, and to provide an initial training capability, the West German navy raised two Type XXIII and one Type XXI submarines for reconstruction with the type of electric propulsion (the diesels being used only as generators) that has been used for all subsequent German submarine classes: the boats became the two Hai and one Wilhelm Bauer-class boats.

West Germany's first operational submarines were the three (originally to have been 12) units of the Type 201 coastal boat with a submerged displacement of only 433 tons, the high submerged speed of 17.5kt and the heavy armament of eight 21-in (533-mm) torpedo tubes for eight torpedoes, but only limited range and indifferent habitability for the crew of 21. Further development of the same basic concept led to the 11 units of the very slightly larger Type 205 class, which was not notably successful, and then the very successful Type 206 class of which 18 units were completed with features to reduce underwater noise and allow the use of advanced torpedoes receiving their guidance commands via a wire system from the submarine's fire-control computer. Germany's latest submarine class is the highly advanced Type 212 with hybrid fuel cell/battery propulsion for considerably

Despite a submerged displacement of only 2,670 tons and an overall length of just over 237ft (72m), the Rubis has good performance and overall capabilities, the boat's primary armament being 14 21.7-in (550-mm) heavyweight torpedoes launched through four bow tubes.

extended underwater endurance.

Design of these boats was undertaken by Ingenieurkontor Lübeck, which has become a world leader in the design of conventionally powered submarines that have secured very considerable success in the export and licence-built markets. Among IKL's designs are therefore the Type 207 class used by Denmark and Norway and the Type 209 used in a number of differently sized subvariants by Argentina, Brazil, Chile, Colombia, Ecuador, Greece, India, Indonesia, Israel, Peru, South Korea, Taiwan, Turkey and Venezuela.

The only southern European country to have designed and built advanced conventionally powered submarines is Italy, whose post-war career in this field started with the four Toti-class attack submarines

optimized for the coastal role and then progressed, via the four larger Sauro class and four Sauro (Improved) class attack submarines optimized for the sea-going role, to the S 90 class modern type with excellent capabilities.

Only one other country has designed and constructed advanced conventionally powered submarines, and that is Japan whose first post-war boat was the Oyashio completed in 1960 with a submerged displacement of 1,420 tons, a submerged speed of 19kt, and an armament of four 21-in (533-mm) torpedo tubes in the bows, and a wholly conservative design based on a whale-shaped hull. There followed the four submarines of the two-boat Hayashio and Natsushio classes with a shorter and fuller hull, good safety features and excellent

The USS Michigan *(SSBN 727) was the third unit of the superb* Ohio *class of nuclear-powered ballistic-missile submarines to be completed for the U.S. Navy by General Dynamics' Electric Boat Division.*

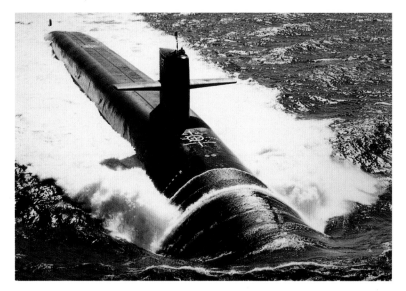

habitability. However, with a submerged displacement of only 800 and 850 tons respectively, the boasts of these two classes were limited to coastal operations. The size was nearly doubled in the five submarines of the Oshio class that followed between 1965 and 1969 as Japan's first post-war attack submarines of the ocean-going type, but Japanese submarine concepts finally began to reach maturity in 1971 with the delivery of the first of seven Uzushio-class boats with a teardrop-shaped hull, a displacement of 3,600 tons, a submerged speed of 20kt, and an armament of six 21-in (533-mm) torpedo tubes located amidships to leave the optimum bow location for the sonar. From 1980 there followed the 10 boats of the Yuushio class developed from the Uzushio class with deeper diving capability and

improved electronics, and the most modern of the Japanese submarine classes, entering service from 1990, is the six-strong Harushio class with a submerged displacement of 2,750 tons, a submerged speed of more than 20kt, and an armament of six 21-in (533-mm) torpedo tubes for wire-guided torpedoes as well as underwater-launched Harpoon anti-ship missiles.

Throughout this period the U.S.A. was forging ahead in the development of the nuclear-powered submarine initially for the attack role and then, in a very considerably enlarged form, for the ballistic missile launch role. The starting point for the concept of the dedicated attack (hunter-killer) submarine was the combination of high underwater performance (especially in speed and endurance/range) offered by

nuclear propulsion once effective quietening features had been developed, and the much enhanced ability to detect and track the enemy's submarines provided by modern sonar (sound navigation and ranging), as the Americans call ASDIC. These features became feasible in the early 1950s, and resulted in two pioneering boats, namely the USS *Nautilus* and the USS *Seawolf* as the world's first nuclear-powered submarines, in each case with an armament of six 21-in (533-mm) torpedo tubes in the bows for the targets located, localized and ranged by the advanced BQS-4 sonar. The first and considerably more successful of the two submarines was the USS *Nautilus*, which was commissioned in April 1955 with a Westinghouse S2W pressurized water-cooled reactor powering two sets of geared steam turbines delivering some 13,400hp (9990kW) to two propellers for a submerged speed of 23kt. The *Seawolf*, which was finally commissioned in March 1957, was less successful as a result of the poor performance of the General Electric S2G liquid sodium-cooled reactor powering two sets of geared steam turbines delivering some 13,000hp (9695kW) to two propellers for a submerged speed of about 20kt.

It was the *Nautilus* and its water-cooled reactor system that opened the way for succeeding generations of American nuclear-powered submarines. It is worth noting at this stage that this pioneering boat retained the type of hull/sail shape introduced by the Type XXI class although on a somewhat larger scale, as indicated by the submerged displacement of 4,092 tons. This greater size was dictated largely by the volume of the reactor system and its associated shielding, and meant that the boat did not possess the same level of underwater manoeuvrability as its predecessors, but experience soon showed that the greater

volume generated by the additional cross section right along the hull was vital to the success of the long submerged patrols made possible by the nuclear powerplant. The length of the sortie in a nuclear-powered boat was now limited not by considerations of energy and/or air but rather by the quantity of food that could be carried and by the habitability of the crew spaces: both of these factors were improved, the second virtually beyond measure, by the greater internal volume now available.

The first nuclear-powered production boats were the four units of the Skate class of attack submarines built between 1955 and 1959. Oddly enough, these were smaller boats approximating to the conventionally powered Tang class in overall dimensions, and had a smaller Westinghouse S3W or S4W reactor powering two sets of geared steam turbines delivering 6,600hp (4920kW) to two propellers for a submerged speed of about 20kt. The boats had the same BQS-4 sonar, but the armament was increased to eight 21-in (533-mm) torpedo tubes by the addition of two in the stern. The success of the Skate class paved the way for the U.S. Navy's complete move into nuclear propulsion for its submarines, and further development into larger and steadily more capable classes was based on the combination of the nuclear powerplant, in increasingly powerful and reliable forms and generally driving a single propeller, with the teardrop hull pioneered by the Albacore, and ever more sophisticated computer-assisted sonar systems relying increasingly on the passive mode for the detection and tracking of target submarines, whose range is acquired only at the last minute by the active ping that can reveal the presence of the ambusher.

The first of these new classes was the Skipjack class of six boats with a submerged speed of about 30kt and an armament of six 21-in (533-mm) bow torpedo tubes for 24 torpedoes, followed by the Thresher (later Permit) class of 11 boats with a submerged speed of about 27kt and an armament of four 21-in (533-mm) amidships tubes for 22 Mk 48 wire-guided torpedoes (or 18 torpedoes and four UUM-44 SUBROC underwater-launched rockets each carrying a small homing torpedo as payload) to allow the

ABOVE
Forward view aboard USS Ohio *(SSBN 726), an Ohio-class submarine at Groton, Connecticut showing a Trident C-4 launch tube.*

ABOVE LEFT
The missile compartment control and monitoring panel station aboard the USS Ohio.

With its buoyancy system, moving surfaces, powerplant, and communications operated with the aid of computers, the control room of a modern submarine is still a complex space, but is less cluttered than that of earlier-generation submarines. The diving planes are operated by a man at a car-type control

incorporation of larger and more sophisticated passive/active sonar in the optimum bow position. This class paved the way for the first very large class, which was the Sturgeon class of 42 boats possessing a submerged speed of about 26kt and an armament of four 21-in (533-mm) amidships tubes for 23 Mk 48 torpedoes or 19 torpedoes and four SUBROC weapons.

These boats were completed between 1966 and 1975, and were the mainstay of the US Navy's hunter-killer submarine capability until the later 1970s, when the first of an eventual 62 Los Angeles-class submarines entered service. Completed between 1976 and 1997, these boats each have a submerged displacement in the order of 6,925 tons, a submerged speed of 32kt on the 35,000hp (26095kW) supplied to one propeller by the two geared steam turbines powered by one S6G reactor, and an armament of four 21-in (533-mm) amidships tubes for a total of 26 weapons, whose versatile fit can include Mk 48 torpedoes, UGM-84 Harpoon submarine-launched anti-ship missiles and BGM-109 Tomahawk cruise missiles in a typical mix of 14, four and eight respectively: the later boats also have vertical launch tubes for 12 Tomahawk missiles, allowing the weapons launched through the amidships tubes to be concentrated on the Mk 48 and Harpoon types, although these can be replaced by up to 78 mines for further expansion of the submarine's operational capabilities.

From the mid-1990s, the Los Angeles-class boats are to be supplemented and eventually replaced by the Seawolf class with a submerged displacement of 9,150 tons, a submerged speed of 35kt driven by a single pumpjet propulsor powered by the 60,000hp (44735kW) provided by the S6W reactor. The armament of these boats is eight 25.6-in (650-mm) tubes for a total of about 50 tube-launched weapons or a considerably larger number of mines.

The American move into nuclear-powered attack submarines was followed by the U.S.S.R., whose first such class was the November class, of which 12 were delivered between 1958 and 1964. The type had a submerged displacement of 5,300 tons, a submerged speed in the order of 30kt on the 30,000hp (22370kW) delivered to two propellers by the geared steam turbines powered by a single reactor, and an armament of eight 21-in (533-mm) bow torpedo tubes for 24 torpedoes. The type was not notably successful because of its considerable underwater noise, and also suffered from the unreliability of its reactor, which was poorly shielded to the detriment of the boat's crews.

In 1968 there appeared the first of the succeeding Victor class, which was developed through three main variants in a programme that lasted to 1991 and was the first Soviet submarine with a teardrop hull. The first variant was the Victor I class that was delivered to the extent of 15 submarines up to 1974 with a submerged displacement of 5,300 tons, a submerged speed of 32kt on the 30,000hp (22370kW) delivered to one propeller by the geared steam turbine powered by two reactors, and an armament of six 21-in (533-mm) bow tubes for 24 torpedoes or 22 torpedoes and two SS-N-15 Starfish anti-ship missiles. Then came the Victor II class of which seven were delivered up to 1978 with a longer hull to provide improved torpedo reload facilities, a submerged displacement of 5,800 tons and a submerged speed of 30kt. Finally, there was the Victor III class of which 26 were delivered up to 1991 to an improved Victor II-class design with a submerged displacement of 6,000 tons, a submerged speed of 30kt, and an armament of two 21-in (533-mm) and four 25.6-in (650-mm) tubes all in the bows for up to 24 torpedoes, or a reduced number of torpedoes to allow carriage of SS-N-15 Starfish and/or SS-N-16 Stallion anti-submarine missiles and SS-N-21 Samson cruise missiles.

Whereas these four classes were each based on a nuclear reactor with pressurized water cooling, the following two types switched to a reactor cooled by a liquid metal, probably sodium. The first of these was the Alfa class with a hull made of a titanium alloy rather than steel for the extreme diving depth of 2,295ft (700m) and a submerged speed of 45kt on the 47,000hp (35045kW) supplied to one propeller by two steam turbo-alternators powered by two reactors. The armament is six 21-in (533-mm) bow tubes for 20

weapons including two SS-N-15 Starfish anti-submarine missiles. The six Alfa class boats were built between 1979 and 1983, and were followed from 1983 by the first of six Sierra-class submarines with a slightly reduced diving depth, a submerged displacement of 8,200 tons, and a submerged speed of about 34kt on the 40,000hp (29825kW) supplied to one propeller by two steam turbo-alternators powered by two reactors. The armament is four 21-in (533-mm) and four 25.6-in (650-mm) tubes for 22 weapons including a variable number of SS-N-15, SS-N-16 and SS-N-21 missiles. The last type of nuclear-powered attack submarine developed in the U.S.S.R. and still in very low rate production for the Commonwealth of Independent States is the Akula class with a submerged displacement of 9,100 tons, a submerged speed of 32kt on the power delivered to one propeller by the steam turbines driven by two pressurized water-cooled reactors, and the armament is basically identical to that of the preceding Sierra class.

These Soviet boats are nothing like as quiet as the American submarines, and also lack the sophistication of the American vessels in their sonar and fire-control systems.

Although China has pretensions to nuclear-powered submarine capability, having produced four or five operational Han-class boats, the only other two countries that can genuinely be regarded as members of this exclusive club are the U.K. and France. The first of the British boats was HMS *Dreadnought* that was commissioned in 1963 with what was virtually the after end and propulsion arrangement of the American Skipjack-class submarine grafted onto a British forward end with British equipment and weapons.

This is the seventh submerged and overall 25th launch of a Trident missile, in this instance by the Lafayette-class USS Francis Scott Key (SSBN 657) off Cape Canaveral in Florida on 31 July 1979.

The following Valiant class, of which five were built between 1962 and 1971, was a slightly larger and bulkier development incorporating a British reactor system for a submerged displacement of 4,900 tons, a submerged speed of 28kt on the 15,000hp (11185kW) supplied to one propeller by a geared steam turbine powered by a pressurized water-cooled reactor, and an armament of six 21-in (533-mm) tubes for 26 torpedoes. Further development of the British concept of attack submarines resulted in the Swiftsure and Trafalgar classes. The Swiftsure class, of which six were delivered between 1973 and 1980 with a shorter and fuller hull for increased diving depth, has a submerged displacement of 4,500 tons, a submerged speed of 30kt, and an armament of five 21-in (533-mm) bow tubes for 25 torpedoes or a mix of torpedoes and Harpoon anti-ship missiles. The Trafalgar class, of which seven were delivered from 1983, is a quietened version of the Swiftsure class with an improved reactor and pumpjet propulsion for a submerged speed of 32kt at a displacement of 5,200 tons.

France has produced only one class of nuclear-powered attack submarines, the eight very small units of the Rubis class delivered from 1983. The type has a submerged displacement of 2,670 tons, a submerged speed of 25kt on the 9,500hp (7085kW) delivered to one propeller by an electric motor drawing current from two steam turbo-alternators driven by one pressurized water-cooled reactor, and an armament of four 21-in (533-mm) tubes for 18 weapons including torpedoes and missiles.

The ability of nuclear-powered submarines to undertake long patrols without surfacing then combined with two other developments, the SINS (Ship's

HMS Resolution (SS22), a Resolution-class nuclear-powered ballistic-missile submarine of the Royal Navy at speed.

steps that allowed the Americans to develop and build these more advanced weapons, but never managed to achieve the targeting accuracies of the American weapons, whose longer range meant that the launch submarines could operate in larger patrol areas in the deeper waters farther offshore, thereby reducing the chances of detection and destruction by orders of magnitude.

The first nuclear-powered ballistic-missile submarines were the five units of the George Washington class, which were built for the U.S. Navy in the period between 1957 and 1961. The design was basically that of the Skipjack-class nuclear-powered attack submarine with the hull cut in half for the insertion of a constant-section missile compartment about 130ft (39.6m) long immediately abaft the sail. This compartment carried 16 vertical tubes for the Polaris missile, and the result was a vessel with a submerged displacement of 6,710 tons and a submerged speed of about 20kt.

The first of the US Navy's SSBNs designed as such were the five boats of the Ethan Allen class, which were built between 1959 and 1963 to a design that was equivalent to the Thresher class of attack submarines with a hull of stronger alloy for the ability to dive deeper, improved quietening features, a towed-array passive sonar for defensive purposes, a submerged displacement of 7,885 tons, a submerged speed of about 20kt, and a primary armament basically similar to that of the George Washington class, namely 16 Polaris missiles as well as four rather than six 21-in (533-mm) torpedo tubes.

Further development resulted in the somewhat larger Lafayette-class boat with a submerged displacement of 8,250 tons, a submerged speed of about 25kt, and an armament of 16 missiles (originally Polaris

Inertial Navigation System) and the nuclear-tipped ballistic missile, to create one of today's ultimate strategic weapons. This is the SSBN (nuclear-powered ballistic missile submarine). This cruises in its patrol area for a long period, ready at command to fire a devastating salvo of missiles which, as a result of the extremely accurate launch position inputted from the SINS, can be targeted with very great accuracy. It is worth noting that while first-generation SLBMs (submarine-launched ballistic missiles) such as the Lockheed UGM-27 Poseidon were indeed comparatively small weapons of the intermediate-range type with a range of 2,750 miles (4425 km) and the ability to carry one warhead, later

weapons were somewhat larger. The second-generation Lockheed UGM-73 Poseidon was enlarged for the accommodation of the fuel providing a range of 3,250 miles (5230km) with a payload of 10 or 14 warheads, third-generation weapons such as the Lockheed UGM-96 Trident I were larger still for a range of some 4,250 miles (6840km) with slightly fewer but independently and more precisely targeted warheads, and fourth-generation weapons such as the Lockheed UGM-133 Trident II are larger still for a range of 7,500 miles (12070km) with between 10 and 12 independently and more precisely targeted warheads. The Soviets sought to emulate the technological

Two British nuclear-powered submarines, the Swiftsure-class HMS Superb *(foreground) and the Trafalgar-class HMS* Turbulent, *are seen on the surface at the North Pole in May 1988.*

USS Memphis visits Souda
Bay, Crete on December
16th 2003. she is the forth
Los-Angeles-class nuclear-
powered attack submarine.

The USS George Washington (SSBN 598) was the lead boat of the U.S. Navy's first class of nuclear-powered ballistic-missile submarines.

but later Poseidon weapons) together with four 21-in (533-mm) torpedo tubes. Construction of these 19 submarines was undertaken between 1961 and 1964, with the generally similar but quieter Benjamin Franklin class of 12 submarines following between 1963 and 1967. As well as their improved quietening, these boats introduced a number of detail improvements, and from the late 1970s were revised to carry the Trident I missile in place of the Poseidon.

The last word in Western SSBNs is the current mainstay of the U.S. Navy, the altogether larger and more formidable Ohio class of boats of which 18 are in the process of being commissioned from 1981 with the

main missile battery increased in size to 24 weapons of the Trident I type in the first eight submarines and the considerably improved Trident II in the last 10 submarines. The size of the missile section is so much greater than those of the preceding classes that the overall dimensions and displacement of the Ohio class are increased dramatically: whereas the Lafayette and Benjamin Franklin classes were based on a hull 425ft (129.5m) long with a beam of 33ft (10.05m) and a draught of 31ft 6in (9.6m) for a submerged displacement of 8,250 tons, the Ohio-class submarine is based on a hull 560ft (170.7m) long with a beam of 42ft (12.8m) and a draught of 36ft 5in (11.1m)

for a submerged displacement of 18,750 tons. The greater size and displacement of the Ohio class meant that an altogether more powerful propulsion arrangement had to be incorporated lest the performance of the submarine fall to unacceptably low levels: the Lafayette and Benjamin Franklin classes had been based on the use of a single propeller receiving 15,000hp (11185kW) from the two geared turbines powered by steam from a single Westinghouse S5W reactor for a submerged speed of about 25kt, but in the Ohio class the single considerably larger propeller receives 60,000hp (44735kW) from the two geared steam turbines powered by steam from a single General Electric S8G reactor for a submerged speed of 30kt. Like its predecessors, the Ohio-class submarine also carries torpedo armament in the form of four 21-in (533-mm) tubes in the bows for Mk 48 wire-guided torpedoes.

Compared with the Americans, who opted for exclusive use of the ballistic missile for strategic purposes after a brief flirtation with the winged cruise missile that ended with the one-off USS *Halibut* nuclear-powered boat completed in 1960 with a primary armament of two Regulus II or five Regulus I missiles, the Soviets opted for a two-handed approach that saw the development of both conventionally powered and nuclear-powered submarines for the carriage of ballistic missiles for the strategic role and winged cruise missiles for the strategic role and also for the operational-level role of tacking the American carrier battle groups whose nuclear-armed aircraft were seen as another major threat to the survival of the U.S.S.R.

The first of the cruise missile types were the conventionally powered Whiskey Long Bin, conventionally powered Juliett and nuclear-powered Echo I classes. The first

comprised a number of Whiskey-class boats converted between 1961 and 1963 with four SS-N-3 Shaddock anti-ship missiles in a process that reduced the type's submerged speed to 8kt, the second totalled 16 boats built between 1961 and 1969 with four SS-N-3 or later four SS-N-12 missiles for a submerged displacement of 3,750 tons and a submerged speed of 14kt, and the third amounted to five boats built between 1960 and 1962 with an armament of eight SS-N-3 missiles, a submerged displacement of 5,500 tons, and a submerged speed of 25kt with two propellers receiving 25,000hp (18640kW) from two sets of geared steam turbines powered by a single reactor. Between 1962 and 1967 there followed 29 Echo II-class boats with an enlarged sail carrying the type of radar that could provide mid-course guidance updates for the eight SS-N-3 missiles, and with a submerged displacement of 6,000 tons the boats could achieve a submerged speed of 23kt on basically the same propulsion arrangement as the Echo I-class boats.

The primary limitation of the Echo-class boats was that they had to surface to fire their missiles, and this tactical limitation was overcome in the following Charlie class of 21 boats delivered between 1968 and 1980 in three subvariants each armed with eight underwater-launched anti-ship missiles: in the 10 units of the Charlie I class these are SS-N-7 Starbright weapons, in the six units of the Charlie II class they are SS-N-9 Siren weapons, and in the five units of the Charlie III class they are SS-N-22 Sunburn weapons. The Charlie I class has a submerged displacement of 5,000 tons and a submerged speed of 27kt, while the longer Charlie II and Charlie III classes each have a submerged displacement of 5,500 tons and a submerged speed of 26kt, in each case with 15,100hp (11260kW)

The SNLE L'Inflexible (S 615) was launched in June 1982 as the sixth and last Le Redoutable-class boat of the French navy's first nuclear-powered ballistic-missile submarine class.

delivered to one propeller from a set of geared steam turbines powered by a single pressurized water-cooled reactor.

The last of the Soviet cruise missile submarines was the six-strong Oscar class of very large boats built in two subclasses as two Oscar I and four Oscar II-class boats, each with a primary armament of 12 two-round launchers for SS-N-19 Shipwreck missiles. The Oscar I class has a submerged displacement of 12,500 tons and a submerged speed 30kt on the 90,000hp (67105kW) delivered to two propellers by geared steam turbines powered by two pressurized water-cooled reactors, while the Oscar II class has a submerged speed of 28kt on the same propulsion arrangement as it is longer to allow the incorporation of improved quietening features in a process that increased the submerged displacement to 13,400 tons.

After development and initial deployment of ballistic missiles in the conventionally powered Golf class, of which 22 were completed between 1958 and 1962 with a primary armament of three SS-N-4 or later SS-N-5 missiles, both of which had to be launched on the surface, the U.S.S.R. moved into the field of nuclear-powered ballistic-missile submarines with the Hotel class, of which eight were completed between 1958 and 1962 with a primary armament of three SS-N-4 missiles, a submerged displacement of 6,000 tons, and a submerged speed of 26kt on the 30,000hp (22370kW) delivered to two propellers by geared steam turbines driven by two pressurized water-cooled reactors. Between 1963 and 1970 the boats were modified to the considerably more capable Hotel II standard with the primary armament revised to three SS-N-5 Sark missiles that could be launched while the boats were still submerged.

Although these boats provided an operational capability of types, the first

genuine SLBM capability was attained by the U.S.S.R. with the 34 Yankee-class submarines delivered between 1963 and 1972 with a submerged displacement of 9,600 tons, a submerged speed of 27kt on the 50,000hp (37280kW) delivered to two propellers by geared steam turbines powered by two pressurized water-cooled reactors. The primary armament of these boats was 16 underwater-launched SS-N-6 Serb missiles, which may be regarded as having been roughly equivalent to the Polaris weapon used by the U.S. Navy, thus making the Yankee class the Soviet counterpart of the Lafayette class, although the Soviet boats were significantly more noisy and, with a 30 per cent larger propulsion section and 30 per cent smaller missile section, generally less efficient than their American rivals.

The next series of Soviet SLBM submarines comprised the four subvariants of the Delta class. Built between 1972 and 1977, the 18 Yankee I-class boats had a submerged displacement of 10,200 tons and a submerged speed of 26kt on the 50,000hp (37280kW) delivered to two propellers by the geared steam turbines powered by two pressurized water-cooled reactors, and carried a primary armament of 12 SS-N-8 Sawfly underwater-launched missiles. The four Delta II-class boats that followed in 1974 and 1975 were lengthened to allow the carriage of 16 rather than 12 missile launch tubes, and with the submerged displacement increased to 11,300 tons had a submerged speed of 25kt with the same propulsion arrangement. Next came 14 Delta III class boats built between 1974 and 1982 with a slightly longer hull and revisions to carry 16 SS-N-18 Stingray with liquid rather than solid propellants, a submerged displacement of 11,700 tons and a submerged speed of 24kt with an unchanged propulsion arrangement.

Finally there were the six submarines of the Yankee IV class delivered from 1984 as a development of the Yankee III class with the SS-N-23 Skiff missile, which is a moderately advanced weapon combining the range of the SS-N-8 with the multiple independently targeted warhead capability of the SS-N-18. The Yankee IV class carries 16 of these weapons, and at a submerged displacement of 12,150 tons has a submerged speed of 23.5kt with an unchanged propulsion arrangement.

The final class of SLBM submarines designed in the U.S.S.R. is the Typhoon class, which is the largest submarine yet designed and built with a submerged displacement of 26,500 tons, a submerged speed of 27kt on the 80,000hp (59650kW)

delivered to two propellers by the geared steam turbines powered by two pressurized water-cooled reactors, and a primary armament of 20 SS-N-20 Sturgeon missiles each carrying up to nine independently targeted warheads. Six of the boats have been delivered since 1982.

The three other countries that have built nuclear-powered SLBM submarines are China, France and the U.K. China's current strength is just one Xia-class submarine with a submerged displacement of 8,000 tons, a submerged speed of 22kt, and a primary armament of 12 CSS-N-3 missiles. France has developed and built three classes of SLBM submarine in the form of the five-strong Le Redoutable class delivered between 1974 and 1980 with a submerged

displacement of 8,940 tons, a submerged speed of 25kt, and a primary armament of 16 M20 or, in one boat, M4 missiles; the single L'Inflexible-class submarine developed from the Le Redoutable class with 16 M4 (later M45) missiles; and the planned six units of the Le Triomphant class entering service in the second half of the 1990s with a submerged displacement of 14,335 tons, a submerged speed of 25kt, and a primary armament of 16 M45 missiles. Finally there is the U.K., which entered the field of the SLBM submarine in 1967 with the commissioning of the first of four Resolution-class submarines with a submerged displacement of 8,400 tons, a submerged speed of 25kt, and a primary armament of 16 Poseidon missiles. From the mid-1990s these are being replaced by the four submarines of the Vanguard class with a submerged speed of 25kt and a primary armament of 16 Trident I missiles.

With the ending of the confrontation between the two superpower blocs in the late 1980s, the rationale behind the construction and operation of nuclear-powered ballistic-missile submarines has been weakened considerably, so it is probable that boats of this type will now be kept in service for as long as possible with improvements introduced in the form of better equipment and updated versions of the current generation of missiles. The flexibility offered by attack and patrol submarines of the nuclear-powered and conventionally powered types is now more important than ever, however, and it is possible that this will result in continued development of these types.

HMS Resolution. *All information on other ships and submarines in the area is fed into the Contact Evaluation Plot in the control room and by this means it is possible to build up an accurate picture of the course and speed of nearby vessels.*

A Polaris A-3 submarine-launched ballistic missile.

A Soviet Foxtrot-class submarine of the Soviet navy with a Royal Navy Sea King from 820 Naval Air Squadron embarked in HMS Hermes *in close attendance. This submarine was detected in the North Atlantic while being escorted to Cuba by the soviet oceanographic research vessel* Nzubov. *1980.*

378, 380, 392
U-507 375
U-Kreuzer 381
U1 372
U 29 397
U117 386
U125 386
U135 381
U139 381
U140 385
U142 381
U151 381
U17 374
U173 386
U20 374
U21 376
U24 374
UA 381
UB 378, 380
UB 133 378
UB I 378
UB II 391
UB III 391
UB-type 375
UC 378, 379, 380
UC I 378
UC III 378
UD 381
UE I 380
UE II 380, 386, 391
UF 381
Upholder 418
Upholder 414
Uzushio 420
V 378, 385
Valiant 424
Vanguard 429, 431
Västergötland 419

Vetehinen 391
Victor 423
Victory 397
W 378
Walrus 418
Whiskey 413, 417, 429
Whiskey 386, 388
Wilhelm Bauer 419
X1 386
Xia 431
XVIIB-class U-boat 402
Yankee 430, 431
Yu 1 411
Yuushio 420
Yuushio 405
Zulu 417
Zwaardvis 418
classes of vessels:
A 124, 131
Active 187
Admiral 66
Admiral Graf Spee 114
Admiral Hipper 216, 225
Admiral Latorre 90
Agano 234
Akatsuki 157
Akitsuki 159, 160
Al Bushra 354
Al Siddiq 358, 359
Alaska 218, 219
Albatros 153
Algérie 216, 225
Allen M. Sumner 144, 148,
174
Alpino 153
Amagi 107
Amatsukaze 130
Amazon 131, 167

Ambuscade 131
Andrea Doria 237
Animoso 130
Annapolis 148
Aoba 230
Aosta 227, 237
Aquila 226
Äran 93
Archer 251
Ardito 130
Arethusa 187, 208
Ariete 154
Ark Royal 242, 247, 251
Arleigh Burke 180, 181
Asheville 358, 359
Assad 357
Asashio 159
Astoria 226, 221
Atlanta 221, 223
Atherstone 142
Atlanta 160
Attacker 250
Audace 126
Audacious 249, 251
Ayah 338
B 124, 132, 203
Baden 101, 114
Bainbridge 227, 236
Baltimore 205, 217, 218,
234
Bande Nere 227
Barcelo 333, 346
Battle 141
Bay 145, 146
Belknap 237
Bellerophon 86
Benson 147
Birkenhead 187

Birmingham 199
Bismarck 113, 114, 117,
119
Bixio 226
Black Swan 137, 142
Blackwood 142
Blücher 86
Bogue 282, 283
Bory 129
Botha 129
Brave 360
Bremen 190
Broadsword 171, 180, 217
Bronstein 175, 177
Brooke 159, 177
Brooklyn 196, 217, 221,
222, 232
Buckley 150
C 124, 132
Caio Duilio 88, 111
Caledon 198, 199
California 237
Cambrian 198
Campania 226
Canarias 215
Canberra 204
Cannon 150
Canopus 70
Capitani Romani 228
Carlisle 198, 199
Caroline 198
Casablanca 260, 282, 283
Casque 130
Cassin 131
Castle 145
Centaur 198, 251
Ceres 198, 199
Challenger 184, 185

Chapayev 237
Charles F. Adams 164, 167,
178
Chester 197
Chikuma 198
Chiyoda 295
Claud Jones 175
Claymore 130
Clemenceau 270, 282
Clemson 131, 146
Cleveland 200, 206, 217,
222, 223, 234, 281
Colbert 237
Colossus 86, 249, 265, 273
Commencement Bay 282,
283
Condottieri type 227
Conte di Cavour 88
Coontz 176
County 151, 178, 193, 202,
203
County (A class) 203
Courageous 241, 244
Courbet 87, 96
Craven 146
Curlew 199
Curtatone 154
CVNX-1 286
CVNX-2 286
D 124, 129, 132
D3 312
Dagger 359
Danae 199, 219
Dardo 155
Dealey 175
de Grasse 237
Delaware 84
Delhi 187, 188, 199, 219

Derfflinger 88
de Ruyter 237
Des Moines 218, 228
Deutschland 112, 113, 197
Diadem 184
Diaz 227
Dido 117, 160, 203, 208, 221, 228
Dogan 347
Dreadnought 70, 79, 80, 82, 86, 87, 88, 89, 90, 93, 95, 96, 102, 103, 105, 106, 125, 183, 184, 186, 189, 299
Duguay Trouin 225, 227
Dunkerque 112, 113, 117
Duquesne 211, 225, 226
Durandal 130
E 125, 132
Eagle 251
Eclipse 190
Edsall 150
Elbing (Type 39) 153
Émile Bertin 225
Esmeraldas 357
España 87
Essex 260, 261, 280, 281, 283
Evarts 150
F-class (Tribal) 125, 129, 132, 133
Fairmile D 300
Fargo 223
Farragut 146, 178
Fiji 209, 210
Flamberge 130
Fletcher 144, 146, 147, 150, 174
Florida 86

Flower 133, 142, 143, 144, 145
Folgore 155, 355
Forrestal 283, 285
Forrest Sherman 178
FPB 57 337
FPB-36 333
FPB-36 type 332
FPB-38 333, 337
Frauenlob 189
Freccia 356
Fremantle 355
Frunze 222
Fubuki 157, 159
Fuso 93, 94, 95
G-class (Basilisk) 126, 132
G3 107, 110
Gangut 88
Garcia 159, 177
Garibaldi 227
Gazelle 189
Gearing 146, 148, 167, 174
Generale 153
Glorious 101
Gneisenau 113, 114
Guépard 151
H145 129
H (Acorn) 126, 132
H3 360
Hamburg 159
Hatsuhara 159
Hauk 343
Hegu 315, 360
Helgoland 86
Hermes 250, 251
Hiyo 293
Holland 151
Hood 103

Huangfen 317, 360
Huchuan 360
Hunt 142
Hunt Type I 142
Hunt Type II 142
Hunt Type III 142
Hunt Type IV 142
Huzzard 130
Hyuga 109
I (Acheron) 126, 132
Illustrious 242, 249, 251
Iltis 153
Imperatritsa Maria 88
Indefatigable 88, 94, 98
Independence 283
Indianapolis 216
Intrepid 130
Invincible 82, 88, 189, 251, 296
Iowa 120, 121
Iraqi 357
Iron Duke 89, 90, 98, 99
Ise 93, 94, 106
J 132, 133, 157
Jaguar 151, 323, 330, 331
John C. Butler 150
K (Acasta) 127, 132, 133
Kaba 129, 131
Kagero 159
Kaiser 86, 100
Kaiyo 295
Kako 230
Kaman 34
Kamikaze 134, 156
Kanin 149
Kara 219, 239
Karlsruhe 185
Kartal 331

Kashin 173, 177, 180
Kasuga 197
Kawachi 86
Kebir 354
Kent 201, 203, 211
Kidd 180
Kiev 274, 276, 288, 295
Kildin 315
King Edward 70
King George V 89, 90, 113, 117, 123
Kirov 211, 225, 237
Kitty Hawk 283
Knox 157, 177
Köln 226
Komar 315, 316, 323, 342, 360
Kongo 90, 92, 106, 111
König 87, 101
Kresta 220
Kresta I 238, 239
Kresta II 212, 239
Kris 355
Krivak 180
Krivak I 174
Krupny 153, 315
Kuma 228
Kuznetsov 295
Kynda 238
Kynda 221
L 127, 132
LM 298
La Combattante 350
La Combattante II 330, 351
La Combattante III 330, 333, 351, 334
La Galissonnière 225, 227
La Masa 130, 153, 154

La Melpomène 151
Lampo 130, 355, 356
Lazaga 346, 347
Le Fantasque 151
Le Hardi 152
Leahy 236, 237
Leander 152, 155, 203, 208
Leone 226
Lexington 107
Lion 90, 113
Livermore 147
Loch 145, 146
London 202
Long Beach 236, 237
Long Island type 281
Lord Nelson 70
Lung Chiang 359
Lürssen FPB-36 322
M 127, 128, 131, 132
Maass Tyoe 152
Maestrale 155
Mahan 146
Majestic 68, 80, 250, 271
Maksim Gorky 237
Manchester 173
Marksman 129, 131
Maryland 110
MAS 299, 312
Matchless (Admiralty 'M') 143
Matka 322, 323, 326
Matsu 173
Meko 360 170, 181
MGB-107 type 300
MGB-62 347
Midway 280, 283
Minas Geraes 86
Minekaze 156

440

Picture Acknowledgements

Military Archive & Research Services, Lincolnshire, England: pages 22, 27 above, 48, 67 left, 71, 79, 87 above right, 88 right, 90, 94, 96, 97, 99 below, 103, 105 right, 106, 107, 113, 114 left and right, 117, 118, 121 all, 123, 124, 148 left, 156, 170 above right, 175 above, 181 right, 182, 185 above and below, 191 below, 192 below, 193, 195 below, 199 both, 206, 214, 217, 231, 234, 245 right, 246, 248 below, 264, 274 both, 277 both, 300, 301, 505, 309, 312, 313, 316, 318, 319, 321, 322, 325, 327, 328, 331, 332, 335, 336, 337, 342, 348, 363, 364, 365, 367 both, 368, 369, 370, 375 below, 376, 377, 386, 400, 405, 408, 428

*Admiralty (Crown copyright): pages 128 below, 131 above, 143

Ann Ronan at Image Select: pages 6, 13, 15, 23, 24, 27 below, 35 above, 38, 40, 41 left and right, 49, 50, 53 all, 54, 56 above, 58, 59, 60 above and below, 61, 62, 63, 65, 67 right, 74 below, 78 above and right

*BBC Hulton Picture Library: page 183

*Blohm & Voss: page 170 above left and below right

*Brazilian Navy, Rio de Janeiro: page 273 left

*Bremer Vulkan, Bremen: page 168

The Bridgeman Art Library, London/British Library, London: page 34

The Bridgeman Art Library, London/British Museum, London: pages 1, 16

The Bridgeman Art Library, London/Christie's Images, London: page 7

The Bridgeman Art Library, London/Christopher Wood Gallery, London: page 4

The Bridgeman Art Library, London/Cider House Galleries Ltd., Bletchingley, Surrey: page 42 left

The Bridgeman Art Library, London/Lambeth Palace Library, London: pages 18 left

The Bridgeman Art Library, London/Library of Congress, Washington: page 19

The Bridgeman Art Library, London/Louvre, Paris: page 10 above left

The Bridgeman Art Library, London/ Musée de la Tapisserie, Bayeux, France: pages 10-11 above and below

The Bridgeman Art Library, London/Museum Maritim Atarazanas, Barcelona, Catalunya, Spain: page 29

The Bridgeman Art Library, London/Museo Naval, Madrid: page 2

The Bridgeman Art Library, London/Palacio del Senado, Madrid, Spain: page 28

The Bridgeman Art Library, London/Private Collections: pages 3, 9, 17, 20, 33, 36 top left, 36-37, 42-43, 46

The Bridgeman Art Library, London/Science Museum, London: pages 8, 25

The Bridgeman Art Library, London/Service Historique de la Marine, Vincennes, France: page 32

The Bridgeman Art Library, London/The Stapleton Collection: page 14

The Bridgeman Art Library, London/Victoria & Albert Museum, London: page 21

The Bridgeman Art Library, London/William Drummond: page 57

The Bridgeman Art Library, London/Yale Center for British Art, Paul Mellon Collection, U.S.A: page 44-45

*British Aerospace: pages 279 right, 281 left

*Built by Hawthorn Leslie (Shipbuilders), Ltd.-now part of Swan Hunter Shipbuilding Ltd.: page 29

*Bundesarchiv, Koblenz: pages 68, 88 left

*Canadian Armed Forces Photo: page 350

*C & S Taylor, Eastbourne: page 344

*Chilean Navy: page 323

*Crown Copyright: pages 151 left, 152 below, 153 right, 239, 258 below, 265 below, 266, 272, 310, 413

*Dartford/Paulley: page 100

*Defence PR Canberra: pages 150 above, 162 right, 271

*ECP/Armées, France: page 152 above

*Empresa Nacional Bazan, Madrid: pages 155 above, 346

*Federal German Navy, Wilhelmshaven: page 329

*Fleet Photographic Unit: page 278

*Foto Drüppel, Wilhelmshaven: pages 119 above, 131 below, 188 above and below

*Fujifotos, Tokyo: page 124 above

*General Dynamics Corp: pages 122, 407

*Hellenic Navy, Athens: pages 334, 387

*HMS Dolphin, Hants: page 372

*Howaldtswerke, Kiel: pages 396, 397, 398, 399, 402

Image Select: pages 18 right, 26, 31

*Imperial War Museum, London: pages 80, 86 above and below, 87 below, 90 left, 90 right, 92 below, 93 above, 95, 98 above and below, 101, 102, 104, 108, 109, 110, 130 above, 132 below, 133, 134 below, 135, 135, 137 all, 138 both, 139 both, 142 above, 186, 189, 190, 191 above, 194, 197 right, 241, 242, 243, 244 above, 245 top left, 248 above, 253 below, 257 right, 371

*Ingalls Shipbuilding: page: 231 left, 230, 232, 233, 250, 251

*Israeli Navy, Tel Aviv: pages 326, 328

*Italcantieri: page 403

*Italian Navy Historical Archives: pages 78 below left, 87 above left, 126, 153 right, 202